THE
SECRETS OF
CHARISMA

Doe Lang, Ph.D

A division of Shapolsky Publishers, Inc.

The Secrets of Charisma

S.P.I. BOOKS

A division of Shapolsky Publishers, Inc.

First Wyden Books edition: August 1980
First Wideview Books edition: May 1982
Wideview Books/A Division of PEI Books, Inc.
First New Choices Press edition: May 1985
First S.P.I. Books edition: May 1992
18th printing: May 1992

The Social Readjustment Rating Scale (Holmes-Rahe Stress Management Scale) is reprinted with permission from *Journal of Psychosomatic Research*, 11, Holmes, T.H. and Rahe, R.H. Pergamon Press, Ltd.

Photos courtesy of Hideoki and Nancy Brown

For any additional information, contact:

S.P.I. BOOKS/Shapolsky Publishers, Inc.
136 West 22nd Street
New York, NY 10011
212/633-2022 / FAX 212/633-2123

ISBN: 0-944007-41-4

Printed in the United States of America

CRITICS SAY:

✳ "**Not since Max Weber** invented political charisma has there been as useful a how-to book on the subject. Doe Lang's book mysteriously draws other books on its shelf closer to it." —William Safire, *New York Times*

✳ "Doe Lang is a woman with charisma, which she says is 'to imagination as electricity is to the wire that carries it.' Her book is **one of the best** self-help volumes I've seen."
—Liz Smith, *New York Newsday*

✳ "**A dazzling** piece of work—perceptive, **witty and wise**—full of delicious surprises!" —Celeste Holm

✳ "Everyone's library should have dictionaries, a thesaurus, the works of Shakespeare and **Doe Lang's wonderful book!**" —Nanette Fabray

✳ "An **exciting** book!" —Rene Dubos, Rockefeller Univ.

✳ "Supremely knowledgeable exercises . . . **A true gift** . . . highly imaginative . . . multifaceted, **extraordinary!** This book is **a treasure.**" —Lisa Curtis

✳ "This wonderful book **will be a bible** for many people for years to come." —Mrs. George Solti

✳ "This book is a **prescription for happiness** . . . A wonderfully **revealing** experience." —Dr. William H. Frey, Dir., Psychiatry Research Laboratories, St. Paul, MN

✳ An **exceptional** book, . . . everybody can find what they need in it—spiritual, emotional, technical, physical . . . Read it!" —Janos Starker

✳ "*The Secrets of Charisma* was . . . an enormous journey, Doe Lang packed virtually everything in the way of liberation, creativity and personal growth into one book . . . ideas that **awaken and energize.**" —Dr. Clark Moustakas

AUTHOR'S NOTE

The Shakyamuni Buddha is said to have uttered a single word, "AH," in such a way that all listeners who heard it understood exactly what they needed to know, in their own language and in a way best suited to them.

Since "AH" is the pure exclamation of wonder and delight, it means to me a kind of magic dream of reaching everyone instantly—the impossible dream of perfect communication, from and to the heart. Moment to moment, it is possible. What I wish for most is that every reader will find something in this book that will make a difference in her or his life and will pass on the affirmation and encouragement they've experienced.

I have seen in my work with people and in the many editions and translations of this book, how self-discovery is passed on to others in widening circles of influence—a beautiful organic process.

I am deeply conscious of my indebtedness to many, many people— scholars, masters, my teachers, students, and clients, and to old and new friends, my family, and others who never knew how much their influence meant. In addition to those I've named in previous editions, I'd like to thank Sherrel Farnsworth, my editor, for her exceptional creativity, taste and integrity in designing this edition.

Doe Lang

CONTENTS

Andrea Lang

TO THE RADIANT, UNDYING SPIRIT
of
ANDREA ILONA LANG

Adored and adoring big sister
of Brian Lang

Incomparable loving heart
her art
her writing
her healing charisma
Lives and inspires others . . .
even who never knew her.
Wherever she was, she created beauty
and humor

our brilliant darling
magical grace
dazzling wit,
her luminous beauty,
song,
laughter

Lost and perished
in the Painted Cave Fire
Santa Barbara, California, June 27, 1990

Dearest Andrea
heart's daughter

phoenix soul

1

Charisma—What Is It?

WHAT IS CHARISMA? Everybody knows, but nobody can tell you *exactly*. In research I conducted with more than two thousand people from all walks of life I got such answers as:

"I don't know—I never thought about it."

"You either have it or you don't—all I know is that when you have it, everybody wants to do things for you!"

"It's sex appeal."

"It's a mysterious charm that draws people to you."

"It's a kind of harmony between the person and his/her audience."

"It's vitality."

"It's energy."

"It's never being boring."

"It's a holistic state—when you're one with the people you're with, and everybody feels inspired, excited, enriched, and enlarged."

"It's a quality of believing your own lies...general confidence."

The majority felt charisma is inborn, but that it could, paradoxically, be developed. I asked people when they themselves had felt most charismatic in their lives. The intriguing (and encouraging!) thing was that nobody, not even the people who regarded themselves as shy and nonassertive, said "Never!"

So apparently everybody has enjoyed some experience with feeling successful, authoritative—times when they felt they were effectively expressing their true selves and were understood and appreciated. Both are necessary for a satisfying experience, according to the majority of people I surveyed.

* * *

I have always had a secret interest in charisma.

Ever since I was very small—when people would say, maddeningly, but in an effort to be kind and helpful, "Be yourself!" I wondered exactly what that meant. Which self was the best one? Even as a child, I knew there were a great many selves wrapped up in the ME that walked around every day, ate, slept, dreamed, talked to people, fantasized, sang, danced, acted, played, and did all the other things children do. Instinctively I sensed, as children always do, that certain selves were more acceptable than others, especially to certain people. But it was not something you could discuss with anybody. Sometimes it was hard to discover exactly what worked best when.

When somebody smiled or frowned, said "Don't!" or "That's not nice!" or "Very good!" that was *some* information but not enough. We're all conditioned to develop certain of our "selves" and not others, but the feedback is often sketchy and confusing.

When I was trying to figure out which "self" to be as a child, I was, of course, dimly aware that certain people received an inordinate share of attention, approval, love. The basis of selection was a mystery.

Some of them were beautiful, some were not, some were smart, some not, some were agreeable, some not. It was very puzzling!

I remember, when I was no more than six, trying to figure out just how my older brother had said, "Good-bye, Mom!" in the morning when he left for school. My mother always answered, "Good-bye, dear. . . ." to him, and it seemed she never said "dear" to me.

What was the secret of his charisma? I had no way of knowing then that the mere fact of his being male had a great deal to do with it. Years later, as a grown-up, I told this story to my mother, and she looked very distressed.

"Oh, why didn't you say something?" she asked.

That had never occurred to me. I suspected that perhaps I was deficient in some way, and that this was why she didn't say "dear" to me. That was too alarming to talk about, or even to voice very clearly to myself. I was far too proud to ASK. . . .

Like most little girls, I grew up an avid student of what pleased people. Since my family was musical and I sang and played the piano from the time I was very small, I was used to pleasing people (as well as myself, it must be admitted) by singing, playing, and later on acting. Mother was a frustrated actress. She used to entertain me by doing little monologues with an Irish accent or crying—which she could do at will—whenever I asked her. This was fun, but obviously it hadn't gotten her anything special—it was just one of those little gifts some people had, which didn't amount to anything important one way or another.

Daddy had a lovely light baritone voice. We enjoyed singing in harmony together. But he didn't like me to sing in my "high" voice. I realized much later that only the sound of an alto voice pleased him, a male sound. I was much praised for singing and playing, but it wasn't considered "important," not the way my brother's interests were.

He was a little envious of me because he couldn't sing or play the piano very well. But it never occurred to me that that was important. Somehow if *he,* clearly the more important person, could not sing, it couldn't be that important to sing! He played chess with my father, who did not offer to teach me. Mother and I were, after all, only women. All the same he expected that I would do very well in school, and I did. But somehow it just wasn't "important."

The mystery of why some people were preferred to others continued to haunt me in a vague underground way. I wanted to be "liked," "loved," but I wasn't sure I had what it took—whatever that was!

Secretly I suspected it had nothing to do with being good, although I was always exhorted to BE good. Perhaps for girls—although this was never suggested—it had something to do with being pretty? So I *secretly* admired the little blond girl who lived across the street, whose face stared down at us from billboards. She was a child model, and always seemed to be exquisitely dressed in blue velvet dresses and white socks. As I studied the cool, distant gaze of models in the magazines and the sultry provocative look of movie stars, I tried to learn how those looks felt from the inside. Somehow, I felt, if I knew *what* to do, I could do it!

I tried so hard! I didn't use bad language because Mother said it was not refined. (In fact I was once sent away from the table by Daddy for using the word *lousy!*) I did my homework faithfully and even with a good deal of pleasure. I suffered agonies at the age of ten when I got a sudden allergic attack (it turned out later

I was reacting to some nose drops, but nobody knew that then), which made me break out, so I wasn't picked to play the lead in the school musical *Blue Belt* even though nobody else could sing as well. I used to creep downstairs and listen outside the auditorium to the rehearsals. I can almost taste the desire I felt for that glamorous proceeding.

After it was discovered that that awful brown stuff they used to put in children's noses was responsible for my pimples, that was cleared up and I got to sing Buttercup in a children's version of *H.M.S. Pinafore*. It was a great success. Mother stuffed my flat little bosom with Kotex so I would better approximate the buxom Buttercup. I warbled, to great appreciation, "I'm called little Buttercup, dear little Buttercup, though I could never tell why. . . ." It was a most appropriate song: Buttercup seemed just as confused about essential things as I was!

In spite of all my efforts I felt no closer to that mysterious and wonderful *confidence* some people had without seeming to work at it at all! *They* could be naughty, outrageous—nobody seemed to mind. On the other hand, I was required to be as perfect as possible. Was it because people thought I wasn't good unless I was perfect? I couldn't be sure but I put on such a great act that a lot of people thought I had *too* much confidence!

Katharine Hepburn once said about her arrival in Hollywood, "I was bringing myself as though I were a basket of flowers!" How wonderful to feel that way and to be able to say it! In my home that would have been considered boastful and immodest—not qualities that were admired or encouraged.

If Hepburn hadn't had her confident sense of "self" she could never have swept through Hollywood as triumphantly as she did. The prevailing ideal in her time was totally different—cuddly, sexy, pretty—nothing like the independent, aristocratic strength, individuality, and racehorse beauty she projected.

People do walk through the door of your expectations! Especially if the expectations are unquestioning and sure. Her sense of self was so powerful that Hepburn not only became a star; as everybody knows, she stayed one for sixty years.

How I admired her! I had a full pantheon of goddesses that I secretly looked to as models when I was a child. Deanna Durbin and Ingrid Bergman were others. And later Audrey Hepburn. Such was the contagious magic of their awareness of their own "charisma" that I actually took on some of their physical characteristics, with the uncanny mimesis of adoration. (You do become what you love.)

People would say, "Oh, do you know, you really look a lot like _____ ." The astonishing thing was, as I see from some of my early pictures, I did manage to resemble my heroines. They were part of my sense of self. They showed me which selves to wear.

And like many little girls, to console myself for not being somehow preferred—although I was certainly treated lovingly—I used to pretend I was a princess. It was very satisfying to know that I had a tiny strawberry mark of my thigh, because otherwise my real family—all kings and queens, naturally—would never be able to find me. I didn't confide this to anyone, but it was a great consolation to know that I was too fine for my own family and my friends—and *they didn't know it!*

Meantime, before the royal talent scouts came, the waiting wasn't wholly satisfactory because I didn't quite know who I was while waiting to *be* a princess. It was fun to pretend to be other people. So I became an actress.

The Tinker Bell Syndrome

The only problem about getting your confidence from performing is that if you depend on it, what happens when you get offstage? Many performers suffer from what I think of as the Tinker Bell syndrome. Unless some audience is crowding round, calling out "I believe! I believe!" and applauds their talent, they don't feel worthy or valid as human beings. There are also negative aspects to being valued for one's talents alone. Other people's jealousy can be very undermining if your personal self-esteem is shaky.

My own experience led to an ambivalence about the business of performing. While I was growing up, I was admired and praised when I sang or played, or (later) acted. But one little girl, who happened to live next door, was bitterly jealous. Years later I found out her mother taunted her by saying, "Why can't you sing and play like Doe?" No wonder she hated me! She herself was a very pretty, bright little girl, but that was apparently not enough for her competitive and ambitious mother.

So I learned: yes, it's good to have talent, but watch out! You may be hated for it. The same is true for beauty, brains, and other gifts. What I kept searching for was *what made a person OK*— that inalienable confidence in oneself that makes it possible to move through life with unassailable joy and assurance. I used to marvel at people who were neither talented nor pretty nor specially bright, but who had IT: charisma.

There is a Sufi saying that if you want young people to learn how to deal well with life, tell them to associate with lucky people! People who have positive expectations usually draw positive events to them.

If you think you're lucky—why, then, you are!

Painful or even tragic events can lift merely lucky people to greatness. Franklin D. Roosevelt was only an extraordinarily handsome, wealthy, carefree young man until he contracted polio. That gave him a great obstacle to struggle against as well as compassion for others' suffering. The combination created a great figure, able to lift a country out of debilitating depression. Only someone who had conquered heavy personal travail and lived through the "dark night of the soul" could say as effectively as he did: "The only thing we have to fear is fear itself."

While going off to Bennington, Vermont, marrying, raising two children, living in Texas and Italy, becoming a singer and theater performer absorbed my energies, the secret unremitting search went on quietly deep inside me—for what? I knew only that I was searching for something, that it was terribly important to me and very elusive.

By chance, one evening at a dinner party, I sat next to a brilliant and interesting woman, who rashly invited me to teach a course at New York's New School, "Public Speaking for Private People."

I had been acting in soap operas and dubbing films. This was a new and intriguing challenge. I accepted.

At first I was a little ashamed to tell people what I was teaching. Heavens, it sounded like Dale Carnegie! So I thought, somewhat snobbishly. But I grew more and more fascinated with the classes.

Suddenly I realized that communication involves people's deepest feelings about themselves and about other people. I also realized that I had something to give them and that I loved doing it. Performing in this way was not an ego trip; I was really of service. I saw how people suffered from low self-esteem, an inability to speak up, and the fear that they couldn't measure up to their own and everybody else's expectations. I began to study everything I could lay my hands on about psychology and, later, Eastern disciplines. I wanted to be able to give people in all their diversity whatever keys they needed to become more comfortable and actualized. I was constantly impressed by the fascinating personal stories people told, how they developed over the course of the semester, the reserves of genius everyone seemed able to draw on.

In the beginning I worried about how could I deal with so many people of totally different backgrounds, ages, interests, and educations. The assortment was wildly diversified, with ages ranging from sixteen to eighty. But I saw that deep down we all have much in common, and had a great deal to give each other.

I had always been a closet optimist about people. Now I was coming out of the closet. Then Beverly Grunwald wrote an article about my course, "Doe Lang's Class in Charisma."

My first reaction was horror. How presumptuous! Did I claim to teach charisma? No, she had simply come to the classes and watched, and that's what *she* said I was doing!

I rushed to the dictionary, and found to my relief that charisma, which comes from Charis, one of the Three Graces in Greek mythology, used to mean the divine gifts or attributes we each have within us!

That was exactly what I believed. I saw my role was to help people to trust themselves; and, through dealing with their fears about public and private speaking, reach very deep places where we could all share our humanness. I soon realized that at that deep level nobody is boring! What most people present at the surface bears very little relation to their real quality and gifts.

Charisma—The Superlanguage

More and more people came to me with urgent communication needs. I began to see that because of the explosion of technology and the rapid changes we have been experiencing, understanding each other was more important than it had ever been. I began to see charisma as a superlanguage, which can be developed so we can achieve a human relation with others and at the same time realize our best potentials.

This was a powerful message. Every time an article about my work appeared or I was on TV or radio I would get letters from all over the world asking how to achieve charisma. Most people were brought up to believe it was either something you had or you didn't. And that there was nothing much you could do about it. How wasteful and how wrong!

Through my work with thousands of people, I have seen that indeed everybody is rich and beautiful inside, if they could only accept that. "We all have the same deep thoughts and feelings. Opening up to them makes a bridge between people," Liv Ullmann said not long ago.

You always teach best what you need to learn. I found some profoundly satisfying bridges to help other people experience themselves in a more loving, accepting way and deal with other people with the same kind of loving concern they now could give to themselves. Political figures wanted my advice on charisma. Big business leaders, actors, architects—people of enormously varied backgrounds—seemed to need affirmation and techniques to learn the increasingly complex and important communication skills. I found it was a nonthreatening way for people to reach very deep areas of themselves, and profoundly affect society as well.

Now I find everything I've learned is truly *useful*. It is my great joy to be able to help people, and that is why I decided to write this book. I want to share the work I have done on myself and with others, because I now know what my gifts—what everybody's gifts—are for.

Charisma is within all of us—everywhere. And it's meant to be shared.

2

Imagination—Its Care and Feeding

Imagination is more important than knowledge.
—ALBERT EINSTEIN

If you learn "tricks," you'll be a caterpillar that flies, not a butterfly.
—BABA RAM DASS

PEOPLE AND EVENTS do walk through the door of our expectations.

"I'm not sure if it's just my imagination!" a client will say to me the first time he or she has tried a new exercise and found it working. We are not yet trained to understand that the world is *created* by our imagination.

I remember my first trip away from my New York home. I was sixteen and went to visit my brother in Minneapolis. Very excited at the prospect of traveling so far, I stood on the station platform and thought, with amazement, "I'm getting on the train because I had an *idea*—to visit my brother!" This seemed so simple, almost stupid, that I didn't share it with anyone. Yet it impressed me very deeply.

Years later, my son, Brian, then ten, wrote a poem:

Ideas are a piece of clay that
keeps developing bigger and bigger.
Until it finally shapes itself into
   a sculpture
which is one specific idea.

Life is an idea—an idea never
   to forget—
It keeps on developing forever.

I was astounded. When it won a prize in a poetry contest and
was printed in *The New York Times*, people wrote in from all over
the country—clearly he had touched universal feelings.

Our expressed and unexpressed ideas control the way we live our
lives. Someone once remarked: **"There are three kinds of people:
those who make things happen, those who have things happen to
them, and those who wonder, 'What happened?'"** Only the first
group is really conscious—or, as the great Russian mystic Gurdjieff
said, "awake."

The human heart can go to the lengths of God.
Dark and cold we may be, but this
Is no winter now. The frozen misery
Of centuries breaks, cracks, begins to move;
The thunder is the thunder of the floes,
The thaw, the flood, the upstart Spring.
Thank God our time is now when wrong
Comes up to face us everywhere,
Never to leave us till we take
The longer stride of soul men ever took.
Affairs are now soul size.
The enterprise
Is exploration into God.
Where are you making for? It takes
So many thousand years to wake.
But will you wake for pity's sake?

—CHRISTOPHER FRY

When we can direct our lives, we feel creative, happy and, most
important, fully alive. As long as we are in the unconscious "victim"
position, our suffering is compounded by the bewilderment and
helplessness we feel.

The Burning Question

In *Man's Search for Meaning* Viktor Frankl described the universal human need to see meaning in one's life—and death. This need can even be stronger than the desire to live. A Zen definition of the purpose of life is "to unroll the scroll of meaning." In other words, we have a profound need to discover what we're here for—not why, but "what for."

I have found this basic human question to be of burning importance to people on all levels. In my workshops for business people, whether their initial motive for taking the course was to speak effectively, handle interpersonal communication better, get over nervousness in front of groups (and more people, according to a survey, are afraid of public speaking than anything listed—including death!), or a dozen other related pragmatic objectives—when I asked what they perceived as the most meaningful part of their existence a hush fell over the room. That told me I had "hit a nerve." It was the silence we have all experienced in a group when something important has happened, something that engages our most basic questions about ourselves.

Michael M., a rising young urban planner, said wonderingly, "I just realized that the most important thing in the world to me is not my work—which I thought was the overriding interest of my life—but my relation to my kids. Everything else is really secondary."

He had made a discovery which changed his view of his own life—what gave it the most meaning.

> Close your eyes, breathe slowly and deeply, and ask: "*What gives my life its meaning?*" Allow yourself to feel the answer emerging without any conscious direction. You may surprise yourself. Take a minute to do that now. . . .

Who's Directing Your Script?

Acknowledging your real feelings is a powerful precondition to becoming the creator and director of your life. A lot of people feel like minor actors in somebody else's production—and a road company at that! They don't like the working conditions, they don't know whether the play is any good or not, they can't tell if *they* are good enough, and they feel at the mercy of the critics, the producer, and possibly the star; life is a misery of anxiety mixed with anticipation:

"When the show opens, *if* it's a success, everything will be OK."

"Suppose the reviews are bad? Suppose my reputation is ruined? Suppose I fail to meet expectations?"

"What if I'm fired?"

Meantime, the stress buildup is tremendous. Everybody's nerves are frayed. Tempers are short. The uncertainty robs good moments of joy.

"How can I play with the kids when I'm worried about business?" moans Donald T.

"I can't get to sleep because I keep thinking about all my office problems and what I have to do tomorrow. I can't relax," says Madelaine, a top government official.

"I can't seem to stop worrying," says a mother of three.

"We wouldn't be as successful and productive if we lowered our stress level," avowed a group of top women radio and TV executives. They were not willing to pay that price!

We tend to equate any kind of "letting go"—even relaxing—with loss of control. In other, more traditional societies, certain days are designed for a mass "letting go" to relieve people's consciousness of the burdens of the tight, structured lives they live the rest of the year. Mardi Gras in Catholic countries, the Indonesian Monkey Dance *(ketjak)*, the festivals in Italy, the Sufi whirling dervish dances—all these are responses to the deep human need for relaxation of tension and freedom from our own and others' expectations of "appropriate behavior." From masked balls to drugs to disco dancing, societies have always provided outlets for the need to "let go." This is a "safety valve" like the "free" period of pillaging, raping, and looting that victorious armies used to allow their soldiers after a hard-fought victory. The curious paradox is: if we are not to lose control entirely, we must occasionally "let go."

My client Henry Geldzahler, Cultural Commissioner of New York, was doing the "I Don't Care Swing" one day, when he stopped and complained, "But Doe, I DO care!" I told him, "Fine! But care only on the inhale. On the exhale, DON'T care!"

It's no longer enough to take a vacation a couple of times a year.

We need to *de-stress daily* to protect our health. Then we can *increase* our creativity and enhance our joy in life.

We are, after all, creatures of rhythmicity: in-out goes our breath. Systole-diastole, up-down, tense-relax, ebb and flow are in our blood. Our functioning is related to the tides of the moon, the pull of the sea, the movement of the planets. In the last few years science has confirmed what earlier societies knew all along: we are creatures of perpetual change, we are all works-in-progress.

As for the contents of our minds—it has been estimated that at any moment it can store a *quadrillion* bits of information. Most of this we are scarcely aware of at all; our cells and life functions take over and run us on automatic pilot. What a power plant of possibilities!

Though internally we are immensely responsive to our environment, most people don't even notice the reaction of their bodies to the stresses of their lives. But the organism is devilishly clever. You can lie to your mind:

"I feel fine! There's nothing wrong with me!"

"That shouldn't bother me! It's a detail! Trivial!"

"Why should I care about that!"

Meanwhile, that magnificently faithful seismograph—your body —is quietly registering (and responding to) the flow of feelings and perceptions you are experiencing, *whether you realize it or not.* Your knees get weak, heart pounds, stomach tightens. You try to pretend none of that is happening. Ignore it long enough and your body will produce some gross imbalance: illness or accident—even hypertension, heart disease, or cancer. That is its way of saying, "Hey, listen to me, you're not paying attention to my feelings!"

Sometimes people who have been overworking will suddenly break down. ("But he was never sick a day in his life!")

Type A people (angry, compulsive workaholics) don't allow themselves to stop until they suffer a heart attack. They are the personality type most likely to be struck down by sudden cardiac collapse.

"Death," as some wag remarked, "is Nature's way of telling you to slow down."

In our Puritan-based culture, we have not been trained to nurture ourselves. Many, many people drive themselves mercilessly on the unspoken assumption that only after you have worked hard do you really have a right to enjoy yourself. Many of us feel deep down that if we do enjoy ourselves, we will be punished for it. Having postponed for so long the human need to enjoy and savor the texture of our lives, we are often unaccustomed to (and uncomfortable with) feeling good. Only being stressed feels familiar. The familiar, even though unpleasant, will seem reassuringly like "home."

The Importance of the Unimportant

Warren M., a brilliantly successful industrialist, had struggled for twenty years to achieve power, wealth, and fame. On the way up, he had risen to every challenge, beaten down every setback and competitor. He came to me because he had now achieved everything he had always wanted, but he couldn't enjoy it. He felt a curious emptiness and hopelessness.

"Isn't there anything else? What's it all *for?*" he blurted out. He couldn't understand why life should suddenly seem so pointless to him. He had used his body like a well-made machine that he had to respect and care for, but he had forgotten to enjoy it. And the inner demon (we are all deeply moralistic in our inmost hearts) nagged at him unrelentingly. He had earned his pleasures and they suddenly seemed worthless. He made love to a succession of desirable women, he drove fast cars, dined in the great restaurants of the world, was a patron of the arts. He was powerful and respected—but the underlying grimness of his drive to succeed had robbed him of the habit of joy.

Joy had, without his even noticing it, been sent packing years ago. We are a product-oriented, result-oriented, end-oriented society. He had fulfilled his own and society's expectations. What was wrong? *Where was the payoff?*

A sense of emptiness—really despair—overpowered him. He felt cheated.

His vision of the meaning of his life was not large enough. When he learned to understand the importance of the unimportant, to get in touch with his unacknowledged inner self and contact all those deeply human centers which had nothing to do with power, success, fame, wealth and were in fact shared with every other living being, his whole feeling about his life changed. Learning to meditate expanded his experience of his own world and opened him to a new sense of value, of lightness, and fellowship with other human beings. During his first meditation, he laughed—it was the first time, he said, in eight months.

Maurice Maeterlinck's famous parable about the bluebird of happiness illustrates a profound insight about the quest for happiness and meaning. The point is not that the foolish hero went around the world looking for the secret when he might have stayed in his own backyard because that is where it was all the time. The point is that he *had* to make the journey in order to experience his own happiness.

We see only what we believe, what we're prepared to see. Yet the clues to a new state of development are probably there all the time if we could only see them. All of us can remember opportunities missed, people neglected, chances we ignored because we were not ready for them.

Our "ideas" were in the way.

Every era produces its own meaningful myths in whatever form is most popular. For us it may be film. A powerful Japanese movie, *Rashomon*, tells the story of a forest murder, based on a 1900s text by Asgatanaka, from the separate viewpoints of the main people involved. At the end of the film, we didn't know if anybody was lying. *Everybody* was telling their truth, although their stories conflicted with each other. Very puzzling! What remained was a basic human mystery.

Today the old certainties are gone. We must be able, in this new age of shifting realities, to tolerate much greater ambiguity than ever before. How *are* we to steer, then, without the lodestar of the old certainties, the old values?

The answer may be that we can only judge the truth by the reality it creates. Let me hasten to add here that this refers to nonverifiable parts of experience—larger issues than "Who forgot to put the cap on the toothpaste?" or even "Who killed President Kennedy?" (This question, which may be insoluble, generates a mythmaking which may reflect our national psyche—much the way a thermometer reflects the patient's fever—if not the nature of the disease.)

What we imagine becomes true because we act as if it is, creating a reality by our very assumption.

For instance, if you walk around with the basic assumption that people are no good, somehow your experience will confirm it. You expect to be cheated—and you will be. If you assume people are not to be trusted, every negative experience you have will reverberate in the light of your inner conviction.

Hidden Assumptions

"People are no damned good."

"I can't win."

"Nobody cares."

"I love people."

"Why does it happen to me?"

"Every guy wants only one thing."

"I'm lovely."

"Somebody up there loves me."

Each of these basic hidden assumptions creates experiences of life that match a perception of meaning. Then whatever happens provides its own justification.

"I'll believe it when I see it" is like saying "I'll go in the water when I can swim." We have been taught, because of the old faith in objective evidence, to see things backward. Yet it is only by an act of imagination (a kind of faith)—before reality provides evidence—that realities begin to happen.

Strangely enough, the old saying "Results count," which used to be the battle cry of result-oriented, materialistic people, is now the touchstone for a new, more organic groping toward human meaning. The question is: "What *effect* does my view/attitude produce?"

We are learning that by imagining we can tap our enormous potential. By imagining we are, as Anne Frank said, "really good at heart," and by imagining that we feel love—or at least by extending our hopes and wishes until they are realized—we can begin to direct energy toward those expanded states of being.

Attention is energy: what we imagine begins to happen.

The Great "As If" Principle

"Act as if," Uta Hagen often says to her acting class. And in life no less than in acting this is how reality is created. In the next chapters, we will explore how to open ourselves to these new enlarged ways of functioning and feeling—tapping our deepest creative potential to express our own gifts and communicate productively with others.

> Visualize a person as perfect, whole, at his/her best, and project that certainty, if possible when that person is asleep. It's not necessary to be in the same place.

One of my students created a very imaginative adaptation of this mental gift giving. She was trying to help a friend who was experiencing a writing block. She thought to herself, "What can I do?" Nothing, she felt, directly. Then she thought, "What if I do three things that *I* hate to do and mentally dedicate the energy released by doing those tasks to my friend?" So she cleaned up her closet, her desk, and her refrigerator. Then she told her friend. Indeed, her friend experienced a certain inexplicable flow of ease and ability to work, perhaps triggered by the generosity of her friend's act.

This was an empathic act—to do something difficult yourself to help someone else. There is, of course, no way of knowing precisely what does help. The alchemy of freeing energy is capricious.

Research tells us it is the right hemisphere of the brain that perceives sudden shifts in feeling. We have all experienced that when a depression lifts, a sudden insight gives a new feeling of lightness, or fear gives way to relief and the world is suddenly bright again.

The left hemisphere is concerned with linear thinking, logic, analysis, sequential thought. It is the plodder, the analyst, the critic and relentness logician. The right hemisphere is intuitive, deals in imagery, spatial and musical matters, and operates swiftly to change gestalt or feeling states, often mysteriously. It is the artist, singer, child, romantic.

We need both to function well. Language, although mainly located in the left hemisphere, also involves music, so when we speak we are using both hemispheres. Western education and thought tends to develop mainly left-brain-oriented processes, and the latest findings have shown that we need to involve learners in more right-brain activities to enhance and facilitate ease and depth of learning.

When you're in a rut mentally you tend to pace up and down. Dance or sing, or paint, jog, or recite poetry—and you free the ght brain and trick the left into accepting some help. *("What's really important is never what seems to be going on!")*

Interrupting or changing the psychophysical processes which correspond to the mental blocks are one way of getting out of our mental traps. The intuitive right brain *would* be responsive to someone's gift of mental energy or positive vision of functioning beautifully, and could immediately integrate that into an entirely different feeling state than the "problem level"—which is full of reasons, history, explanations, grievances, and complaints (rational and "stuck").

Studies have shown that plants that are prayed over grow bigger and produce larger and more exceptional fruit. At Findhorn, a spiritual community in Scotland, the size of the fruits and vegetables has astounded botanists.

A couple of years ago I witnessed a dramatic episode involving the power of group thought. I was teaching at the Manhattan School of Music and one of my students was absent from class one day.

"Where's Kathy?" I inquired.

"Oh, didn't you know? She had a brain tumor, and she's been in a coma for three days!" answered one of the other young women in the class. I was horrified. Although I had never done anything like this before, I gathered everybody—about ten people—into a circle and for the next hour and a half, standing with hands joined, eyes closed, we tried to visualize Kathy as completely healed, and sent her our collective healing energy. Although I had no experience doing anything like this, and no idea if it would work or not, I just felt we had to try to do *something*. That afternoon Kathy came out of her coma. Later I found out that many other people in the school were also sending Kathy healing energy.

William Tiller of Stanford University suggests, on the basis of his research, that the intensity of the coherent group-energy field (which means a group of people on the same wavelength with the same intentions at the same time) is not the sum of the number of group members, but the *square* of the number of people in the group. In other words, the power of a group of 200 people whose energies were coherent would have the numerical value not of 200 but 40,000!

W. Brugh Joy, M.D., writes in *Joy's Way: A Map of the Transformational Journey*, a book about healing with body energies:

The induction potential of a group field can be very powerful. Further-more, one or two individuals with strong energy fields centered at the heart level are capable of igniting the rest of the group into that same level of consciousness.

Of course, this accounts for mass hysteria as well. Anybody who has ever been in an audience mesmerized by a powerful speaker or a great performance has known that sense of exhilaration and oneness that unites the whole crowd. I remember hearing Vladimir Horowitz, the great pianist, play at Carnegie Hall, and I remember being one of 11,000 people at the Albany Woman's Conference, swept away with the sense of exhilarating unity. And who has not been at great football or soccer games, or experienced the power-ful charisma in action of pop singers from Sinatra to the Beatles to Michael Jackson? On the demonic side, we have seen newsreels of Hitler addressing stadium crowds whipped into frenzy.

Tapping Into Your Charisma

Dr. Robert Ornstein, author of *The Psychology of Consciousness*, told a recent medical conference: "Mental control of physical states can show individuals that they have absorbed from their culture a radical underestimation of their possibilities."

Thousands of people have tapped into expanded learning capa-cities through Suggestology, an unfortunately named but remark-ably effective teaching system developed by the distinguished Bulgarian scientist Dr. Georgi Lozanov.

As Sheila Ostrander and Lynn Schroeder report in their book *Superlearning*, Dr. Lozanov pioneered in the mid-1960s a new system of effortless learning and remembering information. He was able to prove what he had suspected—that the human ability to learn and remember is virtually limitless. In the first experiment with fifteen professional people, aged twenty-two to sixty, the group, at first disbelieving and skeptical, learned a thousand French words in one day—almost half the working vocabulary of a language! Using relaxation exercises, stately slow music, and dif-fering intonations for reading aloud the material to be learned, this pilot group not only scored an incredible 97 percent on the test scores, but enjoyed the whole experience. (The usual number of new pieces of information acquired in conventional learning ses-sions is 50–150.)

In subsequent courses, people who tried it noticed that their lives improved—small health problems dropped away, neuroses cleared up, and self-confidence increased along with their ability and pleasure in learning. "They begin to grow into a larger notion of what they are and what they can do." The system worked with people of all ages and levels. Every human being seems to have the capacity to perform at something like a genius level!

Of course there have always been exceptional people and even exceptional groups capable of astonishingly rapid mental calculations and/or feats of hypermnesia (semiphotographic supermemory). Certain yogis in India memorized all the sacred writings in case of some colossal disaster, so that, as long as even one yogi lived, he could restore all the lost knowledge through his own memory. The Maoris in New Zealand were also trained in the same supermethods. A modern Maori chief, Kaumatana, could recite the entire history of his tribe, covering forty-five generations and over 1,000 years *without notes!* It took him three days to recite it. Lozanov studied at many Indian yoga centers. At the Institute of Sri Yogendra in Bombay he met Yogi Sha, who, after doing daily exercises for a year, could instantly recall eighteen-number columns, remember without effort the name and day of the week for any date in a given century, and remember photographically how scores of objects he'd barely glimpsed were arranged. Dozens of people in India had developed such powers, but such techniques were not suitable for mass application. Lozanov himself studied Raja Yoga, the science of concentration, for twenty years. This involves techniques of altering states of consciousness, training in visualization, concentration, and special breathing exercises. With these techniques people can develop "Siddhis," or supernormal abilities supposedly latent in us all, such as photographic supermemory, instant calculation, and other extraordinary mental abilities like pain control, as well as everything from eyeless sight to telepathy.

They also developed spectacular physical accomplishments. Lozanov's research convinced him that when people use both body and mind harmoniously, they can expand their mental capacities, and awaken and enhance their creativity and intuitive abilities. No special equipment is necessary, and it works with young, old, retarded, and brilliant alike. (In Iowa, after a year's teaching in the public school system, Suggestology produced significant leaps in student achievement.)

Originally a doctor and psychiatrist, Lozanov didn't set out to be an educator—he was studying the nature of the human being in all its potential. As Ostrander and Schroeder point out:

Lozanov devised ways to open the reserves of the mind, to heal mental and physical disease. But in investigating what the whole human being can do, he couldn't help being drawn into creative and intuitive areas. . . . Then he became one of the leading parapsychologists in the communist world, and at the same time realized that with his new techniques the average person could develop supermemory, and learn factual information with unheard-of ease.

I was delighted when I read about this remarkable method since it paralleled and reinforced my discoveries in teaching people how to communicate comfortably and effectively, and how to, in effect, *tap their own charisma*. These methods have much in common with Lozanov's system: they work with the whole person—body, mind, life-style. By ironing out blocks in the energy flow—which may be the result of fear, negative self-judgments, momentary tension or early childhood conditioning, poor self-image and/or lack of confidence in one's own abilities—people begin to be able to express their best selves, feel confident and capable, deal calmly and effectively with hitherto frightening communication situations, and best of all—*know that they can always do it*. No more hit-or-miss hoping, or purely verbal or purely experiential approaches. With this holistic approach to communicating well, you master the tools and resources that put you in a state of calm, relaxed, pleasurable functioning. This intuitive, creative state can produce what the Russians call "bio-rapport."

Bio-rapport is the vehicle for experiencing your own charisma. When the "vibes" are good, you feel accepted and liked, you are in resonance with your audience, and they have a positive experience of you.

In *Superlearning*, Ostrander and Schroeder write:

Bio-rapport—messages pulsing in widening circles out of the whole person—probably lies at the heart of charisma. This is the between-the-lines communication of powerful artists and leaders, and of great teachers. It makes the message take, it reaches and moves us, even to the barricades. . . . Underneath the separate surface of things, there

> is a connection, a dynamic network, flashing countless messages everywhere, anywhere, perhaps faster than the speed of light. Time and space do not seem to affect these life signals. We are just beginning to realize how we influence and are influenced by thoughts and feelings pulsing along the network. . . . Like the old telephone system, this is a party line, and we're all on the line. . . . As Donald Hatch Andrews remarked, "In shifting the basis of our ideas about the universe from mechanics to music, we move into an entirely new philosophy of science and a fresh way of looking at things for the rest of us. . . . We form the resonance, we are the music and the message."

Everybody has had the experience of walking into a room feeling great—perhaps you just fell in love! Everyone senses a certain glow about you. When you smile, people respond. When you look or act gloomy or have a chip on your shoulder, the chances are that people will respond to that negative message. Interestingly, negative messages are usually misunderstood! People generally interpret negative feelings as being directed toward them, and may perceive you as angry, sullen, arrogant, snobbish, cold, or mean when you are actually feeling worried, apprehensive, shy, or sad. You are putting out signals on the telepathic network we are all involved in.

Later in the book I will show you how to program yourself for a positive outcome before an important meeting, presentation, or encounter in your life. *People will walk through the door of your expectations—if these are real enough for you.*

Unfortunately it doesn't do any good to say, with the top layer of your mind, "I will do it! I will get that job! I will make a good impression!" If your body is caught up in unconscious tension, your electromagnetic field will not reflect that positive image because it wasn't put in at a deep enough level.

The late Itzhak Bentov, the brilliant author of *Stalking the Wild Pendulum*, asked what happens to your consciousness if you're knocked out in a dark alley. Your body can't worry that your wallet is being stolen. Your waking consciousness is certainly no longer aware of what is happening, but your rudimentary consciousness is keeping the machine going. Your heart is still beating, blood pumping, and you are breathing.

Ben, a wonderfully sunny, funny, spiritual genius used to say that the rudimentary consciousness is like the "janitor who minds the boiler room." Now if you give the "janitor" instructions to clean out all the rooms in the house (translating that into whatever you want to do well, from playing tennis to addressing a board meeting), and your body is tense with anxiety, it's as though you asked him to do a wonderful job cleaning up the house—but left all the doors locked! "Damn," complains the janitor. "How do you expect me to do that? You're lucky I'm taking care of the furnace!" Many people try to bully themselves into relaxing by saying to themselves, "That shouldn't bother me!" or "What's the matter with me anyhow! Shape up! Stop behaving like a fool! Pull yourself together!"

None of this impresses the "janitor." He just shrugs. And you feel angry at yourself for not being able to control your nerves, tension, or scared feelings. Your voice shakes, your legs quiver, you can't remember what you wanted to say, your stomach knots up, your hands perspire. And the more you berate yourself, the worse it gets. In the next chapter we will explore ways for you to change how you react to stressful communication and other situations by learning breathing, psychophysical, and visualization skills that will give you the technique and confidence to be at your best even when you don't feel like it. Through role-playing and courage exercises, and some fun-to-do assignments, you will discover for yourself the secrets of exploring and projecting your true voice, your own insights and perceptions, warmth and feelings, and learn how to read people and situations accurately so that you are really "tuned in."

The ancient knowledge that mind, emotions, and body are all one is now being implemented with new techniques to help you achieve your potential beyond your wildest dreams.

George Leonard, in his beautiful book *The Silent Pulse*, has written about the phenomenon of rhythm entrainment. Our biological cycles are entrained with light, and to some extent by gravitational effects, and magnetic, electromagnetic, atmosphere, and subtle geophysical effects also influence us. We usually get up when it's light and sleep at night. We have electric light so we can vary our biological clocks more than birds, for instance, who go to sleep at dusk. But if you fly in an east-west direction, you experience jet lag. The disruption of our biological clocks when we have crossed several time zones throws our rhythms off, which makes it hard to function for a few days.

Have you ever watched fireflies blinking in a bush, off and on, off and on? Pretty soon they're doing it in unison. Nature likes to do things economically. The Dutch scientist Christian Huygens noticed the two-pendulum entrainment in 1665. Scientists sometimes call this "mutual phase-locking of two oscillators." This is even observable in human relationships. George Leonard writes of Dr. William S. Condon's amazing discoveries about the "subtle, largely unseen conversational dance": listeners were observed moving in precise though unconscious synchrony with a speaker's words. This process appears to be a universal characteristic of human communication. During conversations, people engage in intricate and shared movements across many subtle dimensions, yet all are strangely unaware they are doing so. Even total strangers will display this synchronization.

When people synchronize breathing in a shouting match or singing, chanting, or marching, they feel good about each other. There is some speculation that the brain waves of the participants are synchronized, and a feeling of harmony results. "The closer you move in rhythm with someone," Condon told George Leonard, "the closer you become with that person."

Sensitivity to different rhythms can mean the difference between hostility, incomprehension, or boredom, and a feeling of intuited understanding.

The One-Minute Verbal Free-for-All

Here's an exercise I have found enormously energizing and freeing. I use it with my classes. I ask people to divide into pairs, face each other, and for one minute shout nonstop at each other. The only requirement is that they yell as loud as possible, and not stop for a second, but continue until the minute is up. People who find it difficult to "hold the floor" or grab attention are amazed how hard it is for them to keep it up. They often feel foolish or abashed at first. But once they get into the knock-down, drag-out spirit of it, they find it a tremendous amount of fun, and everybody feels very alive, warm, and energized. In fact, it is one of the fastest ways to bring up the energy of a group of people. The mock battle leaves everybody breathless, laughing, and has the effect of breaking down shyness and inhibition barriers.

If you consider yourself shy, or if you'd like to improve your verbal fluency and spontaneity, try it!

Stand facing your partner (or a wall), set your stopwatch, and begin to talk vehemently, as loudly as possible without straining, for one minute. No less! (If you shout continuously you take in more oxygen, which stimulates more brain activity, and there is a greater flow of energy and ideas.) The loosening of your blocks has the effect of unleashing a veritable flood of rich material. Over and over I have marveled at the funny and imaginative tirades that people come up with out of the reservoir of their own experiences during this exercise—without effort! If you can once break through the barrier of initial shyness, the flow is apt to be torrential!

Sometimes people protest, "But I'm not angry now! How can I yell when I'm not angry?"

This is usually a form of embarrassment at revealing how they might behave when they do let go. Anger is terrifying to many people. They're afraid of simulating it or in some cases expressing it at all. In later chapters, I will show you how using anger productively can enormously enhance your powers of expression, without losing you friends!

The power to switch emotions—to quickly call on and enact emotions you may not be feeling at the moment—gives you access to emotional flexibility and lessens the fearful power of the taboos many people have been burdened with about expressing negative feelings (or, in surprisingly many cases, *any* strong feelings).

Is Your Voice Monotonous?

I discovered a few years ago that people who have monotonous voices almost invariably have been conditioned not to express anger!

If, as a child, you are told that strong negative feelings are BAD, you will tend to cut off *all* strong feelings, because it is so hard to know how to control unacceptable feelings. If some feelings are not OK, runs the internal rationale, then *all* strong feelings are dangerous. This is how people who can't ever express anger also cut themselves off from their positive or joyful feelings. What's left is the boring middle ground—the safe, gray harbor of emotional anonymity:

"If they don't know what I'm feeling, they can't punish me!"

"If I don't show any feelings, I'm safe."

When you've worn a protective mask all your life, it's sometimes very difficult to drop it. Alexandra M., who had grown up in a cold, distant family atmosphere, gave a moving talk in one of my classes on her experience teaching a retarded young man to read after everyone had said it was hopeless. Yet her face showed very little expression. When she did a "scene" where she was supposed to be bawling out a friend for having stood her up, she was so quiet and impassive that everybody remarked on it. Alexandra was genuinely shocked—she thought she'd been showing extreme anger!

The hostility exercise and the one-minute verbal free-for-all gradually had a liberating effect on her. Her whole personality took on a warmth and charm that amazed her friends as well as the class. Originally people tended to think of her as very bright, but standoffish and cold. Because of the change in her personality, she was able to get a job she'd always wanted as a reporter for a top newspaper. She no longer felt shy. She could now talk to strangers and get them to confide in her. She was very happy about that, and it was lovely to see her new confidence and vivacity.

The Keys to Your Charisma

Each of us in our own lives is a vehicle for change. When you make changes in the way you *imagine* your life and its meaning, your ability to impact on others' lives grows powerfully, dramatically. Throughout these chapters, I will give you practical tools for understanding *how* we communicate to other people *what* we are feeling, and *why* our sense of meaning (what is true for us) is communicated clearly to those around us (even when we don't express it openly). Even when we ourselves are not aware of our true feelings, they can change the outcome of our interactions with people.

Imagination has been so undervalued as a practical tool of life that we need to find ways to relegitimize it. Not just for artists, poets, and similar visionaries, but for everybody. You have begun to see how the right hemisphere, which controls our states of feeling, can trick the left hemisphere—the rational, logical part—into dropping its resistance to change, to leaps of imagination, to risks, to confidence. We have to learn to mother and father our unborn selves; we are constantly changing, evolving, growing, shedding old mindsets and personalities which are too limited and limiting for our lives today.

Some of what I will talk about may seem irrelevant at first—but nothing is unimportant. We will commute from the micro to the macro level, and I will show you techniques of reconceptualizing your communication with yourself and people around you so you can be, at once, most fully yourself and most productive with other people.

We will dart acrobatically from inside to outside, from front to back, from body to breathing, to mind, to life-style—because everything counts; *only you—once you have a range of resources wide enough to choose from—can pick a key to unlock the secrets of your own charisma.*

Novelist Elizabeth Bowen once remarked: "A novelist is a person who invents the truth." I have since come to see that we are all artists of our lives. *A person is a truth who invents reality.* Each of us has an inner truth, and we can contact it in ways which I will explore very specifically in coming chapters. *We each have all the gifts we need to live vitally creative lives.*

Many people have remarked, "All children are geniuses!" Marshall McLuhan observed: "Education is a process of shutting off our talents." It need not be. It must not be. With the shrinking of the world into a global village, the rewards and knowledge have grown as great as the risks. We now can know how to contact those unused parts of our selves. With practice, we can become more skillful at tapping into these inner sources of power.

We need to be curious and interested in questions, rather than final answers. Values must be reevaluated, in the shifting light of change.

Dreams—Our Inner Messages

Every human being dreams. A Malaysian tribe, the Senoi, have a crime-free, mental illness-free society because they have learned to work with their dreams—to accept feelings and transform them. In psychodrama workshops, I have been deeply moved time after time by the beauty of imagery, the depth of perception, and the sheer eloquence of people speaking out of their deep feelings, unburdened by clichés from their ordinary levels of existence.

Becoming aware is a prelude to conscious integration at a higher level. Accepting the dignity of your inner gifts makes them real...ized.

Bali is the only society on earth where it is taken for granted that everybody is an artist. As part of religious observances, everybody paints, sings, dances, sculpts, weaves—nearly every possible form of human expression gets free rein. The result is a healthy society and an astonishingly high level of artistic achievement.

Our Western conception of the artist as a suffering genius who has little or no relation to ordinary mortals is part of the old dichotomizing split between mind/body, god/devil, good/evil, pleasure/pain. When we are reunited with all our amputated possibilities, we no longer need to make the artist devil or hero. The Russians, for whom poets have always been the suffering surrogates of the entire popular consciousness, recognize the power of poets and writers to polarize the feelings of the nation. Writers have been thrown into prison, insane asylums, or shipped to Siberia. The Russians know that the fate of poets somehow affects the population very deeply, because to speak truly is to give voice to essential human feelings. Such people are valuable—and dangerous!

Yet people speaking directly from their deep consciousness are as simple, clear, poetic, and moving as the greatest writers.

Most of us have a great deal invested in our automatic ways of behaving, our carefully learned un-consciousness. The process of expanding behavior styles or opening to new experiences, of expressing feelings openly, may be very frightening to many people.

"I feel silly," said Malcolm N., trying to permit himself to do the "I Don't Care Swing". Yet we can't grow properly without laughing. Six somersaults a day—mental and physical—await you in the next chapters. Nothing is irrelevant. The most surprising little memories, actions, and dreams can trigger growth, change, illumination. Irreverence, whimsy, and humor are natural relaxation and survival mechanisms, personal "tuning forks." Humans, like metals, break under too much stress. For all recorded history, one way of diminishing stress has been to *laugh*. The shared experience of celebrating pain lightly provides a feeling of unity that counteracts the most devastating load of private misery.

My adopted Hungarian grandmother, Mimi, who survived endless changes of country, government, mindset, and life-style, once told me, "Laughter is a soul bath." In Nazi-occupied countries of Europe during World War II, jokes were a defiant code that gave people courage and relief. Author Norman Cousins described in *Anatomy of an Illness* how he cured himself of an incurable disease with heavy doses of comedy films and laughter.

Our infinite human capacity to transform and transmute our lives is quickened by the capacity to laugh. Jokes often depend on the juxtaposition of the unexpected with the familiar. But what makes different people laugh? A person who can make others laugh is generally very much valued. The trick is to use humor without straining. (How many of us have winced at jokes carefully, painfully planted in a speech by a speaker who clearly finds nothing a laughing matter?!)

I will show you how to be funny in your own way, by relaxing and sharing in the common experiences of your audience and yourself. NO TRICKS! Instead of tricks, I will show you the processes that will give you the results you want to achieve. When you know how to begin the process for yourself, the results will be like all good performances—surprising, but right and inevitable—the best creative interaction between your own intuition, experience, and feelings and those of your audience.

I'm not going to *give* you a fish; I'll show you how to catch all the big ones yourself out of the rich and surprising aquarium of your own inner resources!

The Technology of Trusting Yourself

Whatever you learn from this book will need to be filled in with insights, feelings, and experiences; all these are your own, yours alone. Call it the "technology of trusting yourself." Then by "merely" imagining (and then practicing!), you can move into a new expanded charismatic self. The discovery of your charisma begins with the cultivation of your own trust in yourself. Much of that depends on garbage removal, clearing away the psychophysical blocks that stand in your path.

When my students begin work with me, I tell them, "People are going to ask you pretty soon what you've done to yourself. Did you have a vacation? A new hairdo? Are you in love?" (This last is really significant, since on over 45 percent of the returns to my Charisma Questionnaire, people replied that they had felt most charismatic in their lives when they were in love.) Most people whom you see won't know exactly what's changed. They will just sense *something* has. A new confidence, a sense of yourself as more valid as a person and more connected to others at the same time— all this will change the way people perceive you.

They *will* walk through the door of your expanded expectations! And that is exactly what happens! It seems like magic. But magic is only a name for what we don't yet understand.

To Grow You Have to Forgive Yourself (and Others!)

We will be exploring many ways you can seduce your left brain into letting go of the small self, the old ways of doing things, and allowing the creative, intuitive, holistic part of your brain—the right hemisphere—to make a quantum leap forward in your development.

It is important to recognize—without self-blame—the fear you may have of changing, the fear of "losing" the self you are familiar with.

"But that's not me!" protests Janet L.

"That's the way I am," says Bruce B. firmly.

These are the last stands of the early resistances of the "small" self. Once, long ago, they helped you to become an individual in ways that were safe in the milieu in which you grew up, which protected you from being overrun, violated, or even destroyed. But that was when you were small. They may no longer be useful. To change, you have to acknowledge their value to you in the past and respectfully ask permission of that resistant part of you to accomplish its goals of survival and growth. This means *not* being angry at yourself for failing to change as rapidly as you would like to.

The only way to grow and move ahead is to throw out self-blame, perfectionism, and anger at yourself for not achieving your ends as fast as you would like, and acknowledge exactly what you feel without feeling it defines you. We are infinitely malleable and, in the process of self-transformation, we must nurture ourselves in order to move ahead as quickly as possible to the next-higher stage of evolution.

St. Francis said, "Be gentle with yourself. Forgive yourself each day." And this is *what works*. The next chapter describes the Anti-Judgmental Notebook—as the initial step in this process.

Just remember that if you can't immediately imagine being confident, charismatic, and all the wonderful qualities you'd like to be and have felt at certain moments in your life you were, have patience. *Feelings change.* Endlessly. Always. They pass like clouds across the horizon, waves across the sea. Patience with yourself gives you the necessary detachment to face your "worst" failings and gently encourage yourself to grow—without judgment.

Remember the story of the two caterpillars inching their way along the ground? Suddenly a bright golden butterfly flashed by them.

"Hmph!" said one of the caterpillars, pausing for a moment. "You'll never get *me* up in one of those things!"

3

How to Stop Putting Yourself Down

(Or Whose Side Are You On, Anyway?!)

Life is a fairy tale in reverse.
—ISAK DINESEN

IN ANSWERING the Charisma questionnaire, one out of four interviewees reported feeling most charismatic "now" or "when I was three [to five] years old." One out of every three said, "When I am in love."

Most of us can remember some time when we felt loved, accepted, in tune with the world. When we feel like that, it's as though we could do no wrong. Our bodies feel light and free (if we're aware of them at all), we feel happy and at ease, life seems full of beautiful possibilities. The world seems friendly. It's hard to imagine we'll ever feel differently. The sun shines for us, and we are in tune with everything.

Remember, nobody who answered the questionnaire wrote that he or she had *never* felt charismatic! It appears to be part of our natural heritage. Why, then, is it so difficult to hang on to that marvelous sense of being totally "at home" in the world? More important, *how do we get back to it?* This chapter is about how.

To discover, nurture, and enhance your own natural charisma, you have to play detective with your own mind and body and feelings. By discovering what roadblocks you put up—which first take the form of negative thoughts, and then are translated into physiological symptoms and interferences with full natural breathing and functioning—you will have the tools to "clear the way" to the kind of natural easy functioning we've all experienced at good moments in our lives. You will learn how to make them happen at will.

Imagine for a moment a garden hose spraying water full force. The force of the spray is very powerful; the water shoots across your garden in a splendidly concentrated arc. Now imagine that you bend the hose, make a kink, a small stoppage at one point in the line. This is comparable to what happens when you have a negative thought and your body tenses. *Your electromagnetic field literally weakens.* Your breathing grows shallower; less oxygen is reaching your brain, which uses three-quarters of your oxygen supply, and so you can't think as well.

When I was a young actress going for auditions I was so nervous I'd forget the names of the people I met. "What's the matter with me?" I wondered. "It's as though there's a hole in my head. All the information I get when I'm nervous falls right out. I feel so stupid!" I didn't realize then that I had practically stopped breathing. Holding your breath when you're nervous is what most people do without realizing it. It's guaranteed to lower your IQ instantly, at least for a spell.

If you want to demonstrate to yourself how your negative thoughts and feelings literally weaken you, try the following experiment: stand facing a friend and put your left hand on his or her right shoulder. Now ask him to extend his left hand, palm down—elbow straight, wrist slightly higher than the shoulder (you can reverse it—it's not important which side is used). Tell him to think of something very pleasant. When he's ready, tell him you're going to try to push down his extended hand and he should resist your pressure. (The idea is to test his strength, not to suddenly overwhelm him and knock the arm down.)

Put your fingers on his arm just past the wrist (between the elbow and the wrist) and press down. Notice how strong the resistance is. Now ask your friend to close his eyes and think of something very negative. Give him enough time and ask when he is ready. Then put your right hand on his arm again the way you did before and press down again. You'll be surprised—and so will he—when his arm goes straight down, as though there were no strength in it at all! Then let him test you. The same thing will happen. People are always amazed by this test.

This kinesiological testing can also be used to test foods and drugs, to see if your body finds them positive or negative. (To do the test with foods, drugs, or vitamins, hold the substance at the center of your chest with one hand, and test as usual with the other. It doesn't matter whether you know what you're holding or not. For instance, if you wrap up a cigarette for a smoker, the reaction will be very weak even if the person is an unregenerate smoker and "likes" cigarettes! The test isn't affected by your likes and dislikes, but by what is really strengthening or weakening for your system. Again, the body doesn't lie!)

It's impossible to be relaxed and anxious at the same time and that's not as obvious as it sounds! In this chapter, using this clue, I am going to show you how to free your energy flow and unlock your charisma.

Since we know that everybody has had the experience of feeling charismatic—i.e., comfortable, at ease, effective, alive, and in joyful communication with the world, i.e., bio-rapport—we're going to learn how to produce that psychophysical state quite deliberately. This is a four-stage process:

1. Identifying the interferences (the "kink" in the hose—the "water" is your energy flow) when they're
   a. thoughts and feelings.
   b. physical tensions and irregular breathing.
2. Learning relaxation techniques to deal with the specific tensions that *you* experience.
3. Practicing new breathing processes that will change the chemistry of your consciousness and help you maintain a calm, powerful energy flow—even under stress—so you can be at your best when you don't feel like it!
4. Learning and rehearsing unfamiliar "power amplifiers" so you can be on a natural "high" *at will*—and you will learn to function with a heightened energy flow.

A good detective needs a greedy eye for detail. Your clues will be the trivial moments that trigger negative feelings. Sherlock Holmes, Hercule Poirot, and all good detectives unravel the most complex mysteries by their keen attention to the significance of details. Most of us are more like Watson in our unawareness and disbelief; when we start paying attention, we say, "Elementary, of course!" The "crime" is the fatal leakage of energy and confidence caused by negative thoughts, experiences, and tensions.

So you'll use your "trivia triggers" to "clue" you in to the secret of your own mystery. Since we need to find the negatives that interfere with the flow of creativity and power, I have found it most productive with thousands of people to start with the negatives—the Anti-Judgmental Notebook.

Nothing is irrelevant or arbitrary here. Every question has a direct bearing on how we unconsciously sabotage our own power. You will find it surprising, possibly painful. But please bear with the process—there is a positive payoff within only a short time, and I'll explain that immediately after the Anti-Judgmental Notebook.

"Who was the most negatively critical person in your childhood?" I asked a group, as I always do at the beginning of the course. People shifted in their seats, smiled, looked surprised or uneasy. What did that have to do with communicating well? Public speaking? Charisma? A great deal, as you'll see.

"And what," I asked, "were some of the verbal and nonverbal messages you got as a child, about what you were or should be or do?" Now the answers poured out.

"My mother: she always told me I was clumsy."

"Both my parents: nothing I did was ever right."

"My older sister: she kept telling me I was stupid and I'd be found out."

"My father: he said people were no damn good. He also gave me the feeling that whatever I felt or did was somehow not important. He just wasn't interested. I was expected to do well, but when I did, it just meant I didn't get yelled at. There wasn't any positive reinforcement."

"My grandmother: 'Stop, you're being a bad boy. You must never get angry. Don't be disobedient.'"

"My older brother: 'You're a dumb klutz—you're clumsy, awkward. You're ugly.'"

"My aunt: she said I should be a little lady; 'You're too shy.'"

Many women often had heard the messages:
"Be a lady!"
"Keep your elbows in, your legs together."
"Do what's expected of you."
"Be nice."
"Don't raise your voice."

Often people reported contradictory instructions. One woman, a writer, said she was told, "Be aggressive, don't be shy," and at the same time, "Be obedient, do what you're told!" An amazing number of people, including some high up on the corporate ladder, had been told they were "stupid." One executive, who kept deploring that he exploded regularly at his subordinates, said he just couldn't stop. He stuck out his jaw like a rebellious little boy: "That's the way I am, I can't help it!" he declared. His early message, from his father, had been that he was "stupid." He began to see that every time he ordered himself to do something—"Every morning I yell at myself, 'John, today don't be such a jerk, don't yell at everybody,' and then I go right out and do it!"—his inner self would rebel against that bossy voice that talked to him exactly like his father who called him "stupid."

Knowing what your hidden self-put-downs are can save you from sabotaging your own performance. I have found it absolutely crucial to help people unearth their negative self-images —only then do they realize they're not true!

Most of us suffer from at least an occasional nagging doubt. It's important to recognize these little devils when you're making a speech, meeting new people or new challenges. Perhaps you say to yourself:
"I'm not clever enough."
"I'm not attractive enough."
"I'm not young/old enough."
"I have no right to be happy/successful/famous."
"My vocabulary's not good enough."
"They'll think I'm a hick."
"They'll think I'm boring."
"Who am I to sound like an expert?"
"I'll probably louse this up."
"THEY will resent it if I act sure of myself."

"THEY won't like me—why should they?!"
"THEY won't be interested in me."
"I'm not as good as _____"
      (. . . I was
      . . . he/she is
      . . . I should be)
etc. etc. etc.

You may not even be aware that you have some doubts and negative beliefs about yourself, but when you're in a new or challenging situation, they may show up and shoot you down *if you are not aware of them!* Recognizing them as temporary roadblocks will prevent them from taking over.

On the surface, you may be capable, attractive, and apparently sure of yourself. But if a small inner voice tells you you're really going to mess up, and this little imp constantly nags you when you're not paying attention, watch out. It's practically impossible to fake an air of authority and ease. (When there is a conflict between verbal and nonverbal signals, studies show it is the nonverbal ones that are believed.) You may find you shrink, bluster, stumble, fall silent, laugh apologetically, talk too much or too little, betray by a hundred little signs that you're not feeling very comfortable. Afterward you beat yourself about the head (mentally) and think of ten splendid things you could have said but didn't. You can't understand why you didn't think of those things in time, but it is, alas, too late to retrieve the situation.

(This is known to the perceptive French as *l'esprit de l'escalier* —"the wit of the staircase"—what you think of as you're leaving, going down the stairs.) *Each time you don't speak up when you have something to say makes it harder to do so the next time.*

Your Verbal Polaroid

Get yourself a small (three-by-five-inch) spiral notebook. *Take this everywhere*—in your purse or pocket, keep it with you. Whenever something triggers a negative judgment (it may take some noticing at first to realize exactly what is or isn't a judgment and I'll get to that) write it down along with the date, the time, and (if you know) a brief note on what set it off. *The only essen-*

tial is what you said to yourself. Do add what you felt in your body when the painful thought occurred to you.

Important: don't be misled if your trigger moments seem trivial. What's really important is never what seems to be going on. That's one of the cagey disguises of our inner messages. We often feel ashamed to acknowledge that something so *trivial* as a chance remark or tiny incident or an unfavorable comparison with someone that we ourselves make can upset us.

"Don't be ridiculous—that shouldn't bother me! It's so petty!" This lightning inner response can make the original perception slink back into the underbrush, cowed, discouraged. You have no *right,* you're telling yourself, to feel this way. Not so! At this point stand up and say ALOUD:

"I HAVE THE RIGHT TO FEEL WHAT I FEEL!"

Say that three times. Go ahead! How does it sound? Angry? Defensive? Apologetic? Practice saying it AS LOUD AS YOU CAN —at least three times a day until it stops feeling foolish and silly or frightening. *What you say inside your head is not the same as saying it aloud.* One of the most important prerequisites for beginning to feel you have the right to speak up in any situation, and share your information, experiences, and perceptions with others is GIVING YOURSELF PERMISSION TO FEEL WHATEVER YOU ARE REALLY FEELING.

The problem is that many people are afraid if they have feelings they don't approve of; acknowledging them will mean they're giving in to those feelings. They identify character with feelings like this: "If I have jealous feelings, I must be a jealous, rotten person. I don't want to be that!" Or "If I'm so angry, I must be a bad person. Anger is bad." Many people, having been brought up by parents who themselves did not know how to handle anger, are convinced that natural, normal feelings of anger—which everybody has sometimes— are evil, that *they* are bad or undeserving if they experience such feelings. Sometimes the parents expressed anger themselves but didn't allow their children to.

Scraps of psychotherapeutic jargon often become weapons in the war against the self. "You're neurotic!" is the latter-day version of the old message to a child: "You're bad, you have a devil in you!"

Many people put themselves down for feeling something they don't approve of by telling themselves, "That's sick!" or "I'm being compulsive again!" The discouragement of succumbing to a negative pattern is compounded by self-blame—or used as a justification; hopeless, helpless, or defiant—"That's the way I am."

I remember a student in one of my classes at Columbia who flounced into a department meeting where she had been asked to explain why she hadn't done any work in her courses. She stared defiantly at the assembled professors and announced, "Well, I can't help it. I'm an anal compulsive personality." With that triumphant announcement, she swept out of the room.

Whether you take refuge in a LABEL or JUDGMENT or are cast down by it, it prevents you from moving ahead to another stage.

Part of this is a misunderstanding about the nature of emotions. We all are capable of innumerable feelings from ecstasy to blind rage and it's important to recognize that this doesn't make us bad or evil beings. Emotions are, as many Eastern writings have taught us, like clouds passing across the sky or waves across the ocean. Our mind is a screen across which changing emotions and scenes pass. If we identify with any of them and hang our self-image on them we'll be unable to let go of the negative emotions, unable to go on to experience others.

As Buddhist philosopher Chogyam Trungpa Rinpoche remarked:

> Negative emotions are like manure. If you recycle them and work with them, they become like a compost heap, they nurture growth. If you don't deal with them, but just push them aside, or ignore them, they are nothing but a pile of shit!

We've all seen little children playing together. Suddenly a great fight erupts. There is a lot of yelling and wrangling, maybe even hitting. Suddenly, as though nothing had happened, they'll be playing together peacefully again. This is a perfect demonstration of what happens to feelings when they're fully expressed. There is an almost magical transformation; having been expressed fully, the anger disappears. Often it is not convenient or appropriate to express feelings openly in a social, personal, or business setting. Then what do we as adults do? The same principle applies. *The key to letting go of negative emotions is full acknowl-*

edgment without judgment. (You may have to talk to yourself quickly!)

Imagine a little girl or boy who comes crying to you because he or she skinned a knee or had an argument. You can say: "That's not important—stop crying. Don't be a baby!" Or you can say, "You really feel bad, don't you? That really hurt when you fell down!" Which response is going to feel better to the child? Try it. You'll see: the first will make your child cry harder and feel worse. The second will be comforting.

We tend to think we have to *solve problems* for people. We offer advice, suggestions, pep talks. We do the same to ourselves. And the child part that is feeling anger, hurt, fear, gets enraged at this message that seems to say, "You have no right to feel what you feel," or "If you feel like that you're no good," or "Get on with it! You're being an idiot, ridiculous, babyish!" Result? You feel discouraged, blocked, depressed.

We're all complex combinations of many different states; sometimes we feel grown-up, sometimes childish, sometimes detached, sometimes emotional; our needs change. It's important to recognize that feelings are just our emotional equipment. If we lay judgments on them, it becomes impossible to follow the Ariadne thread to the minotaur in the cave and find out what the real monster looks like. *The monster is not us.* The deeper you go, the better the news is. Messages of doubt, put-down, self-hate prevent us from using our true gifts—our real charisma.

The monster is *ignorance* of our true feelings. CRITICAL VOICES are not the voice of truth, simply taped recordings, old messages that aren't true, that you do not have to identify with. Not anymore!

Notice your judgments (sometimes they're elusive). That's the first step. Sally R., a beautiful woman in her thirties, said, "My sister who was seven years older and very jealous took care of me. She always used to tell me I was stupid in math, that I couldn't hide how dumb I was; I'd be found out. So I want to deal with my math anxiety and fear of public speaking—then *at least it won't be that which will stop me.*" She didn't realize as she spoke that her negative tape was saying in a leapfrog judgment: "Well, kid, you can get rid of one or two fears but *you'll fail anyway* because those old messages were really true—you *are* stupid and you *will* be found out!" When I pointed this out to her, she gasped: "Oh, my goodness, I guess I really feel deep down that I am all those things—I didn't even notice I was being judgmental then!" That awareness was the beginning of change. Most of us never stop castigating ourselves, and have completely forgotten that originally those down-putting messages came from adults, and are *not* the voice of Truth.

Lawrence the stockbroker was a dignified, highly respectable individual—who rarely smiled. When he told me he was angry about the Anti-Judgmental Notebook, I asked him to explain. "Well, I was horrified—I realized this week that I'm judgmental about everything in my life, all the time. With my friends, my wife and children, my colleagues, my business associates—I'm always involved in a running dialogue of put-down and self-criticism. And I had never been aware of it before! It was pretty shocking, I can tell you. Now what do I do? No wonder I find it hard to speak up in a group or be spontaneous! This inner critic is telling me all the time I'm going to botch it up. By the time I've subjected what I wanted to say to my inner scrutiny it's no longer appropriate to say anything."

WRONG DOORS!

That brings us to the next step. When you have become aware of all your hidden judgments, you can identify "wrong doors" and cut off the old tapes. Once you realize that these critical voices are tapes from your past, and not real evaluations, it's possible to shake free of their heavy judgments and begin to appreciate and acknowledge yourself. *That* is the beginning of true growth.

"But my mother didn't *mean* to be so negative," protests one woman, distressed. "She meant to be a good mother."

Let's detach right now from blaming your parents for the negative messages they gave you. They probably were programmed that way by *their* parents. You *are* responsible for having responded to the message in the way you did. The point of the Anti-Judgmental Notebook is not to lay blame at the door of others or your own, but just to recognize that these are mere messages, not the "truth!"

Inside, everybody is an instant moralizer. Even people who on the surface do not admit their doubts to themselves or anybody will blame others or act them out, and will then be bewildered about why they behaved the way they did.

Ronnie R. said he had no trouble talking, but he said other people complained that he didn't listen. He was, indeed, a good speaker. He did not show up for the breathing exercises because he thought he really didn't need them. People wondered why he had taken the class (I wondered too!). Then I invited him and four other students to appear on a TV program. The others had never been on TV before. The host of the program was a young, attractive man who had only recently been promoted to network TV from the "sticks." Before the show, I asked him, "Bill, would you mind my asking what fears or uncertainties you had when you started?"

"No, that's fine," he answered. But evidently he really did mind, because when I asked him that question on the show, he snapped back angrily, "Fears? I have no fears! If I did, I wouldn't be in this business!"

"Oh," I retorted innocently, "congratulations! You're the only person in the world with no fears!" Bill was so furious that he turned to Ronnie and blasted him: "Well, what about you? Are you blocked?" Poor Ronnie was so stunned he couldn't speak. I saw him freeze. I knew he was trying to figure out what to do. Should he make a joke? Hit the host? Be pleasant? He was totally immobilized. Finally, Bill turned to the next student, who, fully prepared by long, slow breathing, answered him coolly and with poise. (Ronnie was so dismayed by his own inability to function that he took the course over again. This time he learned the breathing exercises. "Now, my wife says I listen!" he said proudly. "It's changed my life!" He had become *aware* of his own feelings *and* other people's.)

Jennifer L. said she was unable to understand why she had forgotten a very important party she had agreed to go to. She had noted it in her appointment book, but had forgotten all about it.

"I feel I'm losing my mind! How could I forget a thing like that?" she complained.

"Did you have any ambivalence about going?" I asked her.

"Well," she admitted, "I really wasn't crazy about the people giving the party, but I told myself I should get out and socialize more and *I shouldn't feel that way about them.*"

I pointed out to Jennifer what had really happened. She had given herself information about her feelings and had then told herself that she had no right to feel them! So like mischievous gremlins they had crept underground and undermined her conscious decision to go to the party. It's as though the unacknowledged, unrespected feelings said, "Aha! You won't listen to us, we'll fix you! We'll put you in a trance and you'll do what *we* want, not what *you* want, and you won't even know what hit you!" In Romans, chapter 7, verse 19, St. Paul puts it this way: "For I do not do the good I want, but the evil I do not want is what I do."

Rosalie M. gave her first talk in class on the Alexander Pope quotation "The proper study of mankind is man." Never having gone to college, Rosalie found the challenge of marshaling her thoughts on a philosophical subject very exciting. She prepared carefully and rehearsed thoroughly. Her talk was excellent until she got to the end, which was the statement of Pope's maxim. Suddenly, she stopped dead—she could not remember the quotation! I asked her, "Did you feel you had *no right* to talk about this?" Rosalie nodded. I explained that it was as though her unconscious judge were saying, "Who do you think you are? You don't have a college education. You have no right to talk about philosophy!" The inner doubt she felt, which she had not allowed herself to acknowledge, sabotaged her speech by making her forget the most important part of it!

Why do we try to hide our feelings from ourselves? For three reasons, mainly.

1. We're afraid we will take on unpleasant qualities of negative emotion we feel. ("Your face'll freeze!" Grandma used to tell me when I cried.)
2. If we recognize it, the emotion will be fed and will increase.
3. We're being self-indulgent and self-pitying.

Curiously, far from fanning the negative thoughts, full acknowledgment leads to the release of those painful feelings. Allowing yourself to experience the pain of whatever feeling you're experiencing, noticing its exact location in the body ("When I see my husband out with another woman, I feel jealous. My throat tightens and my chest hurts, and my heart beats so hard I feel it'll burst my chest"), is the first step toward feeling better and changing patterns of behavior, even though for the moment it feels worse!

Allowing yourself to notice all the feelings you *are* feeling, not just the ones you *approve* of, gives you more information on which to base your action; it gives you choice. For instance, if Jennifer sat down and wrote out her thoughts:

POSITIVE
"I'd like to meet more people."
"They've invited me and I know I could meet some people at their party."
"It's fun to be with new people sometimes."

but:

NEGATIVE
"I don't like Tim and Jerry."
"I can't stand their smoking."
"Their taste in music isn't mine."
"I don't like their friends."
"I don't feel good around them."

THEN, with this full range of information, she could decide whether to:

a. go for a short time
b. set up another appointment so she would have a reason to leave early
c. not go at all, but take a rain check
d. seek out other friends and social situations that would respect her needs but not conflict with her preferences

In short, she would be able to make a *real* choice, one that satisfied her.

Next time you find yourself making one of these judgments, STOP. Take out your notebook. Write it down. Try whenever possible to record your feelings immediately. Should you find yourself in a social situation where this might be awkward or difficult, make a mental note and write it down later, but always the same day. Don't let more than a day pass; if things pile up, they'll never be written down at all.

You'll recognize the importance of recording (and immediacy) over time. You'll be able to determine a pattern of judgmental behavior. You'll probably find out, as most do, that your times of discomfort and alienation from yourself are confined to a few situations and are not global at all. You'll observe that you're confident at cocktail parties but not at the office; that you're generally at ease over dinner with friends but not at family gatherings. Being able to monitor your unique patterns will yield insight and attention to those facets of yourself that require more "work" than others and those that require no work at all. As a log of your growing self, the Anti-Judgmental Notebook will become your best tutor: a set of guidelines by, for, and of yourself.

The act of making a choice is always more satisfying than being led around by unconscious drives. Acting out unacknowledged feelings makes one feel helpless, out of control. The mere recognizing and voicing of your desires, doubts, and feelings is, strangely enough, more important than getting what you wanted.

If you can't communicate well with yourself, you'll find it harder to communicate with others. Speaking up has to start at home. The first line of communication has to be a check with your inner feelings. Otherwise you'll soon find you don't know what they are.

When I was a little girl, I remember my brother asking my grandfather, "Grandpa, what's so terrible about lying?"

"Oh, nothing much," he answered innocently. "Just one little problem. After a while, if you keep lying, *you won't know what the truth is!*"

Not being honest with ourselves has the same result.

How can the Anti-Judgmental Notebook help you get in touch with your real feelings, liberate your courage, and open the door to a new expressiveness and charisma?

Just observing your feelings dispassionately gives you a sense of detachment and greater control. Then it's suddenly very clear that *you are not your feelings*—you *have* feelings and they change. You no longer confuse character with behavior, behavior with identity. By getting in touch with the repetitive "tapes" you may be running in your head, you can separate those "messages" from your "automatic pilot" and unmask them for thieves of your charisma.

There is a very big difference between saying "I never do anything right" (and the accompanying "sinking" feeling) and "I never do anything right . . . oh! that's judgmental—throw it out!" At least you're not identifying with your own persecutor anymore!

Wrong Doors

WHOSE SIDE ARE YOU ON ANYWAY? Somebody once said, "If there's no answer to a question, it's probably the wrong question!" Yet some of the most painful questions we put to ourselves seem unanswerable. How often have you tortured yourself with these:

"Why ME?"

"Why can't I ever get things right?"

"Why does everybody let me down?"

"Why can't I find love?"

"Why do other people have so much more luck than I do?"

"Why am I such a loser?"

The sense of helplessness, frustration, and low self-esteem such questions produce can be almost unbearable. When you were an adolescent you probably wondered, "Will any girl/boy really like me?" "Will I ever stop feeling clumsy, awkward, and uncomfortable?" As time went on, your problems probably lessened or disappeared. You didn't notice, however, the exact moment when you got an *answer* to the question. Or, indeed, whether you got an answer at all. At a certain point, the question simply seemed irrelevant. I remember saying to my mother in a panic, "How can I go to high school? . . . I've never been!"

Is there a question that you ask yourself over and over again that has tortured you for years and seems to have no answer? I call that a WRONG DOOR. Once you recognize such a question as a dead end that leads nowhere, you can, the next time it comes up, say to yourself, "Uh-oh! That's a WRONG DOOR!" and don't go through it. A WRONG DOOR is simply an unproductive question that will lead only to anguish, nothing else.

There is an odd paradox here. Emotions are usually based on old thought patterns or early assumptions:

"Mommy doesn't love me because I'm unlovable."

"I always goof up because I'm stupid."

"People laugh at me because I say the wrong things and have the wrong feelings."

"It's bad to feel mean."

"Nobody believes me when I tell them how I feel."

"Men don't like me because I'm small-breasted."

When one extricates the WRONG DOORS and early messages from the negative feelings, it is then possible to isolate a lot of mechanical, automatic, pain-producing mechanisms and just turn off the power!

You're still aware of thinking those things, but now they're almost "in quotes"; *you know they're not real.* Remember the old joke about the psychiatrist who told his patient, "Madam, you don't have an inferiority complex—you *are* inferior!" Most people are afraid that in some way this is really true of them. But when you're in harmony with yourself, you feel you have value, human worth, and capacity for love, and then all fear and pain from negative self-image drains away.

As you saw in the first chapter, we can look at the same group of facts and, according to what they're named, wind up with entirely different results. It's the old "is-the-glass-half-full-or-half-empty?" story.

"Bah! Humbug!" said Scrooge. We have a habit, in our puritanical Judeo-Christian culture, of imagining that being tough on ourselves is "realistic." Actually, having confidence in ourselves works much better and, happily, this is a skill that can be learned. Most people, I find, need to increase their self-affirmation. If you were fortunate enough to have grown up in a family that gave you a feeling of "OK-ness" about yourself and your feelings, you'll have had a head start. But as a friend of mine observed, most people have led "wounded" lives so that most of us need very much to increase our self-affirmation. This means changing habits of thought.

Most people are confident in some respects but not in others, which is why we all need to expand our powers and skills in communication. I've never met anyone who was perfect or perfectly at home in every communication situation. Maybe it isn't even possible! Some people are very comfortable talking to a few people, but uncomfortable with large groups. Others are at home with multitudes, but uncomfortable with a few. (I recall the very famous conductor who announced his personal career plans to a huge audience at one of his concerts, plans which he had not confided to a soul among his close family and associates.)

It's often a surprise—and a source of encouragement—to my class members when they realize that someone they had perceived as highly competent and effective is, in fact, feeling insecure and nervous.

Like many techniques in this book, new ways of doing and being need to be learned, practiced, and reinforced. They are not quick gimmicks that will instantly transform your image and self-image, but skills that, once acquired, will serve you in every aspect of your life. Realizing that other people put themselves through the same painful "hoops" will amplify your compassion for others and increase your ability to listen "between the lines." Understanding your own processes gives you the tools to see people as they are, rather than as extensions or projections of your own fears. And you will begin to see that you have more margin than you think—you don't have to be "perfect" to be charismatic! ("You don't have to bat 1,000," said my old friend, the memorable comedian Wally Cox.)

When someone is unpleasant or hostile, the WRONG DOOR question is: "Why doesn't he like me?" and the sinking feeling that follows leads to the old trap, "Nobody likes me!" The right question (one that will yield an answer) is: "What's he feeling?" You may not always be able to find out, but just asking this question will shift the focus of your attention, probably more realistically. You may think (and feel free to give your imagination full play):

"He had a fight with his wife and is feeling grumpy."
"Big parties make her feel shy and uncomfortable."

"When his ideas are challenged, he feels his right to exist has
    been threatened."
None of your guesses may be right, but at least you won't have
involved yourself in the line of fire between another person and
her or his private problem.

When my daughter, Andrea, was about seven years old, she
asked me one morning, "Mommy, are you mad at me because
of something I did or because you got up on the wrong side of
the bed?" I was amazed that she was able to make that distinction. Certainly, at her age, I couldn't have. Many adults I know
see everything that happens to them as a reflection of themselves. Everything negative is their "hard luck," or "it could only
happen" to them. Transactional Analysis calls these negative
expectations "scripts"; that is, people have made unequivocal
decisions early in life, usually below the level of awareness on
which they operate for the rest of their lives unless they ferret
out unrewarding patterns and decide to change them. If you're
convinced that all men are beasts and that it's dangerous to
love a man because he'll leave you, you'll probably choose part-
ners who fulfill your unconscious expectations. If you think all
women are bitches, you'll be drawn to the ones who will treat
you badly. If, because your older brother laughed at you and
constantly interrupted when you tried to speak up at the dinner
table, you find your voice is mousey and timid, you may actually
feel it very *dangerous* to talk louder even though you're perfectly
able to.

Lucy S. came from a family of "interrupters." Now middle-
aged, she had a husband and children who never listened to her.
In my class, she was so timid that she asked if she could remain
seated while she spoke. Why was she taking my class? I asked.
"Well," she said with a nervous, apologetic laugh, "I want to
learn how not to be so boring. I can't hold people's attention. At
a dinner party, I can't even finish my sentences. People start
talking and I never get to say what I want to, so most of the time
I don't even try." Lucy held her shoulders hunched around her
ears. Her eyes darted timidly back and forth. She spoke so softly
and hesitantly it was difficult to hear her words. Her expectation

was that nobody would listen to her because of her assumption (judgment) that she was "boring." To her, it was actually frightening to stand up and say what she felt.

By the time she had completed the course, she was standing up straight and speaking in a firm voice. Two years later, Lucy was directing a volunteer program for reading aides in her local schools, training new volunteers for (and speaking on behalf of) the whole program to community groups. The change began when she kept her Anti-Judgmental Notebook, noting whenever she told herself she was "boring." She learned to tell herself, "Judgment—WRONG DOOR!" and to drop her old, negative expectations.

People are always amazed to find that they can *choose* to change the characteristics they think they're "stuck with." Being "boring" is not like having blue eyes; it may be learned, but it is not genetically determined or immutable. Have you ever noticed how people pick up the speech and behavior patterns of those they associate with? Even dogs seem to acquire personalities like their owners'!

It's fascinating to see how differently people react to similar situations. In the class with Lucy was a young engineer, Bob R., who said, "I come from a family of interrupters, too, but I talk louder than they do! You can't stop me!" Bob's judgment of himself was: "I can't let anybody get behind my facade because they won't like me if they do. I'm really *not likable* unless I'm being witty or giving information." Secretly, he too felt he was boring. But how differently he projected his judgment! Some of his family messages had been:

"You can't trust people."

"Don't let anybody know you well."

"People are no good!"

The upshot: Bob never looked anybody in the eye and never stopped talking! Through my listening exercises he found that he didn't *have to talk* to communicate with another person. Gradually, he began to change his self-image as he allowed himself to trust other people a little more. It was a hard struggle for him to let go of his wariness and his need to chatter. For Bob, the meditation exercises (see p. 323) and the discovery that people *really wanted* to be helpful and supportive gradually calmed him so that by the end of the term he was able to look people in the eye, listen, and really hear what they were saying. He reported with pride and pleasure that people at work had remarked on how much he had changed for the better, and that "I actually like some of them now!"

Some people have an inner dialogue which is challenging but not destructive—a kind of "pep talk" that helps them get moving. "C'mon, now, let's go! Get your act together and stop horsing around!" one woman told herself when she got upset. She was very judgmental of herself and of other people, but she was able to notice that she was being "melodramatic" and cut short the "garbage" without feeling put down.

It's not so much what you say, but how you feel about it that counts. If your inner dialogue has a painful quality, and leaves you feeling low in self-esteem and depressed, that's perfect material for your Anti-Judgmental Notebook. Whip it out and jot down as briefly as possible whenever you hear yourself saying something, aloud or to yourself, that is a judgment or a WRONG DOOR. Note down the date, the time, and what you feel physically (e.g., my stomach is all knotted up, my heart is beating very fast, I have a throbbing headache, I have a "dull" feeling all over . . .). Notice also what happens to your breathing. "I'm tense—I almost stopped breathing and blacked out," a lawyer told me, "when I felt I couldn't make a good impression in court. Until we started to do the breathing exercises [see chapter 12], I never realized that I practically stopped breathing when I got nervous. That's why I was always afraid I'd black out and faint in court."

For a week or two, keep your little notebook with you. If you're not able to write it down immediately, go to the bathroom to make your notes or update your book before you go to bed at night. DON'T LET THE DAY PASS WITHOUT WRITING IN IT. This is your instant VERBAL POLAROID for checking what you're actually feeling.

Working with the Anti-Judgmental Notebook

The Anti-Judgmental Notebook, then, is a running account of the times and the words in which you "put yourself down." I ask each class member to keep the notebook handy at all times and keep making notes of everything they said to themselves that was negative:

"Why did I do that? That was dumb!"
"I said the wrong thing!"
"I'm so disorganized."
"I messed up again!"

Someone asked, "How do I know I'm being judgmental? For instance, how can I improve if I can't correct myself when I've done something wrong?"

"That's easy!" I answered. "When you have a purely pragmatic 'should,' like: 'I must get to the bank by three o'clock so I can get some cash before it closes.'" This is straightforward and "nontoxic." But watch out for a little hook of anguish, a little catch at the heart, when you say something negative to yourself ("Why am I always late?"). THAT'S how you know you're being judgmental; those are the "tapes" left over from early messages, now counterproductive and useless.

Sometimes you'll get the feeling without words. It could be the look someone gave you or something somebody did or some piece of news that triggers a feeling of anger, jealousy, hurt, self-mistrust, or loss of self-esteem. (Gore Vidal once said, "Every time a writer sees another writer have a success, something in him dies a little.")

To escape painful emotions we experience we often distract ourselves by talking, smoking, drinking, eating, or burying ourselves in some activity—playing cards, watching television. Bad idea! If you're feeling judgmental, disgusted with yourself, it's because you haven't gone deep enough. You can be sure that *if you go deep enough* the news is good! It's important to learn to observe one's feelings *without blame*—only then can you make any real changes.

"But," objected one student, "if I don't criticize myself, how can I improve?"

"Tell me," I asked him, "when you put yourself down, how do you feel? Does it make you want to go rushing out and do a dozen good things? Or do you feel dispirited, discouraged, maybe even *immobilized?*"

"Yes, that's true," he admitted. "When I put myself down, I don't want to do anything." Heads nodded around the room. Someone asked, puzzled, "But why should that be?"

In *Inner Tennis*, Tim Gallwey described what he called "Self 1 and Self 2." "Self 1" is the critic, the "teller" who keeps up a running tirade of directions, judgments, and (often) abuse.

"What a ninny! Why did I do that? What a stupid thing to do! Won't I ever learn!"

"Self 2" is the "doer," unconscious, automatic. It includes the memory and the nervous system, never forgets anything, and is anything but stupid.

We have all noticed that there seem to be several voices inside us—and not always friendly ones, either!

One way to look at those voices is to remember the right and left hemispheres of the brain. The left brain (logical, sequential, deals with formulating language and rational thinking) corresponds roughly to the critical "Self 1." "Self 2" has a lot in common with the right hemisphere (intuition, music, spatial thinking, feeling states or emotions). It's more like the child in us, plunging eagerly into new activities, learning without quite knowing how or why, certainly not stopped by inhibitions, fears, and worries about whether we'll make fools of ourselves or annoy the neighbors!

In other terms, you might also think of "Self 1" as the critical parent (as in Eric Berne's Transactional Analysis) and "Self 2" as the free child, spontaneous, impulsive, and uninhibited.

First off, the part of us that's impulsive and free will do something joyously, spontaneously—only to have "Self 1," the critical side, jeer and criticize. Then, poor "Self 2," exactly like a child that has been bawled out, will balk. Will he/she jump to improve and change? No! He/she will figuratively fold his/her arms and sulk. "Oh!" that self seems to retort silently. "If you're going to be so nasty, I'm not going to do a damn thing! Try and make me!" Scold, urge, cajole, try as we will, we don't budge. We have effectively locked ourselves into a double bind.

Result? Inaction. Frustration. Discouragement. And, like an angry executive yelling at his employees, we are bewildered and helpless at our own "stuckness."

When we are very small, our minds are like the untouched wax of a phonograph record before pressing. Each experience makes grooves in our neurological system which become embedded in our mind/body armor. Each time the message is repeated, the groove is deepened. This is why, as adults, we lock in messages we have forgotten, sometimes physically. One middle-aged man was sensitive along his arms and chest. He couldn't bear to be touched there. He didn't remember that he had a bully for a father whom he was not allowed to hit back. The stifled impulse to return his father's blows had recorded itself on his muscles even though he had no conscious awareness that he had internalized his angry response to his father's brutality.

The messages we absorbed from the important authority figures in our childhood become so familiar that we forget who originated them; now we say them to ourselves and think they're true!

This is rather like the story of the monkey who belonged to a British colonel in India. Whenever the monkey misbehaved in the colonel's rooms, the colonel would slap his pink bottom and throw him out of the window to teach him a lesson. Soon, the monkey was so well trained that when he misbehaved, he would slap his own bottom and jump out of the window!

By the time we've reached adolescence, we make full-scale, harsh judgments of ourselves, thereby causing ourselves a lot of misery.

"I'm ugly!"

"I'm stupid!"

"I'm clumsy."

and so on and so on.

It helps to recognize that whatever we find difficult to do, we have some good interior reason for feeling as we do about it. When we're able to accomplish something that is hard for us, our own acknowledgment solidifies our "ownership" of it. The importance of this cannot be overemphasized.

A cynical father I know once berated his wife: "Why are you so encouraging to the children? Are we supposed to applaud because they don't 'make' in the middle of the floor?" Well, what about that?

Many, many people come from families who expect them to do well, but who give neither praise nor encouragement for success. Achievements are taken for granted and elicit no appreciation. We learn from realistic feedback. If there is *no* positive feedback, it's not easy to reinforce or even to *know* what we're doing right.

Evelyn M., a troubled young woman who had a disastrous family history, spoke very little during our first few sessions. Her alcoholic father had deserted the family. Her mother had committed suicide. Evelyn had had several breakdowns and was seriously overweight. It was clear that she had a very poor self-image. Yet she was bright, articulate when she did speak, and eager to learn. Her first talk, candid and interesting, elicited a warm response from the class. The following week, Evelyn came in and told us, "I did something yesterday that I've never done before! I read aloud to a group of writers a short story I wrote, but I'm very upset."

"Why?" the class wanted to know. "Didn't you get a good reaction?"

"Oh, yes," she answered, "everybody said very nice things, and they all seemed to think highly of my story. But afterward the teacher spoke to me and I couldn't get away! I really had to leave because I had an appointment, but I just couldn't tell her! I just stood and waited until she finished." Evelyn's distress was evident. Her lower lip trembled and her face flushed.

"But don't you see what a remarkable thing you did?" I asked her. "You've always considered yourself so shy, and now you've read your own short story aloud to a group of strangers! That was really courageous!" Heads nodded around the room.

Shaking her head sadly, Evelyn said, "But I couldn't get away from that teacher! I just didn't know how to tell her I wanted to leave. I'm so ashamed of myself!" We could not console her. She was so used to thinking of herself negatively that she had to seize on one tiny part of a remarkable achievement to reassure herself that she was still a failure in her own eyes! The act of acknowledgment was so foreign to her that she could not allow herself to enjoy her own progress. And so it was lost to her. "Awareness of transformation," as George Leonard observed, "IS transformation."

The Three A's: Acknowledge—Appreciate—Absorb

Do you deny yourself the pleasure of your own good moments? The power of *your own* acknowledgment and appreciation can give you an experience of success and pleasure which is the foundation for expanding your more positive experiences.

"Nothing suceeds like success," we say. It's true, so why not learn from it? Take time at the end of your day to appreciate the good moments in it. If you did something well, allow yourself to feel pleased about it—even though it might have been a small thing that would not have meant much to anybody else, but was not easy for you. Perhaps you cleared your desk or made a difficult phone call. Close your eyes, breathe deeply, and spread the pleasure of that small achievement throughout your whole body. Feel it in your fingertips, your arms, your toes, your solar plexus. You're nourishing yourself in the most practical way, feeding your positive expectation. Next time will be easier! After a while, the good moments may become the major part of your day!

Do the Acknowledge-Appreciate-Absorb exercise at least three times every day.

Many of us walk through our lives with a pall hanging over us. Nothing is really terrible, yet the whole world seems gray. Lawrence, the dour stockbroker who told me he was angry with me for making him do the Anti-Judgmental Notebook, was horrified to find that he constantly made judgments on himself when he dealt with his associates, colleagues, friends, even his children.

"It never occurred to me to take *pleasure* in anything I did," he said in an astonished voice. "I was so busy being dissatisfied with myself that I felt gloomy all the time and didn't even realize it!" At the end of the course, people were telling him he looked, sounded, and acted ten years younger. He smiled, laughed, and displayed his considerable wit to the delight of the entire class.

When we realize that our judgments are not US, we feel lighter about ourselves and about other people.

"I'm OK, But That Other Guy's a Bastard!"

The next step is to let go of judgments of other people. Write down a description of the person you dislike most.

"He's a rotten son of a bitch!"

"She's obnoxious!"

"He's a real pain in the neck!"

This is typical of the descriptions I got when I asked people in the class to describe somebody they disliked or hated:

"She's a pill!"

"He's a bastard!"

Everybody was having a lot of fun with that, grinning as they unleashed their verbal brickbats, until I asked, "How much information does that give you?"

People looked surprised, a little crestfallen. "Not much," admitted Margaret L., "but it sure feels good!"

"How do you feel about the person you hear making nasty remarks about somebody else? Does it make you trust that person?"

"No. As a matter of fact," remarked one man, "it gives me a kind of funny, uneasy feeling. I think, 'Well, if he talks like this about so-and-so, what does he say behind MY back!' "

"Does it give you information about the person he's talking about? Does he make you feel the same way about the person?"

"No," offered another student, a woman. "All we know is that the speaker feels strongly. We don't know why—and there's no reason for *me* to feel strongly."

"Then, in terms of communication and persuasion, judgments haven't been very effective, have they? Now, think of that person you dislike so much again, and describe the behavior that bothers you."

Now the responses were informative, detailed, interesting— and persuasive:

"He never listens to anybody and has no regard for other people's feelings."

"She's constantly criticizing others. She's never satisfied with anybody's behavior."

"He treats people as though he has nothing but contempt for them."

"He flies into tantrums when he doesn't get his way. You never know if he's going to be nice or unpleasant when you see him next."

"All right," I said. "What's the difference between describing behavior and judging character?"

"Well," answered an eager young social worker, "for one thing, I feel sympathetic when I hear about the behavior because I'd probably react the same way the speaker did. At the same time, I don't feel he's being vindictive, so I trust him more. And I know a lot more about the situation than I did when I just heard the judgment. That gives me a good feeling that the speaker has trusted me with his observations and experiences."

"Good! What else?"

"I get the feeling that the person the speaker is describing *could* possibly change," offered a retired police captain. "So I think it helps me to feel that people can change their behavior. They're not locked into certain patterns forever."

"Yes," added his wife, "don't we tend to see people according to our expectations of them?" She looked mischievously at her husband. "For instance, for years you were sure I was going to mess up my checkbook and I expected you to be clumsy in the kitchen, and we went right ahead fulfilling each other's expectations!"

"Right!" he laughed, a trifle wryly. "But now that I've taken Chinese cooking lessons and you've somehow gotten much better with your checkbook, I'm sorry I made you feel stupid all those years. Actually, you're one pretty smart lady!"

They beamed at each other, having overcome their own early judgmentalism.

In a massive study of shy people at Stanford University, Philip Zinbardo found that 90 percent of the sample felt they had been shy at some time in their lives. Here's the only difference between those who considered themselves shy now and those who didn't:

The shy-now group would complete the statement "I feel uncomfortable at a cocktail party where I don't know anybody . . ." by adding ". . . *because I'm shy.*"

Those who didn't think of themselves as shy simply added a period, so that the statement read: "I feel uncomfortable at a cocktail party where I don't know anybody."

So people who damn themselves with the judgmental word *shy* blame themselves for their feelings. Worse, they set up the expectation that the same thing will always happen. Ergo, when they go to a cocktail party they expect to be uncomfortable because, according to their judgment, that's their nature, i.e., being SHY! They've "programmed" themselves into a little box. That makes it very difficult to have a different experience the next time.

To confuse behavior with character is dangerous whether you do it toward yourself or other people. Nobody, child or grown-up, does well when the worst is expected of them.

Try this exercise: watch your language for one whole day and see if you can avoid making judgments of other people. (If you've been keeping your Anti-Judgmental Notebook, I hope you aren't judging yourself by this time.) If you catch yourself in a negative remark about someone, immediately reword your statement to avoid using any "judgment" words (*arrogant, lazy,* etc.) to describe the person or his behavior. You'll soon learn that some parts of speech are "happier" than others.

One of my students, a seventy-five-year-old patent lawyer who made a very successful second career acting in commercials, told me that this one exercise had changed his "whole way of being in the world."

"I come from Boston," he told me, "and up there, there was a lot of judgmentalism. Mine was an old WASP family, you know, and I really didn't even *see* a lot of people who were automatically considered OUT by my early family and social standards. I was terribly narrow. Now I go into the subway and catch someone's eye. It doesn't matter who or what he is. We have a moment of eye contact, and I feel close to that person because he's human just as I am, even though his background and experience are totally different from mine. You have no idea," he added, "how that has changed life for me. I really feel at home anywhere and I just don't meet anybody I don't like! I know that sounds Pollyannaish, but it's true."

One time, he told me, his son had come to visit him, and they went to a coffee shop run by a "really crabby woman" who never had a good word for anybody. " 'Wait,' I told Don," he said. " 'By the time we leave she'll smile at me and be my friend.' And, by God, she did!" There's always some good reason why people behave badly. They're having family troubles or something else is wrong, but if you're pleasant, eventually they just have to respond.

This reminded me of a story I heard about two men who walked to work every day past a newsstand owned by a very disagreeable man. Every day, the first man would greet the grouch pleasantly despite the fact that he received no response other than an occasional surly grunt. Finally, his friend said, "Why do you bother? That guy is so nasty!" "I'm just not going to let him ruin my day!" the first man replied. Sooner or later, the newsman would respond. It was inevitable.

If you find yourself going around with a chip on your shoulder, take the responsibility for your angry feelings and make a small step toward transforming them.

There was a period in my life when I yelled at strangers a lot. Why were they always doing things to aggravate me? Finally, I realized it was my own anger that was bouncing off everybody because I didn't dare express my feelings to the people who were close to me—only to strangers.

In the chapter on anger, you'll learn how to use the power of anger—its energy and information—in ways that are productive for your charisma. Properly used, this is a great natural resource.

Best of all, practicing detachment from other people's anger helps lessen your own. If you cut down on your judgments of yourself, you'll feel less anger toward other people.

Begin to collect Pleasure Points. Find three moments during each day when you're aware of experiencing pleasure. Spreading your Pleasure Points gives you a natural protection against low-level judgmental anger. Once you have found what pleasures you (the play of sunshine on your roof, an unexpected smile from a stranger while you're both awaiting the elevator, or a little child's pudgy fist waving in the air) notice how your body FEELS.

What is the difference in local-area body sensations between the "shock" of recognition when you unexpectedly see a friend and the joy of contemplating a beautiful painting? Memorize each sensation.

Next, take three opportunities during the day to produce Pleasure Points *without any occasion*, without any external stimulation whatever. I mean pure, free-floating pleasure!

Now, are you ready for a real challenge? When you've acknowledged your judgment, transform it into pleasure. Let go. Relax your shoulders, your stomach; slow your breathing; straighten and relax your back. *FOR NO REASON* . . . ENJOY! You're entering new territory—the unfamiliar, yet deeply remembered, world within the heart that is always yours. In the next chapter, you'll learn how to retake it at will, how it can shelter and revitalize your charisma, first for you, then for everybody else.

4

Your Tension Inventory

> "What I was going to say," said the
> Dodo in an offended tone, "was
> that the best thing to get us dry
> would be a Caucus-race."
> "What is a Caucus-race?" said
> Alice.
> "Why," said the Dodo, "the best
> way to explain it is to do it."
> —LEWIS CARROLL, *Alice's
> Adventures in Wonderland*

OUR BODIES know a lot that we're unaware of. Some people deal with their bodies as though they were enemies. Others ignore them until they break down. Many people are becoming aware that treating the body intelligently (and making it move the way it was meant to) yields extraordinary dividends of mental and emotional health, clarity, pleasure, and fulfillment.

In a Charismedia workshop, Barbara R., a capable, attractive fashion executive, did the One-Minute Verbal Free-for-All (p. 29) with great facility and enthusiasm. When it was over, a look of shocked surprise came over her face. "My goodness, my heart is beating so hard and so fast—I feel as though I'd just done something very dangerous! I had no idea I felt like that! I thought it was easy for me to yell—I've done so much of it!" The fact that her body could tell her things she *didn't know intellectually* impressed her so deeply that it was the beginning of a real breakthrough in letting go of some very old problems. She had found an extraordinarily "new" ally—the information and feedback her own physical tensions could give her.

Getting in touch with your body and finding out where your tension points are is a crucial part of unearthing and enjoying your charisma. Your body and mind are the wire through which your electricity flows. If you blow a fuse because the wire is frayed, there won't be any light at all. Reduction of energy or burnouts result either from underutilizing or overloading the circuits.

Luckily, the body is a very responsive instrument—if you're prepared to tune in to it. We get messages from the interior and the exterior all the time. Yet many of us try to ignore them as long as possible. We pay no attention until they become so insistent that we are forced to deal with what has turned into a big problem—an ulcer, a bad back, stroke, arthritis, even cancer. We don't want (most of us) to be hypochondriacs. On the other hand, most people have a secret feeling that the body is beyond their control anyway and, with a shudder of almost superstitious fear, hope that not noticing aches and pains will, somehow, make them go away.

Faith in technology has fostered a habit of turning over mechanical problems to specialists. Go to the doctor and he'll give you a pill or potion to fix the difficulty. There was little sense of interconnectedness between problems of the body and the mind. A few years ago, a medical joke recounted the story of a proctologist and a psychiatrist who opened an office together and called it Odds and Ends. For a while people whispered darkly about psychosomatic ailments. "Oh, I'm having heart palpitations but the doctor says it's psychosomatic" (slightly shamefaced).

"Oh, it's all psychosomatic" meant to many people you were either faking or that your ailment was not serious—certainly not quite respectable. We're so quick to de-legitimize our suffering!

As early as the fourth century B.C. the Greek philosopher Plato avowed that "all diseases of the body proceed from the mind or soul." People have always reacted physically to their emotions—cried with joy or grief, paled with fear, reddened in embarrassment or anger, thrown up in fright or disgust, trembled in anguish. Only poets or philosophers paid attention. Language, being more intuitive than we are, is full of expressive reflections of the true connection between our minds and feelings and our physical bodies:

"My heart is heavy."
"I feel light as a feather when I'm happy."
"There's a stone in my chest."
"She's all tied up in knots."

What are *you* experiencing physically and emotionally? Where do *you* feel tension in your body when you experience apprehension, anger, or nervousness? (Later you'll use a checklist to notice where you feel joy, satisfaction, pleasure, and I'll also show you how to capitalize on your findings so you can actually *produce the desirable feelings at will*. First, though, it's important to deal with the negatives—the obstacles that *stop* us from enjoying our own power and gifts, our charisma, and block the flow of biorapport with others.)

Here are some physical feelings most commonly reported by people in my workshops and private counseling when they're uptight or nervous or unhappy, in public or in private:

Stomach knots up, hurts
Shoulders and back of neck tense
Hands clench
Knees lock
Butterflies in stomach
Trembling
Palms perspire
Throat gets tight
Lower back aches
Legs shake
Heart beats fast, thuds
Mouth becomes dry, or else too much saliva
Voice gets high, squeaky, shakes, or gets weak
Feel faint
Nausea
Dizziness
Pounding of the temples
Flushing or blushing
You suddenly have to go to the bathroom
Your hands, toes, nose feel cold
You can't hear well
You don't see well
You break out in a cold sweat
Armpits perspire
Head hurts

It's hard to breathe
Chest feels tight
etc., etc., etc.

Obviously, a lot goes on!

While the autonomic nerves tense and tighten muscles, the heartbeat speeds up, blood vessels constrict, raising the blood pressure and almost completely closing the vessels just under the skin. Your face muscles may contort, but stomach and intestines temporarily halt digestion. The muscles controlling the bowels and bladder loosen. Many people have experienced embarrassment ("I was so scared I wet my pants!"). Soldiers terrified of battle have lost control of their bowels.

While all this is happening, autonomic nerves directly stimulate the adrenal glands to release some thirty hormones—the surest signs (in lab experiments) of stress. Your cholesterol level shoots up without your having eaten a thing! Epinephrine, thought to be associated with fear, produces the heady exuberance (mixed with anxiety) that we call "the adrenaline flowing." This is by no means all bad. It's meant to help in moments of danger or trouble so you can leap higher, lift greater weights, run faster, achieve faster reaction time. Many performers, musicians, and sports figures feel they need that heightened sense for their best moments.

The tricky part is that our bodies go into an elaborate and complicated stress reaction even when *there is no physical danger,* no actual threat or need—when we can't return the system to normal by either fighting or running away. Your boss may have said, "This report is late. I don't like the way you're handling this project!" Suddenly your mouth goes dry and your heart races; you are experiencing a fight-or-flight syndrome. Or your friend or lover says, "Why do you treat me this way?" Or somebody gives you a nasty look. Or the most important person in the room walks out during a presentation you're giving. Or you're terrified of making a speech—a thousand triggers, large or small, can set off these reactions. Your *feelings are causing real physiological changes.* Imagine what a stress-filled business lunch does to your system—think, eat, be on your toes—no wonder many executives get ulcers! (I'll show you later how to de-stress—actually eliminate or transform—the biophysical changes and stress.)

Here your Anti-Judgmental Notebook and attention to trivia will pay off, combined with your sense of what is happening in your body. An amazing number of people never think about their bodies except when something breaks down. They are astonished to discover that their bodies *never lie*. By respecting physical signals as we learned to do the emotional ones, we can clear the path to being centered and using our charisma.

Reactions are highly individual, so what upsets you might leave someone else quite cool and undisturbed, and vice versa. And what bothered you a year ago might have very little effect today. What you find stimulating at one time might be a stress at another. Don't judge yourself or be angry if this happens. That only prevents you from being aware of, acknowledging, and then releasing the stress. Body sensing with detached interest is of immense value and a skill that has to be learned.

We have many different ways of "seeing" things.

The great St. Bonaventure, a favorite philosopher of Western mystics (the great Doctor Seraphicus of the Church), wrote that humans have "three eyes," three ways of gaining knowledge.

The "eye of flesh" sees the external world of space, time, objects, and living things. Animals also have the eye of flesh—if you throw a stick down, a dog will respond; a rock won't. The "eye of reason" deals with philosophy, logic, the mind itself. You can't smell or taste mathematics, and no one has ever seen a square root or an atom. But no one would deny that these mental realities have drastically changed our physical world. The "third eye," the "eye of contemplation," transcends the mental realm. It gives us a sense of our oneness with the cosmos—which is that inexpressible and wordless sense we all experience at some time in our lives and have no real words to describe. Psychologist Abraham Maslow called these moments "peak experiences." Jung talked about the "oceanic consciousness."

Lawrence LeShan, in *The Medium, the Mystic, and the Physicist,* described what all three have in common when they are at their best: one is not aware of oneself as separate from the rest of the world; there is a sense of unity—past, present, and future are all rolled up in one. For some people, this may be a religious experience; for others the sense of oneness comes while making love, performing or listening to music, communing with nature, running, or dancing. Some people have experienced it under the influence of drugs. Terminal cancer patients who were given LSD experienced a sense of peace, calm, and oceanic oneness with the cosmos, even if they had no religious background or belief.

(At this moment, close your eyes, breathe deeply, and go back within to a place where you were completely happy and relaxed. Be there for a few moments, totally. . . .)

This experience of ultimate reality that comes through the "eye of contemplation" we also know as the "sense of flow." When you are experiencing a feeling of your own charisma, you are in that "state of flow."

Selye's General Adaptation Syndrome

Dr. Hans Selye, the famous Canadian stress researcher, worked out a detailed sequence of behavior, the aftermath of stress. He called it the General Adaptation Syndrome.

The first part, or "alarm reaction," roughly corresponds to a "fight-or-flight" response. Each additional stress makes everything harder to bear. There is a sort of "cost-overrun" of the original stress. If you had a fight with your wife at breakfast, after a pleasant walk to the office, although you thought you were completely calm again, when the elevator in your building shows no sign of appearing you suddenly feel angry enough to yell at somebody—whether you do or not, you feel it! In the second part, the "resistance stage," the stressed animal's functions normalize and its resistance to further stimuli rises. If severe stress continues (the third and last stage), total exhaustion may set in. This time when the alarm symptoms appear they are irreversible; a laboratory animal dies.

Instead of more oxygen you feel you're getting less under stress, that your senses are *not* taking in as much information as usual. In general, you're actually suffering from impaired functioning. Our systems get the signals mixed. When we can't fight or run away, the buildup of symptoms is no longer functional. The effort not to show what you're feeling adds to the stress you're already under. Denial adds to the stress. As you have seen, this increases the physiological and emotional toll of the original stress. Now we can understand why (according to the U.S. Senate Committee on Nutrition and Human Needs, chaired by George McGovern) most of the deaths in this country can be traced to stress-related diseases. One out of three men will die of heart disease or stroke before the age of sixty and one out of five women. (Undoubtedly, as women move into more and more high-level positions, that figure will rise.)

Two psychiatrists, Thomas Holmes and Richard Rahe, of the University of Washington's School of Medicine, have created a Stress-Measurement Scale so people can score themselves on how much life stress they experienced within a two-year period before taking the test. According to their findings, if your point total for each year is 150 or less you have a 30 percent chance (1 out of 3) of getting sick in the next two years. A score of 150–299 gives you a 50-50 chance. Watch out if it's 300 or above—you have an 80 percent chance of falling sick. The chance of getting a serious illness such as cancer, heart disease, or psychosis is greater for those with scores above 300.

What's the Point of Scaring Yourself to Death?

Awareness and acknowledgment—remember these keys. If you recognize what a stressful time you've been having (your marriage broke up, you changed jobs three times, you became a vegetarian and remarried), that recognition alone reduces the stress! Positive events like buying a home, getting an award, or getting married also carry a stress quotient. As Will Rogers noted, "We know lots of things we used to didn't know, but we don't know any way to prevent 'em happening."

Factory tests showed that workers who were about to get married made more mistakes than usual during the week or two before the ceremony!

Holmes and Rahe asked 400 men and women of varying ages, religions, and marital status to compare marriage with forty-two other events (all known from clinical tests to be stressful) and gave each event a numerical value higher or lower than 50. Mar-

Holmes-Rahe Stress Measurement Scale

Life Event	Number of Points
Death of Spouse	100
Divorce	73
Marital Separation	65
Jail Term	63
Death of Close Family Member	63
Personal Injury or Illness	53
Marriage	50
Fired from Work	47
Marital Reconciliation	45
Retirement	45
Change in Family Member's Health	44
Pregnancy	40
Sex Difficulties	39
Addition to Family	39
Business Readjustment	39
Change in Financial Status	38
Death of Close Friend	37
Change to Different Line of Work	36
Change in Number of Marital Arguments	35
Mortgage or Loan over $10,000	31
Foreclosure of Mortgage or Loan	30
Change in Work Responsibilities	29
Son or Daughter Leaving Home	29
Trouble with In-Laws	29
Outstanding Personal Achievement	28
Spouse Begins or Starts Working	26
Starting or Finishing School	26
Change in Living Conditions	25
Revision of Personal Habits	24
Trouble with Boss	23
Change in Work Hours, Conditions	20
Change in Residence	20
Change in Schools	20
Change in Recreational Habits	19
Change in Church Activities	19
Change in Social Activities	18
Mortgage or Loan under $10,000	17
Change in Sleeping Habits	16
Change in Number of Family Gatherings	15
Change in Eating Habits	15
Vacation	13
Christmas Season	12
Minor Violation of the Law	11

Count up the number of points that apply to you and add up your total.

riage was used as a comparison point since the most severe stress apparently comes from family relationships.

Critics have pointed out that the Holmes and Rahe scale seems to overemphasize male problems. Such crucial events in a woman's life as menopause or mastectomy are not mentioned.

Sally M., in two years, saw her last child go off to college, and her husband left her. She also had a hysterectomy and went back to work as a bookkeeper. Through all the crises she had undergone she had held up remarkably well, but when she began to meditate as part of the charisma workshop she complained that it made her tired; she was sleepy all the time. Meditation had made her aware of really feeling the accumulated stresses of her life. The tremendous strains she had undergone demanded rest and repair. If she had not started to meditate, she probably would have suffered a physical breakdown because she was driving herself without rest or recognition of what she was really feeling. After a month or so, she found she no longer needed excessive amounts of sleep; and the meditations brought her renewed energy, as they usually do.

People often handle extraordinary crises remarkably well, as though the body knew it couldn't afford to fall apart; sometimes sheer survival depends on the ability not to. During the war, a friend survived hair-raising adventures: escape from a Nazi labor camp; near death by shooting, bombing, and minefields; loss of his parents and most relatives and friends. He lived mostly on dry bread and bacon which he could carry in his pocket. *He didn't even get a cold.* Such stories are not uncommon—this superhuman strength seems to be a common protective mechanism. After the danger is over, we can afford to collapse.

But if you live your whole life as a long, unrecognized battle (or have suffered grievous emotional losses) you don't realize what havoc this is wreaking on your body. During a time of great national or international crisis and upheaval, people's best qualities often emerge. The heightened danger provides heightened opportunity to be of service, to act and feel like a worthwhile human being. (The Chinese pictograph for crisis is a combination of the symbols for danger and for opportunity.) During the London blitz, the English experienced their "finest hour."

We've all heard stories of superhuman feats ordinary people performed at extraordinary moments—a woman who cannot swim jumps overboard to save her child from drowning or a man finds the strength to lift a car to save a friend trapped under the wreckage. At such times, we seem to be able to tap into near-miraculous reserves of power. The satisfaction of meeting such challenges seems to offset a great deal of the negative stress of crisis.

Even happy events can cause stress. If you're irritable or jumpy after something exciting or pleasant has happened in your life—winning a prize, having a baby, getting a promotion—it's the change that is affecting you. Of course, we'd all much rather have that kind of stress than the other! "Oh, I can deal with that," said one man with a broad grin when he was asked how he would feel if he won the Sweepstakes.

Anything can contribute to stress. It's important to *know* what you're experiencing, since acknowledgment is a dandy detoxifier even *if nothing else changes*. Thinking aloud with someone sympathetic amplifies the de-stressing effect. You can set up your own tension inventory if you're not feeling at your best. *Self-communication is the first line of defense against stress*. Some sources of tension need to be checked every day, others only occasionally; it's like maintaining your car. The habit of noticing stress will enable you to be more and more *in touch* so you can intuit changes, handle unexpected situations, be centered and moving at the same time.

Everything in the world is moving. The only security is not to stand still and resist, but maintain your center so you can flow with events in a way that feels right to you. We always know it when that's happening. Here's another paradox. People who cling to old ideas or ways of doing things find themselves increasingly bewildered by the world they live in. They know when they're not with it.

What Year Is Your Right or Wrong?

"I don't know . . . Young people today are no good. . . ."
  "Children should be seen and not heard."
  "A lady never swears."
  "A woman needs a man to protect her."

"What's the use—you can't beat the system."

Pessimism is a perception of the dark side of life, never the whole. If your general attitude is pessimistic, it probably means loss of personal control.

Even pessimists can be charismatic—when their inner vitality and life force belie their ideas. Matt M., a brilliant and dynamic man, who had been a Jesuit, a Marine, a professor, and a theater director, was confined to a wheelchair through a series of accidents and iatrogenic illness. When he was with people, his ebullience, charm, and personal magnetism amazed everybody. "He exemplifies grace under pressure," a friend observed. Since he had always been handsome, brilliant, charming, and talented, everything had come easy to him before his accidents. The best avenue for reaching the kind of audience he had commanded easily before his disabilities was writing and lecturing. Since this meant designing, inventing, and actively promoting his own interests, this was now terribly hard for him. His secret liability had always been an intense and harsh self-judgmentalism. Yet he was proudly aware of his abilities. He was a generous and loyal friend and had been a powerful and effective advocate for worthwhile social causes, but his inner voice said, "You're great, but maybe you're not good enough!" That made it impossible for him to shift the arena of his activities now that it was so necessary. It's the Tinker Bell syndrome again. So many performers suffer from it, the nasty little voice that says, "If somebody else believes in you, you're OK," or "If somebody loves you, you're OK." Otherwise you're not!

Everybody is multitalented. When you locate your inner charisma and trust your intuition, if you then can't move in one direction you'll find a good way to move in another. You'll dance with the world, even without legs.

Knowing that the world comes to meet you at least halfway, you can act "as if." Try acting "as if" you are in love for a single day. What is the feeling? Self-acceptance and joy and the lovely sense that wonderful things are happening and that more are still about to happen will change the way you feel about every moment of your day. Other people will remark on how well you look: "Have you had a vacation? Are you in love?"

Your Ideal Listener

Before a difficult interview, close your eyes, breathe deeply, and visualize sharing a story or discussion with someone who really listens, who appreciates and enhances your sense of self-worth. Talking to a person like that, everything you say feels more interesting, richer, more exciting. May L. said ruefully in a group discussion, "The only creature I can think of who gives me that kind of loving attention is my dog!"

Still, it worked for her. When she pictured herself telling something that was important to her to her little dog, she saw his shining eyes, his excitedly wagging tail, his air of absolute devotion, and it gave her the first sample of the feeling she needed: total acceptance. She felt silly at first describing to her puppy a new product that she wanted to market, but she realized then that she could transfer that enthusiasm, eagerness, and zest to *any conversation.*

In chapter 8, I will show you how to come across the way you want to by using this technique of imagining and then transferring sound, expression, inflection *without feeling phony.* Energy, life force, appetite, enthusiasm—we need several hundred ways to evoke these qualities in ourselves because they are the true substance of personal charisma.

Now, how do you check out your Tension Inventory? The main categories are: body, breath, mental, emotional, and social sphere. (I am indebted for much of this formulation to Sidney Lecker, M.D., from his *Natural Way to Stress Control.*)

There are two kinds of tension you will want to notice. One is the *emergency tension* you feel when you're on the spot. (I'll give you emergency first aid later in this chapter for some of the most common problems.) The other is more long-range—the negative judgments that come from early negative messages and how they may be affecting your mind, body, and social self. All symptoms are important and potentially useful as sources of information.

When you realize that everything is relevant, you can direct your energy flow toward enhancing your charisma by eliminating roadblocks and potholes. You'll become increasingly ingenious about making small changes that produce a different feeling, a feeling of control and mastery. (What's really important is never what seems to be going on.)* Whether you decide to run downstairs in your building instead of taking the elevator, cut out sugar and cut down on salt, take up Sumi painting or T'ai Chi or chamber music or crystallography or simply walk to work by a different route, you have, by choosing change, cut down stress and opened up the channels to your charisma—magnetism and joy in life.

In questionnaires filled out by people who took my workshops, the largest percentage (approximately 70 percent) said they felt tension under fire of a stress-producing situation in the throat, neck, head, shoulders, or chest. When you remember that this is where speech emanates, these answers seem very understandable. Another 30 percent felt tightening or pain in the stomach (an assorted miscellany experienced other symptoms). So here's emergency first aid tension release.

Whenever you face a tough situation, *stop*, recognize the feelings you're experiencing (mental sensations and physical symptoms), and begin very slow breathing. Verbalize your feelings, aloud if possible, mentally if that's not practical. You'll feel better within minutes.

Here's another stress evaluation scale. Score as follows (each score shows how true OR the amount of time you believe that statement is true for YOU):

0 = not at all true for me
1 = somewhat true or true only part of the time
2 = fairly true or true about half the time
3 = mainly true or true most of the time
4 = true all the time

* Buckminster Fuller

STRESS STATEMENTS*

_____	1.	I feel inferior and inadequate compared with others.
_____	2.	I feel unworthy and guilty when criticized and condemned.
_____	3.	I am easily frustrated.
_____	4.	I have a compulsive need to prove my worth and importance.
_____	5.	I am anxious about my future.
_____	6.	I have trouble making decisions and sticking to them.
_____	7.	I am afraid of death.
_____	8.	I am easily angered.
_____	9.	I resent people who don't do what they should.
_____	10	I am badly upset by disappointed expectations.
_____	11.	I have a strong need to dominate and control others.
_____	12.	I blame myself for my mistakes and defeats.
_____	13.	I have a strong need for confirmation and agreement.
_____	14.	I habitually put off doing what I should do.
_____	15.	I have an intense need for approval and acceptance.
_____	16.	I am fearful of undertaking new endeavors.
_____	17.	I am sensitive to social pressures.
_____	18.	I have an intense fear of failure.
_____	19.	I have trouble admitting I am wrong.
_____	20.	I worry about my loved ones.
_____	21.	I am pressured by responsibility.
_____	22.	I am afraid to let others see the real me.
_____	23.	I have a compulsive need to meet others' expectations.
_____	24.	I have a compulsive need to win.
_____	25.	I am impatient and worry about getting things done in time.

_____ PERSONAL STRESS FACTOR (PSF) (sum of all scores)

* Stress Inventory No. 25. Copyright H. L. Barksdale. Courtesy Barksdale Foundation, Laguna Beach, Ca. 92651.

A stress factor of 5 indicates an essentially stress-free life. A PSF of 15 is a definite handicap to your emotional well-being. A PSF of 25 indicates a severe handicap, and one of 50 or more indicates serious emotional problems and a definite threat to your health. Achieving sound self-esteem is definitely the most effective remedy for eliminating stress.

How to Change the Chemistry of Your Consciousness

This is easy to do when you know how, but it takes awareness and practice. So practice BEFORE you experience an acute difficulty.

1. Sit down and time your breaths (counting each breath as one inhalation and an exhalation) for one minute. Most people breathe somewhere between twelve to eighteen breaths per minute. If your rate is higher, you are operating under too much stress. If you breathe seven breaths a minute or less, you will be seen as more composed, more authoritative, more "together," and indeed you actually *will* be.

2. Now, consciously slow your breathing.

HERE'S THE BIG BALLOON

Exhale fully with a big, audible sigh (particularly if you're already stressed) and stay empty for a few seconds. Let go of any tightness you feel build up in your face, neck, jaw, shoulders, head, back, chest, and belly. As the air is coming through your nostrils, imagine you are breathing it between your legs as though you're filling a balloon from the bottom. (The balloon is your lower belly.)

Imagine the balloon as very beautiful; make it your favorite color (whatever comes to mind first). Never mind the actual physiological process; this visualization gives you access to an instantaneous, complex de-stressing which will remove the build-up of lactic acid from your taut muscles, calm and oxygenate and revitalize your whole system *within seconds*.

Hold—check to see if your shoulders are relaxed.

Exhale steadily to a very slow count of seven. See the balloon deflating slowly as you exhale.

Hold for a count of one.

Keep this up for five minutes or as long as you like.

In chapter 5, I will explain why this exercise is a magic weapon to be used anytime, anywhere.

It's important to practice this when you don't need it so it be-

comes so easy and natural you can do it whenever you want, without giving it your full attention. Since giving so much attention to a usually completely automatic process is very unusual for most people, it's absolutely essential that you practice it when nothing else is going on. That way you can explore how it feels. Otherwise you will never, in the hurly-burly of panic, excitement, tension, and crisis, remember to breathe slowly. Your conscious mind would probably say, "Oh, shut up and leave me alone—I have important things to deal with—don't bother me with BREATHING, for God's sake. I've got enough on my mind as it is!"

There is almost a feeling somewhere buried in our psyche that by breathing harder we're *helping* ourselves handle the problem; that's how we recognize "this is serious!" We identify so closely with the problem and the emergency that we actually *push* it with our breath out of some feeling that this will help. Can you remember the last James Bond movie you saw when 007 was teetering on the edge of a cliff and the whole audience was holding its breath and saying "ooh-ooh"—as though that could help the hero?

If you were pushing a great load with twenty other people, your hard breathing *would* actually help mobilize the strength you needed to perform some feat beyond your normal strength. But most of the time holding your breath or breathing irregularly or shallowly—as most people unconsciously do under stress— makes it much harder to deal with the emergency. Your brain is deprived of the increased oxygen it needs and the tension of the alarm reaction interferes more and more with the superfunctioning the original stress reaction was designed to provide.

The mental equivalent of that strained sympathetic breathing is worry. Most people worry because they unconsciously feel it's going to help; it shows to themselves (that tough inner censor) that they're good, that they care, that they're concerned, responsible. ("If I worry about doing a good job, I'm worth what they're paying me at work." "If I worry about my children, I'm a good parent.")

Arthur L. said, "I *need* anxiety to get me worked up so I can accomplish things." He was in the habit of taking Valium to cut the level of anxiety to manageable proportions. After he began the breathing, he found he didn't "need" the anxiety anymore; he was productive and relaxed at the same time.

Unfortunately, worry is no more productive than shallow breathing. By identifying with fear and limitation, we cut our supply lines to intuition, resourcefulness, and inner strength. So do practice the breathing when you have nothing else to think about. You may be surprised to find, as many people do, that it's rather scary, at first, to breathe slowly; it brings you smack up against an awareness of your own mortality.

Billy R., a young, athletic lawyer in my workshop, said, "Gee, it's so much *work* to breathe slowly—I felt exhausted when I finished. My stomach was tense with anxiety. I couldn't wait to get the next breath—I had to gulp in air." I asked him if he knew whether his birth had been a difficult one. "No," he said slowly, "but when I was an infant, I almost died of a serious intestinal problem and they cut out part of my intestines before I was a year old." His body and nervous system had retained the physical memory of that early trauma, and his breathing reflected a fear of dying that was an early infant experience.

I invented a gentle self-massage exercise for him which in twenty minutes totally changed the way he had been breathing all his twenty-eight years. After that, he was able to do the slow breathing and sense with his whole body the deep ease and relaxation it brings.

Malcolm N., a political candidate who was a successful industrialist, came to me because his speaking style was choppy and he didn't always project with authority. He too had a very uneven breathing pattern. He too was surprised to find it felt very alarming to breathe very slowly.

"I don't know why that's hard," he said slowly, "but I find myself gasping for air after the long exhalation, desperate to get in another breath as fast as possible. I can't seem to take it in slowly."

Since I have noticed that breathing difficulties sometimes go back to traumatic births, I asked him if he knew anything unusual about his own birth.

"Well, as a matter of fact," he said with a look of surprise, "I almost strangled at birth—the cord was wrapped around my neck!" Buried inside this fifty-five-year-old man was a terrified infant struggling to get enough breath to survive—*with each breath*. After he had flashed on that memory, he was able to breathe more easily. For the first time in his life he was able to breathe slowly and consistently. Interestingly, this simple breathing change gave him more concentration and improved eye contact. He had remarked that people complained he didn't really listen to them, and his wife, a sharp observer, criticized him for constantly looking around while people were talking to him. Breathing slowly and consistently, once it became habit, changed the quality of his awareness. He found he had more patience, was able to center himself in the NOW instead of always thinking about what had just happened or what was going to happen, and really listened to people when they talked to him.

This gave him more opportunity to observe the totality of what people were communicating. He found them much more interesting than just their *words*, which he had tended to jump ahead and impatiently complete for them. He now found he was getting subtler and more complete information and also better feedback from people. They in turn knew that he really was interested in them. They felt flattered by his steady attention and gaze. It was a remarkable series of changes—all triggered by the change to slow, even breathing. His charisma in the next political campaign was much more powerful. In fact, he won!

Another client, a brilliant Freudian psychiatrist in his forties, also noted with astonishment that he went through a real panic reaction the first few times he did the slow 8-4-16 breathing (see chapter 12). He reported with great satisfaction the following week:

"I determined to stick it out even if I died in the attempt—and it felt as dangerous as though I was faced with the prospect of drowning. Knowing I could choose to go through with it gave me the strength to do it over and over. Finally, it was no longer frightening. I know now I can control any panic I suffer before giving one of my lectures, because it'll never be as bad as that again! This sense of potential control gives me enormous satisfaction. I'm very pleased with myself that I was able to overcome my terror and stick with it."

His face, habitually rather gloomy, broke out in a triumphant grin. Gradually through that first crucial victory he was able to liberate his sense of humor and enjoyment of speaking, and he has become a popular and successful lecturer.

The Rush Act

Now you're ready to learn a very effective secret weapon against the stress of rushing. All of us have moments when there are nineteen things to be done and far too little time to do them. This is an extraordinarily effective way to be efficient, calm, and collected while rushing! The secret is: *the more rushed you are, the more slowly you should breathe,* even if you find internal resistance or an obligation to worry ("What are you doing? I *have* to breathe fast to move fast, stupid!").

The best way to practice (before you're under stress) is by walking first slowly and then increasingly fast. Experience the complex sensation of slowing your breathing as you increase your pace. Make sure your shoulders are relaxed; we shouldn't see any evidence that you're breathing deeply. A certain mischievous pleasure comes with this contrapuntal breathing. You'll feel a delicious satisfaction in the fact that you *seem* to be rushing, and nobody knows but you that actually you're moving very slowly (since your breath carries the movement) and you have all the time in the world. What's happening? Your actual perception of time expands, unfolding like a paper flower in water.

Here's the usual jerky, spasmodic, uncoordinated behavior that characterizes rushing—"Oh, my God, where are my keys? What did I do with my briefcase? Did I turn off the stove? Lock the door? Remember to call the plumber [carpenter, wife, boss, children]?" You know the kind of last-minute details that fall out of our heads like dropped papers when we're rushing around. "Chicken without a head" is a perfect expression for that feeling of being "headless" which rushing often produces. Instead of all that almost spastic lack of flow, now you're moving in a continuum of slow, gentle breathing which utilizes all the adrenaline shooting through your system, sending energy and information to the brain. This creates such a detailed, complex perception of every micromoment that in the expanded sensorium there is *time* for everything you need to accomplish and a feeling of sailing easily through crisis.

The Throat Clutch

One of the most common difficulties people report is that their throats close up or tighten. Voices rise embarrassingly or get practically inaudible, which can ruin anybody's confident and authoritative image.

Mary B. told her group, "I was so humiliated. I'd just started to give a presentation for twenty men and felt my voice shaking and actually cracking. It was all I could do to get through it. What can I do? I don't ever want that to happen again!"

Here are exercises to keep your throat open and your voice grounded in the body so you can use your full range even when you're nervous. All these too must be practiced when you *don't* need them.

First, YAWN! That's right, a nice rude yawn. If the yawn doesn't take over and do *itself* after you've started, you're not really yawning. Yawning is one of the great natural relaxers, like laughing. If you have trouble starting the yawn, lift your lips up, away from the teeth, as though you're snarling, inhale, crinkle up your eyes, and then open your mouth as wide as you can, in all directions, so that the muscles in your neck stand out and you hear a roaring in your ears, YAWN. No halfway measures, please! Only by exaggerating can you really get into the feeling that will take over and thoroughly relax your whole face, neck, and throat. You're learning to imitate your own natural processes, so you can use them when you need them. Try that a couple of times, until it's easy for you to do at will. If you feel silly doing these exercises, try them in the privacy of your bedroom or bathroom, but full out! Otherwise, they won't hook into your natural relaxing mechanisms and won't be any use to you.

You may find that once you get started it's hard to stop! Good! Keep going until you are all "yawned out."

Once you've got that so you can induce a yawn any time you want to, *do it with your mouth closed*. Everybody can remember doing this when you're bored and don't want to show it—at a dull meeting or party or with someone who bores you. Now, however, be very aware of your muscular reactions. The tongue is as low as possible at the back of the throat and lying on the bottom of the mouth, the tip flat (not drawn back), and the sides in contact with all the gums; press the middle of the tongue down as hard as possible. This enlarges the space inside the mouth. Imagine there is a huge ball of helium in your mouth, pressing the roof up, the back out against the back of your neck, and the sides and bottom down.

THE HELIUM BALL YAWN

If you put your fingertips against the sides of the neck in back, you should feel the muscles expanding outward and downward when you yawn, either with mouth open or closed. Your ears go back too. The back of the tongue goes down. If you want to help get the feeling, put a spoon on the back of your tongue the way the doctor used to use a tongue depressor when you were a child to see the back of your throat. If you expand the throat downward in back of the tongue, you won't gag when you do this. Gagging means you've closed the throat up at the back.

Once you can do this helium ball expansion at will, begin to hum, with a *phmmmmmm*. Notice if you start the sound of the hum with a little click in your throat; that's called the glottal catch. When I was acting in TV daytime dramas, we referred to certain emotional scenes as "glottal stop scenes." They all started with a very effective catch in the throat: "Oh, John, please . . . I can't . . . I . . . I . . . I (gasp) . . . I, oh . . . I don't know what to do . . . Aren't you . . . are you? . . . I know but . . . I . . . I can't!"

The glottis is that little fleshy protuberance atop the vocal cords in the back of the throat. A "glottal catch" means you start a word that begins with A E I O U by momentarily closing the throat to start the sound. It's an effective way to emphasize the word. But many people begin *all* words there, and the sounds get trapped in the throat, deprived of the rich vibrations that your breath can give coming through the trunk and mixing with the sounds your vocal chords produce and send up through the head cavities. When the throat closes, you cut off three-quarters of your resonating space.

It's important for your charisma that you free and use your whole, true voice. (See chapter 7.)

Jaw Looseners

A great deal of tension settles in the jaw. Here are a couple of jaw looseners.

To free the throat: open your mouth as wide as you can, scrunch up your eyes, and stick out your tongue as far as you can. Now, press your chin in with your index finger and hold the chin steady—don't let it move! (It will try to get in the act!)

Now circle your tongue all around your mouth, keeping it extended as far as possible. At first it may be very unwilling to move smoothly, but keep trying until it makes a complete circle as smoothly and continuously as though it were being pulled around by an outside hand. Try to aim for touching your nose on top, your cheeks on the sides, and your chin on the lower part.

When you've circled your tongue slowly clockwise, stretching as far as you can three times, reverse and do it three times in the other direction. (This brings blood to the throat area as the circulation increases—great for a sore throat!)

You will find that your throat feels more open and lighter when you are finished.

Now take your chin between your thumb and first finger and, letting your mouth fall open, wobble your head back and forth between your fingers by moving the jaw. Don't move the jaw itself; let the fingers do the moving. If your jaw is very tight, you may find that the hinge doesn't want to move at all at first. Keep trying until the whole hinge moves and shakes your head when you push it back and forth with your fingers.

How to Free Your Face

Have you ever watched a horse as it stands in the sun, swatting away flies and blowing gently? That's what you're going to do to loosen up your face.

THE HORSE LAUGH

Start with your lips tightly together as though you were going to say *P*. Blow outward to let your lips ripple continuously like a little motor. Hardly a child alive has not tried this at some time or another. It's impossible to be dignified and do this, so be prepared again to feel foolish. So what? But don't laugh until you run out of breath! Do this over and over until it's easy. Now sing a little, running up and down the scales as you do it.

"My goodness, I can't do it at all," mourned one tense young woman, Jane S. "My lips just won't move!" That shows Jane needed the exercise badly; tension will prevent you from being able to do it. As with so much else, you do this by NOT trying. Just let go of your lips and make them as limp as you can.

If you're having trouble with this, try Idiot Fingers. Making a small continuous sound, move your index finger up and down rapidly across your absolutely lax limp lips—as kids used to do when they were playing Idiot! It's guaranteed to make you feel pretty idiotic! The virtue of this "dumb" exercise is that you'll get the feeling of loose lips, and that's vital for relaxing the face and jaw tension.

Now you've got the feeling of loose lips. If you need an image of what that looks like, remember Charles Laughton, whose lower lip always seemed to be hanging open. (I didn't say it was necessarily attractive!) If that picture doesn't appeal to you, you can tune in a mental image of Marilyn Monroe's luscious, half-open lips. Feel what it would be like to have your mouth be exactly like that.

THE WIBBLE WABBLE

Now, keeping your lips limp, make a small continuous sound and shake your head rapidly from side to side as though you're saying "No-o-o-o-o." Important: let your cheeks and lips wobble, as though they were hanging off your bones. (The láte S. D. Szakall and Charles Coburn of the movies had the wonderful wabbly-wobbly jowls that this exercise suggests.)

If your head gets stuck or the movement is jerky you have a lot of neck tension. Keep at it till the movement is fast, continuous, and smooth.

The Pleasure Purr

Now, yawn again with your mouth closed and hum *phmm*. This time think of something you love doing—eating chocolate mousse, making love, stroking fur, smelling burning leaves—whatever sensual memory turns you on. Spread the feeling of glow all around your head, throat, and neck, keeping your throat open and relaxed with your tongue lying low and flat. See if you can distribute humming vibrations evenly throughout your head and neck, as though you were massaging the inside of your skull with sound. You *are* actually doing that! Make the hum as quiet as the purr of a kitten or a very fine Rolls-Royce motor. Make sure you start each sound with the breath snorting through the nostrils (lips relaxed, though), a *phmm* so it does *not* start from the glottal catch. Make it as even, easy, and continuous as you can. Breathe deeply, close your eyes, and turn on the motor.

After five minutes you will feel thoroughly relaxed and pampered. (By the way, this low "white sound," turned down as far as you can without catching, is a wonderful way to put yourself to sleep. Breathing slowly, you purr away and you'll automatically fall asleep.) Anytime during the day when you feel stressed, just begin to use this helium ball hum (the bottom of your chin should visibly expand to look like a duck-billed platypus, as the tongue presses down the glands under your chin). And keep purring.

Here's the beautiful payoff:

If you've faithfully practiced these exercises so you can do them easily anytime (even if waked up in the middle of the night from a deep sleep), then, as you get up on a platform to speak, all you have to do is open your mouth slightly, allow your lips to be as limp as possible, and, gently, silently blow your breath past your lower lip. This will *remind* your whole face of the entire sequence of exercises that you practiced so faithfully and will achieve exactly the same results as if you had *done the whole series!*

Warning: This will *only* work if you *have* practiced the whole series beforehand so your face will pick up the cues it remembers from that final moment.

* * *

The aim of all of these exercises of course is to change your physical sense so that you instantly put yourself in a relaxed state with any part of the body, face, or breath. When you practice the exercises your body is learning a new way to experience itself. This should return you to a sense of freedom and ease you haven't felt since childhood. It's no accident that many of these exercises are things children do idly all the time while growing up. *If it makes you feel silly, it's probably good for you!*

It's instructive to notice what makes you feel foolish. If you can allow yourself in the privacy of your own home to do things that make you feel "silly" you've broken down some of the shyness barrier that prevents you from expressing your charisma. Remember it takes relaxation, freedom from tension, *and* practice in new behaviors, to give you the full freedom you need to be truly expressive and eloquent.

Your Inhibition Inventory

Score yourself as follows. Privately (or with one person) or in public each statement is

    0 = not at all true for me
    1 = somewhat true (part of the time)
    2 = fairly true (about half the time)
    3 = mainly true (most of the time)
    4 = true all the time

	In Private	In Public
I would feel silly (or embarrassed) to		
1. cry	___	___
2. yawn	___	___
3. dance	___	___
4. run	___	___
5. shake or move my body rapidly	___	___
6. do any kind of physical movement	___	___
7. move my pelvis back and forth	___	___

8.	shake my shoulders	_____	_____
9.	shake my feet or legs	_____	_____
10.	tell a joke	_____	_____
11.	open my eyes very wide	_____	_____
12.	open my mouth very wide	_____	_____
13.	yell	_____	_____
14.	scream	_____	_____
15.	admit I'm wrong	_____	_____
16.	apologize	_____	_____
17.	accept compliments	_____	_____
18.	make a mistake	_____	_____
19.	act in front of people	_____	_____
20.	sing for people	_____	_____
21.	be asked to read aloud	_____	_____
22.	have to play charades	_____	_____
23.	wear a costume	_____	_____
24.	express emotions	_____	_____
25.	express opinions	_____	_____
	TOTAL	_____	_____

Add the score for both columns. 0–15 = You don't always use discretion or listen to others enough. 16–50 = You go with your gut feelings, are expressive, enjoy life, have a good sense of humor and a balanced attitude. 51–90 = You envy people who are more relaxed, you are more timid than you'd like and less spontaneous, you fear rejection. 91–130 = You feel that everything you do is not good enough, you're afraid of social disapproval, you seldom depart from routine, you don't like to make a fool of yourself. 131–170 = You are held back by many fears, you're easily shocked, you don't like to take chances, you have rigid expectations. 171–200 = You feel life is dull, boring, meaningless, your inhibitions overwhelm you, your self-esteem is very shaky, and you're unable to express your potential. Your health is affected.

I hear you saying, "But why do I have to feel silly? I'm a grown-up! I want to have more control, not *less*, in my life! You're asking me to behave like a child and I don't see the point—I certainly wouldn't want to behave like that in public! In fact, it's a secret nightmare of mine that I *will* do something silly in public—you're asking me to deliberately practice silly behavior! I don't get it."

OK, OK, don't go away mad!

Let me explain! Relaxation from stress is essential to break up the buildup of tension. Between birth and age six, children learn more than at any time during their lives. There is now evidence that children have more brain synapses than adults. Children are more physically active and use their senses more fully. The constant stimulation of the cerebral motor cortex and the challenge to all the senses stimulate greater development of the complex brain centers and fantastic leaps in growth. By returning to some of the child's repertoire of vocal and motor exercises, we stimulate our own regeneration (growth) and give ourselves a welcome antidote to gravity: levity! Everything begins to seem so grim when we're adults that we cannot relax and play. The best work is always accomplished in the spirit of eager play. The natural curiosity of a child, and instinctive use of all the senses, is something we have to painstakingly find our way back to as grown-ups—so here is a Child/Adults' Garden of Absurdities.

Give yourself permission to behave like a fool. To change your behavior style from A to D you have to go way out to X. That's the Bluebird Principle: it isn't the destination but the journey that make the difference! When you have allowed yourself to be silly, use some of your expanded sensorium, and let go of your dignity. At this point, results *don't* count! But having done some absurd and extravagant exercises will loosen you up in your daily life, with very little special effort.

SIX SOMERSAULTS A DAY

(Please be careful—I don't want any injuries!) Roll over as limp and roundbacked and relaxed as you can—and be sure to have something soft under you!

THE SILLY SUPER SHAKEOUT

First shake out one hand, then the other, then shake your head like a rag doll (let your mouth hang loose). Then shake out each leg (just adding each limb, keep up the ones you began with!). Then hop, shaking the other foot. Then jump and wiggle your pelvis and throw your arms and elbows and hands all around every which way and make some noises while you're at it! Keep this up for three to five minutes.

THE SEXY DANCER BIT

Turn on some jazzy music, turn the lights off, take your shoes and socks off, and dance for fifteen minutes, or until you fall exhausted—whichever happens first. Try to move parts of your body that you don't usually move. Move everything. Flail your arms about. Your legs. Shake, rattle, and roll. The harder the better. Really throw yourself into this. You may find you're inhibited even when nobody is there. Good! Now you know what you have to overcome. Nobody's watching, so knock yourself out. Then reward yourself by lying on your back for fifteen minutes and letting go completely. Be aware of exactly what your body is feeling. Feel your heart beating, your muscles vibrating with the unexpected exertion. Enjoy the luxury of letting go completely. Feel supported and caressed by the floor.

THE CAT STRETCH

When you wake up in the morning and any other time it's convenient, stretch as slowly and luxuriously as a cat. Feel the energy going down to your toes and beyond, out through your fingers and beyond. Don't let it short-circuit halfway. Visualize yourself as Nureyev or Ann-Margret or your favorite dancer, sexy and lithe. Really get into it; whatever shape your body's in doesn't matter. Feel the beautiful, supportive structure underneath, and STRETCH. Breathe. . . . Stand up. Feel your rib cage pulling up out of your waist, your waist up out of your hips, your hips pulling away from your thighs, your thighs pulling downward toward your toes, your knees and calves reaching downward; feel the energy pulling down to your feet and up through your hands to the ends of your fingers.

RAINBOW POWER

Now breathe deeply and bend your hands backward at the wrists, so the palms are facing upward, fingers extended as straight as you can, as though you're supporting the world on your flattened palms, arms straight. Now raise your arms straight above your head. Keeping the palms facing upward, the heels of the palms forward, the backs of the hands pressing down, slowly move your hands outward as though your body were being pulled apart, in a rainbow arc of power. Keep the energy flowing all the way out through your fingertips *and beyond*, as taut and stretched out as you can. When you have brought the hands down to shoulder level, feel your upper back muscles stretching and the inner arms stretched as though you were outlined in fire.

When your hands and arms are level with your shoulders, hold for ten very slow full breaths. Keep mouth closed, shoulders down, neck long. Your fingers will probably tingle! Keep resisting the air with your palms, as though you were pushing away two walls at the ends of your hands.

Now move your whole torso as far to the left as you can, as slowly as possible, turning your head to lean into it—breathe in and stretch as far as possible, then return to center, exhaling. (Bend left knee as you stretch.)

Now push to the right side, again following the movement with your head and eyes, bending your right knee. Your feet are solidly planted about two feet apart. Feel the stretch along the opposite side when you lean in each direction. Make sure your body remains straight, not tipped over, so your head, shoulders, and arms keep the same relation to each other. Do this stretch five times in each direction.

THE SWINGER

Clasp your hands behind your back (if you can't, put your hands on your shoulders, keeping the shoulders down). Swing your whole torso and head to the left, breathing in. Then swing to the right as you exhale. Do this twenty times. Imagine there is a point in the middle of your chest and you're suspended from the ceiling by a string attached there. Feel the two "wings" of your back touching—your chest very open.

You will feel completely energized and shoulder tension will be greatly relieved.

Another great SHOULDER AND MIDBACK DE-TENSER for when you've been bending over a hot desk or stove all day:

stand with your back to a desk and place your hands on the desk behind you at your sides. Bend your knees a little, curve your whole body forward as though you were deeply ashamed, and bow your head. Now press down on your hands, inhale (mouth closed, of course), and stretch backward until your body is arched like a bow, head as far back as it will go. Rise on your toes, press them against the floor, and hold for a count of four. Then exhale and slowly curve over again. Do this two to three times. (The height of the desk should be a little lower than you can put your hands on easily—so you have to bend your knees a little.) This is the best and fastest back de-kinker going.

When I did a TV series on how to de-stress at your desk, these were the most popular exercises because they're quick and effective. They don't take much time. They do need to be done with full attention.

Here is the all-time champ of neck relaxers:

THE POINTILLIST NECKLACE
(also known as the Drunken Head Roll)

Drop your head from the first vertebra until your chin practically rests on your chest. Now imagine there is a necklace around your clavicle. At each point someone will press gently, and that will move your head. It's going to start moving of its own weight without your help. At each point, moving as slowly as possible without actually stopping, ask yourself, "Is my head as heavy as possible? As heavy as a cannonball? Is my neck as long as possible? Are my shoulders relaxed?" Imagine there is a ball bearing inside your temples that is moving your head around because its weight shifts—don't lead with your face, but with that imaginary weight inside your head at eye level. It makes your head roll slowly, slowly around. As slowly as possible, circle clockwise. When you hear cracks and clicks, gently go back and "iron" them out. Three times around and then three times in the other direction.

Result: wonderful when you're tense, as a general relaxer, as well as the best exercise for neck and shoulder tension. Do it anytime. It's excellent before going to sleep. Most important—do it as SLOWLY AS POSSIBLE. Imagine your head's going to rest on your shoulder, your back, your other shoulder, and your chest.

Keep breathing steadily. If it hurts at some point, and it may because you're unkinking a lot of accumulated knots, just breathe more deeply (you can open your mouth a little, but breathe mainly through the nose) and RELAX the rest of the torso.

Tips: remember to keep shoulders relaxed; don't hunch them around your ears! Don't let your body tip over—stay upright. Keep your stomach relaxed.

Between each exercise, scan your body from the inside: notice how you're breathing; lie down and enjoy the expanded sense of ease, space, and power; memorize it so you can get back into that state with less and less exertion as your body begins to learn how to produce that natural unstressed state with less and less effort. Consciously, let go more and more. You may find you're feeling lighter and more relaxed than you have in years. Many people report that their breathing eases, they feel suddenly more cheerful, hopeful, and energized. Lie down and enjoy your well-earned rest. . . .

Ready to get up? First rotate your limp hands at the wrists, as though you were oiling the joints by rolling them around. Make the movement as smooth and sinuous as you can. Now try rolling them in the other direction. If you hear a snap, crackle, or pop, make the movements even gentler and subtler and more snaky. Then draw your knees up like a baby, and begin to rotate your feet at the ankles. You'll probably hear a lot of snapcracklepop there; our poor feet, mostly encased in shoes, don't usually get enough expressive movement to free the energy locked in there. It's lumpishly dropped at the bottom of the elevator shaft that is our bodies.

So you're waking up your system by activating the sensitive micromuscles in your feet and ankles. Like your hands, they can be as expressive as energy terminals. In foot reflexology, you dissolve body tensions by massaging the feet because every part of the foot has a corresponding energy center in other parts of the body.

Roll the feet around as smoothly as you can, keeping the hands going too. (If this is hard for you to coordinate at first, do the feet alone, then add the hands.) If you are really up for a challenge, try rotating clockwise with the hands. Not easy, but new brain pathways are made when you practice coordinations that had been difficult or impossible! You actually make yourself smarter when your physical functioning gets more adroit and sophisticated.

Take it at your own pace, and don't be discouraged if it seems impossible at first. Stop a moment, knees up, and do it MENTALLY for a few minutes. Then do it again physically. This kinesthetic practice greatly enhances functioning.

In experiments with sounds, clinical researchers found that when people *thought* a certain sound, there were tiny movements in the middle ear, and athletes who mentally practiced their skills could cut practice time very substantially. Golfer Jack Nicklaus always rehearses his plays by seeing them in his mind's eye and mentally feeling himself going through the moves. You can greatly enhance your own coordination with little or no muscular effort by this kind of mental rehearsal.

After you have done the circling about ten times with both feet and hands, rub your hands together vigorously until you feel they're very warm; then rub your feet together hard, grab your knees, and rock back and forth gently on your spine. Then when you feel it is the right moment, sit up. You will be immensely ALIVE, AWAKE, REFRESHED.

•

NOW LAUGH FOR THREE MINUTES! You think this is easy? Try it! I guarantee you'll feel revved up, stimulated, totally energized. At first it may wear you out; laughing continuously takes a lot of energy, but it also produces a lot by relaxing a great many involuntary muscles and stepping up oxygen consumption and circulation. Try it with your friends and family.

One very entertaining variant that I often do with business groups is to have everybody lie down, each person with his/her head on someone's stomach; then the first person begins to laugh and soon everybody's roaring. It's an amazing feeling to feel that tide of laughter sweeping through everybody's gut and vibrating the floor underneath you.

Here's an easy private one to finish off—your personal HEART RELAXER.

Every half hour or so, if you're having a hectic day, drop your jaw suddenly. As you do that, breathe, shrug your shoulders, and rotate them fully—back, front, up, down, in generous smooth circles as high, wide, and handsome as you can make them. When you bring them around to normal position, make sure the back muscles of your shoulders have really relaxed. And when you shrug, keep the jaw dropped and relaxed. It's a little like patting your stomach with one hand and rubbing your head with the other!

Holding on produces a tight jaw and sore shoulders. People who carry a lot of burdens generally have tight shoulder and neck muscles. You're beginning to tighten up for the fight-or-flight syndrome. "Crouched for action" can whip the heart into a spasm. If you do this exercise for ten seconds every half hour, it will counteract the buildup of the heart's tendency to spasm. The brain wave, which slows down in older people and those with heart disease, will switch to a normally functioning one.

After a while, you can begin to get the exact "feel" of this relaxed-heart brain wave. Even Type A uptight personalities can help prevent heart attacks by practicing this normalizing exercise and feel the new calmer functioning that it engenders in their brains and hearts.

THE CAVEMAN WHUMP

If you feel a lot of anxiety in your chest, lock yourself in the john and lightly beat your chest, shoulders, and back with your fists for two or three minutes. (A low, steady *ughghgh* helps!)

This will break up the tight feeling and stimulate circulation. For more daily and emergency tension-reducers, see pages 323, 332, 333, 334, for the I Don't Care Swing, the hostility exercises, the Steam Engine, and the Woodchopper. You'll discover which ones feel best and most effective for you. Try them in the suggested sequences. Then, by noticing what feelings they produce, you can have a short or extended routine that will always keep you in condition to handle the tensions that result from challenges, whether speaking in public or dealing with difficult interpersonal situations or just a time pressure.

Now you know WHAT, WHY, and the beginnings of HOW. From here on, the Dodo—who was no dodo—said it best: "THE BEST WAY TO EXPERIENCE IT IS TO DO IT!"

You're becoming aware of your internal thought, emotional, and body processes, and have some new tools to deal with the most common tension problems most people experience. You may find that the breathing alone will make the difference between handling a situation well and feeling out of control. Breathing may even make it possible for you to stop smoking, if you are a smoker (more about this in chapter 12).

If you have chronic tension problems, some exercises in this chapter and later will help to undo the accumulated knots that your life and experience have tied up your inner gifts with.

You're beginning to stretch and experience the full magic of your own body/mind. Now you'll find out how you can get in touch with your "heartfelt" inner self, and share it (safely!) with the world around you; how to create your own inner radiance and resonate with the warmth, love, and acceptance that is waiting for you in others.

5

De-Stress Yourself

ONE MORNING the phone rang. It was Margaret L., a distinguished author of many books on health, lecturer, and president of several organizations. She was in a panic.

"I've got a radio show to do this morning to publicize my new book and I'm absolutely frantic! I don't know why. I've done lots of them before, but suddenly I'm so nervous and frightened and I can't remember anything in my book. I can't even talk straight! What'll I do? You've got to help me!"

"Don't worry, Margaret," I assured her, "it'll be okay. First tell me what has been going on. Has something else happened to make you feel anxious?"

"Oh, yes, well, I've been visiting my sister, and our mother is very ill again, and I've been terribly worried about her and I feel so *helpless!*"

"First of all," I told her, "put your right thumb over your right nostril and exhale through your left nostril. Then inhale through the same nostril. Do this for twenty-six long breaths. Each time you exhale, release all the fear and anxiety and let it dissolve into the universe. Every time you inhale, imagine you're cleansing your whole brain and body and taking in all the energy of the universe. Imagine that the breath—they call it prana in Yogic philosophy—is sweeping past any obstruction in the nose and clearing an enormous radiant space in your brain. Each time you exhale, let go more and more of the fear, pain, and distress we all carry with us, even from years ago. With each new inhalation, start fresh and fill up with all the energy in the world. It's all out there, if you take it!" There was a silence while she did the exercise, then a deep sigh.

"I feel better now," she said, "but why did that happen?"

"Oh, your body is feeling the stress and anxiety of your mother's illness. That contaminated everything. The body doesn't know the difference between one kind of anxiety and another. That's why tension escalates. It may be triggered by one thing and then something that wouldn't have bothered you at all another time becomes an unbearable irritation or pressure. Remember, *it's impossible to be relaxed and anxious at the same time.*"

How to Be at Your Best When You Don't Feel Like It

In this chapter I'll show you how to make the BODY-MIND-BREATH connection work for you, so you can keep your charisma flowing even when it seems to have deserted you!

We know from the Charisma survey that nobody says "I've never felt charismatic!" This is our natural heritage, and although most people don't know how to *make* it happen, everyone has experienced moments of feeling tuned in, at one with themselves and the world. At such moments, life is good, and we have a natural confidence, ease, and vital enjoyment of being alive.

"The universe," says Tarthang Tulku, the Buddhist teacher, "is confident." That's why it's so creative! By eliminating the "roadblocks," we can stimulate the natural flow of energy which has been cut off or dammed up.

Since we live in a holographic universe, every cell encapsulates the entire development of the organism. This means that starting from almost any point, we can bring ourselves back into a state of "flow" or balance. Our body is our vehicle, our musical instrument, our expressive channel, a seismograph of our feelings and history. And if we pay attention, a wonderful guide to our inner journey. The energy body radiates outward and elicits love and acceptance from others.

Michael Colgrass, the Pulitzer Prize–winning composer, once came onstage at Carnegie Hall before a concert and stood on his head. "The body is the first musical instrument," he told his audience, "and I've just tuned mine!" Most of us never think of "tuning" ourselves, although we have to "play" (relate to) all kinds of different people and situations. As you saw in the tension inventory, our communication needs at this time in history have expanded overwhelmingly. More and more people are becoming aware of the life-threatening effects of stress overload. We face enormous challenges to planetary survival as well as in our own lives. De-stressing and "tuning" the body are the tools for realizing personal charisma and connecting with others. Imagine how different world events might be if political leaders de-stressed and meditated together before an important conference!

If you have a problem with your body, look at your mind. If you have a problem with your mind, look at your body. If you have problems with both, look at your life-style!

"The body," wrote Samuel Butler, "is a pair of pincers set over a bellows and a stewpot, and the whole fixed upon stilts!"

"The body is a temple" according to nearly all great religions.

Most people ignore their bodies' distress or pleasure signals except when they get too urgent, and we tend to be harshly critical of physical defects. These days the mirror of the world is only kind to those who are thin and fit. Not only do fat people have a poor self-image but studies confirm that they are actually less well received in personal and work situations than slim ones. The handicapped are only now beginning to assert their rights in a society that has all but ignored their needs, preferring not to notice them at all.

The Inner Mirror

What if we look at our bodies from the inside? Without judgments and disapproval, we can begin to get in touch with our marvelous arsenal of emotional and intuitive as well as physical resources. We need to pay attention to how our bodies feel inside and out, to sense how the flow of our energies is functioning. Our inner images of our bodies, though mostly unconscious, deeply affect our health, enjoyment of life, and charisma.

Through biofeedback, visualization, and relaxation techniques, we are beginning to appreciate the responsiveness of our bodies to our thoughts and feelings. That's the beginning of our control of our own health and well-being. Few of us could duplicate the feat of a yogi who could produce a cyst within minutes on his body, and then, while spectators watched, make it disappear! But the training in relaxation and concentration that produced such feats is now available to help us achieve more control over our lives and increase our respect for the healing powers of our own bodies. It also opens up the channels to personal development and growth through the evolution of our nervous system. Here are paths to feeling very much at home in the world, challenged by possibilities yet comfortable with people, a path to confidence and charisma, living at the peak of our powers.

What does the body need? Strength, balance, and flexibility. What do our minds and spirits need? Strength, balance, and flexibility. The path to all three can be opened through body awareness. It's vitally important to be a gentle, dispassionate witness of what your body is *actually* experiencing, not caught up in disapproval of it.

"Oh, I hate my body," moaned Gloria M. As she happened to be a ballet dancer, with long, exquisite legs and arms, the ordinary mortals in our workshop were baffled, annoyed, and envious.

"What are you talking about?" asked Marion L., a slightly dumpy advertising executive, rather impatiently. "Are you just fishing for compliments?"

"Why, no," answered Gloria, her eyes widening in surprise. "When I gain a couple of pounds or have a little roll of flesh on my hips, I hate myself, I don't feel good. It's a constant struggle. It's not even that I look better and dance better when I'm thinner; I don't *like* myself unless I'm perfect."

Practically nobody is really satisfied with her/his body. Much of this has to do at least as much with social, media, and parental external ideals of perfection as with optimal functioning. But "I don't like myself unless I'm perfect!" carries a depth charge worth examining. "The perfect is the enemy of the good," someone once remarked.

For a dancer, model, or sports figure, the attainment of a physical standard of maximum fitness, strength, and symmetry is a professional necessity. The drive to increase one's physical abilities and improve appearance can, of course, provide valuable spurs to achievement. But there's a hidden trap. The current rage for physical fitness and media emphasis on "beautiful people" is both valuable and damaging.

On the plus side, people are becoming aware that using your body will increase your brain power, aid relaxation and health and your pleasure in life. But the pressure to be "perfect" (or at least superior) is increasing our own disgust with ourselves for not living up to our ideals of physical perfection, aggravated by the visible signs, on every side, of people who seem to have managed it!

The Ugly Duckling Syndrome

We're looking for short-cuts, prescriptions, miracles, instant trans-formations. We're looking for answers no outer mirror can pro-vide. We're all hoping somebody will magically declare that we too are swans. Our star worship, even with its new parade of acceptable vulnerabilities, still separates us from a sense of our own uniqueness. Only the inner mirror can provide that. The fact is, no body is perfect. Even the wonderfully developed ones that belong to dancers and athletes are uneven in some way or sub-ject to injury. The body is a part of our developing exploration of our relation to the world. It is also a metaphor for how we feel about ourselves and other people. Part of this is genetic. Most women seem to put on weight in the trunk or in the middle and have thin legs, or have slender waists and get bottom-heavy. Paunches, double chins, and wrinkle patterns run in families. Genetics and environment are our history. Body language speaks through structure as well as function. By becoming aware of what your own body is expressing, you'll be able to utilize hitherto unexpressed feelings and release a tremendous amount of locked-in energy. When you're physically in touch and expressive, your charisma quotient increases radically. The paradox is: you have to let go of the clutching need to be perfect to realize your body's real gifts and capacities.

The down side of the current passion for physical fitness is that feelings of self-worth are too often dependent on whether you're exactly the right weight or measurements or proportions or not. Luckily, there is a countermovement to allow greater acceptance of individual differences—ethnic, physical, and social. But still an unmistakable elitism pressures us to revere those who exemplify —like the Bionic Woman—our physical ideals.

"I'm so mad at my damn leg," said John R., who had a slightly crippled leg from a childhood bout with polio. Through exercises he practiced feeling tender and affectionate toward this vulnerable part of his body. Then he visualized it as functioning well. Eventually he was able to restore some of its functioning. Equally important, he began to walk with an assurance and dignity that he had never had. Now his limp seems distinguished rather than apologetic. He holds his head up. You see the full power of his eyes and strong torso. He feels centered and balanced and gives an impression of immense strength and dignity, although his leg will never be as strong as the other.

How's Your Body Image?

Do you have a negative body image? That can seriously interfere with your ability to project your charisma. To get a clear idea of exactly what you *do* feel about your body, try this little experiment. Take a large sheet of brown paper and draw an outline of your body. Fill in the parts of your body that you like best; use colors that you like to color them. Now fill in the parts you like least or hate. At the side of the page, write the "messages" you got about the parts of your body you don't like from (*a*) parents, (*b*) peers, (*c*) your loved one, and (*d*) the media.

Draw in all the locations where you've suffered pain, accidents, illness, injuries. Then color (with other favorite colors) those body parts that give you the greatest pleasure or joy. Which parts do you consider vital and healthy? When you've finished this part of the drawing, look at yourself and try to sense which parts of your body project charisma, i.e., vitality, to other people. Do your eyes shine? Are your hips expressive? Your hands? When you've figured out your exceptionally vital parts, color in the auras projecting outward from them on your drawing.

Make one drawing for the front and one for the back.* You may be surprised to find that your negative feelings about parts of your body are related to media messages. Nell M., for instance, admitted, "I'm ashamed of having small breasts. Most of the men in my life prefer Playboy Bunny types."

Nell is not alone. Although the woman's movement now encourages greater self-acceptance for a woman's natural endowments (even if she has suffered a mastectomy), the Playboy Bunny ideal is very much with us still. Our culture glorifies big breasts. In the hit musical *A Chorus Line,* one dancer sings a song about "Tits" and how she became successful after an operation which gave her bigger "tits." Yet small breasts can be more sensitive and responsive during lovemaking and certainly don't sag as much when a woman grows older. In other societies, small breasts were considered charming and desirable. (The French ideal was that each should fit into a champagne glass!)

Men don't escape physical stereotypes either. They have long been programmed to believe that you need a large penis to be a successful lover. Many men who feel underendowed still suffer agonies of shame and feelings of sexual insecurity.

When self-hate is triggered by a "fall" from physical grace (or a lack of it), we become alienated from ourselves. It is then so much harder to reconnect with a sense of being loved and charismatic. "I'm always thinking about being overweight," reported Celeste J., a pretty young arts administrator, plump but by no means fat. "It's like a gloomy shadow that's always with me, raining guilt all over me! When I meet people, I'm sure they're thinking, 'Oh, look at that blimp,' and, if they're fat, I can't stand being with them. I guess I should be more tolerant, but I *hate* fat people."

Often, as a defense against unpleasant or unacceptable experiences, we numb ourselves to feeling. Allan S., a trial lawyer, said, "I really don't know where I feel any tension in my body. In fact I'm not very aware of my body." He also remarked, "I think I'm

* This exercise is partly based on one in Ken Dychtwald's *Bodymind* and is very useful for getting in touch with your own feelings about different aspects of your body.

just about perfect! It's other people I can't stand! People are always doing something that I find annoying. Why can't they do the right thing?" Since he, unlike most people, suffered from being hard not on himself but other people, I asked him if he would like to reduce the stress he suffered in relation to other people.

"Oh, yes," he said. "My kids annoy me. So do my colleagues. And, of course, my wife drives me crazy! *People* give me a headache!" (He reminded me of Shaw's Professor Higgins in *My Fair Lady* who asked plaintively, "Why can't a woman be more like a man?" blissfully unaware of his own fallibility.)

After a couple of weeks, Allan noticed he *was* indeed feeling definite tension in his neck, shoulders, and head. "When I get annoyed with people," he reported, "I feel a pain right here," and he pointed to the top of his head. He had never realized that he literally got a headache from annoyance.

His wife, Merry, on the other hand, was painfully aware of all her tensions. She seemed terrified of making a mistake. She constantly interrupted, eager to prove she had understood. Self-doubt gnawed at her, the fear that she couldn't stand on her own feet. Although they displayed such very different personalities, both Allan and Merry had developed their patterns of tension in childhood as a defense against invasion of their privacy. Allan was an older child, very brilliant. His parents adored him but wouldn't leave him alone. He outstripped them and his brother very quickly, and then needed to protect himself against their efforts to "take over" and live his life with him.

Merry, on the other hand, said, "I'm always daydreaming. I can't concentrate and I'm always late. I don't have much physical energy. But when I'm interested in a project, I can go on forever." Merry's mother had constantly overprotected her and the "messages" for Merry were "Watch out, you might get sick." "Let me do it for you." Merry then translated them into the assumption "I guess I'm not able to do it for myself." Her way of escaping from her mother's pressure was to daydream. Allan numbed himself; she remained open and too vulnerable, but full of nervous distraction. On the surface, she was eager, almost frantically attentive—but incapable of real concentration.

As we worked on the "inner mirror" that observes body sensations (and includes thoughts and feelings as they are translated into the body), Allan gradually grew more aware of what he was really feeling underneath the numbness he had imposed on himself since childhood. He became so interested in the new "textures" of experience he was feeling in himself that he began to be much more patient and empathetic with Merry, his children, and his colleagues. By focusing on his own neglected sensations, he reduced the unnoticed buildup of pressure that had been his way of reacting to other people since he was very young. He no longer got headaches from sheer annoyance. He felt more detached about other people's failings and foibles because he was so interested in watching his own reactions. His friends observed that he seemed more responsive to people and more charming. "They think I'm less abrasive," he grinned wryly, "and certainly I am feeling different. For some strange reason people don't annoy me as much anymore!"

Merry, who now recognized that her daydreaming and lack of concentration, her nervousness and inability to be on time, all stemmed from her early need to protect herself against her mother's negative messages about her self-worth, paid more loving attention to her body and what it was telling her. She stopped assuming she was always "wrong" and just watched the flow of sensations and tensions, which was a great surprise to her. She found that it was *not* difficult to concentrate when she had relaxed her body through muscular relaxation or deep slow breathing (see chapter 12) because her anxiety level dropped. "I can't believe how marvelous it is to know that there's nothing wrong with me!" she exclaimed, her eyes shining. "I just thought I'd never be able to control my mind and my actions. It makes me feel—" she paused, and laughed a little shyly, "well—grownup! Here I am with two children, nine and seven. It's about time, isn't it!"

The need for authentic expression is very powerful. I'm amazed and awed when I see people instinctively find outlets for deep feelings. For instance, for all of Allan's supposed indifference to his physical sensations, Merry reported: "Allan loves massage, so he really is more interested in his body than he admits!"

The power of feeling (and intention) is so profound that even if a person is physically disabled it's possible to express feelings through the body and change the quality of that person's experience. Manfred Clynes, in *Sentic Cycles*, describes an emotional cycle he devised for seven basic emotions: anger, hate, grief, love, sex, joy, and reverence. People press down with their third finger on a simple machine (he calls it a sentograph) while recalling these emotions. Going through these cycles for half an hour seems to set off an amazing emotional catharsis that's satisfying and therapeutic. One woman, a quadriplegic from the neck down, discovered she could express grief and frustration by pressing down her chin, the only part of her body she could move voluntarily. This brought about a remarkable change in her inner sense of life. Gradually she began to draw some pleasure from her existence. She could sleep better, enjoy music, and she suffered less pain; her state of mind improved so much that "it came to be a real pleasure to be in Mrs. C. N.'s company; a radiance seemed to issue from her that affected others who came in contact with her." However limited your body, the power of your mind to amplify your experience is almost limitless.

If muscular tension restricts our responses, the feeling quality (texture) of perception suffers. Sometimes the tension is a defense against sexual feelings. For some people who have been trained to "control" themselves at all times, it can be scary to feel floating or falling or lightness sensations, as though one had lost control.

The most important prerequisite is to get beyond "right" and "wrong," "good" and "bad" when you look in your inner "feeling" mirror. Just observe with interest and patience and you'll begin to be amazed at your own resources of grace, strength, balance, and intuition. They only need to be evoked, to come trooping out, shy at first as woodland deer, and full of unexpected subtleties.

When you let go of judgments and tension, you begin to discover a whole world within a moment or two. When was the last time you "lost" yourself, perhaps listening to music or during lovemaking, skiing, lying on the beach? Curiously, the more attention we pay to what's happening in and around us (rather than to thoughts and feelings about the past and the future, which usually involve anxiety or regret), the more free we feel and the less constrained by fear of failure and what people may think. (In *Limelight*, Charlie Chaplin played an old vaudeville comedian trying to make a comeback. Claire Bloom, a young woman he had rescued when she tried to commit suicide, asks him, "Why do you want so much to succeed?" He looks at her for a moment and

106

gently replies, "It isn't that I want to succeed so much—I just don't want to fail!" He spoke for our culture.)

Practice in reproducing a state of relaxed awareness is invaluable in training us to be charismatic. If you're dismayed by how difficult it is to concentrate or sit still or enjoy the flow of feelings for a few minutes, remember: as your anxiety level drops and your skills increase, it'll get easier and easier, more and more pleasurable. It's like learning music. When you first heard a song, you may have noticed mostly the rhythm or only the melody. With experience, you can listen to the rhythm, the melody, the words, the scoring, the dynamics, and be aware of a dozen things at once.

It's a paradox: to free yourself from the body, you first have to pay attention to it. Who's running the show? It or you? If you are, you have to check out all the elements and take charge. In the privacy of your own room, take a good look at your body (nude) in the mirror. But this time, don't disapprove of weak arches or extra flesh or other physical attributes you have been accustomed to deploring. Look at your body like a sympathetic stranger, and notice if one side is stronger, one shoulder higher (or other imbalances). Your body and mind are reflections of each other. I was very amused when I realized that my feet are very thin-skinned. When I was a little girl, my mother said: "Dear, you're too sensitive!" She was right. Now I value the sensitivity for the insight and awareness it gives me. I also know how to stabilize my nervous system to avoid falling prey to my sensitivity. I don't always succeed!

Muscles, bones, and muscular coordination are all involved with how we have lived, what we have eaten, what we have done, and how frequently, and how we felt doing it.

Even your skin is meaningful. Is it rough? Smooth? Is the skin loose or tight? If it's not elastic there may be a lot of pain locked in between the skin and bones. (Chua K'a, the Mongolian warriors' massage, rolls the skin between thumbs and fingers until the psychophysical knots in the flesh yield. Warriors used to massage the pains and wounds of battle out of each other's body. Rolfing, a more brutal massage, also releases emotional traumas from the body.)

Gently massage your body several times a week, every day if possible. Particularly in tension areas—neck, shoulders, head, hands, and feet. Start by stimulating energy in your hands by rubbing them together hard! Reflexology is the art of stimulating all the body centers through massaging the feet or hands. The Chinese, who knew all about these meridians thousands of years ago, avoid drugs by using acupuncture for anesthesia in operations.

If you were depressed for years, your shoulders slump. Your eyes are dull. Your body may look meek and passive if you're used to "taking it." We all get instant subliminal messages about people from the way they hold their bodies and heads. Look at yourself as a sympathetic stranger would. See if you get a subliminal impression of your personality preferences and overall feelings and tone. You may have to let your eyes go "soft-focus," let them blur a bit so you can imagine it's not you but someone else in the mirror.

Five factors shape our body/minds: (1) heredity, (2) physical activity and exposure, (3) nutrition, (4) environment, and (5) emotional and psychological history and current functioning. In *Bodymind,* Ken Dychtwald writes:

> Emotional stimulation of muscles can have the same effect on the body as purely physical activity, except that it is usually more difficult to detect the source of stimulation and the way it has been selectively, and often unconsciously, exercised. The body begins to form around the feelings that animate it, and the feelings in turn become habituated and trapped within the body tissue itself. The bodymind, then, when seen from this perspective, is to some extent the continually regenerating product of a lifetime of emotional encounters, psychological activities, and psychosomatic preferences.

Dychtwald suggests that when all these forces are merged in the creation of a human being, the force of the aware psyche is the most powerfully formative of all.

In the West, we split the body and mind in two—the psyche, which is supposed to be somewhere in the skull between the eyes; and the body, living and moving underneath. All our institutions and cultural processes reflect this split and fragmentation both personally and socially. A few years ago a man in Colorado left a will offering a million dollars to anybody who could find the exact location of the soul—so far there have been no takers.

Eastern cultures consider the body and mind inseparable, as the Greeks did. We are beginning to apply this concept of harmony. It is encouraging to know that to a large extent we do create ourselves in our own image. Our cells and thoughts are directly connected.

Dychtwald's description of the most common body and body-mind splits and imbalances provides a provocative way to look at the body.

Right-Left

The right side of the brain controls the left side of the body. This is usually considered the feminine aspect—emotionality, passivity, creativity, holistic expression, visualization, yin or receptive forces, music. The left hemisphere (with its predominantly logical, analytic, verbal, and mathematical functions) controls the right side of the body—the "masculine" side. The right-side personality traits are assertiveness, aggressiveness—the yang force in Chinese cosmology.

Reaching out with the left hand is passive, receptive, while gesturing with the right is active, aggressive. This doesn't seem to be much affected by whether you're right- or left-handed.

Dychtwald tells the story of a woman in his workshop who shed tears of rage—from the right eye only! When her crying changed to sadness, the left eye was the one that shed the tears! (Emotional states are right-hemisphere activity.)

Actor John Barrymore was able to cry out of either eye, *or both*, whenever he wanted to! Once when he was making a movie, he asked director Elia Kazan, "Now, how do you want these tears—all at once, or one group at a time? Which eye—or would you like them simultaneously from both?" (He claimed that he practiced his crying techniques from the time he was a tiny child.)

Oriental facial diagnosis explores the left-right relation in great detail. For example, the right cheek represents one's mother's influence, the left the father's. If you look closely at someone's face, in most cases you will notice that one cheek is usually a little wider than the other. Usually that turns out to mean that the yang cheek (or more contracted one) represents the dominant parent in the person's life. Try it. It's surprisingly accurate.

Meet Your Bottom (and Your Top) Half

The lower half of the body, the part that contacts the earth, is concerned with stability, moving, balancing, rooting, supporting, feeling grounded. The top half deals with seeing, hearing, introspection, *emotional* stability, homeyness, dependency, and the alternation between motion and stasis. Outward expression and interpersonal communication, socializing, self-assertion, personal aspirations, manipulation, and action are concerns of the top half.

Have another look at your own body: How is the weight distributed? Where is your center of gravity? Are you bottom-heavy or top-heavy? Forget about disapproval and let's examine the implication of these divisions.

When the lower half is larger than the upper, the person usually feels more at home dealing with the grounded private aspects of his/her life. Usually this person cultivates a life-style that reinforces these relationships. The top half, remember, is concerned with self-expression, self-assertion, and communication. Which parts of your personality have been given the most attention and support throughout your life? Think how your friends, children, and strangers respond to you and you'll find out.

Most women find one breast is slightly larger than the other. Usually, the larger one corresponds to the side of her personality she has been using more. If the left side is larger, the more feminine, passive side of her nature has been dominant in her life; if the right side, it's the more aggressive, active parts of her personality. This is uncannily accurate, based on observation and informal questioning.

If you overdevelop the private (lower) aspects rather than the expressive upper, you may feel more comfortable expressing inwardly than outwardly. Emotions express themselves naturally and are released through hands, chest, heart, mouth, jaws, and eyes (the windows of the soul).

"Feeling" or "being" is more characteristic of the lower-dominant person. She/he may find it hard to express feelings to other people. An apparent paradox: many women who have lived homebound, family-oriented lives are "feeling-" or "being-" oriented; they come to my workshops to learn how to express their feelings openly, how to speak up and hold their own. Yet women generally are more conditioned to be *aware* of their feelings than men, even if they don't express them. Many upper-oriented men, who have no trouble expressing themselves, are extremely uncomfortable voicing feelings!

A top executive in one major firm told one of my groups, "I don't feel I have the right to feel all my feelings! I shouldn't be afraid or weak." I've noticed at Thanksgiving and other holiday dinners that the men will often pass off a toast with a joke or a light remark, afraid of seeming sentimental or exposing their real feelings. Older men especially have learned wariness and sometimes find it hard to contact feelings they haven't expressed in a long time. *Yet true charisma comes from being able to own and voice your feelings fully, touching other people as well.* Practicing expression of your feelings encourages your ability to discriminate about when and how much to disclose. Keeping a tight lid on them leads to reduced expressiveness or the possibility of an explosion or inappropriate show of emotion.

Watch for a correlation between ease in using your body expressively and being able to speak without difficulty. Eloquence, agreed 88 percent of the Charismedia questionnaire answers, is "crucial for charisma." My hunch about this connection was confirmed by an informal experiment devised by an imaginative biochemist, Dr. William Frey, at the Ramsey Medical Center in St. Paul, Minn. Frey invited twenty people to a dinner party and notified them that no one was to speak. "I explained to them that this was an experiment in communication. They agreed on a three-hour time span during which I served dinner. Everybody came in identical togas. And they were strangers to each other. Some people couldn't stand not talking and left. What I found fascinating," he added, "was that the people who are the most verbal normally were the ones who found it easiest to communicate *without* words!"

This confirms my experience that when you become less inhibited moving your body, you also become verbally freer. And it's wonderful that you can move in either direction, from the body to the mind or reverse, depending on which is easier.

Biofeedback techniques help migraine sufferers avoid headaches by warming their hands and extending muscle warmth out to their extremities. Whenever you have a problem in one part, the most productive tactic is often to attack something else entirely! For example, many people ask, during a presentation, "What shall I do with my hands?" So we immediately do a centering exercise for balance and groundedness (see p. 119) and then the following exercise:

PRE-PRESENTATION WARM-UP

Rub your hands together as hard as possible until you've built up a nice feeling of warmth; then spread it to your arms, chest, head, back, legs, feet, and all around you.

When you're surrounded by warm vibration, take a deep breath and fling your arms out as wide as possible (as though you were welcoming a 300-pound fuzzy gift). Hold your breath and stretch, stretch, stretch until you can't hold anymore. Your fingers will tingle.

Then bring your hands in and lay them powerfully, slowly (the right hand over the left) on your chest as you exhale—and spread all that golden warmth through your heart and body.

Repeat three times.

THE GIMME GRAB

If you have trouble using your hands expressively or they feel awkward, practice stretching your arms out, fingers very wide. Then grab hard at a huge imagined object and, fists clenched, swiftly pull it in toward your body. The important thing is to stimulate your hands to reach out and grab what they reach for. The energy finally gets all the way out to your hands. "Hey, I feel selfish when I do that!" reported Myron L., an insurance executive. Grabbing for his own had been a no-no. Given permission, he gained visibly in confidence. He practiced the Gimme Grab every day, feeling increased confidence in his ability to focus on, express, and get what he wanted.

At the end of these exercises you won't have any problem with your hands! And your whole body will be warm and relaxed.

Since the upper half of the body is the communication center, it's not surprising that this is where most people feel tension before or during speaking. Sharon L., a training consultant at a large corporation, had a timid voice and used small, ineffectual gestures (all below-the-waist hand movements look weak and ineffectual) when she gave her talk. She was not very persuasive and she knew it.

"Sharon, please run in place and start your talk again," I asked her.

Sharon looked startled but agreed, feeling, as she said, predictably "silly." She began to laugh; it felt so funny to be running and talking. After a minute or so, her voice became fuller, because she was breathing more deeply. As she jogged, the lower half of the body became more grounded; her upper half became more relaxed and expressive. As though to match the flailing, pumping motion of the legs, now the arms, released from inhibition, began to make big gestures of an appropriate scale and size. She stopped jogging and went on with her talk, newly convincing. Her gestures were now quite large, and instead of looking as though she were pleading for a hearing, she was dynamic and forceful. Just changing the size of the gestures made them look completely different! There was a spontaneous burst of applause from the rest of the group when she finished. When Sharon saw the playback on video, she was amazed at the difference. Any instructions about what to do or not do with her hands would have left Sharon feeling as awkward and uncomfortable as ever.

The two halves of the body can learn from each other. The "stuck" lower part, through jogging and stimulating action, feels more active, and the immobilized upper becomes calmer and freer. When you're stuck in one area it may be a good time to get going in another. Then the momentum of that success can be transferred to the "stuck" area. Suddenly, what was difficult becomes easy and natural and you didn't even work on it!

The "action" or "doing" person may have a large chest, skinny legs, contracted buttocks. The assertive, outgoing, upper-dominated person may very well be an "oral" type, interested in eating and drinking. (The stereotype of the old-fashioned Hollywood producer!) The weak legs and thin hips may reflect a lack of groundedness—stability and emotional self-support.

Now take a look at the relative grace or awkwardness of your body's various parts. What are you secretly vain about? Disgusted by? Deposits of fat are considered by many body therapists as stagnant energy. Dychtwald suggests that if you're more talented with the upper body and awkward in legs and hips, you're probably more involved in upper-body aspects of your life. The reverse (healthy, active legs, a troublesome spine, clumsy arms) might suggest overemphasis on lower-body aspects.

Not surprisingly, the best-coordinated parts also escape injuries more than the others. Imbalances may turn up in the opposite ends of the body. The bottom-oriented person might be subject to tension headaches, asthma, arthritis of the wrists, or nervous stomach. Underdevelopment of the lower half may show up in sprained ankles, varicose veins, sexual dysfunction, or flat feet. But as with right- and left-hemisphere activity, there is often a crossover of functioning. It's possible to have tension headaches *and* flat feet!

To some extent most of us are "double-decker" people. Dychtwald suggests we can further pinpoint areas of health or disease by dividing the body still further into quadrants, top-bottom, right-left. A woman who finds it hard to be assertive might have tension in her right arm. This may produce weakness in the joints, tight muscles, or a tendency to injury in that area. If the same woman has trouble asking for love or accepting it, the tension might show up in the left arm.

Someone who has a hard time "taking a stand" (our bodies are very literal-minded!) might have problems in the right leg. Pain in the legs often indicates a fear of taking action; foot pain is a fear of being oneself.

"That's ridiculous!" Annette R. protested. "Can I help it if I was born with flat feet?"

"No, of course not," I told her, "but I want to suggest that there's an emotional component to every physical characteristic. Our bodies give very clear clues as to our personalities, weaknesses, and values."

Alicia L. was living with a husband who had left her once for seven years and then returned. They were quite content living with each other again, but Alicia didn't trust him: "This is the way he used to be at the beginning; I suppose it could happen again!" They were furnishing a new apartment when she developed a pain in her left leg. This suggests an inability to take a stand in a receptive way. If you're afraid and can't run away, you may feel tension in the legs. If you're in a situation you really enjoy and are afraid someone may force you to leave or spoil it for you, tension may show up in the legs, although it may seem it's for exactly the opposite reason! Body wisdom is almost impertinently literal!

FRONT-BACK SPLIT

This is the third important psychosomatic separation. Your front side represents the social (conscious) self: what is "presented," the side we see most often, look at most affectionately (or angrily) in the mirror, the clearest "image" of ourselves.

The private, unconscious elements are reflected by the back side. All that I don't want people to see or probe—emotions and feelings. Back trouble often shows up in people who're not used to exploring their own emotions or facing some of their darker feelings. There is some evidence that men are more prone to back trouble than women, possibly because they have been conditioned not to look at their feelings. Lower back pain has been interpreted as a repressed desire to shit on the world, to get back at it. At one time, most of the top executives of a major New York newspaper were suffering from lower back pain! Happily, with men's liberation there will be fewer such complaints.

Women also have these problems. Lisa H. often suffered from lower back pain but in between attacks was an excellent ice skater, horsewoman, and tennis player. Although she was preoccupied with her symptoms, she paid very little attention to her feelings. She and her mother, a southern belle, had spent their lives manipulating men to get material possessions and power. Denial of feeling was one of the ways they practiced Christian Science (a misapplication of the Christian Science principle of healing yourself through faith).

The Inner Mirror Views the Outer Mirror: Centering

Now see if you can feel where you are centered. Is it the head? Stomach? Legs? Solar plexus? Be aware of whether you feel balanced. Imagine a plumb line running from the sky through the crown of your head, your forehead, throat, heart center, solar plexus, navel, genitals, and plunging to the ground between your legs. Now with your eyes half-closed, gently transfer all your weight to the right foot, lifting your left a little. (Don't lean onto your hip.) Keep breathing easily (we tend to hold our breaths when we make an effort!). Keep imagining that plumb line and breathe easily. Hold your balance for six slow breaths. (Later you can expand that to ten, twelve, and then twenty.) Feel the floor supporting you (it is!).

If you feel comfortable, extend your arms to the sides and balance yourself easily, lightly again for six breaths. Then return to center and gently transfer your weight to the left leg (don't sink onto the hip—imagine the weight is still centered between your legs). As before, hold your balance for six full breaths, each consisting of an inhalation and an exhalation. Anytime you feel off center, do this centering exercise, and you'll immediately feel lighter, calmer, and at the same time more solidly balanced and supported.

Now stand centered and at ease. With your inner mirror tuned to your balances, look in the outer mirror and begin to notice, with detachment and nonjudgmental vision, any outer imbalances. The major ones to look for are: a great difference or inconsistency between front-back, top-bottom, right-left, head-body, torso-limbs. These observations are going to be very useful to you in "reading" other people as well.

Don't tell yourself, "Oh, God, I must go on a diet!" or "I hate my knobby knees!" Just get a sense of how you are formed at this moment. Ask: Does one side seem larger, more powerful, or more healthy than the other? Ken Dychtwald suggests in *Bodymind* that you ask which part of you projects a glow of vitality toward other people. Allow this sense to fill you with affection for your "vital parts." See the underdeveloped parts not as weaknesses but as untapped resources to be nurtured and developed. If you want to change, appreciate yourself as you *are!* It's another odd paradox that feeling affection for your body makes it easier to change what you don't like.

There are often good reasons why fat settles in one area. It may represent stagnant energy or the body's successful attempt to literally cushion you against emotional pain.

Madeline R., an actress who had been very slim and lithe, was very distressed about her thirty-pound weight gain. Most of it settled in her stomach, which looked almost pregnant. Her husband of twenty years had left her suddenly for a seventeen-year-old girl, and for three or four years she had struggled to regain her balance. She was able, being a strong and gifted woman, to recover and begin her career again. Now a character actress, she was a great success. But the weight would not come off. Then, as in Alicia's case, her husband returned to her. Still she could not lose that weight, and she was despairing about it.

"I don't want anyone to see me like this," she said (even though she'd be enacting on stage!). "I can't bring myself to go to an exercise class or have a masseur see me. I used to be so proud of my figure!" When I suggested that the weight in her stomach was the protective action her body had chosen to shield her from the unbearable emotional pain she suffered, she gasped, "I used to wonder where the pain went? I couldn't feel it! I knew it was there, but I didn't know where it was." The first time I massaged her stomach, she suddenly burst into deep, racking sobs with the release of old stored grief. Within a few weeks, her stomach began to soften, and as she lost weight she gradually got rid of her unwanted bulge. But *as long as she only hated it, it wouldn't budge!*

Recognizing the pain and her body's ingenious device to protect her from emotional annihilation, she was able, at last, to dissolve its tight hold on her—by appreciating how it had protected her! Body wisdom is profound. How we need this kind of "carnal knowledge"!

We all act on subtle body language cues which form an unspoken base for communication. They affect whether or not we like others, or they like us. But we don't have to know all the details of people's lives to "read" and "speak" their body language.

Here is a technique to help you establish bio-rapport without saying a word!

Mirror Matching

Notice how the person you're talking to is sitting or standing. Is he leaning back, legs crossed or uncrossed, hands clasped or unclasped? Then match his posture (reversed of course, if you're sitting opposite). If it seems too obvious to copy the other person's gestures right away, do it a moment later. At first you may feel absurd and think the other person will suspect you're mimicking him. Oddly enough, if you're unobtrusive about it, people do *not* notice. When people get along very well, this is often exactly what happens automatically! When you breathe or move like another person, you are, as the saying goes, on their wavelength. The result is bio-rapport.

Here's an astonishingly effective device for making yourself comfortable when you feel uneasy with this mime for one reason or another. If you're at a cocktail party and you are not comfortable talking to someone, try mirroring her/his posture, angle of head, hand position, feet position. Also mirror the level of energy they send (unless it is very low, in which case you'll both fall asleep!). We've all seen this at work when one person leans forward and the other then leans forward with great interest. It seems very natural. It is.

In films of successful negotiations the matching of gestures and body language is strikingly evident. People who communicate well do the mirror matching instinctively. So we're utilizing natural techniques that you do automatically when everything is going well. It is extremely valuable to know how the process works. Then, when there isn't a flow of rapport between two people you can actually start it because you know HOW. And if you succeeded in overcoming the first discomfort with this strategy, it very quickly elicits a warm response, which in turn makes you feel *more* comfortable. Very soon no more deliberate effort is necessary.

Vocal mirror matching can also be a powerful way to turn a potentially negative hostile encounter into an experience of solidarity. Suppose one day your boss storms into your office and shouts: "This is terrible! The orders were not in on time and we've lost that account. It's got to be done over again."

What do you do? If you quietly apologize, you feel mealy-mouthed, ashamed, and humiliated. If you deny or defend yourself, he'll get angrier. The answer, as in aikido, is to "blend." With the same energy he used when he bawled you out, you reply, "Yes, I'm really upset about that. I'm giving you my personal guarantee that I'm not going to leave the office until the rewrite is completely done, no matter what happens."

Your tone is very strong, assertive, but *you're on his side!* This is an amazingly effective style. Your former antagonist feels instinctively backed up. He is all but certain to drop his truculent tone, mollified by your response.

Tim R. couldn't get over the effect this had on the way he felt when he got a dressing-down. "I used to feel like slinking away with my tail between my legs," he told the group. "This time, after practicing this new style, I noticed my boss calmed down immediately, and I felt strong and independent, not as though I'd knuckled under. He actually seemed grateful to me for my concern. The same afternoon, he asked my advice about a business matter he'd never discussed with me before. Clearly he had more confidence in me. And I certainly had more confidence in myself!"

How to Avoid Getting Defensive

One of the hardest accomplishments in a tense situation is to avoid getting defensive. The minute you do, you've lost ground—and charisma—and it's not easy to recover.

Ann M., a mother of three young children, reported that her oldest child's French teacher had complained that her child wasn't paying attention in class. "She leaned forward as though she were attacking me. Her voice grew very loud.

"I would have reacted very badly to that before," admitted Ann. "I felt as though my 'honor' as a mother were at stake. This time, I looked at Miss Cook, leaned forward too, and I said, 'Isn't it awful? I really need your help on this. What can I do that would be helpful? I'm furious with him!' She immediately softened, and said, 'Well, maybe something is bothering him. He's really a very bright, nice little boy and I know he *wants* to do well. Don't be angry with him! I'll try to get him interested in a special project. Maybe he needs a little extra attention.' And do you know, it worked!"

Important: if you're going to "blend" (join) your antagonist, it's crucial to keep your own strong center. Keep your consciousness at the "hara" center (as the Japanese call it) or kath center, two inches below the navel. Otherwise you'll feel as though you are collapsing or toadying to the other person, which is totally unsatisfactory.

"But how can I be sure that I'll react this way, even if I know the right thing to do?" many students ask. This is where the Visceral Rehearsal comes in.

Rerunning the Day's Film

Every night about an hour before bedtime (don't do it just before or it will keep you up!) run over the day's events in your mind, backward, like a film. Stop and enjoy moments that were particularly warm, satisfying, pleasant (particularly small ones: a look somebody gave you, the color of a leaf or a flower, your awareness of the good weather, the smell of baking bread from next door, an insightful or valuable remark you heard or read). Internalize the three A's: Acknowledge–Appreciate–Absorb.

Every day check whether you had at least one pleasant positive experience with each of your senses. Here's how:

The Pleasure Checklist
Did I see something beautiful and feel pleasure today?
Did I taste something good and savor it today?
Did I smell something fragrant and enjoy it today?
Did I hear something beautiful and enjoy it today?
Did I touch something pleasurable and enjoy it today?
Did I feel any warm, loving thoughts and spread them through my body?

Keep a record for one week and notice whether you tend to have more pleasant experiences with one sense than the others. Are any of them totally neglected? If you find that, for instance, you had a lot of good "eye" nourishment but no "smell" or "touch" checks, consciously make an effort to be aware of good smells or feeling experiences (fur, velvet, cotton). Award yourself at least three of each every day.

Looking for pleasure can have extraordinary results. An attractive, vital man, Jim N., head of a large reference book firm in the Midwest, came to me to get over his inordinate fear of public speaking. When I asked him the first day what gave him pleasure, he replied promptly, "Nothing!" I was amazed when he insisted that he had no hobbies and there was nothing that *really* gave him pleasure. As an assignment I asked him to find three pleasurable experiences for each sense before we met again the following day.

The next day, he reported, astonished, "I suddenly remembered a lot of things I used to enjoy—sailing, painting, the pleasure of exploring libraries." His face was alight with his rediscovery of his own Pleasure Points. When he acknowledged the many interests he really deeply enjoyed, his entire attitude toward public speaking and toward his work changed.

"I suddenly realized," he told me, "that it's ridiculous for me to take forty-five-minute lunches, come in at eight o'clock, and stay till five. My job is to be creative, and when I am relaxed, one hour of uninterrupted thinking will produce enough work for everybody so I don't have to even be there for several days, even weeks! I'm going to look for more pleasure in the whole quality of my life. I see my creativity tremendously enhanced by it, so even from a business point of view, not to mention the quality of my life, it makes sense. I could be traveling more, making more contacts with libraries—which I love to do." He grinned. "I'm going to enjoy this!" When he saw himself on video playback, he laughed ingenuously. "Now I see why I get such good feedback!" he exclaimed. "I thought people were just being kind!"

People connect with their Pleasure Points in different ways. The important thing is to look for them; then the appropriate form for *you* will appear as if by magic. It may be something so apparently trivial that it seems like nothing, but if it works for you, you have a potent tool that's all your own.

Maud L. told us she enjoys sitting down in the middle of her busy day as a social worker. She shuts the door of her office and closes her eyes, then begins to stroke her left hand with the fingers of her right hand as gently and softly as possible.

"I try to imagine that it's somebody loving, sometimes my mother, or my boyfriend, and I see how light and tender I can make my own touch. It's so relaxing that within a few minutes I feel all smoothed out. It really does a lot for me. Sometimes in a hectic meeting when people are attacking my proposals (I used to pick my cuticles), I remember to stroke part of my hand with a finger of the other hand. It can be a very small, imperceptible gesture, but if I'm consciously sending tenderness to that contact, it reminds my whole body to breathe deeply and relax as though someone were taking care of me and making it easier to handle the stress of the meeting. It's interesting how different the sensations are from one place on your skin to another, even right next to the first area. When you move lightly and subtly you begin to discover all kinds of variations. Then you're breathing more softly, and even that seems like an internal massage."

Bannon M. laughed. "I'm afraid that wouldn't work for me. When I want to relax quickly, I just close my eyes and go back to a tiny village between Granada and the ocean, where it's very white and very quiet. That's my retreat, and within seconds I am totally relaxed. I can feel all the tensions in my body letting go."

Different strokes for different folks! See which works best for you.

PART II THE VISCERAL REHEARSAL

In your rerun of today's "film" stop at any episode you didn't like. Was there something else you could have done? Could you have behaved differently? Would it have made a difference, either in what happened or your feelings afterward? If so, run it again, and this time program the new behavior; see yourself responding as you would like to. For example, if you didn't speak up when the cabdriver overcharged you or refused to stop smoking when you asked him to, prepare what you want to say and then rehearse the scene. Or if you snapped defensively at someone who criticized you, try the new nondefensive way of responding. Practice relaxing when attacked instead of automatically tensing. Remember that your self-worth is *not* at stake, no matter what the accusation, and rehearse your new response. By going through the new responses in your imagination, next time a similar situation comes up your visceral response will be the newly learned behavior. Please notice that whatever unpleasant situation happens, something similar will happen again—until you learn how to deal with it. "The universe," said researcher Bentov, "is a learning machine." You can do one of two things: respond externally in a different way or change your internal reaction if no outward change is possible.

In chapter 12, you will see how using the new slowed breathing at times of sudden stress will help you change your old unsatisfactory responses so you'll be able to tap into better ways of dealing with people and situations. When you're mentally rerunning your daily tape, *remember to breathe very slowly and evenly, and if you feel a flash of anger or fear or other negative emotion, deliberately relax your body and slow your breathing before you go on with the visualization.*

"It's funny," said Laura C., a psychologist who wanted to project more confidence, "with certain people, I feel so clumsy! I find myself stumbling all over the place. That was one of the early messages I got in life, of course: 'Laura's so clumsy!' Now before an important meeting, I visualize myself floating through it with infinite grace. I plan exactly what I'll wear that'll give me the right feeling. Then I imagine," she laughed, a little embarrassed, "I'm a tall slender flamingo moving with perfect calm and coordination. I don't know why, but that image really works wonders! I've always admired flamingos and I seem to know just how to move and be with that image in the back of my mind."

Jason R., a burly management consultant, said, "Well, my image for myself is a smooth basketball—light but substantial and able to really fly! I used to have a tendency to get into confrontations with some of my clients. I guess I'm a rough diamond!" he grinned wryly. "But when I was doing the Visceral Rehearsal one night the image of a basketball popped into my mind. It keeps me agile and on my toes and I can really move! I don't knock people down now. I just challenge them and we *play* together. It sounds crazy, but my work is more fun now. We 'make baskets' together. Both they and I feel good about that! With that image in mind, I rehearse things coming up and I think of ways to handle things that never would have occurred to me before!"

Robert C., a successful young lawyer, uses the previsualizations to prepare his court cases. "I can generally 'see' what the other lawyers and the judge are going to do, and it's very helpful. When I go in, I feel very prepared because I've seen the whole thing in my mind the night before, maybe three or four different ways, so whatever comes up I can handle it. Relaxing my body when I'm visualizing the scene not only makes it possible for me to see all the conceivable alternatives, but somehow I find the next day that I can stay in that relaxed state when it's actually happening. And I used to almost black out in court!"

Studies have shown that the feeling of control that comes when you have reliable techniques you know are going to work adds immeasurably to self-confidence, more than any single form of training such as biofeedback, desensitization, hypnosis, etc. I've seen it happen time after time.

Elaine L., a magazine editor who was terrified of speaking up in a regional meeting, always uses the I Don't Care Swing, the Elbow Propeller, and the Steam Engine (see pp. 323, 321, 334) in the ladies' room before she speaks. Now she's in great demand by her company because she is such a dynamic, effervescent speaker. "I love it," she confessed. "I've always secretly seen myself as a star. Now I really can make it happen, just like my childhood fantasies! I feel terrifically charismatic!"

Gradually, throughout this book, as you try the suggestions you'll be able to observe how these feel and assemble the techniques that work best for you. Just remember, it's impossible to know in advance which ones will prove most effective. You have to try them with a "beginner's mind," as they say in Zen. What's most meaningful for you may not be for someone else. "Be greedy!" I always tell my students. Do *want* to explore experience and use your new knowledge. What you're discovering is not a decoration or a frill but a process of self-definition that will make you the charismatic person you want to be—*all* the time.

6

The World Inside Your Heart

Within the city of Brahman, which is the body, there is the heart, and within it, there is a little castle which has the shape of a lotus . . . within it dwells that which is to be sought after, inquired about and realized.

. . . Even so large as the universe outside is the universe within the lotus of the heart. Within it are heaven and the earth, the sun, the moon, the lightning and all the stars. Whatever is in the macrocosm is in this microcosm also.

. . . Though old age comes to the body the lotus of the heart does not grow old . . . untouched by any deed, ageless, deathless, free from grief, from hunger and thirst, its desires are right desires and its desires are fulfilled.

—CHANDOGYA UPANISHAD

"Tears Before Bedtime"

An English friend of mine told me that when she was a little girl if she laughed a lot playing during the afternoon, her nanny would warn, "Tears before bedtime!" The message was: laugh and enjoy now; pay later. It's risky to be happy.

An American student, Aileen M., said she grew up with all kinds of superstitions. "Wear red against envy." "Don't tempt the evil eye." "Now I have real proof," she said firmly, "that when I say something good has happened, something bad will follow. For instance, I say, 'I haven't had a cold all year,' and then I get one. Or I say, 'My friend loves me,' and then we have a fight. So," she added, eyes flashing, "when I say I know my husband loves me I'm taking a *big* chance. I'm not *supposed* to say these things aloud. It's OK to think them as long as I don't say them out loud! I'm always controlling things, to take care of the waiting devil."

"How?" I asked.

"Oh, when I leave my house in the morning everything has to be spotless—even if I'm going to be late parking the car. I *can't* leave if anything's out of place. The dishes have to be washed, everything sparkling, clothes hung up. It's like stepping on a crack when you're a kid."

"What else?"

"I always tear toilet paper evenly." She laughed, embarrassed. "I know it sounds crazy, but I *have* to do it. And I have little scraps of prayers I say. I remember a little bit in Hebrew—first I take care of everybody else—the world, my family—I ask that no harm come to them, that there shouldn't be famine, wars, that there should be social justice, and then I ask for myself. *Last.* That way I make sure I'm covered. Oh, I have hundreds of rules I hang on to so I won't tempt the evil eye." She looked at me with a troubled, pleading face. "Oh, I'd really like to enjoy my life a little more!"

When you're afraid, you attract what you fear or actually produce it in your life. By focusing on what you fear, you make it the most real thing in your world. But what can you *do* when you *are* afraid? It's no good to tell yourself *not* to think of something!

A wonderful story by Isak Dinesen tells about a young prince who received a visit from a genie.

"I'm going to show you a great treasure," said the genie to the young prince, "and perhaps it will be yours—if you do exactly as I tell you."

Then he led the prince to a casket. When he opened it, the prince saw the most magnificent ruby that had ever been seen. "Oh!" gasped the boy. "Tell me what to do so I may own that— that's the most beautiful jewel I have ever seen. I must have it!"

The genie smiled. "Very simple," he said. "All you have to do is NOT think of this ruby for a year and a day and it will be yours."

If you're determined *not* to think of something, of course you're not likely to succeed.

Many people, like Aileen, try to propitiate some controlling force by ritual. Aileen was more aware than most people of how dependent she was on outside elements for her peace of mind. She admitted, "I depend on other people for my sense of self-esteem, for amusement, for validation. I *need* my house, my clothes, I *need* to feel men admire me, I *need* to feel tanned and fit; otherwise I hate myself and don't know who I am. And yet I have a lot of power, mostly negative I guess," she added with a laugh. "Sometimes if I'm sitting in the hairdresser's and I'm mad, he'll drop the comb, even though I haven't said anything or even given him a dirty look. He can *feel* what I'm feeling. My sister is ten times worse. It's as though she had a huge cloud hanging over her all the time. She's so smart she could do anything, but people don't like to be with her because she makes them feel that big dark cloud all the time. It's really heavy. She doesn't enjoy *anything* in her life."

When you're wearing heavy emotional armor it's hard even to imagine that dancing, playing, swimming, and making love are pleasurable. In one workshop, Frank L. reported happily after he had done the *Anti-Judgmental Notebook* and the *less hostility exercise:* "I can't believe it! For the first time in my life I can dance!" He had felt too inhibited before, too worried about what people might say.

Why Do You Act That Way?—The Power of Early Messages

In the movie *Twelve Angry Men* Martin Balsam asks another man, "Why are you so damn polite?" "Same reason you're so rude—that's how I was brought up," retorted George Voskovec.

Jansen B., a handsome investment banker who was half German and half South African, came to me to "become more expressive." He was reserved to the point of being almost withdrawn. He barely spoke up at all. People found him boring. He had spent his early childhood years fleeing across Europe from the Nazis, forced to be very quiet for fear of discovery and arrest. His early childhood messages had been: "be proper," "don't show feeling," "never get angry." This was not only the message of his family but of the upper class he grew up in. He found it impossible to lift his voice above a very quiet, cultivated monotone. The only release he enjoyed was lovemaking. He was extremely correct and apologized frequently.

When he began to still the internal censor that constantly chipped away at his spontaneity, he found himself laughing and enjoying himself more. When he shared some of the secrets of his childhood, he began to talk louder. His voice suddenly had more color; his personality seemed less formal, warmer, more appealing.

I am impressed with how often people find extraordinarily adroit ways of tuning in to their inner capacities, even when everything else in their lives seems confining. Jansen told us that when he used to prepare for exams, he was very nervous about not doing well enough to live up to his family's expectations. Suddenly, a vision of a beautiful female body would float into his consciousness and he would meditate on that while driving to the exam. He had never told anybody about this, and was ashamed of it. Not only that, he had taken the injunction against speaking up so literally that he had never told anyone, not even his wife, the story of his childhood flights across Europe. "I don't want to burden people with it," he said. "They wouldn't be interested."

What Are You Passionate About?

If there is a large part of your life that you've never shared with anyone, chances are you feel cut off from expressing very deep feelings. This has a subtle dulling effect on your ability to communicate directly and warmly to people. It's as though your inner self, deprived of the right to speak, lost confidence in its own nature and retreated into an impersonal, "safe" grayness that would neither offend nor call attention to itself.

To be charismatic, you must have "heartfelt" connections with what you're saying. This means giving yourself permission not only to know what you really feel about your experiences but to express your inner thoughts openly. *If you can talk about something personal openly, then you can talk about something open personally.*

THE PASSION PLOY: VOICE YOUR FEELINGS

That's why the first talk I ask people in my workshops to give is three to five minutes on something they feel passionate about. Once you share your true feelings with a group of strangers, it's much easier to talk about business, politics, philosophy, or anything else that interests you.

A lot of people have a very hard time with this assignment. "Nobody will be interested!" said a student.

"I'm not passionate about anything," a middle-aged advertising executive mourned. "I was shocked to find that out. When I was young, I was passionate about so many things, but gradually they all faded away. I got discouraged, apathetic, indifferent."

Stuart M., a corporation executive, gave a talk on his hobby, biophysics. As he spoke, he kept rubbing his nose with his hand, an unconscious signal that he didn't think the audience would understand or appreciate what he was saying. When I asked him if that *was* what he felt, an embarrassed smile spread over his face. "I'm afraid that's just what I was thinking!" he answered.

Are you worried your audience may not understand? If you observe and acknowledge that you're feeling doubts, you can go ahead without being undermined. Otherwise your energy level will swiftly and mysteriously drop and you'll telegraph uncertainty and lack of confidence to your audience.

Martin B., a professor and author of eight books, took the class because he was terrified of getting up to speak. He was comfortable enough seated as part of a panel, but he turned down speaking engagements. Martin gave his first talk on the FCC. Although he had written a prizewinning book on it and was deeply interested in the subject, nobody would have known it from his platform behavior. His face was expressionless, his large, burly frame slouched miserably, his voice was toneless and uninteresting. "Martin," I asked, "please give us a talk on something personal!"

The following week he got up and gave one of the most memorable talks of the semester about three risks he had taken. The first was riding the white water rapids in Colorado with his daughter. Braving the rough waters and feeling he had held his own turned out to be an enormously exhilarating boost to his self-esteem. The world looked a little different to him after that adventure. The second risk was taking the Charismedia workshop. The third was that "for the first time in twenty-five years, I talked back to my father-in-law." The change in Martin was remarkable. His face was animated, his voice colorful. He even stood up straighter. We were all fascinated. We felt we really knew him because he had shared important experiences and perceptions with us and allowed us to know his vulnerabilities. He was, suddenly, very human and appealing. (I later found out his father-in-law was a world-famous songwriter who was a notorious curmudgeon!)

The Charm of Being Vulnerable

If you admit you're not perfect, and share that with the audience, that's very engaging and warms everybody; we can all relate to imperfection. Perfection is not only unlikely and unreal, it's boring! Programmed as most of us are to revere success and equate it with perfection (the impossible dream), it's a great relief to hear about someone's bumbling efforts to master a personal problem. Lewis Thomas, the wise physician, says in *The Medusa and the Snail* that "the capacity to leap across mountains of information to land lightly on the wrong side represents the highest of human endowments. It may be that this is a uniquely human gift." He claims if we were not "provided with the knack of being wrong, we could never get anything useful done."

What a relief it is if we plunge ahead and not only admit but are amused at our mistakes! It enhances communication. People feel they know and like you. Of course, you want to be "right" in an important report for your company or a research paper, but it's marvelous practice to speak openly of personal feelings without having to be "right" when you want to connect warmly with people.

Check your "passion quotient": Could you give three talks on subjects you're passionate about? Remember, anything you care deeply about you're probably expert on. You don't need weeks or even days of research to prepare a talk about something you're very involved with.

Name your passions:

1.

2.

3.

The first two should be about feelings and experiences, not public issues: perhaps "The Most Important Decision of My Life" or "My Passion for Driftwood." Do *not* write out the whole talk. If you do, you'll feel you have to read it, which will kill all spontaneity. When you read a speech without looking at the audience, you tend to lose connection with it; it'll sound impersonal or dull. Randomly brainstorm your ideas for a day or so; jot them down, not necessarily in order. Gradually you'll begin to organize the structure. Be sure to *know* your opening sentences perfectly; half the battle is getting a fluent, running start. Rehearse it *out loud*. Doing it in your head is not the same.

Now, give yourself permission to say the same thing twenty times with as much expression as the first time.

"But that feels phony," you protest.

For your audience it *will* be the first time. Remember, *spontaneity is the product of great preparation.* The preparation can be a lot of rehearsal or a lot of experience. The aliveness and enthusiasm of spontaneity is an important element of charisma; 89 percent of my questionnaire respondents listed eloquence among its essential ingredients. Eloquence is not just *what* you say but *how you say it.*

To find the tone of greatest interest and connection with your audience, close your eyes and visualize your ideal hearer. It may be your mother, sister, husband, colleague, a childhood teacher, or even your dog!

Elizabeth S. remarked, "You know, that's really hard for me to do. I keep seeing my family interrupting me which makes me tense, so I want to bludgeon through before they stop me."

Other people experience the reverse—they feel uninteresting and shrink back, sometimes without saying anything at all. Mary R. protested, "I could never get a word in edgewise in my house. But I just flashed on an old lady I met in the country last summer who loved to hear me talk about photography, my hobby. When I talked to her I felt everything I said was interesting and important. I'll concentrate on her!"

Trial lawyer Jimmy M. laughed and remarked, "The first thing that came into my mind was the look on the face of a girl I took out when I was sixteen. We were madly in love and talked a lot about what we wanted to do. She was the first person who really listened to me. It was because of her that I applied for and got into law school. Now most of the time, I see adversaries when I'm talking, but it certainly changes things to visualize my first girl." Next time he tried it he won his case!

Emma L. said, "Believe it or not, my best listener is my ten-year-old son. Everything interests him! I love to tell him what I'm thinking and he really listens."

If you signal mistrust of your hearer or show doubt of a listener's willingness (or capacity) to take in your message, you automatically lose your audience. Worse, you may come across as unpleasant, weak, discouraged, even snobbish. Remember: whenever there is a conflict between verbal and nonverbal signals, the *non*verbal ones are believed!

Here's the key: what makes you an interesting speaker is *your own interest in what you're saying*. It doesn't matter whether you are passionate about orthodontics or semiotics, Glagolithic script, stamp collecting, or rock 'n' roll. *Behave* as though your listeners are just as fascinated as you are; then they will be. That's the "entrainment process" of charisma. Plunge right in. *Never* begin with:

"I am going to talk about _____"

"Today I want to tell you about _____"

"I'd like to share with you . . ."

You can start with a provocative sentence: "September 8, 1964, may have been the most extraordinary day in my life."

Or a question: "Who would have guessed a few short years ago that the Australian dugong would become the world's most desirable mammal?"

Or an outrageous remark: "The worst thing about living in this town is the animal population."

Or a quotation: " 'When I feel like exercising, I lie down until the impulse goes away,' said Alexander Woollcott. I used to feel that way, too."

If you're inexperienced, just throw away your first sentence (the one that begins "I'd like to tell you about _____") and start with the one where you're really into the topic.

Go through your main points, noting a couple of "key words" for each on three-by-five-inch cards to help you remember the order. Keep your notes brief; resist the temptation to write everything out. Don't get bogged down in trivia. Feelings are important and the audience can identify with yours. Save your medical complaints for a friend!

Then decide on your last sentence or last two sentences. Work on tying up the main points of your talk. End with a quotation or powerful sentence so your hearers are left thinking about what you said. *Don't* say "In conclusion . . ." or "I'd like to close by saying . . ." Make your audience know it's the end by the weight you give your closing words and the silence and eye contact after you've finished. Never mind the wit who defined an optimist as "Someone who puts his shoes on when Hubert Humphrey says 'And, in conclusion . . .' "

Practice talking about something personal because you need to validate your feelings and be convinced by demonstration that nothing is more interesting to any audience than what you bring yourself—your "baggage" of knowledge, experience, feelings, and reactions. That special combination is a unique package. It's heartfelt. "Heartfelt" is charismatic. And keep it simple. Simple is clear.

According to scientist-researcher René Dubos, no need is more pressing in the world. Humans are the only creatures able to change their fate by making decisions based on their view of the future and their review of the past. A short, pithy phrase—often an image, if it's the right one—can accomplish more than thousands of words. The term "population bomb" probably helped trigger the tremendous drop in the birthrate in the United States and Western Europe during the last ten years.

When Rachel Carson finished a book about ecology, her publisher said, "It's an important, remarkable book, but it'll never sell. We need a catchy title." A few days later, Ms. Carson received a letter from an old friend. It read: "I found two more robins dead on the lawn today; I guess it's going to be a *silent spring.*"

"Aha," said the publisher. "Perfect! That's our title."

Finding the right *simple* words is far from easy. The larger your vocabulary, the more choices you have of what to say and how best to say it. You'll also see more subtleties when you have more ways of expressing your thoughts. When talking about passions, guard against clichés: "Oh, it was just wonderful." "It was really terrific, a marvelous experience." "It really pisses me off!"

If you want your hearer to share your experience, fill in details; use your memories of sight, sound, taste, feeling, hearing so we can journey with you through your adventure. Allow yourself meaningful pauses. Don't be afraid to relate problems you encountered. It's more interesting to hear of an occasional setback than an unbroken string of successes. The audience will enjoy your success story even more. Every "passion" is an adventure.

Marjorie L., a writer in my workshop, told us she had become intrigued with a prehistoric boat that had been found in England and decided to write a book on it. She told us how she had written to all the people and organizations she could track down that might have something to add to her story. Then she described her frustration when she got a flat turndown from the woman who owned the property on which the relic had been found; and how the little old curator of the local library invited her to tea and then cajoled the woman into admitting her onto the estate. She told us how her car broke down, her money ran out, her husband had helped her, and how one clue led to another. Finally she showed us the completed book, just published. We all had listened entranced as the story unfolded, because she shared with us all the disappointments, dead-end leads, and sense of growing excitement. She took us into her life.

This is what you do when you talk about a passion. You take your hearers into a whole world. It is important to prepare a strong ending so you know where you are heading. We must feel you are in control of the point you want to make. If you shape your talk, you can decide which details will enrich and clarify and which are irrelevant or repetitious. The act of making these choices will give you a feeling of exhilarating command —since *you* can create whatever impression you want to. Imagine your ideal listener, and think of the questions she/he might ask at different points:

"What happened then?" with eager eyes.

"But didn't you get discouraged?" at another point.

"What made you pick that particular road [or bowl, or day, or city, or whatever]?"

"What did it-he-she-they look like, feel like, sound like, talk like, act like, etc.?"

What would *you*—if you were listening to this talk—really want to know?

Every solo talk is a dialogue even if the audience is silent. When you know roughly what you want to say, it's time to start saying it out loud. Don't make the mistake of using a mirror. It's going to leave you feeling lost if you practice with a mirror and then speak to real people! Use a mirror to check on a particular expression, or phrase, or gesture, but don't get hypnotized by your own image. If you do, you'll be lost without it when you face an audience.

It also helps to practice louder than you normally speak. You raise your energy level and increase your vocal and expressive range when you speak louder. You'll feel stronger, more in charge. Don't be surprised if you feel silly at first. Practice talking to a tape recorder. Set it up across the room, as far as possible.

Expanding your style means changing. What feels awkward and unnatural at first will become easy, comfortable, and effective with practice. All new behaviors need to be rehearsed. To give yourself new confidence, practice for enlargement; don't try to be "good" at first. Try for outrageousness. Be as loud, as exaggerated as you can, *without* self-parody. (One client, a partner in an accounting firm, saw himself as a politician.) You'll probably notice your heart beating very rapidly, as though you were doing something very dangerous. The more you practice, the more quickly that will subside. After rehearsing four or five times, three times as loud as you normally speak, reduce it a *little* but not much. This is a process. Don't inspect each attempt like a finished product, not until you've done it twenty times!

If you have an ideal listener in the house, ask him or her to check you, but for *loudness only*. Don't ask for anything else at this stage. Politely but firmly explain that you're just practicing and don't want their reactions—yet.

One writer, a serious, extremely intellectual young man who had grown up as the foster son of one of the wealthiest American families, was a guest on the Dick Cavett show one evening. His publisher had asked me to watch. To my horror, I witnessed a small massacre. The host and another guest, the brilliant, acerbic playwright/actor Robert Shaw, decided to lambaste—I shall call him Ashley—for his literary style. They opened his book, read some of his prose—and ridiculed it. "Your style stinks," one said. Poor Ashley, unaccustomed to such rudeness, was completely nonplussed. He began to defend himself at excruciating length. It was a painful scene.

When he came to see me I asked him what his first impulse had been when they attacked him. "What did you *feel* like saying?" I asked. He looked surprised. "Oh," he answered slowly, "I felt like saying, 'For *this* I came on the Cavett show?'"

Of course, that would have been an excellent response. The audience, able to appreciate his position and sympathize, would have applauded. He probably would have had no further trouble with the hosts. They only wanted to create controversy and an interesting show. By taking a deep breath and tuning in on his intuition, he would have uttered the "heartfelt," natural response that would have been the best riposte. And charismatic, to boot!

A TV panel show not being a social situation, the ordinary rules of courtesy do not apply. It is a *simulated* social situation, something quite different. Remember, it's a show, and there's very little time to make your point. Images, metaphors, quotes, and colorful stories help get your points across in the shortest possible time. A senatorial candidate from a New England state asked me how to handle reporters at a press conference who asked broad, general questions such as, "What do you think of the prospects for the economy next year in our state?" He felt himself getting hopelessly long-winded in such situations. When we role-played it, he answered with a slightly bored, exasperated look, and droned on for five minutes.

"You see what I mean?" he said despairingly. "I can't seem to give a short answer!"

"Who is the youngest person you enjoy explaining things to?" I asked him. His face broke out in a smile. "My nine-year-old daughter, Christina."

"OK," I said, "then, how would you explain the economy to Christina?"

"Well," he said promptly, "you see the economy is like a three-legged stool. One leg is farming, one is tourism, and one is industry."

"Perfect!" I told him. "Not only is that a clear and interesting image, but it's brief and to the point. You give the reporter an opportunity to ask the next question, and you won't be contemptuous of your audience if you think of your little daughter; we're all nine-year-olds on matters in which we are not experts. Will Rogers remarked, 'Everybody is ignorant, only on different subjects!'"

Life is so complex that we're almost all what Miguel Unamuno called "vertical savages." He meant that most people would have a difficult time explaining the basic inventions of our age. I've often thought that if I were whisked back to the eighteenth or nineteenth century, I'd have a hard time explaining the radio or an airplane, let alone the theory of relativity! We need to be humble about our inability to absorb the leaps of the past seventy-five years. Nobody can possibly know everything! We're all ignorant children in some fields. If you want to communicate, show a respect for the hearers and a desire to really get through to them.

By imagining what questions an intelligent uninformed listener might raise, you'll know how to phrase the information. You'll be able to put it in small enough chunks to be understandable and provide space and time for feedback. A really thoughtful listener is regarded as charismatic. Remember too that our attention spans are more or less "programmed" by the fifteen- and thirty-second commercial. Television has altered our nervous system and given us shorter attention spans. Can you imagine an American or European audience sitting through an eight-hour opera as a Chinese audience might, or listening to a story for four hours as they do in India? No way!

When your eyes express concentrated pleasure and interest in what you're talking about, people feel it and are drawn to you as if by magic. Someone estimated that the human face is capable of about 20,000 expressions.° But the eyes are still the "windows of the soul." If you are tuned in to your heart center, there is a change in your electromagnetic field.

Incessant intensity of gaze among strangers in a public setting is sometimes considered threatening. In a study of eye contact, people were comfortable with an 85 percent ratio of eye contact. More than that was regarded an invasion of privacy, less was equated with evasiveness or untrustworthiness. The subliminal cues we give are so subtle that most people are not even aware of them or why they react as they do. They may call it "chemistry" or "instinct," but whatever it is, people do respond.

If you're talking to a group, small or large, be sure at some time in your talk to include everyone in your gaze. Look at all parts of the room. Be aware of the sides and back and even behind you, although it's a good idea to arrange not to have anyone behind you, if possible. Find a friendly face and address a sentence or two to that person. Then transfer your attention to another. Really connect with the person you're looking at for at least two or three statements. A nervous darting eye scan doesn't satisfy anyone.

You may find yourself instinctively looking more toward one side than the other. One client had trouble looking to his right; then he realized he *always* ignored people on his right! Once he was aware of it, he got new glasses!

° Facial expression is an international language. Intense emotions like joy, sadness, fright, and wonder are instantly comprehensible to people from almost all cultures. Paul Eckman of the University of California at San Francisco took photos of six different emotional states and compared interpretations of people from five different cultures. A high percentage of the associations were the same. Even blind and/or deaf children who cannot imitate facial expressions they haven't seen express feelings the same way (according to studies made by Eible-Eibesfeldt). To be human transcends all national and physical barriers.

Look up or over your audience's heads when you're reflecting, remembering, or visualizing. If the audience can see you thinking, they stay in touch and are interested. Looking down is like garlic: a little goes a long way! It cuts people off from what you're thinking. It also may give the impression you're shy, nervous, or ashamed. No need to give these messages!

When your heart center is open, people feel that and respond to it.

"But how will I be able to protect myself from people who might try to exploit or take advantage of me?" you ask.

Being open doesn't mean you're a sucker. On the contrary, your instinct becomes so sharp that you protect yourself when necessary without even making a special effort. There is a story of a Zen master who was always "one-pointed" and perfectly relaxed. When a bandit tried to attack him from behind, the master cut him down with his sword with a lightning sweep so fast that *nobody saw it!*

This is very different from the fearful self-protectiveness that makes some people constantly check on locks and walk around half-expecting an attack, worrying about cancer, the bomb, and being robbed or mugged. Aileen, who depended on "magic" to get her through the day and lived in fear of the "evil eye," is an extremely bright young woman, yet she felt she had little control over her life. Her charisma was buried under her "armor."

Do you have too much armor to enjoy your life? If you're constantly expecting disaster or wary of being ill-treated, regardless of your experience, you're living in a state of tension or fear and cannot use your full human capacities. Your personality will seem guarded, constricted, or tense and hostile to people. The warmth of your charisma is hidden under your armor.

Let's explore how finding your center and being able to go inward for refreshment and strength can enhance your joy in life and help your charisma emerge more clearly.

After Aileen complained that she would like to enjoy her life, I asked her to close her eyes and breathe slowly and deeply. Her body began to relax. Her breathing grew slow. Her stomach rose and fell.

We have all experienced a sense of floating, ease, and well-being on a mountaintop or with a great open expanse of sky. When we hang on, out of fear, to possessions, attributes, relationships, we feel "stuck," aware of limitation and pain. Through breathing and visualization we can transform our sense of being alive, so that the moment is enough—being in the quiet inner world of the heart is so satisfying that nothing else matters.

"Close your eyes," I told Aileen, who relaxed in her chair, hands in her lap, "and feel a great space between your eyes . . . now feel the space between your ears . . . be aware of the space between your shoulders . . . between your ribs . . . between your sides . . . between your hips . . . now feel the space within the body . . . visualize yourself floating in the spaces and just be there . . . be aware of any emotions, thoughts, pain that is your body and dissolve them in the space flowing through . . . watch the colors as they change, flowing through and around the space . . . let all the spaces around your body, under the chair, over your head, flow through the body and melt with the space flowing out through the walls, up into the sky, down below the earth, into the sea, and past the endless horizon, all is swirling lightness . . . feel that you are all space . . . it is dissolved in you and you in space . . . no boundaries anywhere . . . just a flowing of lightness . . . space and radiance . . . allow yourself to let go of your body completely . . . imagine yourself letting go . . . dissolving easily . . . you are diffused through the universe . . . exhale . . . and let go . . . after a long pause now choose to be born again . . . as a tiny baby anywhere and any way you wish . . . you choose your new life . . . when you open your eyes you will see everything as though for the first time . . . you are reborn . . . with each breath you die, as you exhale, and let go completely, and with each inhalation, you are born again . . . rested, fresh, new. . . ."

Aileen opened her eyes, smiled, and sat silently for a few minutes. Then she said, "Oh, that was wonderful! I have never been able to relax like that. At one point, I had the most wonderful image: I was an angel flying over me with outspread wings. That was the first time in my life I ever felt *my own angel* watch over me. It was peaceful and exhilarating. Until now I was only aware of my devil. I just feel this is one of the most important things that's ever happened to me."

She sat quietly, a smile on her face. "You know," she said, "I'm breathing really deeply but very gently—it feels so easy—the way babies breathe—it's no effort at all. And my whole body feels soft and light. The strange thing is that it's as though I knew this all along—*it's like coming home.*"

The World Heart Embrace

I asked her to stand up and stretch. "Inhale and hold out your arms as though you are embracing the universe," I told her. "Really feel you're stretching to embrace the whole world. This is the most life-affirming gesture, the primal loving welcome of the eternal mother. Muscle testing shows that merely seeing this gesture strengthens your life force. Making the gesture opens your heart center and expands your electromagnetic field; your charisma is moving out to strengthen others. Now hold that stretch and visualize that you really are including the whole world in your arms.

"When you've held your breath as long as you can, slowly, lovingly, bring your arms closer together until your hands fold over each other and rest on your breast. Feel that you have brought the love of the whole world to your own heart; feel the warmth of that flowing into you through your fingers. Now again stretch and embrace the universe and then allow all this concentrated love to sink in and nourish every cell of your body; spread it to your fingertips and your toes, to the topmost cell of your brain, and every single muscle, ligament, and neuron; feel all of you warmed and bathed in the warmth and radiance of that love . . . spread it with your soft full breath through your body and beyond the boundaries until the world and you are one—there is no distinction; all warmth and energy is flowing to you, through you, and you feel with every cell love pervading everything. . . . Do this three to nine times."

THE ANGER TRANSFORMER

If you feel anger toward somebody or something in your life, do this before the World-Heart Embrace:

1. Anger Discharger

Stand or sit straight, bend your arms at the elbows, and put your hands up about a foot in front of your face very gently, palms facing away from you as though somebody had said, "Stick 'em up!" Make little circles in the air with your hands. Gradually, with bent elbows, move your hands toward the right. Your head follows, eyes soft-focused looking just above the hands. When you get all the way to the right, make a sudden very violent pushing motion with both hands, as though you're straightening both arms and pushing hard, throwing away something you want to get rid of. Throw it as far as possible! Let a sound come out of you ("UGH!") at the moment you do the violent push.

Immediately afterward, gently begin to move your hands in the little circles toward the center, continuing until you get to the far left. Then do exactly the same thing: SHOVE AS HARD AND AS SUDDENLY AS YOU CAN, flinging away the person or problem you have negative feelings about! As you say "UGH!" the air is forced out of your lungs and your flung arms extend, straightened. Then immediately do the very soft, small circles with your raised hands, palms outward, until you get to the far right again. Then again fling away the person or problem you hate as suddenly and as violently as possible, the *ugh* escaping from you as you do it. Do this cycle five times, alternating right and left.

2. Transformer

Then expand, inhale, open your arms, and embrace the whole world, stretching upward and outward as fully as you can, as though your heart center were the world being stretched and opened and you become larger than life. Hold for at least sixty seconds. Bring the whole world into your embrace and gather that love and lay it on your breast, your hands on your chest, pressed gently. Do that four times. On the fifth time, *transform the negative image you pushed away, love it, bring it toward you, and lay it on your own heart, transformed from hate or dislike to love.*

This is an amazing exercise. It really works and has a wonderful healing effect on your life. If you find it hard to transform the negative image, then practice the world embrace alone. Really internalize the good feelings this produces. Another time, do the Anger Discharger, remembering to start softly and gently and then with all your might flinging away ("UGH!") the person or problem you hate.

I have watched this exercise revitalize and refresh all kinds of groups. In a business workshop, it eases the tensions that build up in the room because of business problems. The warmth and currents of ease that flow through the group as they finish are always visible on people's faces and in their bodies: smiles, a relaxed look, laughter. It's a marvelous, safe, nontoxic way to discharge the buildup of anger and tension that produces constraint and discomfort in so many groups. This exercise works for everybody regardless of the causes of the friction. And there is nothing competitive about it. Anybody can do it. It doesn't look "better" or "worse," depending how you do it, and it requires no athletic nimbleness. People who resist "exercises" don't resist this.

Alternating very gentle, easy-moving small motions and the sudden violent discharge of feelings is like the hidden movements of the emotions themselves. We think we're very calm ("That doesn't bother me!"), and suddenly there's a terrific flash of anger or rage. It's disarming to start off so softly and gently and then experience a satisfying surge of power when you suddenly fling away *without* warning everything that may have been secretly bothering you. The most mild-mannered people throw themselves into this exercise with great abandon. The violent motion happens so suddenly that one can lie low and play "meek" right up to the moment of explosion. Like the flow of your feelings, you allow yourself to go from a gentle state to a fierce and total discharge. It's safe, yet swift as an adder's tongue. Busy with what you're doing, you don't watch anyone else, and the violent part is brief enough, followed again by the soothing massage of slow, gentle small hand circles, so that you get both a release of sharp violent feeling and a sense of instantly renewed control.

This is very characteristic of Tibetan Kum Nye relaxation exercises, a wonderful system of detailed psychophysical stretches and releases that tune the mind and body and even out emotions. I recognized the origin of this style of release when Walt Anderson did this exercise at a Washington conference for the top 100 government policymakers and the leaders of the human potential movement who had come together to brainstorm and "soulstorm" the "possible society." People had come from very different mindsets; there were some tense confrontations. It was amazing to see how the atmosphere in the room changed after we did this exercise. Defensiveness melted, barriers eased. It was possible for people who had argued before to go out of the room together, smiling and talking to each other.

When communication breaks down because of anger and dissension, nobody's charisma can prevail. Perhaps there is such a thing as group charisma—when the bio-rapport is so powerful that *everybody* feels enhanced, richly effective, and turned on. Someone who makes a marvelous speech makes everyone feel he/she has spoken for *them*. When you can directly express what's in your heart, other people who might not have had the courage (or be completely aware of what they felt) feel *understood*, validated, supported.

In Frances Vaughan's *Awakening Intuition* she has an exercise where you ask yourself in a deeply relaxed state, "What mattered most in my life?" as though asking it on your deathbed. If you breathe quietly and just let surface whatever comes up, you may be surprised by the answers.

Ask yourself that question now. . . .

"What Matters Most in My Life?"

I remember spending Easter weekend a few years ago with Swami Muktananda. There were hundreds of people there, and I was full of skepticism. Everywhere people were telling stories of what "Baba" had done for them. I had been meditating for a number of years, but I had the typical Western reluctance to "surrender" to a guru. In the early morning hundreds of people, having left their shoes outside the door, entered the carpeted meditation hall hung with enormous pictures of various gurus, venerable teachers in a great lineage. When everyone was seated on the carpeted floor, a beautiful young woman entered, carrying cymbals and some incense. As she started playing the cymbals, the fragrant vapors of incense curled lazily toward the ceiling. A young man seated in the lotus position accompanied her on a small harmonica. Songbooks were passed out. For an hour we chanted various sacred songs of Sanskrit. After that, the room was darkened and we were left to meditate. Muktananda, wearing dark glasses, entered, was seated on a kind of throne with fresh flowers in front of him. He was wearing an orange robe and a knitted cap. A great scepter of peacock feathers was at his side.

Toward the end of the meditation, odd things began to happen. Muktananda had been quietly walking around, touching people gently with the plumes of peacock feathers. When he came to me, he pressed his fingers gently on the ridge of my eyes, just below the eyebrows. Since I was wearing contact lenses, I was a little nervous at this. I wondered if he knew, but I said nothing. I began to hear strange sounds: crying, gasping, laughter, growling, and what sounded like wings flapping. People were shaking, sometimes flailing arms and legs about. At first when I heard what sounded like exaggerated sounds of human beings in extreme pain, I thought to myself, "Oh, come on. That's just plain self-indulgence! Some people will take any opportunity to yell their heads off." Some of the sounds were positively spine-chilling. At the same time I noticed with some surprise tears were running down my face, although I was not feeling any sadness. I had come with some idea of what I wanted to ask, but suddenly all that fell away. I had an immediate perception that this was a Christlike human being who communicated love through his presence. If it was possible for a living human to actually be that, all I wanted was to *be like that*. I felt I had never wanted anything so much in my life. To be able to live in perfect love seemed both miraculous yet completely real and attainable.

When the meditation was over, people spoke up and shared their experiences. One man, who had uttered a loud, fierce growl, said, "I want to tell everybody what I was feeling when I made that sound. It was not an unhappy sound; I was experiencing a great triumphant joy, and I was thinking, 'I am the only son of the only father!' I wanted to share that with you because I heard people make what sounded like pretty scary sounds so I thought you'd like to know, in case it sounded frightening, what I was feeling when I uttered those sounds. All my life I've suffered from having been rejected by my father at a very early age, and in that moment during meditation after I had received the *shakti* (energy) from Baba, all of that was wiped out. I felt I had been restored to my true place."

The people who spoke were Christian, Jewish, agnostic; their images were all different. But they all *felt* something very deep that would change their lives. The form it took for each person depended on their history and background.

Recent brain research explains that our feelings and emotional reactions are deeply embedded in our brains. Our memories, experiences, emotions, and thoughts are all mixed up together. Everything is connected—biochemical, emotional, sensory, mental, and spiritual. Our nervous system is like an astonishingly complex switchboard, emitting electrical currents at each contraction. We can measure the electrical activity of the brain. (Electroencephalographs register the pulsing waves on the surface of the scalp.) The current generated by the heart can produce as high a charge as a hundredth of a volt on the chest surface. Sensitive instruments can pick up the electromagnetic field of the cardiovascular system several feet away from the body.

Who does not remember sitting in a classroom and mentally concentrating on the back of somebody's neck at the front of the room? As if by magic, that person after a while will turn around and try to see who is staring at him! Aileen's remark that she experienced "power" because her hairdresser could feel her anger, even when she said nothing, is an example of this common "energy transfer."

We seem to be like radio transmitters. If there is a lot of static (i.e., stress) we get a great deal of noise and disturbance, and very limited programing, mostly rock music and murder reports. When we fine-tune and get FM programing, the choice will be much wider: more interesting music, poetry, information of all kinds. Meditation is a practical method for this fine-tuning, or stress release. When we are able to drop our fears, hates, and old wounds, we have access to more of ourselves and intuitive understanding of the world.

It's always easier to see the connection between events from the top. Patterns become clear. A beetle doesn't see the tiny blade of grass he laboriously crawled over a minute before; that's already in the past. But for the falcon, the hill he flew straight up over fifteen minutes ago is still there. He has a larger view of the present. This is what enables mediums, mystics, and physicists to accomplish their remarkable feats; they report that at their creative best, time is unified: past, present, and future are one.

Ordinary people suddenly find they have access to extraordinary capacities.

Having been brought up a rationalist-skeptic-agnostic, it took a long time for me to convince myself that all this really works. When I saw incontrovertible evidence, I thought, "Well, for other people, maybe. But not me! I'm absolutely not the least bit psychic!" Then an interesting thing happened. A writer client of mine had submitted her manuscript to a publisher and was very fearful of its being turned down. She needed the money urgently and had been turned down by three publishers before because the subject was very controversial. She called and said, "Would you do me a great favor? Please go with me to the Muktananda center and meditate with me Friday—I'm expecting to get the verdict Friday afternoon on whether they'll take the book or not, and I'm terribly nervous about it."

At six in the morning we walked up to the apartment house near mine where the center was then located and deposited our shoes outside the door. Five or six hardy souls were already seated on cushions. Then we went in, sat down cross-legged, and meditated in front of the little altar with flowers and pictures of Baba Muktananda. I was only doing it to give Ellen moral support, with no expectations of any kind. After we had sat for an hour meditating, we left, feeling pleasantly calm and peaceful. I bought her a small pot of African violets to sweeten the hours of waiting and we parted.

That afternoon at about four, in the middle of a lesson, I suddenly *knew* she was not going to hear any news that afternoon. Ten minutes later, the phone rang. Ellen wailed, "I just got a call that the publisher took the manuscript home with him for the weekend—oh, how can I stand this suspense?" Sunday evening, without knowing I knew, I got the distinct feeling that Monday would bring no word either. Sure enough, the next day the publisher was still out of town. That evening, I *knew* in the same mysterious way that the next day she would hear from the publisher and he *was* going to buy the book. I wasn't sure I was right, that I could trust my sense, so I didn't tell her. But it happened exactly as I had seen. I was astonished. What had happened? The meditation had "fine-tuned" me so I could receive the information. Ellen's great anxiety, on the other hand, was a stress "static" that prevented her from receiving the same information.

That first Easter weekend, I had felt mistrustful of all the adulation of Baba. What was all the business about "surrender" to the guru? Wasn't that giving up your free will? Abandoning your precious right to choose? "God is within you—love the God within" read signs all over the ashram. Then why surrender? I didn't even know what they meant by "God." I'm extremely wary of groups that talk about God. Religious wars caused more suffering in the West than any plagues or natural disasters. Just what were you surrendering to when you surrendered to the divine in Baba?

When I got home from the weekend, I found that I had lost my menstrual period. It had stopped abruptly, something that had never happened before. I went to bed with an unexplained pain in my ovaries. Suddenly, I thought rather angrily, "OK, let's see what happens if I turn *this* over to Baba! That's what they said one could do, and he would take away the pain." Feeling a little ridiculous and completely skeptical, I thought, "OK, Baba, I'm giving this to you. Take away this pain!" To my absolute amazement, the pain actually went away. And I didn't believe in him!

Suddenly I understood what "surrender" meant. When we're suffering or stressed, we operate out of a limited spectrum of sensorimotor frequencies—our "radio transmitter" is out of tune, limping along; fear or pain or any negative emotion produces a contraction of the electrical impulses. We cling, as fearful as a baby. In that condition, when we "surrender" the problem, turn it over to a higher power, we're deeply de-stressing. ("It's out of my hands!") We permit ourselves to relax and connect with the infinite powers of the universe.

"Letting go" allows the natural homeostatic powers of body and mind to heal and make us whole. Of course, people who pray know this. They tune in to their higher selves, that synchronicity of the individual self with the universal mind. One of the hardest things to do when you're sick or frightened is to let go of fear, to detach and *trust*, to visualize health as the present reality. Turning the problem over to a higher will provides that deep relaxation, that dissolution of the small self that opens the door to restoration of health or the solution to one's problem.

"Believing" is hoping, not knowing.

Sometimes when people pray, they're really only bargaining: "please make me well [or rich or send me a mate] and I'll be good [or give you money], God." Or whatever promises people make in their desperation. But real prayer doesn't ask for anything. It just experiences that return to a unitary consciousness where all things are present and possible, that deep quiet, the "secret world of the heart."

In our anxiety to "control" our lives at a time when we feel less certainty (and more fear) about our capacity to control than ever before, probably our deepest need is to release our stranglehold on the limited reality that our usual functioning provides. It just isn't good enough. It's as though we're in a desperate race to get somewhere and stay alive with 10,000 bandits pursuing. We have to stop time, get off the track. Later I'll show you how you can tune in to your own creative consciousness, which is part of the collective consciousness of everything that exists. ("Not only is the drop of water contained in the ocean, but the ocean is contained in a drop of water."—The Upanishads)

Like someone who has not ridden on a bicycle and can't *believe* it could possibly stay upright, you can't imagine this unless you've tried it. Yet everybody has *experienced* it. The un-self-consciousness of a child is a state we long for instinctively because it allows us to "flow," be one with the world. In that unstressed state, our senses function with great subtlety. The human eye can discern more than 10 million colors. We have very elaborate awarenesses for touching. We can sense temperature, heavy and medium and light touch. Smell and taste, equally mysterious, reverberate to memory.

Chinese Taoist literature harps on "no-mind," not unconsciousness but *un-self*-consciousness. This is a state of spontaneous flow. The mind functions easily, naturally, effectively, without Self 1 standing over it criticizing and making matters difficult. In a more restful, free state, without judgment, right action is possible. The necessary decisions will come without the chatter and racket of the judging mind. That only gets in the way, makes us feel "not good enough," and prevents us from realizing our potential and connecting with others.

When we communicate with people effectively, when our charisma is clear and shining, we "touch" the hearts of others. We all know people who are intellectually brilliant but quite insensitive to other people. They do not have, in psychologist Bruno Bettelheim's phrase, the "wisdom of the heart." (Arthur Koestler, the author, has a wonderful name for such people: he calls them "mimophants." A mimophant is a person who is as sensitive as a mimosa when it comes to his own feelings and as insensitive as an elephant when it comes to others' feelings.)

By de-stressing, you expand your senses and open up your evolutionary capacities for learning and evolving. By opening your heart center, you expand the power of your brain, that still largely unused palace of potentiality.

The instruments of your development that enable your charismatic gifts to unfold are awareness and intention. You see the possibilities like a wonderful garden that lies just beyond the wall. You despise nothing trivial that may lead, like a golden thread, to the essential mystery and answer.

The deeper you go into your inner world, the more you can let go of old fears, hatreds, tensions, and emotional wounds, and the more easily you can relate to other people. By connecting with other people in a satisfying and human way, you activate your charisma and theirs.

The experience of feeling your own heart center open, loving, and radiant will expand to others. They too are "touched" with the light of the extraordinary brain and the limitless powers of the heart.

7

The Magic of Sound

O what is it that makes me tremble
so at voices? Surely, whoever
speaks to me in the right voice, him
or her I shall follow.
　　　　　—WALT WHITMAN
　　　　　("Vocalism," *Leaves of Grass*)

Voices—I think they must go deeper
into us than other things. I have
often fancied heaven might be
made of voices.
　　　　　—GEORGE ELIOT

She has a voice full of money.
　　　　　—F. SCOTT FITZGERALD

SOUND has the power to change worlds. And the sounds of our
own voices change with our own changes. They deeply affect
how we perceive ourselves and how other people react to us. A
whopping 90 percent of respondents to the Charisma questionnaire agreed that voice was one of the most important elements
of charisma.

Often in one of my workshops or lectures I ask people if they
would like to see me undergo a complete personality change in
one minute. Everybody is immediately curious and skeptical. The
room gets very quiet. I stand still and concentrate hard for a
second or two (at one point in my life, I used to sound the way
I'm now about to talk; these days it takes a deliberate effort).
Then, speaking from the face, feeling no connection with my

body at all, I say in a dull, innocuous voice, "This is the way I sound when I talk with no vibration at all. That's the only change I'm making. But I'd like you to notice any difference you see in my personality!"

Usually I hear gasps . . .

"You sound so boring!"

"You don't even look like the same person. . . ."

"You look inhibited. . . ."

"Your voice sounds thin, unsure. . . ."

"Right, uninteresting, not friendly . . ."

"You seemed to shrink. . . ."

"Yes," I add, "and I also feel very different. I feel timid, unassertive, dull, rather fearful. I'm aware of a tightness in my shoulders, neck, and head. My head feels very far away from my feet. I'd really get a headache if I kept that up!"

Amazingly, I told the group, the only change I made was that I *used no vibration,* either in the head or the body. I spoke from the throat and face as though my face were a mask and there was nothing behind it or below it.

I remember so well the feeling that voice gave me when I was very young and unsure of myself. I didn't know then, of course, that it was possible to change one's feeling about oneself by simply using the full vibration of the body with the voice. Like most people, I was barely aware of the psychophysical and physical force of my discomfort. I just felt when I was uncomfortable that it was an effort to be audible. When I felt happy and at ease, my voice felt rich and full. It never occurred to me that I could put myself in that state at will. That was to come much later.

Ever since the first century A.D. when Quintilian, the Roman rhetorician, described vocal quality and quantity, poets, phoneticians, philosophers, and physicians have been fascinated and baffled by the elusive characteristics of the human voice. The ancient world knew that there was a profound connection between voice and personality. The word *personality* itself comes from the Latin *per sona,* meaning, literally, "through sound." The *persona* was the mask actors wore through which their sound (their characters) emerged. In classical Greece, with its stable authority system (people even rebelled according to set rules!), conflict arose from individual opposition to the system, but there was no concept for the self as we know it today. (Homer's poetry doesn't even have a word for "person" or "oneself.") Gradually *persona* came to mean not the mask but the actor himself, then the "person" in drama.

> Persona—a type of personality conceived as the full realization of oneself; a character in a play or novel.

Eventually the word meant *any* person and lost its original association with the human voice. But the dim awareness that there was a profound connection between the voice and personality remained.

The first systematic attempt to analyze the voice in terms of human emotions was made by Giovanni de la Porta, a medieval Florentine physician and playwright (considered one of the six great men of science in his day). Nothing more seems to have happened until Freud, along with Abraham and Ferenczi, investigated conscious and unconscious speech expression and their links to neurosis. About forty years ago Wilhelm Reich and later his disciple Alexander Lowen (founder of bioenergetics) showed how people's voices and speech patterns reveal character structure.

Today, the "masks" of modern communication—records, tapes, telephone, movies, radio, TV—flood our consciousness, and the cult of "personality" is a dominant part of our culture. For the first time in history, humanity can *hear* itself mirrored. (Before photography was invented, there were painted portraits, but there was never any acoustic equivalent.) Most people are surprised and less than pleased when they first hear themselves recorded ("Gee, do I sound like that?"). The sound we hear inside our heads is, of course, apt to be very different from the sound other people hear. Students tell me:

"God, I sound so boring!"

"My voice is so nasal I can't stand it!"

"What a flat sound I have—I can't believe it!"

"I never knew I said 'uh' so much. That's awful!"

"I sound like a hick!"

etc., etc.

Taping or recording your own voice can be extremely helpful.

Now you can hear yourself and learn to sound as interesting and expressive as you were meant to be. Everybody instinctively responds to the power of a fascinating voice. (According to Mehrabian's studies, if you remember, 37 percent of the communication is affected by voice quality itself.)

Since behavior changes consciousness and you become what you act, if you use your voice fully to express your true feelings and develop its timbre and range, *your* "persona" *will* involve your full self, not a facade. This kind of authentic and organismic voice can give you a sense of integrity (wholeness). People with interesting voices unquestionably have a decided advantage: they seem more fascinating, more attractive. And how disappointing it is when a beautiful person opens her/his mouth and out comes a high, unpleasant or thin, weak sound! Your charisma emerges with an interesting voice and people begin to respond to it.

Voiceprints are as individual as fingerprints. Now computer devices are used in business and police investigations to spot lies, confusion, or mixed motives. Apparently changes in attitude and feelings show up as alterations in pitch—not always audible to the naked ear. (That's why speakers are often surprised that the audience doesn't realize their nervousness, even though *they* can feel the changes in their own voices.) Of the three complex variables in the human voice—pitch, loudness, and complexity—pitch is the easiest to measure. When you feel a stressful emotion, the hypothalamus gets the message and sends it instantly to your larynx, or "voice box." The larynx gets tighter or looser, depending on what you were feeling, and that changes the pitch. Computers can be programmed to measure these changes and determine the depth of emotion behind the spoken words. Pitch changes, beyond certain well-defined limits, usually indicate confusion, lying, or fear.

As usual, involuntary physiological response is more reliable than conventional testing results. Commercial market research has found this to be of particular value. Consumers are not always able or willing to consciously verbalize their real feelings—for instance, when children are asked about soft drinks or teenagers about sex. Voiceprints can also be used to find out if psychiatric patients with anxiety or depression are getting better or worse. Studies have shown that "personality disorders" (which used to be called "neuroses")° and schizophrenia can be spotted through voice and speech patterns alone.

Everybody who has suffered from nervousness before a speech or a performance or the prospect of meeting someone important has experienced vocal unsteadiness, dry throat, pitch changes. We all recognize the sound of irritation or annoyance accurately, whether or not the words match the message. It's only when these aberrations are constant, when the voice quality is consistently "out of sync" with what the person is saying, that a personality disorder is indicated. In the last years of her life, Judy Garland's voice held a throbbing vibrato of near hysteria no matter what she was saying or singing. The disturbed patterns of her life, the constant turbulent emotionalism, had become part of every sound she uttered.

When your voice says one thing and your words another, it's the real message that gets through—your underlying feelings—even when you think you're hiding them. Martin M., a trial lawyer, came to me to improve his courtroom style and communication with his clients. They tended to find him abrasive, he said. He got annoyed with people easily and often found them irritatingly "stupid." When I asked him to do the hostility exercise (see p. 332) and shout "You bastard" he said, "I don't want to do that. You see, I never swear! I *never* use any four-letter words."

He smiled proudly when he said this. "One of my clients called up my partner today and started screaming that he was furious at me. 'He abused me, called me names,' he said. 'He swore at

° Interestingly, the American Psychiatric Association has just revised its diagnostic terms in its new *Diagnostic and Statistical Manual of Mental Disorders* (Third Edition). "Neurosis" is out and "panic disorder" is in. This is a healthy shift from a flat judgment to a process-oriented description. It's easier to prescribe treatment if you describe the problem more exactly. This is an index to our changing view of people from the medical model to the growth model. All states are changing all the time. Here is another clear reflection of the new concepts in physics and the influence of Eastern thought. With so many psychologists and psychiatrists studying meditation, transpersonal psychology, Zen Buddhism, Mahayana Buddhism, the amalgam of Eastern disciplines packaged by est, and others, there was bound to be a profound effect on the way we see ourselves. A paradigm shift, as Karl Pribram remarked, is a new way of looking at old problems.

me.' My partner, who knows I never swear, said, 'Now exactly what did Martin say? He never swears! Ask anyone who knows him!' The client sputtered a minute and then said, 'He called me an—ashtray!' " Martin grinned broadly.

"And did you?" I asked him.

"Yes," he said. "That's right, I did."

"Well, it's very clear that he got your meaning, isn't it? He knew you were actually calling him an asshole."

"Yes, but I didn't say that!"

"He understood you very well. So you really abused him even though you didn't swear. Your voice told the story as clearly as if you had."

> I would rather be kicked with a
> foot than be overcome by a loud
> voice speaking cruel words.
> —ELIZABETH BARRETT
>   BROWNING

Martin smiled sheepishly.

"Would you do the hostility exercise with 'You rat!' instead of 'You bastard'?" I asked him. "If you allowed yourself to ventilate your anger privately, you wouldn't have to release it directly at clients. You saw by the satisfaction you got that you *needed* to release it. You were really fooling yourself by pretending you weren't swearing at the poor man!" Martin's relations with his clients improved dramatically after he acknowledged the power of his feelings and vocalized them in private.

> "I'll discuss it with you," she said,
> in a voice that could have been
> used to defrost her refrigerator.
> —REX STOUT

Never Yell at a Chrysanthemum

Not only people are sensitive to anger. Plants are, too. Dr. John A. Pierrakos, reporting experiments with his colleague, Dr. Wesley Thomas, tells us that when a person shouted at a chrysanthemum from five feet away, it lost its blue azure color and its pulsation diminished to one-third. The poor plants that were kept near the heads of screaming patients (three feet away) for more than two hours a day withered within three days and died!

The more we know about the "invisible," the more we see that everything is a form of vibration and all vibrations are related, sometimes translatable into another form.

I remember singing the St. Matthew Passion with the Collegiate Chorale. Robert Shaw, the conductor, began the first rehearsal by drawing on a blackboard the musical lines as they rose and fell in the opening bars. To our astonishment, they formed soaring spires—the magnificent form of a Gothic cathedral. That was my first insight into the mysterious synchrony of sound and form.

Sounds and colors are related, too. When his mother yells at a small child in an angry voice, the child's energy fields lose color and slow down. If you shout angrily and bang on the table, your field becomes red, streaked as though with porcupine quills, and the pulsatory rate doubles. The auric field of a person sobbing convulsively becomes deep purple, particularly over the chest, and the pulsation increases.

The voice expresses or blocks vibration from the very ground of our being. Since we are not "solid" (as we thought before the theory of relativity and quantum mechanics turned our ideas about "reality" upside down) but patterns of waves, our thoughts, emotions, actions, and relationships with others create constantly changing designs of colors, lights, sounds—a dazzling kaleidoscope of shifting energies. Human consciousness is capable of astonishing feats when we begin to respect and work with these subtle emanations.

Since vibrations are life force, sound has a mysterious potency. "In the beginning was the Word," begins the story of Creation. Logos (the Word) is sometimes translated as law or, more deeply, archetypal pattern. The Greek philosopher Philo wrote: "His image is THE WORD, a form more brilliant than fire—the Logos is the vehicle by which God acts on the universe and may be compared to the speech of man." The "word" must have been sound. Pythagoras, too, wrote that sound is a creative force.

The knowledge that music is therapeutic for the body is very ancient. According to the Mystery Schools, rhythm is related to the body, melody to the emotions, and harmony lifts our consciousness to spiritual awareness (perhaps because it blends the individual with the group, the solitary wave with the throbbing force field of its environmental sea).

The history of civilization could be written in terms of vocal expression. Nobody knows exactly how many languages and dialects there are at the moment; the guess is that there are at least 3,000. We know from the evidence of ancient fossils that languages originated more than a million years ago. Through all recorded history, humans have raised their voices (the primary musical instrument) to control nature and each other, as well as to express their joy, sadness, anger, fear, or yearning, through sheer sound.

Our very first breath becomes a sound, a life-giving cry of protest. To speak up is our birthright! The baby quickly learns to associate pleasure, comfort, and food with his mother's voice and touch—the first harmony in its life. His breathing and vocalizing reinforce each other. Later, when we're frightened or upset, the coordination between voice and breathing is disturbed. That throws off the normal rhythms of vocalization and very likely plays havoc with the heartbeat's steadiness as well. Since everything is connected, we then feel and sound thoroughly off balance and uncomfortable.

It's fascinating that all over the world children begin to articulate sounds in the same sequence—regardless of what language their parents speak! The sequence starts from the lips (*p, b, m*) to the tip of the tongue (*t, d, l, n*) to the back of the tongue (*k, g*).

Babies often sing before they speak, and long before she/he understands words the child has already learned much of the vocal language of emotions. The acoustic impressions with which they pick up other people's moods and the kinetic urge to recreate sounds begin before words. The early impression of these sounds is very acute and explains some of our adult reactions to voices. For instance, once associated with fear, a particular sound will always have that meaning—even though as an adult we have no idea why. "My father used to scream at me when I was little," remembered Rosa N., "and then he'd beat me. Whenever I hear a man yelling, even now, I get very frightened."

La-La—or, the Fun Starts

Babies have perfect voice production! Their breathing (at least in happy babies) functions perfectly, and the vocal cords operate in complete harmony with the breath. Babies never get hoarse! If mothers sing to their babies, the child's development moves easily to the next stage. If children aren't allowed to vocalize freely, there may be serious disturbances in breathing and speaking later.

To get in touch with the mischievous and playful freedom a very small baby has, try this:

1. Breathe deeply (all exercises start with that "clearing the decks") and empty your mind of words.
2. Pretend you're a tiny baby, and play with sound combinations just to feel the pleasure of making sounds through your voice, lips, and tongue. (Forget about the usual way you pronounce words. It'll probably feel very silly and aimless; if it does, you're doing it right!) For instance, try: *ma-ma-ma-ma-ma; da-da-da-da; la-la-la-la-la; ooooooooooohoooooooooookoooooooooooooo-ooooo; dee dee dee dee dee dii dii dii dii dii da-doo da-doo da-doo.*
3. Keep your lips very, very relaxed and say *bhu-bhu-bhu-bhuh* and other sounds that are not in the English language but which a baby discovers for itself. (Sanskrit has fifty letters, the only language in the world that includes all the sounds that infants make as they are learning to speak. This is one of the reasons the yogis were able to come up with mantras which have profound effects on the human organism—because they *include all* the possible sounds.)
4. Notice how it feels physically and how the vibrations affect you —*muh-muh-muh*—as though you had nothing in the world to think about except the feeling of these sounds. Try bubbling (not very adult, for sure!) and keeping the little sound going for a while as though it were a delicate thread of sound you are spinning out of your mouth like a snail's trail. See how many places in your mouth, tongue, and throat you can combine—and which you don't ordinarily use in speech.
5. Vary the pitch and the length.
   For instance, after *puh, puh, puh, puh* (with the cheeks puffing lightly), do it in a sustained way: *puuuuuuh, puuuuuuuuh, puuuuuuuh.*
6. As "research," observe a real baby and notice all the sounds it is making.

7. The last step is to internalize the pleasure of using your tongue, lips, throat for nothing but sound. Add breath before, during, or after and see how a sigh or a quick breath or a slow intake changes the sound.
8. Do this entire exercise with small subtle sounds, like the very beginning of speech—which it is.
9. At the end you'll feel very relaxed and somehow tuned up. It'll be a pleasure to put together words after having gone back to the dawn of speech!

Around the first year, the child begins to learn words. Its echolalia (rhythmic repetition of sounds and syllables) gives way to one-word, then full sentences. A small child knows exactly how much air she/he needs to speak and figures out how to breathe quietly through the nose with small amounts of air and deeper inhalation through the mouth, using more air just before speaking. As always, body wisdom is instinctive and accurate. (Retarded children manage this less well.)

BLAH BLAH BLISSOUT

To further relax your lips and tongue and get in touch with that delightful stage of totally relaxed and playful experimentation, try the following (use as big a vocal range as you can):

> Bluh, blah, bluh, blah, etc. (start slow, get faster until you're going at top speed).
> Bidda, bidda, bidda, etc. (again slow and then faster).
> Puddah, puddah, puddah, etc.
> Matta, matta, matta, etc.
> Kicka, kicka, kicka, etc.

Go back to the beginning and start again (*bluh, blah,* etc.). This time, take away the *b,* until your tongue is flipping back and forth in a continuous *l.* Try your own combinations, all loose-lipped and -tongued.

In nursery school a child meets other children and a teacher. At this point, if children are told "You can't sing!" or "You talk too loud!" inhibition will set in that permanently affects their voices, self-confidence, and sense of well-being.

Paul S., a tall, very thin financial expert, came to me to get over his shyness in giving presentations. He had not had overly critical parents, but when he thought back to his adolescence, he flashed on the painful experience of being called on to stand up and read in class.

"I was the tallest kid in the grade, and everybody made fun of my skinniness. When I had to get up to read, it was agony. My voice cracked, and I felt horribly embarrassed. I guess I always associate getting up and speaking with that adolescent torture! Deep down I'm sure people are going to make fun of me the way they did then!" He looked surprised. In his mid-thirties he had become very successful in his career, and it was only now that he realized that he couldn't go any further until he could get over that early painful association. He was still narrow-chested and breathed shallowly. The Elbow Propeller and Whole Body Breath (see pp. 321, 326) developed and expanded his chest. They helped him feel like the authoritative adult he really was when he got up to address his business associates. His whole personality noticeably expanded when he overcame that early association. The fear of being humiliated had locked him into a   timid sound and body posture.

Author Elizabeth   also had a painful childhood memory which affected her voice. She was understandably worried. Whenever she spoke in front of more than two people, she lost her voice. She had to go out on a lecture tour when her new book was published and she was panicked that her voice would disappear as it always had. When I asked her about her earliest painful association with speaking, her face grew white and her eyes suddenly filled with tears.

"My father died of pneumonia when I was ten. I remember one day the teacher asked every child to stand up and tell what her father did. By the time my turn came, I was absolutely unable to tell the class that my father was dead. I felt like fainting—I just stood there, unable to say a word until the teacher took pity on me and told me to sit down. During the time he was sick, I had to go around on tiptoe and never speak louder than a whisper." The realization of the source of her difficulty, combined with breathing and courage exercises, gave her the confidence to begin to speak up—within a few weeks she was enjoying her new sense of maturity (it still felt rather dangerous) and confident expression. Before that she had only dared to express herself on paper. I have found that to be true of many writers;

no matter how bold they may be on the typewriter, speaking directly in their own voices is a very different challenge.

Babies and primitive societies use a much freer and more expansive range of speaking and singing than most adults. Many people are vocally very inhibited, even though they consider themselves otherwise free. Practice in voicing your most outrageous thoughts *aloud* (in your head doesn't count!) has surprisingly liberating effects for everybody. Not only does it help your voice, but it stimulates the flow of energy and ideas and produces a carefree spontaneity that might have seemed impossible a short time before.

MOVE IT!

THAT MOVES ME. . . .

GET A MOVE ON. . . .

MOVERS AND SHAKERS . . .

To move (vibrate) is to live. The phrase "that turns me on" gives us a very vivid image of some powerful inner motor being turned on. "I really like the vibrations here" is not just a figure of speech. We can feel other people's sonic fields. They're as individual as fingerprints and they're made of sound vibrations or soundless ones.

A leftover from the eighteenth century rise of rationalism is our unspoken instinctive attitude that what we cannot see, hear, or touch is somehow not real. But how can we maintain our literal-mindedness when we sit and watch images on a screen that are not there (TV) or hear the shifting kaleidoscope of sounds on tapes and records fill the air as if by magic?

She has "a voice that shatters glass," sang Professor Higgins in *My Fair Lady*. Sounds can have amazing effects on matter. The eighteenth-century German physicist Ernst Chladni scattered sand on steel disks and watched the changing patterns in the sand when he played a violin. He had discovered that inorganic matter (in this case, sand), vibrated with nothing but sound, creates *new* organic shapes both moving and still.

Every time you raise the pitch of notes on the musical scale, the form changes—a static pattern becomes a moving one. Raise it again and a new, different static pattern is created. Lawrence Blair in *Rhythms of Vision* observes that:

> we see a parallel here with the evolution of civilizations, which consolidate into giant patterns of static form, crumble into phases of

movement and creative vitality and get again into periods of conservatism; like the altering Chladni figures, their points of change or "metanoia" are marked by a return to chaos, to a lack of any coherent pattern, before the society begins to respond once more to the new vibratory frequency, or perhaps to the same harmonic, but in a different key.

Not for nothing was the first act of a new Chinese emperor to set—or restructure—the musical scale.

"WHAT HAS ALL THIS TO DO WITH MY CHARISMA?"

When you connect with your charisma, you become acutely aware of being in harmony with yourself and your world. It is possible to take yourself less heavily, to be less troubled and stressed by the difficulties of your life, when you are able to feel both your uniqueness and your connectedness. Each of us is a field of resonances, interacting with other oscillating fields contracting at different speeds at different times. When our voice resonates in the head, chest, belly, and throughout the body, we become intensely aware of being alive. In fact, our electromagnetic field expands and affects others powerfully. When our voices are constricted, our expressive capacities are limited and we feel less than truly ourselves. Our effect on other people is much less than when we are fully resonating. Most people, I find, are not aware of what it means to speak with the body.

"My throat tightens when I have to talk in public."
"My voice gets high and shrill."
"People say I can't be heard. I don't know why."
"People don't listen to me."
"My voice feels unreal and far away when I get nervous."

These are some of the most common complaints from people who want to learn to speak comfortably in public or private. You can't feel charismatic if your voice is small, tight, or strained. Children have clear and ringing voices—no vocal problems. What happens when we grow up? We have seen the irresistible alternation in nature between static and dynamic that is true in our own development as human beings, too. We learn, we acquire knowledge, concepts, information, power. Then we must ask ourselves what we *want* from all this and very quietly allow the answer to arise from the unsuspected depths and begin to form the new shapes of becoming, growing. We don't have to will it—just allow it to happen. We are stuffed with information, overloaded with stimuli. We need to go deep inside, then express freely the fruits of our secret intuition.

Too often, in the process of learning, people are conditioned *not* to express fully. It's impossible to be fully charismatic unless you give yourself permission—especially if it was once withheld by the authority figures in your life—to express your feelings vocally. This means the whole range of human expression from a whimper to a shriek, from crying to singing, from talking to laughing. This is why we need "silly" exercises, the one-minute verbal free-for-all, and all the other vocal exercises in this book that may make you balk or wonder "What has this to do with being charismatic?"

Through your voice you'll be known—and know yourself. You must voice your feelings to really know what they are. As a baby you did it instinctively. Now, of course, it's not always possible or desirable to express them to other people. (Look what happened to the chrysanthemums!) That's why you must liberate your "inner child" and energize yourself and express yourself as vocally as you can (at least in private)—without feeling guilty, ashamed, or foolish. It is *not* the same if you never *utter* the sound!

Music has always provided a marvelous neutral outlet for expressing the full range of emotions. Singing or playing a wind or brass instrument deepens the breath and provides a new voice —an intimation of new ways to be alive and expressive, which is deeply satisfying. Something within us longs to know the full range of our possibilities and leaps at the chance to express in new ways—each human is like a prism with infinite facets. When a new facet develops, the gem glitters more brilliantly, the self expands, and we have more ways to interact with the world— one test of a satisfying life. Most powerful of all is singing— with words.

George Bernard Shaw, that charismatic, indomitable genius, grew up in a household full of music. His mother was a singer and when he was quite small, a singing teacher named G. J. Lee "found his way into our house, first by giving my mother lessons there, and then by using our drawing-room for rehearsals." He remained grateful ever after to Lee for teaching both him and his mother an effortless method of singing. Having heard an Italian baritone named Badeali, who at eighty had a perfectly preserved voice, Lee figured out how it was produced. (The other Dublin teachers were only interested in Badeali, Shaw writes, because he could drink a glass of wine and sing a sustained note at the same time!) Shaw's mother "lived to be Badeali's age and kept her voice without a scrape on it till the end."

When Shaw's adolescent voice broke, he insisted on being taught how to sing properly.

> When following my mother's directions, I left my jaw completely loose and the tongue flat instead of convulsively rolling it up; when I operated my diaphragm so as to breathe instead of "blowing"; when I tried to round up my pharynx and soft palate and found it like trying to wag my ears, I found for the first time in my life, I could not produce an audible note. It seemed that I had no voice. . . . But I insisted on being taught how to use my voice as if I had one: and in the end the unused and involuntary pharyngeal muscles became active and voluntary, and I developed an uninteresting baritone voice of no exceptional range, which I have ever since used for my private satisfaction and exercise without damaging either it or myself in the process. . . .

Notice that Shaw admits unashamedly that he had no talent for singing, nor did he claim any for playing either. Yet he never for a moment questioned his right to sing or play to his heart's content. All his life he got extraordinary satisfaction from doing both. Certainly this "hands-on" in-depth involvement in music was invaluable for his career as music critic, "probably the best that ever lived," according to W. H. Auden. But "Corno di Bassetto," as he signed himself, was doing it to please himself.

Beyond that, I have a strong hunch that his early singing and music making contributed a great deal to his exceptional confidence in his own powers. Certainly he had the courage to be outrageous, sure of his right to express anything he pleased. (After all, he valued his *pleasure* in singing above his talent!) All this played an important role in his extraordinary vitality, productivity, and longevity. The sheer energy and scope of his many-faceted genius are amazing.

> The root of beauty is audacity.
> —Boris Pasternak

According to author Kurt Vonnegut, respect is an absolutely essential form of human nourishment. Interestingly, 65 percent of the people who responded to the Charisma questionnaire wrote that they had felt most charismatic when other people responded to them with love and/or admiration and *respect*.

People who are disappointed in their persona or image or voice usually sense that they don't command the respect or authority that they would like. They find it hard to "make themselves heard." It's impossible to be charismatic with a flat, uninteresting voice. Everyone responds to the magnetism of great voices—although some people are wrapped in "situational" charisma—the magic of high office or high heroism, which may have nothing to do with vocal qualities. Still, the rolling tones of Henry Kissinger and Abba Eban and the pounding intensity of Hitler certainly had much to do with their impact. Richard Burton said he developed his voice by shouting Shakespeare at the sheep in his native Wales. The curious underlying rhythm in Sir Laurence Olivier's remarkable voice exerts a hypnotic fascination. Or the richness of the vibration will roll over the hearer like a kind of deep sonic massage—Orson Welles's marvelous baritone, for instance. Tallulah Bankhead, Marlene Dietrich, Charles Boyer—voices can be extremely seductive.

In 1939 Welles shook the country with his famous radio show based on H. G. Wells's *War of the Worlds*. Even though announcements were made that it was only a dramatic representation and not an actual event, the newslike coverage with the impressive, stirring sound of Welles's voice mesmerized the country. Thousands of people panicked, convinced we were being invaded by Martians. (Nowadays the voluptuous authority of that memorable voice is mostly employed in commercials. What a waste!)

A voice that commands respect, fascination, belief, interest—all this, then, is essential for charisma. Since there are more overtones in a low voice, a high, thin sound can't have much range or expressiveness. Usually when people get nervous, their voices get pinched or high or flat or all three. If you stick your chin out, you cut yourself off at the throat, and it's impossible to connect with the breath and strength of the rest of your body. This is how we get "uptight" when we're tense. The center of gravity shifts upward, everything "upstairs" gets tense and tight, your throat closes, and you lose your sense of being in control—both of yourself and the audience.

We all make instant assessments of people based on their voices. We're also subliminally very responsive to vocal changes in people close to us. When you call home and your husband, wife, boyfriend, or mother answers, you immediately know just from their "hello" if something is wrong. How do we make these split-second inferences?

Our computerlike brains, putting together vibratory information, plus our instinctive and learned knowledge that certain sounds indicate certain emotional states, can pick up awareness in a flash.

For instance, you decide to go on a trip with the children and not stop at your mother's house.

"That's all right, don't worry about me," she says, but her voice, trembling slightly, says very clearly, "I'm hurt, very hurt!"

So often we hear someone say something which she/he clearly doesn't mean; the tone and the inflection provide the dead giveaway.

Try this exercise for yourself. Say both versions aloud:

You Mean It	You Don't
I'm really glad to be here!	I'm really glad to be here. (downward discouraged inflection—somebody dragged you to the party!)
She's a nice person.	She's a nice person. (dead voice—you don't think so.)
I'd love to go!	I'd love to go. (resigned, with a sigh)
I'm sorry.	I'm sorry . . . (sarcastic, or with a smile or flippant shrug)
We must get together.	We must get together. (light, indifferent, eyes roving)
I believe you.	I believe you. (sarcastic)
You did OK. (with warm approval)	You did OK. (grudgingly)

I feel fine.	I feel fine. (apologetic smile— you don't want to complain.) (or angry, denying) (or confused, desperate, faint)
Don't do that.	Don't do that. (inviting, seductive, or unsure)
it was nice meeting you.	It was nice meeting you. (unsmiling—actually it was a big strain. Or indifferent. Or with an unspoken addition "And I hope I never see you again!" (with a curl of the lip)
You look lovely.	You look lovely . . . (. . . considering . . .) (or, forget it, you couldn't.)
That was wonderful.	That was wonderful. (I really didn't like it much.)
I don't mind, really.	(What's the use?—I'm helpless) (or, you're always taking advantage.)
I'm not upset.	(I'm mad! or I'm not going to let you know I am!) (through clenched teeth)

You'll notice that you and everybody you know sometimes say things you don't mean—out of politeness, annoyance, fear, indifference, or a dozen other motives. Sometimes, though, people misunderstand what we say because our voice does not express what we are really feeling. If you've been conditioned not to show your feelings, you probably never sound as enthusiastic as you may actually feel. Do you feel silly when you have to repeat an enthusiastic remark? Practice it—as though each time were the first and most spontaneous. If you have a good deal of free-floating hostility or anger, your voice may sound sharp and sarcastic even when you don't intend it to.

*   *   *

"That's me," Harriet R. sighed. "I can't understand why people think I'm sharp-tongued. I'm always trying *not* to hurt people's feelings!" Denying that you have the right to negative feelings has the paradoxical effect of creating "anger leakages"—when the anger you never express for fear of hurting feelings "leaks out" without your knowing it. Other people do! There's no hiding hostility. (See chapter 10.)

Oddly enough, I have found that people who lament that they "talk too much" are those who are secretly afraid to assert their real feelings. When we do the one-minute nonstop talkathon, those people, along with the shy, quiet ones, find it impossible to keep talking. Having been given permission to "talk too much," they suddenly feel shy! Their "talking too much" is a way of "getting back" at people who would shut them up, without taking responsibility for rebelling. "I can't help myself," Wilma L. complained. "I don't know what's the matter with me—even though my husband tells me all the time I'm talking too much, I can't seem to stop—and I say the same things twice. I go off on tangents and I can't seem to stop. I keep repeating—oh, there I go again!" She stopped and laughed ruefully.

Wilma had completely "bought" her husband's judgment and was not aware of resenting his continual put-downs, since she humbly thought he was right. He even belittled her to their seven-year-old son, who started to put her down too.

The turning point came one day when a woman at a cocktail party "cornered me and in this loud, overwhelming voice of hers started complimenting me until I just wanted to crawl away and get out of there. In fact, I left the party and sat shaking in my car. I was so upset I just wanted to go somewhere and calm down before seeing anybody. Now what can you do about somebody like that?" (She was still "blaming" someone else.)

"Could you tell her that all the compliments make you uncomfortable?" I asked her.

"Oh, no, that would hurt her feelings!" she answered, horrified.

"It's always legitimate to tell someone what you *feel*," I told her, "without saying 'You're impossible or you did this and this wrong.' In fact, it's much kinder because then people know where they stand with you. As it was, your running away from the party could have been misunderstood by several people. The hostess may be insulted, or the man you were talking to before this woman came along; you can't know all the repercussions. You were so shaken by this incident because you felt you had no control—you felt bullied. Isn't it so?"

She nodded. "Absolutely."

"It's important not to let anyone bully you, because then you feel like a helpless victim," I said. "The 'I have no control over what's happening' feeling, as you saw, is the most stress-producing feeling of all. Since it's hard for you to speak up when somebody is running you down or riding roughshod over your feelings, let's role-play that. You interrupt her and tell her very firmly, 'All this flattery makes me uncomfortable; that's how I feel about it.' Nobody can argue with your feelings, especially if you preface it with 'I know it's silly but . . .' "

"Pat," Wilma said to another woman in the workshop, "you know Joyce. You play her."

At first it was hard for Wilma to speak up and assert her rights. She laughed and discounted her feelings. But after a few tries she was able to say it firmly. Her voice was clear and her manner friendly but firm—and she stopped Joyce cold. We all applauded. "But *why* does she do that to me?" complained Wilma.

"Ask instead what is she feeling when she tries to manipulate people? Do you think her self-esteem is high?"

"No, I guess not. I never thought of that before, but actually she has a pretty empty life—I guess she's afraid we'll all stop inviting her if she doesn't butter us up."

"What shall I do when I feel I'm starting to talk too much?" Wilma asked later. This is the exercise I gave her to "ground" herself and quiet down. It's powerfully effective.

THE "NO BARS" HOLD
(For people who feel they talk too much!)

1. Press your toes firmly into the ground. Hold. Increase the pressure.
2. At the same time, breathe in slowly (mouth closed), continuously expanding your lower abdomen and back to a count of seven.
3. Hold one count.
4. Release your toes and exhale for seven slow counts. Make sure your shoulders don't go up.
5. Repeat. Keep it up.

Practice tensing your toes and *nothing else*. At first, tensing your toes and *not* tensing your stomach and hands may feel like the old game of rubbing your stomach and patting your head at the same time. You'll soon be able to coordinate with your breath. Breathe very smoothly and noiselessly.

This has all the advantages of the Basic Buddha Belly (p. 318) plus one more: pressing into the ground with your toes will literally "ground" you and prevent you from "flying high" when you don't want to. It'll also help you slow down and say only what you really want to say. All the other advantages—such as being able to listen better, being perceived as a calm, excellent listener (and actually functioning that way), and getting over nervousness—are amplified and reinforced by the toe press.

You'll be reminded that you're literally being supported by the ground. Sir Laurence Olivier° has said that this awareness is *the* most important part of his preparation when he goes on-stage. Once when he played Richard III, he made his entrance appearing in a doorway and stood with his *back* to the audience for fully a minute before he whirled around and savagely began the famous opening speech, "Now is the winter of my discontent. . . ."

When I asked why he made the unusual choice for the opening moment, he said thoughtfully, "Well, you see Richard is a hunchback. It's crucial for me to get my balance established so I can feel the ground supporting me when I begin. Since Richard is off balance because of his deformity, I needed time to establish the feeling of centeredness in myself before speaking or my voice wouldn't feel or sound right. The shock value of starting with my back to the audience gave me time—I could take as long as I needed to establish the groundedness that's so important—then the rest of the act was no problem." I was fascinated that Olivier

° I've always admired Olivier as the greatest English-speaking actor in the world. When I was singing at the Hotel Pierre in New York, I was thrilled to be asked to entertain at a private party given for Sir Laurence at the Waldorf. Afterward, to my great delight, he asked if he could see me home. This was when he had just appeared in New York in *The Entertainer*, playing a seedy English musical hall performer. We had an absorbing discussion about theater. I told him how much I admired him for being able —after playing all the greatest Shakespearean heroes—to play a third-rater so magnificently. "Oh, no," he replied merrily. "I'm really very much like that, you know!"

felt his being supported by the ground was important enough to dictate his choice of how to stage the crucial first entrance.

Olivier also described his search for an image while preparing to play Oedipus. This is how he found the right sound for the shattering scream in his classic performance. "To make the pain real, I had to think of animals," he said. "I thought of foxes screaming, with their paws caught in the teeth of a trap. Then I heard how they catch ermine in the arctic. Trappers put down salt, and the ermine comes to lick. And his tongue freezes to the ice. That's what I thought about as I screamed." The perfect vowel sound for screaming "wasn't an *ah* or an *ugh*—more an *err*." It was the living image that gave him the sound he wanted.

Everything is connected. As infants and children, we use our entire animal vocal range and breath freely to express feelings. In order to develop vocal and emotional richness speaking—so necessary for your charisma—it's important to expand the limited sound spectrum you've been operating with for so long. Loosen up! Limber up! Let fly!

I'd like you to think about your own voice for a moment. What instrument is it like? What color? Colors? How heavy? How light? Is it thick or thin? Do you enjoy it? Do other people? Is it responsive to your moods? Does it hide your feelings? What fabric or substance is it like? (Wood, stone, velvet, sandpaper, metal?) If it were a fragrance or smell, what would it be? Where is it mostly located? In your face? Head? Nose? Jaw? Chest? Eyes? Throat? Is it a true representation of you? Is it weak? Strong? Monotonous? Varied? What animal is it like? What kind of landscape does it most resemble? Desert? Mountaintop? Lake? Forest? Has it changed much? Since you were a child? An adolescent? In the last five years? In the last ten years? Do you like it? Do you listen to the sound of what you say or only to the words? Do you find words juicy? Dry? Is it too soft? Too loud? Does it envelop you or issue from a small opening? Is breathing easy or an effort? In chapter 13, using some of these questions, you'll be able to chart your own vocal portrait. The spontaneous images you choose (and there are no *wrong* ones!) will give you access to unsuspected resources. They provide a tool for instant expansion and deepening of your vocal charisma anytime you want it.

8

The Sounds of Your Feelings

The most beautiful words in the
English language are *cellar door*.
—J. B. PRIESTLY

WE ALL HAVE certain half-conscious associations with words
and their sounds, and for each person certain sounds are more
pleasurable than others. Since we know that the sound of what
we say is often more important than the meaning of the words,
it's valuable to discover the inner palette of sound that pleases
you most. When you enjoy the sounds of words, you're more expressive, persuasive, and charismatic.

Sometimes I ask Charismedia students to say a word like *soft*.
When they do, with no preparation, it might just as well be
hard or *June* or *stone*. The word has no particular distinguishing
associations, and we certainly can't tell the meaning from the
sound.

Then I ask for some associations with the word *soft*—we go
around the room: "Feathers." "Fur." "Clouds." "Velvet." "Skin."
"Pillows."

"Now," I ask the group, "let's hear the word *soft* again, keeping some of those images in mind."

Now when each person says "soft," it really *sounds* soft. If you
have a mental image, it changes the way a word sounds even
though your hearer has no idea of what picture you have in mind.

Subliminal Onomatopoeia

You can trigger instant acceptance of your words by making them so "juicy" with association that people automatically feel attracted by what you're saying. This works even with controversial concepts.

Carol Bellamy, the brilliant president of the city council in New York, came to me because people criticized her for talking too fast. She is an excellent speaker, but some of her words got lost when she slurred over them. I asked her to improvise a talk on some topic that she might be speaking on during her week. Without hesitation, she began to speak very fluently about something called—I had to strain to catch it—an urban development action grant.

"Hold it!" I called out. "Is that something your audience knows all about? You dropped your voice and said it in a rush, as though you yourself were rather bored with it."

"No! Oh, did I?" she asked. "On the contrary, this would be the first time they've heard about it. Even the legislators don't know about it yet."

"Oh, then it's important to break it down and make each word interesting and attractive. First, *urban.* Can you think of a positive association for *urban?*"

"Well, it suggests the complexity of the city . . . the planning, the variety and wealth of resources and people," she shot back.

"Now, keeping all those good associations in mind, say the word again!" I told her.

"Urban," she said, smiling a little. Now it was more deliberate. It sounded tempting already.

"Now for *development!* That gives us an impression of growth, as though good things were in the offing, a change for the better, auspicious planning. Say it that way!"

"*Development,*" she said, taking time, this time, to emphasize the second syllable thoughtfully and promisingly, as though she were visualizing growth.

"Good! Now the next word, *action,* is certainly a very positive concept, especially with so much *inaction* and red tape in government. So say *action* very powerfully!"

"Action," she grinned, pronouncing it with a crisp glottal attack that sounded like the starting gun in a race.

"Now for the final coup, *grant*. That's a very positive word. It suggests generosity, a large gift; in fact, a magnificent present everybody would like."

"Grant," Carol said firmly. The *r* was juicy and the final *t* crisp and decisive. The subliminal association with granite added an underground feeling of solidity and reliability.

"Good. Now let's put them all together," I said. "But here's the challenge: make each word LIVE with its own association and rich suggestion background instead of running them all together as though they're all the same or running downhill in declining importance so that by the end of the sentence the audience can't even hear what you're saying. A common failing in speakers is dropping their voices completely at the end of a sentence even though they're not at the end of their talk. Remember: dropping your voice is like lowering the curtain. It signifies the end. It's much more interesting if you keep your inflection at midrange at the end of a sentence so your listeners instinctively know you're going on. Otherwise the audience may either mentally tune out or miss your point altogether or figure you're ashamed of it!"

The melody of her inflection at the beginning had been like this:

```
Urban
     Development
          Action
               Grant
```

Now it sounded like this:

```
                    t   Act
          vel      n
               e         ion   Grant
Urban  De   op  m
```

It was clearer, more distinct, more varied, and definitely more persuasive. There is another benefit. The act of applying concentrated attention to each word increases the amount of energy projected in the phrase. That automatically makes it sound more

enthusiastic, positive, and interesting. And increases your charisma!°

Sometimes a negative assumption by the speaker about how
people will respond robs his words of energy. Suppose you know
there's a lot of resistance to a certain plan among the audience.
Anticipating opposition may lead you to sound defensive, negative, or uncertain. Since this happens largely unconsciously, it's
important, whenever you feel there may be hostility or resistance
or lack of comprehension, to put *more* energy into your words
(to make up for the drainage of confidence). Be careful, however, not to fall into a "justifying" or complaining tone. Nothing
is less convincing.

Some people are so unsure of being believed that almost everything they say has a petulant or aggrieved sound. People, as
you've seen, respond to the *tone* of what you're saying even
more than the content. Do you tend to sound complaining? If
you do, remember that this comes across as lack of authority.
Give yourself this little tone test:

1. The cabdriver has ignored your instructions and taken a different, longer route. Now you're stuck in traffic and late for an
   appointment.
   "I *told* you not to go that way!"
   told
   I   you not to go that way!
   (Your forehead wrinkles and your head juts forward.)
2. Your friend has ignored your advice and bought the wrong
   color paint for your apartment, insisting on his way. Now it's
   clear that the bright yellow you wanted would have looked better, as you originally thought, than the tan he chose.
   "I *told* you this wasn't a good color!"
3. You scold a child for breaking a toy after you warned her that
   throwing it on the floor would damage or ruin it.
   "I *told* you not to throw it on the floor!"
4. An employee has disobeyed your instructions and sent out the
   wrong letter to an important client.
   "I *told* you to be careful about that letter!"
5. Your friend or relative, who tends to be late, has arrived fifteen
   minutes after the movie starts. The tickets are sold out. She had
   insisted that it would be time enough if you both got there
   fifteen minutes before the movie started.
   "You're *never* on time!" (Do you sound aggrieved?)

° On the Charisma questionnaire, 73 percent of the answers cited "per-
suasiveness" as a powerful ingredient of charisma.

6. You went to a party against your better judgment and had a terrible time. Then you find you got a parking ticket on your car. You say to your escort:

   "I didn't want to go in the first place!"

7. Your butcher gives you a cheaper cut of meat to save you money. But you're preparing dinner for a party and the dish doesn't come out as well as usual. You're embarrassed and annoyed at the butcher.

   "I really wish you'd given me the usual!"

8. You go to a new hairdresser (or barber), and he persuades you to cut your hair much shorter than you wanted it. You're not pleased with the effect.

   "I wish you had just done it the way I asked you to!"

9. Your boss throws another assignment at you before you've finished the other two you're trying to complete.

   "I can't do all of this at once!"

10. You're annoyed with a friend who doesn't call you as often as you call her.

    "Why do I always have to be the first one to call?"

11. Your teenage son has left a mess in his room. For the hundredth time, you yell:

    "How can you live in such a pigsty?"

12. The garage mechanic has just told you your car needs a new gas line.

    "But you fixed it only a couple of weeks ago! You told me I wouldn't have any more expense with it this year!"

13. You're annoyed at some neighbors:

    "We're always inviting them to our house for parties, and they never invite us back!"

14. You call up the super, who never seems to be around when you need him.

    "We haven't had any heat for three days! Why don't you answer my phone calls?"

15. Your parents don't like your new boyfriend.

    "Why are you always criticizing my friends? You never like anybody I do!"

Then there are the self-pitying complaints. Fill in for yourself:

"You always expect . . ."
"You never let me . . ."
"You always wait until . . ."   (there's no time, I'm exhausted, it's too late, etc.)
"Why don't you ever . . ."
"Why must I always . . ."

Notice which of all the above statements sound complaining or whining. Now say the same things in a tone of *detached interest*.

You'll find that you have much more credibility, and the chances are you will get a more satisfying response. Most people get defensive or angry when they're complained at. There's something about the sound of someone feeling sorry for her/himself that is weak and powerless as well as irritating.

This vocal checkup can be a useful guide to unacknowledged feelings. If you find that you tend to have a complaining inflection rather often, this is a clue to you that there is a good deal of hidden anger poisoning your system. Are you an injustice collector?

Sentences that begin "I told you . . ." or "Why did you . . ." (or "Why didn't you . . .") are also likely to act as communication stoppers *if* the tone is complaining.

Others are:

"Don't be ridiculous" (or any down-putters, sure to produce either ice or fire).
"That's the way I am" (and don't intend to change).
"It won't work."
"What are you trying to do—make waves?"

Accusations, reproaches, even if delivered in your normal tone, will probably produce a counterattack, almost by reflex.

Shoulds, coulds, the great wistful wasteland of the subjunctive ("You should have . . .," "I would have . . .," You could have . . .," "If only . . ."), the country of regrets and disappointments and lost opportunities—they all torture us. If somebody is always "right," the other person is terribly "wrong"—a painful place to be. If any emotion is involved, you must abandon the heady temptation to prove yourself right, because if you "win," the other person loses. That's not a rewarding resolution of the conflict. It triggers resentment. Grievance collectors are forever "proving" they're right and everybody else is wrong. By their tone you shall know them.

If you find yourself complaining a lot, examine your life to see if there are any positive steps you can take to change your passivity. The passive role is basically unsatisfactory, and turns other people off as well. First, acknowledge that you're experiencing a lot of anger and frustration and are "dumping" on possibly innocent bystanders. Next, if the amount of anger is out of proportion to the offense, that's a clue that you have to take responsibility (*not* blame!) for dealing with your feelings rather than blame them on other people. Meantime, the *sounds* of your feelings are getting through, loud and clear.

Often, in conversation, we hear someone express feelings she/he's unaware of or that don't match the situation. It's impossible to know what their mental buildup was. I'm reminded of a man who found himself out on a dark country road late at night when his car broke down. He decided to knock on the nearest door and ask to use the telephone. But it was very late and he began to imagine that the people who lived in the house would get angry at the disturbance. In his mind he saw them getting furious and saying that not only could he not use the telephone but he had a "hell of a nerve" waking them up at that hour and to get out before they called the police. By the time he rang the bell he was thoroughly worked up. When a woman answered the door and before she had a chance to say anything, he yelled in outrage at her, "You can keep your lousy telephone if you're gonna be so rotten about it!"

Ella M., a retired schoolteacher, constantly complained in class, "Nobody cares about human misery or politics. I'm always giving people newspaper articles, and do you think they ever act on them? No! I'm very disappointed in groups of people. I seem to be the only person that cares."

The rest of the class grew very impatient with Ella. "She is always telling us what to do. It's very annoying," one woman observed. "Also she hogs attention all the time." With her complaining voice and all her constant criticism of other people, Ella was terribly hurt when someone criticized her! She fit Arthur Koestler's definition of "mimophant" given earlier in chapter 6.

Ella's need to be "right" and her constant disappointment in people who didn't behave the way she thought they should left her angry, lonely, and bewildered, but the combination of her demands for attention and her self-righteousness produced a good deal of resentment against her in the class. She couldn't grasp that nothing annoys people more than being told what they SHOULD do and how deficient or negligent they are for not doing it. A large part of it was her tone.

"You SHOULD write letters to your congressman; otherwise

you are a bad citizen!" That was Ella's style and everybody bristled. Meditation and the hostility exercises helped her release the great unexpressed load of old anger she carried around with her. Gradually, she stopped trying to manipulate other people. All of us who need to persuade—and that means everybody at some time or another—must be able to suggest a course of action in a tone that's nonjudgmental and nonmanipulative.

If you're asked for advice, a neutral, nondirective statement of information leaves the other person more freedom to consider it without feeling pushed. For instance, your friend asks you what to do about a problem involving her family. If you take her side, she may resent them more or take some action she'll regret later and then blame you. If you take theirs, she'll get angry and accuse you of not appreciating her feelings. This would apply to a boss-employee relationship, a student-teacher conflict, or any interpersonal problem where someone brings you a problem with a third person.

Fanning resentment is unproductive. So is defending the other side. What can you do?

First, mirror the other person's thoughts by restating what she/he has said. "You feel he deliberately kept you waiting for spite?" Invariably, the other person will then explore his/her own feelings more fully. You can then restate what you hear as the other's emotions: "You felt really abused when he didn't show up twice in a row."

Describing someone else's feelings is a nondirective way of helping them ventilate their feelings so they can move on to others. ("Well, I was mad, but he did have a really good excuse—his boss kept him late both times. I guess I really want to forgive him.") Most important, you're not *telling* anybody what's right and wrong. That would be irrelevant and, worse, not helpful. It simply escalates the other person's sense of grievance. For your friend, being able to share angry or hurt feelings with you, willingness to listen productively and not make value judgments, is a tremendous boon. When someone is emotionally upset, this also allows the person to process his own anger by turning it over on all sides, so that it is completely explored. Then she/he will be able to let it go or to act on it in a satisfactory way, not hasty and ill-considered.

If someone constantly asks for advice, you only foster their dependence by feeding it. ("It's better to give a person a fishing rod than a fish.") Usually neutral information, plus the implicit trust that you know your friend or relative or colleague can handle the situation well, are more effective and satisfying than direct help.

Molly went to her friend Evelyn who had been the chairperson of her organization before her and asked her to help her organize a benefit. She felt unable to handle it now that she had been elected president. Evelyn took over, only too happy to have her old powers back. Molly felt resentful and pushed aside. She came to the Charismedia class and asked how she could reestablish her authority at board meetings. Evelyn was running things her own way and now treated Molly as though she were unimportant and had no ideas worth considering. Molly had brought the situation on herself by panicking and running for help. Evelyn was convinced she was indispensable and happy to take over, which was not what Molly wanted.

"How do I get my authority back?" she groaned, very distressed. We role-played a meeting where she would acknowledge all of Evelyn's contributions in the past, thank her for them, and ask her now to let some others in the organization share in the planning: "Please save your comments until they've spoken; we need to have everybody's input." Molly had to practice saying it calmly and authoritatively. This worked out well. Evelyn subsided when she realized Molly was going to be firm in controlling the meeting herself. She was satisfied by the acknowledgment of her past contribution and respected Molly's new authority. Molly realized that she *could* run the meetings herself, and was happy that she was able to control the situation without creating an open break with her demanding predecessor. Others on the committee came to her privately and thanked her for handling Molly so well; everybody had been feeling overrun by her.

If you're asked for information or help, give it neutrally, without a stake in whether or not the help is used. Don't let your self-esteem depend on whether your advice is taken! We all have only a part of the picture anyway. Your considered opinion about the best thing for the other person may not be the best at all when all the information is in. This doesn't in the least lessen the value of your insights; only you must realize that we're all blind people touching a part of the elephant and mistaking our sensations for the totality.

Everyone has a right and a need to get as much information as possible about a problem situation. Only on the basis of maximum information (outside facts and inner feelings) can we make the most productive decisions. A respect for the innate good sense of other people also removes the horrendous need to be RIGHT all the time—which clearly nobody ever is. The ultimate responsibility for our actions must rest with ourselves.

With the triple beacons of respect:

a) for the unknown depths of others,
b) for their right to make their own decisions,
c) for the assumption that they too are trying to do their best,

your persuasion power will rise sharply.

Ella dropped her aggressive, hectoring tone ("You *should* write letters to your congressmen") and said, "If you write to your congressman, we have a good chance of getting this legislation passed. We must make some noise about what we believe in so the legislators know what their constituents want. It's up to US to do that."

I congratulated her. By saying "us" instead of "you," you include yourself and detoxify the pointing finger of "Do this!" or "Do that!" which everybody finds objectionable. You want to stimulate and inspire people to act, not bully them into it. They must believe that whatever you want to persuade them of is in *their* best interest.

In general, by expecting the best of people and taking for granted that they're acting out of valid motives (though you may not think so), you'll get better results.

A woman complained to her friend that the druggist in their neighborhood gave her terrible service and she was very annoyed with him. The friend promised to speak to him. A few weeks later they met again, and the first woman said, "What did you say to him? He's been wonderful. You really must have given him a good bawling out!" The friend smiled. "No, as a matter of fact, I told him you had remarked how extremely helpful and cooperative he always was!"

I experienced a somewhat similar situation one day dealing with a belligerent maintenance man at a school where I was teaching. We were having a TV session in the auditorium that day and I decided, on impulse, that I'd like the piano opened so I could accompany one of the students in a song. Ordinarily it was kept closed. (Of course, I should have made arrangements ahead of time!) When I found the maintenance man, he was in no hurry. I'd have to wait, he said, until he finished his coffee. It was clear he would be happy to throw as many road-blocks in the way of opening the piano as he could think of.

"You should have filled out a written request," he glared at me. "Yes, you're right—I really should have. I'm sorry about that," I answered. Not much mollified, he finally, at a snail's pace, grudgingly got the keys for the piano. When we reentered the auditorium I called the class's attention to his "kindness in opening the piano for us." He threw me a suspicious glance, sus-pecting sarcasm, but I WAS grateful at that point, and deter-mined to acknowledge him for it. (After all, it had been hard for him to accommodate me when he was so full of resentment and annoyance at being asked anything at all out of his ordinary routine!) When he saw I meant it, his attitude changed. Sud-denly, he *did* become cooperative. When I asked if we could have the use of the piano for the next hour he said expansively, "Sure, as long as you like—don't worry about it!" He departed happily to a wave of appreciative applause from the class. Had we gotten embroiled in who was "right" and who was "wrong" I have no doubt he wouldn't have opened the piano at all.

A small incident, but a telling one. It is necessary to LET GO of your own resentment and anger if you use this approach. You have to be innocent; otherwise you sound and feel false and it won't work. The biggest difficulty is that your usual impulse is to get defensive when someone is critical or hostile, to prove you're right. In dealing with antagonism:

1. Don't be defensive. Recognize when you feel threatened and repeat to yourself, "I am not less valuable or worthwhile even

when I make a mistake or someone challenges my ideas or criticizes me." Breathe deeply as you say this!

2. Recognize whatever you can agree with and express it. If there is *one* small element you can accept in someone else's tirade, do it. It takes you off the barricades, enables your antagonist to start listening to you and stop attacking. This is useful with children as well as grown-ups.

"You're always interrupting me!" shouts your child.

Our impulse is to say, "Well, you never let me get a word in!" or "I am not!" and the battle is joined. A better way (it requires some hors de combat rehearsal so that it "takes" viscerally and you can remember to do it in crises) is "Yeah, that's a terrible habit. I'm sorry. Be sure and let me know when I do that. It *is* very annoying to be interrupted all the time!" Or simply "I'm sorry." The explosion will instantly subside. You also have established a principle: it's not good to interrupt people. Next time *you're* interrupted, you'll get a fair response if you ask for equal time. You've provided a model for improved interaction. You're also demonstrating you're strong enough to admit you're wrong.

If you can't agree with one single thing the other person says, you can always say, "I see this really bothers you a lot" or "You really feel very deeply about this." (Be careful to use an interested, sympathetic tone, *not* reproachful.) This brings up the third way for dealing with antagonism:

3. When the other person is very angry, *never deal with the issues!* That's not where the action is. *Acknowledge the feelings* and encourage the other person to express them fully. This ventilation always lowers the temperature of the argument, removes the need for defense or attack, and brings you both to a third place. A HIGHER LEVEL OF CONSENSUS CAN BE REACHED THROUGH WELL-MANAGED FRICTION.

When you ask, "Why do you feel so strongly about this?" (in a sympathetic, nonchallenging tone), you'll be amazed at the results.

The first time I tested this principle, I wasn't at all sure it would work, but the effect was so dramatic I was astounded. I was a guest on a radio talk show. The topic was Pornography and Obscenity in the Theater. The other guests were two producers and a psychologist. One producer (whom I will call Edmund) had a long-running, charming musical fairy tale on Broadway.

He was ranting about the evils of pornography. His style was that of a fulminating nineteenth-century preacher. Nobody could get a word in edgewise.

"Obscenity is ruining our youth, corrupting our society's morals, and cheapening our theater," he declaimed. He had a point or two, but they were lost in the torrent of invective and denunciation he unleashed at us. I was beginning to wonder why I had come. The host of the show had actually left the studio! Nobody but Edmund was able to get in a word. I thought to myself, "What am I doing here? I might as well go home! OK, I've got to do something. I don't know if this will work, but here goes."

I said to Edmund, "Mr. ———, why do you feel so deeply about this?" To tell the truth, I didn't expect much, or even that he'd stop and respond. To my surprise, he stopped dead. That was the first boon! Then he said, in a quiet voice, very different from the thundering tone he'd been bombarding us with, "Well, you see, when I was a kid growing up in New York, my father—he was an Italian immigrant and he didn't know much English—used to use all the dirty street talk. I'd beg him, 'Pop, please don't use that gutter talk, it's not nice, you're embarrassing me,' but he didn't listen to me. He kept right on doing it."

We all sat silent, stunned and moved. All our antagonism at him for monopolizing the panel dissolved. We felt tremendous empathy for the child who had suffered because of his father's "dirty talk." No wonder he hated obscenity! Then the other producer, a man of about thirty who had a nude musical running, remarked, "You know, Edmund, I understand just how you feel. All my life, I've heard four-letter words and they didn't mean a thing. Now that I've got this show, I hear them so much that I wouldn't care if I never heard another one in my life!"

It was an astonishing turnaround. He had agreed with Edmund and demolished his point at the same time! (Clearly *he* had *not* been corrupted by obscenities and bad language, as the older man had insisted was bound to happen.) There was a warm feeling among the group. We went on to a much more productive general discussion. Edmund dropped his lecturing tone and was able to share the floor with the rest of us.

This was my first dramatic demonstration of the principle: WELL-MANAGED FRICTION CAN CREATE A HIGHER

LEVEL OF CONSENSUS. If pressed to a statement, you can say something like "I see the problem from a somewhat different angle" or "I can understand your feelings about this." If somebody stands up in a meeting and makes totally negative remarks, which you don't want to get into, you can simply say, "Thank you for sharing that with us." Nobody can argue with that! If you *want* to argue the point, do not attack the person or his ideas or "judge" them. Among the no-nos: "That's ridiculous!" "What a stupid remark!" "You don't know what you're talking about!"

Some adults deliberately go for the jugular when they get angry. They say cruel, hurtful things with an uncanny instinct for your weak spots, your own secret fears and insecurities. Using the power to hurt is *not* a sign of strength. Truly strong people are loving as well. When someone's caustic tongue intimidates you or hurts your feelings, remember to ask yourself, "Why does that remark [or action] lower my self-esteem?" It probably confirms some secret fears or insecurities you have. So you have "bought" the put-down. Often people accuse others of failings that they dislike in their own nature. Or they dislike people who remind them of their own weaknesses. Is that you? Then say to yourself, "I can *choose* my reaction. I *choose* not to be hurt." Change channels; tune it out! Use a visual image of a wall that no one can get over.

If you're on the receiving end, think carefully before you indulge in a sharp put-down. Beware of making a lifelong enemy. Put-downs may be a great short-term satisfaction, but they work best with people you'll never see again. The more elaborate the put-down, the better. Disraeli was once attacked by another peer in Parliament who shouted at him, "Sir, you will either die on the gallows or of a pox!" Lord Beaconsfield replied quietly, "That depends, sir, on whether I embrace your politics or your mistress!"

Another put-down answer, just as effective, is to treat the slap as a compliment: "Please, no flattery!" Americans are not very accomplished at slurs. Probably no group exceeds the virtuosity and range of the Hungarians (famous for blasphemy) or the Irish. The Yiddish language is also rich in expressive put-downs ("May you have a palace with 1,000 rooms and be unhappy in every one of them").

Few of us could think as fast as Mark Twain when a French-man remarked to him, "When an American has nothing else to do, he can always spend a few years trying to find out who his grandfather was."

"That's so," drawled Twain, "and when all other interests pall for a Frenchman, he can always try to find out who his father was."

Many of us think only too late of what we would *like* to have said when someone takes us unawares with a question or a rude remark. A friend told me what she *wished* she'd said when a casual acquaintance surprised her with "Why did your husband leave you?" at a party just after her divorce. "I see," she wished she had remarked, eyeing his rather plump middle, "the only exercise you get is jumping to conclusions!"

If someone catches you off guard, maliciously or not, the first thing to do is breathe deeply and say nothing. That'll keep you from stammering or stumbling while you try to collect your thoughts. Sometimes your silence is enough to abash your questioner. A slight smile gives you an all-knowing air.

Wait at least ten seconds before saying anything (breathing quietly and deeply all the time, gazing calmly at your questioner). It's amazing how often, faced with this kind of composed, smiling silence, people will retreat, mumble apologies, and take you off the hook. If you feel an answer is required after that, you can murmur (smiling, of course), "I never give personal information between 3:00 and 6:00 on alternate Fridays" (or whatever time it happens to be). Don't forget to look your questioner straight in the eye with a pleasant, searching expression.

It's a good idea to write down (as I ask participants in the Charismedia workshop to do) ten questions or remarks that make you uncomfortable and *prepare* your response. Remember: it doesn't necessarily have to answer the question. You're not obliged to answer whatever is thrown at you. It's worth studying diplomats' and politicians' answers and nonanswers to questions. You, too, can give people exactly the kind and amount of information that pleases you.

It's important to discover honestly what kind of question bothers you most. When I work with top executives of large corporations, I ask them to prepare a list of questions that they would find difficult to answer about their business. This is exactly the kind of question a shrewd interviewer or newscaster will seize on. Then we rehearse not only the answers, but the way the executives look and sound. The way you behave when you're answering is crucial. Remember: if there's a conflict between verbal and nonverbal language, it's the nonverbal that's believed! Rehearsal is the key to handling uncomfortable moments well. Nixon looked wonderfully sincere in his "Checkers" speech because he'd rehearsed it thoroughly. Canadians who heard the Nixon-Kennedy debates on radio thought Nixon had won because they didn't *see* him with his giveaway nervousness and shifty-eyed facial expressions. If you don't rehearse, your underlying discomfort at a question will come through and will probably be misinterpreted. Negative messages are almost always, as we have seen, read wrong.

Sometimes a question may seem innocuous to an outsider, but for some reason it bothers you. One young lawyer in my group hated to be asked at a party, "What are you doing?" He had taken a couple of years off after law school to look around, see how he felt about himself and law, survey his options, and get his priorities in order. He sounded apologetic when he told us this. We rehearsed his saying, "I'm very fortunate—I've been doing some private research on projects I'm interested in" until he felt comfortable with that. It was true; he only needed to choose *what* and *how* he wanted to disclose to take the discomfort out of the question.

In a large meeting it's a good idea to repeat the question and address the answer to *other* members of the audience so you don't get trapped in an extended dialogue with one person. In President Carter's town meeting TV chats, he unhesitatingly said, "I don't have the answer to that, but I'll have someone on my staff get back to you with the information."

Another good way of responding is to say, "That's a good [or a very interesting] question," and then go on to make a statement which may or may *not* answer the question.

If it's not appropriate, tell the questioner, "Can we put that aside for now, sir? I'll be happy to discuss that after we've dealt with the agenda before us. Please see me at the end."

A client of mine who had been a political candidate decided not to run, and asked me how to handle his press conference.

The truth was he was fed up with the drubbing he'd gotten from the press during the year on some intrastate matters he'd been involved in. He planned to read a formal statement, which sounded totally impersonal. Yet because he was uncomfortable, he gave the impression he was hiding something!

I asked him to choose a positive statement he could say with conviction—because it was the truth, though not the whole truth: "I have decided not to run now. It seems more important to me to support the candidacy of X——, who has been a superb governor, and devote my energies to the international problems I have been interested in." He felt good about this statement and said it with conviction and authority. It also opened the door to a job appointment which he preferred. He avoided having to air his rancor against the press, which would have been disastrous. And he maintained his image of a dynamic pubic figure who knew what he was about and who could be trusted to take steps in the public interest as well as his own.

If you do decide you want (or should) answer a question you're being asked, there are many ways to do it. Choose an answer you're comfortable with and practice saying it with pleasant authority. A flip answer has to be unusually good keep the questioner at bay. If it's a question about your age (and most women don't like to answer that after thirty), you can (a) lie, (b) say "old enough."

1. not to answer questions when I don't want to."
2. to have accomplished such and such—or to have a grown daughter and son."
3. to know I am still growing."

Barbara Marx Hubbard said, "The older I get, the newer I feel." (But then she announced she was forty-nine.) I sometimes say, "Younger than I was ten years ago." Which is true! (c) Say, with a smile, "What an indelicate question!" and *say no more.* (d) Do a really elaborate variant on "I only answer questions like that on alternate Shrove Tuesdays in Leap Year!"

The elderly and very feisty mother of a client deliberately shaved ten years off her age (which was ninety-three) when she went in to the hospital, because, she said, "They treat you better if they think you're younger."

Lies are, of course, invariably risky, but reconceptualizing information is not only legitimate but necessary. One executive said that when he only had a shipping clerk's experience he had told interviewers that he had "been in charge of production supplies" for his company. Look for the positive components of your work (they may not have been included in you title) and add those to your statement. This will also give you a more positive feeling about your qualifications.

Ronnie Eldridge, then Special Assistant to the Mayor of New York, said that most women whose main life experience has been running a household, don't realize that they have had most of the experience necessary to run government: handling budgets, supplies, personnel, inventory, etc. Many women, returning to work after having raised a family feel apologetic about their "lack of qualifications."

> **Practice in answering "difficult" questions will help you meet the world with confidence and present the image you want.**

Write down the questions you find most difficult or unpleasant to answer, then the put-downs you most dislike:

	Tough Questions	Uncomfortable Put-Downs
1.		
2.		
3.		
4.		
5.		
6.		
7.		
8.		
9.		
10.		
(etc.)		

Now *choose* your responses by asking:

1. How much do I want to disclose?
2. Do I want to answer the question or just appear to?
3. Can I state what I want to tell people in a positive, confident way, feeling good about it?

4. How can I phrase the facts I want to disclose in a positive, confident way, telling some but not too much? (Now practice aloud.)
5. Does it sound convincing when I rehearse it out loud? (This is very important! Rehearse until it does. Try it with a friend or supportive relative.)
6. Does this question require any answer at all?
7. If not, what responses can I prepare that will cover all contingencies?

Jackie R. hated to go home to Ohio because her mother and father were not interested in her career. They kept asking, "When are you getting married? Your cousins are all married!" Exploring how she felt, using the above list of questions, she decided she didn't want to explain or defend her life or why she had no intention of getting married in the near future. I suggested she address herself to their well-meaning concern for her, while side-stepping the question. (You don't have to join other people's games if you don't like the game!)

She practiced saying "Dad, Mom, I appreciate your concern. I know you want me to be happy. Right now, things are going very well. I'll certainly let you know when I plan to make any changes. You must trust me to make the right decisions about my life."

It might not be necessary or desirable to say *all* this at once. The first sentence or two might be enough. But Jackie's attitude had changed. Again, as in the antagonism situation, it's not the issues you address; it's the attitudes. If you can appreciate and acknowledge someone's concern, your own response is apt to be non-defensive and hence more satisfying. Nobody like to JUSTIFY himself—and w don't *have* to. Instead of accepting terms that are not your own, you can bring people onto your turf. They may find it unfamiiar and bewildering, but you'll be a lot happier and avoid unnecessary conflict.

When Jackie went back to Ohio after rehearsing the confrontation with her parents, she had the happiest visit in years. As in all truly productive conflict solutions, EVERYBODY was happier. They didn't get an answer to their question (which was rhetorical anyway), but they felt she appreciated their concern about her and she didn't blow up as she usually did. The whole visit was a great success. They even promised to visit her in New York and expressed interest in her career for the first time.

What if a question is less benign? Often we think a question is meant as a put-down merely because we feel uncomfortable about it. A small part of you may feel guilty when faced with the accusing question "Why aren't you married?" or "Have you had enough experience for this job?" or "Why haven't you called me?" Suppose you're worried about your weight. A friend says, "I love your dress! You really have to have a good figure to wear a dress like that!" That may sound like a put-down to you even if none was intended.

If it *was* intended, don't inhale! All chronic put-downers suffer from low self-esteem, though their arrogance often fools people. Since negativism is a communicable "dis-ease," a common way of shoring up group and individual insecurities is to indulge in cruel banter, racial jokes, and mean gibes. Allowing such remarks to pass is tacit encouragement. "Say, that's pretty unkind" or "That sound rather bigoted!" will call other people's attention to the slur and often elicits a hasty denial or even an apology. People may derive satisfaction from being nasty or prejudiced, but they don't want to be perceived that way. Low-key social pressure can fight prejudice and put-downs by saying clearly that they *aren't* all right. By the same token, avoid denunciation of the critic; your objection is to the behavior, not the critic—a person always has the potential to learn.

If a remark wounded you, observe that you're hurt, even if it's only a slight, stabbing pain. Repeat your "comfort sentence" to yourself immediately: "I am a worthwhile person; nothing anyone can say can diminish my true value." Next, ask yourself if the put-downer feels threatened by or envious of you!

Marlin P., a young artist, complained that his boss often made remarks like, "You could never make it freelance!" or "Why can't you get along with anybody?" even though Marlin's talent was generally admired and he got along well with people. I asked Marlin, "Does your boss feel threatened by you?" After thinking about it for a bit, Marlin answered, "Yes, I guess maybe he does. He knows he's not as talented as I am, or as young, and he thinks I want his job." Knowing why others feel threatened by you helps take the sting out of their put-downs. You may have to shore up their self-esteem or have some good responses ready—or both.

In a Charismedia group, I asked people to practice attacking a fellow student so that the "victims" could sharpen their responses. One man said to a pretty young student, "Why do you wear dark glasses all the time? To hide your sexuality?" At first she was terribly flustered by his question. I suggested that she practice turning the question back on the questioner. With a wide-eyed, innocent look, she turned to him and said, "Oh! Really? What makes you think that?" The attacker stammered, suddenly put on the spot by his own question. Now *he* sounded suspect. This technique of repeating the question can gain time and catch the questioer off guard. When you seriously call the question into question (without appearing resentful) the spotlight is turned on the person who asked it, and you may never have to answer the question at all! Again, the principle is: don't play other people's games if you don't want to!

You can also answer with a wild exaggeration. If someone were to ask (unforgivably) how much money you make, a flippant response is in order: "Well, I've decided not to buy the Koh-i-noor diamond this year!" or you might prefer to give a sober but evasive answer: "Well, I can't complain, but, these days, with inflation, money just isn't worth what it was." You have to decide exacty what shade of impression you want to convey. A well-known author told of going as a little boy to buy clothes with his mother, who dressed him in his worst to look poorer—so that she could bargain better with the storekeeper.

Seeming to answer while giving very little real information is an art familiar to every political figure. Watch "Meet the Press" or "Face the Nation" on television, and observe political statements in the news with an appreciative eye for old and new effective ploys. Different levels of disclosure are appropriate for each situation. You don't have to "tell all" to an interviewer or casual acquaintance. The head of a leading executive search firm told me that women reentering the job market tend to tell too much in a job interview, as though talking to a personal friend. As we way earlier, if you share your feeling fully with someone or with your private journal, then you can decide how much or how little to tell a stranger, and exactly how you want to do it.

One of the secrets of good communication is judging how much the person you're talking to needs to hear and can take in. Lynn S. needed a ride home because of trouble with her car. When she met a fellow teacher in the hall, though they had only five minutes between classes, she went into a long story about her day's misfortunes before asking her question. All she had needed to say was: "Could you give a lift home? My car broke down."

Make your own Commonplace Book where you collect the uncommon, quotable sayings, aphorisms, observations of the great and near-great or unknown. Collect the most entertaining and effective put-downs you come across. You may never use them, but it gives you a pleasant glow of security to know you can if you choose. They will also help you use *humor*, which takes the sting out of most put-downs and keeps you from sounding angry and losing face. Every barb should be accompanied by a smile. The Chinese assert that the first person to become angry has run out of arguments and has lost face. Certainly, when you remain calm and unruffled, you seem much less vulnerable to attack.

If a put-down is powerful, it often outlives the relationship that triggered it. One of the oldest is attributed to Heraclitus. When a nobleman sneered at him for his low birth, Heraclitus replied, "The difference between us is that your family ends with you and mine begins with me." In the same vein, when the renown artist, Whistler, was asked by a snob in a London drawing room how he had come to be born in such a nondescript town as Lowell, MA, he answered simply "I wanted to be close to my mother."

Adlai Stevenson, who enjoyed needling other politicians, was once annoyed by a man from California. Stevenson said, "He is the only man I know who could chop down a giant sequoia, then stand on the stump and deliver a speech on conservation." (The beauty of that denunciation is its extravagantly fantasied scenario.)

Dr. Reinhold Aman, who edits *Maledicta, the International Journal of Verbal Aggression*, claims that the art of cursing is socially important—as it releases pent-up emotions without violence! He says, "Insults should be aimed at behavior, something a person can change": "When I see you," he told his department chairman, "my feet fall asleep." (He had already been fired, so he had nothing to lose!)

The art of hyperbole is very useful, but practice flexing it on yourself rather than jumping to put down others. Nine times out of ten there's a better way. Making other people look foolish is a dangerous game. Most people can never forget a really telling slur, nor forgive the perpetrator—especially if it holds the victim up to

194

tease, ask yourself or the tease-ees if you're causing pain. Ask yourself how you would like being on the receiving end!

Knowing your feelings, acknowledging them, and taking appropriate action to express them in ways that you want to are essential to your charisma. If you never insult anybody, practice inventing the most imaginative insults you can, simply to flex you creative imagination. *Don't* unleash them on the people who bother you!

Using images always gives a powerful boost to your persuasion power. Practice finding images for describing qualities that annoy you, trouble you, or delight you. Successful communicators do this almost automatically. Warning me about a talk show host who flitted from topic to topic in a maddening way, a writer told me, "He has the attention span of a spastic dragonfly!"

Keep notes on particularly effective images
that you hear or read.

Sometimes putting *yourself* down, ruefully and without gravity, can be very disarming. I cherish an early remark my then-husband made about me. "You're the only person I know," he said lovingly, "who can eat ice cream in bed and make crumbs!"

In the happy event you're deluged with compliments, lightening the weight of all those tributes with a little humor makes everybody more comfortable. Again, it's a question of balance.

Don't Duck the Flowers

"I'm always uncomfortable when people say nice things to me." "I usually mistrust people who pay me compliments. . . ." When I ask in Charismedia workshops, "How many people find it hard to accept compliments?" most people raise their hands. Nearly everybody sometimes enjoys admiration, but if you were brought up to be "modest" and self-deprecating, naturally you were also supposed to pretend you were unworthy of compliments, or, worse, you actually feel you are. All this makes it very difficult to accept compliments gracefully.

Does it matter? Yes! If you don't accept with pleasure, the complimenter feels pretty foolish or even put down, as though you had refused a gift or, worse, questioned his judgment or taste. Which in a way you have!

How many times have you heard someone say, in response to a compliment about appearance or dress: "Oh, this old thing!? or "It only cost $2.98" or "It's dirty!" or "Really? *I* think I look terrible! Or the other person hastily compliments you back. In many cultures, a half-buried superstitious fear of attracting the "evil eye" dictates a modest disclaimer. Most Europeans and Orientals would consider a response like "I like it too" immodest and possibly arrogant. (It's also dangerous to admire something too effusively in a Chinese home—hospitality would demand that your host give you the admired object!) Many people also fear envy and jealousy implied in flattery. The Greek idea of "hubris," or overweening pride or arrogance, suggests a disastrous fall awaits those who are too pleased with themselves.

Gift giving is often a power play that leaves the recipient at a disadvantage—in the giver's debt. Someone says to you, "Gee you look great!" You notice he or she is not looking so well; nevertheless you hasten to respond, "You're looking wonderful too!" feeling like a shabby hypocrite.

Resist the impulse to give back the compliment as though it were a bomb that might go off if you held on to it. "I appreciate that" or a simple, smiling "Thank you" or "You're very kind" or "That's nice to hear" are better. And . . .

Don't worry about deserving the compliment.

There is a rough justice in human affairs. You'll probably find things you deserved recognition for are sometimes overlooked, so you can aford to accept an undeserved compliment once in a while.

Sometimes people will value an action or remark that you take completely for granted. "It was so wonderful of you not to call attention to the fact that I was fifteen minutes early for my first appointment," a client remarked to me once. I was surprised that she found this "wonderful," but for some reason of her own, it was important to her.

Some compliments may be so effusive they surprise you ("It was wonderful of you to come—you made the party!) Although you don't need to agree with equal effusion, you should accept such compliments simply and gracefully. Although they may be part of a social ritual, they are not necessarily insincere.

If you *need* constant praise to keep going, your basic self-esteem is dangerously low. Ideally, neither praise nor blame should determine your life-path. In practice, most people need a fair amount of encouragement. *Too much* can boomerang. Tell a child he's "wonderful" and he'll promptly pull his little sister's hair or do some other mischief to prevent your having such unrealistic notions. Serves you right for putting an unfair burden of expectation on him!

The Art of Giving Compliments

> I can live on a really good compliment
> for months!   —MARK TWAIN

Compliment giving, like other gentle arts, has suffered a considerable decline since Twain's time. Maybe that's why, in this anxious age, people need more of them to achieve the same sustaining effect. A really good compliment shows a subtle appreciation of the person you admire. When you can praise a quality or action that the person values, too, you have enhanced creativity and self-image.

**Appreciate—Acknowledge—Absorb,
not only your own by others' good qualities**

This is the nurturing ground of further growth and development. In an era of increasing consumption choices, there is simply too much going on to keep track of without help. Critics offer a consumers' guide in the commercial jungle, but the critical attitude itself creates divisions and rifts. If "ugh" and "wow!" are your usual responses, you're missing a whole range of reactions in between.

*What five things would you like people to think or say of you?
Which five compliments do you dislike the most?*

Consider your motives for chosing each one.

It used to be said that a beautiful woman wants to be admired for her brains and a brainy one for her beauty. This was before we realized that brains and beauty are not mutually exclusive!

Sometimes a bouquet can masquerade as a barb. Paul Tabori, the Hungarian-English writer and humorist, was a great humanitarian. Always quietly helping the steady stream of exiled writers and artists who fled to London and New York to escape tyranny of one kind or another. So the word went out: "Don't go to see Paul—he'll get you a job!"

Don't compliment someone on the obvious. It's almost insulting to gush, "You have a lovely voice!" to a great singer or "You're so talented!" to a recognized artist. The more detailed and specific you make your points of admiration, the more valid and appreciatd it will be.

"I love the way you phrased that final section in the Mozart!"

"You have redefined that piece for me!"

Your handling of irony is masterful, especially in the 'bird-dog' story!"

"I've never been so moved by a performance of _____"

"You handled that situation with a great deal of tact."

"I liked the way you presented your points in that paper."

Informed appreciation is rare and treasurable. I once called a researcher who did the fact-checking for an article about my work in a major magazine to thank her for the accuracy of her reporting. She said, "Oh, I can't tell you how much I appreciate this! Nobody ever notices what I do since I don't have a by-line. This is the first time anybody's called to thank me."

When you praise a child, be just as specific: "I like the way that line curves down the apge; you used interesting colors." "I admire your backhand; you get a good swing to the racket."

A good compliment gives insight and warmth, and is, therefore, a real gift. In our Charismedia workshops, I ask each person to hear compliments in turn from each of the group. Everybody is asked to offer each person something valid and positive. Even though people have to come up with something different from the coments of others who preceded them, it's remarkable that everybody is *able* to find *something*, given a few guidelines. "Don't waste time on trivia like items of clothing," I caution them when somebody says something like "I like your tie!" "Stick to appreciation that is meaningful, even if it's slight or elusive." Forced to make distinctions, people come up with subtle and valuable messages that they otherwise might not have hunted for. like: "I really appreciate your warmth in sharing with the group; you always have an insightful comment." Or "I learned a lot from listening to you." Or "I enjoy the little half-smile with which you tell us something new." Often warmth and helful feedback might otherwise never have been expressed.

The habit of defining what you appreciate,
like describing your image flow, sharpens you pleasure and
stimulates the very qualities you admire.

Everybody learns from feedback and what we nourish develops, positive or negative.

Try expanding your vocabulary; learn a new word every other day. the richer your appreciation of language, the more eloquent and articulate you can be. Those are important aspects of charisma.

In general, our culture encourages us to express negatives more freely than positives. "I wish I had told him I loved him!" Rosalind L. sobbed about her father who had died suddenly. "I never did! And now I'll never be able to!" Many people find it hard to express their true feelings of love and appreciation to those they love most.

If you want to correct or improve a student, employee, friend, or colleague's performance, give positive feedback *first*, before criticizing. And don't say *but!*

"You did a good job—*but* it could have been more thorough."

Better: "Your points were excellent—on the rewrite it would be good to add more detail to points 6, 9 and 12."

One of the most frequent complaints in business and academia is "I don't know what my boss wants! He never tell me when I'm doing well!" Expressing positive feelings is related to giving honest and constructive compliments. Both can be deeply satisfying and enhance your relationships and the quality of your life. Earlier you saw

> how important it is to give positive feedback to yourself. *Giving it to others and being able to accept it ungrudgingly from them is the other side of the coin!*

The increased flow of information and warmth provides the foundation and energy for improved communication. New and unexpected things begin to happen. People who are energized act more creatively in their own lives and begin to interact in more life-enhancing ways. You raise the energy level, and your own charisma quotient shoots up when you exercise your capability to voice positive and valid perceptions about other people and to accept theirs about you.

9

Anger: Fire in Your Boiler Room

WHAT ABOUT YOUR ANGER? Is there any value in it? How do you use it productively? How do you keep from hurting yourself and other people with it?

> Anger is a brief madness.
> —HORACE

On the other hand:

> Anger is one of the sinews of the soul; he that wants it hath a maimed mind.
> —THOMAS FULLER
> (1608–1661)

> Anger makes dull men witty, but it keeps them poor.
> —attributed by Sir Francis Bacon to QUEEN ELIZABETH I

Everybody gets angry now and then, except some very advanced souls who have outgrown it. Often people were brought up with very conflicting messages about anger. Mostly it's: "If you get angry, you're bad." The unspoken part is: "Only we parents can get angry—you children must not!" Other messages: "Anger means hatred." "Anger means you don't love me."

My students tell me: "It's more manly to get angry than to cry and show I'm hurt." "When I get very angry, I burst into tears." "Anger is frightening. I'll do anything to avoid it." "When I get angry, watch out. I let it out on anybody and everybody around me. I have a short fuse, but that way I'll never get an ulcer!"

Anger's two powerful components are: information and energy. When people deny their anger because they don't approve of getting angry at all, they lose contact with the information as well as the energy. Depression very often is anger turned inward. Depression is immobilizing, unproductive, and painful. Often people don't know why they're depressed because they have successfully hidden the messages in their anger, even from themselves.

Some people think "positive thoughts" on the conscious level, although underneath they are experiencing fear, anger, and conflict. Nobody is fooled except the person himself/herself.

Anna A. came into class one day after having been beaten by her husband. In a high thin voice she said, "He can't help himself—but I'm not angry at him; I just want to help him." Her hands twisted a handkerchief and her knuckles were white (as though she were wringing his neck) but she was unaware of her real feelings because she was determined to have only "positive" thoughts. Her anger was clear to everybody in the room, but her voice was flat, colorless, *unconvincing*.

Denying your true feelings robs you of your charisma. Your feelings, perceptions, and experience are the gifts that comprise the inner landscape of your soul. Real feelings, no matter how negative, are better than sham ones. If you think of emotions as clouds passing across the sky or waves across the sea, you can allow yourself to flow with the negative feelings so they can become new feelings that may be quite different.

If you're keeping your Anti-Judgmental Notebook, you'll be able to spot your anger and begin to observe it with detachment. ("Oh, I feel so angry—isn't that interesting!") The next question is: If you're not going to deny it, what do you do with it? It's like a hand grenade that people toss gingerly from hand to hand until it explodes. Obviously that's not a very satisfactory way of dealing with hand grenades or anger. Innocent people get blown away.

"Damn him, why does he treat me like this? I'm a person, can't he realize that?" "My wife is always cutting me down in public. I could kill her." "Man, you touch my things, and you won't know what hit you!"

Anger and hurt usually *want* something. Dissonance—as in music—yearns for resolution. Angry people often think they want revenge, but their real *need* is deeper—to protect or affirm their sense of dignity, self, or value as a person or that of others (as in a social reformer). An angry person *can* be charismatic, if the level of intensity and emotional power meshes with others' needs.

Demagogues like Hitler, Stalin, Napoleon, Joseph McCarthy, even Lumumba, voiced the rage and fear of the masses they addressed. The "angry young man" of John Osborne's plays, the brooding intensity of James Dean and Marlon Brando, touched some responsive chord in audiences for whom they personified larger-than-life feelings. Even now they exert an enduring fascination.

Anger can be a constructive spur to social and political reform and personal growth—if the energy is not short-circuited by fear. But if you don't examine your feelings you may be completely in the dark as to what they really are. The Important Question: *Are you running your anger or is it running you?*

If you must get angry, make it a *conscious* decision on your part. Then, as Shyam Bhatnagar, the eminent yogi, says, "You will be ANGRY, not ANGER." Words are potent weapons, so when you use them to fight, *do not hit below the belt*. Avoid vicious, bitter remarks that may boomerang or scar people for life.

You can probably remember idle or deliberately cruel words that were hurled at you once and penetrated so deep that you'll never forget them. There is no way to take back or un-say words like, "You'll never amount to anything!" "You're stupid!" "You're ugly!" "I never loved you!" "I never wanted you—I wish you'd never been born," or "Your sister doesn't do half as much for me as you do, but I love her more." From the time she was nine, a fifty-year-old woman has never been able to sing, even for her own pleasure, since a teacher pointed to her in choir practice and said, "You! Listener!" and sent her to the back of the room where she was not allowed to sing.

The desire to harm someone you're angry at eats you up inside. When you take responsibility for dealing with (and dissolving) your own anger, the desire for revenge will fade.

HOW TO LENGTHEN A SHORT FUSE

In personal life, continual anger is likely to be an explosive turn-off. If you are always simmering or "on a short fuse," people may be afraid of you or avoid you.

"I haven't had any tantrums this week," reported Marie, very pleased with herself. "I did the long, deep breathing, and did not explode once. That was a good feeling. Even though my life was not so great, I handled it very well. I felt power and control because I used my anger in a more productive way than usual. My nineteen-year-old son called long distance to tell me he was thrown into the brig in the Marines. Instead of yelling at him, I was able to talk calmly to him. To my surprise he admitted he was at fault—something he's never done before. I could tell he respected me more because I didn't yell."

Some people constantly "blow up"—their rages are an attempt to prove to themselves that they're not weak and fearful. Underneath, like Aileen or Marie, they may really be terrified of losing love and respect; feel compelled to hang on to their possessions, for fear of being left like a turtle without its shell, intolerably vulnerable. The yelling is a "Don't step on me" message that says: "I exist. I *have* to yell to prove it to myself and you."

"I don't get ulcers—I give them," declared one corporate giant proudly. Another successful but inwardly frightened businessman was extravagantly generous with his employees. He bought them all health club memberships and raised their salaries far beyond the norm for the jobs, but periodically he raged irrationally at his colleagues and his children. People never knew what to expect from him. He could be charming, perceptive, and gentle one moment, a furious tyrant the next. He was a fiercely competitive striver, who needed to earn more and more to assure himself of his own worth. No matter how much money he earned, he didn't feel safe.

Disproportionate anger in his case was (as it often is) a sign of inward panic, weakness, and fear which he managed to disguise most of the time in frenzied activity. Some people, you'll have noticed, yell deliberately, as a strategy. It's one thing to decide to get angry, quite another to find yourself out of control.

If there is a raging authority figure in your life, it may help to remember the next time he/she screams and yells that those may well be cries of pain and insecurity. ("If I don't yell, nobody will listen to me.") Real authority doesn't need to rant and rave to make itself felt.

John C., who came into the group to learn to communicate better, admitted that periodically he would get drunk, yell at his children, and furiously break everything in sight. "I don't know whether I drink because I'm angry or whether I get angry because I drink," he said sheepishly.

I asked him to keep a Judgmental Notebook and for a week to put down all his feelings whenever he became aware of them. At the end of the week, he realized with amazement that what he was feeling most of the time was not anger but fear. Once he had discovered this, he no longer had to drink and break things. He could begin to confront his real problems.

Lee M., a paddle tennis champion, came to class one day very discouraged. "I got so angry this week, I really behaved like a bitch," she said sadly. "First I grabbed the phone from my eighteen-year-old son and yelled at the travel agent, who had screwed up reservations for the fifth time. I was afraid Timmy wouldn't get back to school on time. But I shouldn't have grabbed the phone. I apologized to Timmy later. Then the next morning, in the airport, the clerk was having trouble with the computer, charging my reservation. So I said, thinking it would help her out, 'Oh, I'll pay cash for it.' Then she snapped at me, 'Well, you might have told me before!' I yelled back at her. 'You're supposed to be a service person; you don't have to be rude! Now you just void that ticket!'" Lee looked mournful. "I'm ashamed of myself. I don't know what got into me. But I just couldn't help myself; I felt so furious!"

Jason R., an architect, reported, "I yelled at an associate in my office yesterday. He does everything possible to be uncooperative. I completely lost my temper. Now, of course, everything is much worse."

Whatever the trigger for your anger, if you want to deal with it productively, it's important to separate the information from the energy. First, take responsibility for feeling angry. Recognize that whatever someone else does, it's *your* anger. There will always be negative and annoying people around! *You* must decide what to do with it. An explosion may cause irreparable damage to others and repression may hurt *you*. (Such illnesses as arthritis and ulcers are now correlated with repressed anger. As we saw earlier, what your mind won't recognize, your body will internalize and may express in the form of illness, injury, or disease.)

Often people find that a series of little irritations and unnoticed anxieties build up until a tiny incident (as with Lee) suddenly produces an unexpected explosion. Many of us have a backlog of unexpressed angers simmering just below the surface. Your cholesterol level goes up, your heart races, all the stress hormones are pouring into your bloodstream, lactic acid builds up in the muscles. WHAT ARE YOU GOING TO DO WITH ALL THAT?

Next, separate the information from the feelings before responding to the situation. It's not easy. But since neither an explosion at the person who triggered your fury nor repression is a good idea, you need other ways of releasing the anger so you can discharge the stress buildup and begin to think coolly. As long as there's "blood in your eye," it's like trying suddenly to reverse a car going ninety miles an hour without going into neutral first. You'll strip the gears and maybe wreck the car!

We've all seen children get angry, blow up, yell, and five minutes later go back to happily playing together. Somewhere on the way to adulthood, we're taught to dissynchronize the free expression of anger. What was once a total release through voice, body, and speech becomes a strained, painful double bind. Part of you says "Let go!" The other part commands "Hold back!" I devised the hostility exercises to reintegrate our original happy coordination of body, thoughts, voice, and feelings and safely discharge all that massive buildup of anger not *at* anyone else, but privately, where no one can be hurt by it.

Strangely, to obtain relief from angry feelings it's neither desirable nor necessary to vent them on the people who triggered them. We get the same satisfaction from physically and vocally discharging rage with nobody present (though at first this may feel foolish). The first impulse of an angry person is to get back at the "enemy," but it's seldom the action we take on cool reflection. The hostility exercises give you a safe, swift release for the powerful anger buildup, so you can shift to neutral and decide exactly *how* you want to handle the problem in a way that will be most effective and satisfying. It's impossible to make the best decision until you've acknowledged and released your feelings offstage, away from the conflict.

What to Do:

Close the door to your room and warn your family you're going to make some weird noises and not to worry! If you're concerned about what the neighbors will say, put some loud music on or turn up the TV set to drown out your yelling.

1. THE PILLOW POUNDER

Put a couple of heavy sofa pillows on the floor or stand next to a firm bed. Inhale, raise your arms as high as possible so you feel the stretch all the way down to your stomach. Then bring your fists down as powerfully as possible while you bend your knees and yell "*EEEEEYuhhhhh!*" Keep your throat open and relaxed. Do this five to fifteen times, or more if you like, as powerfully as possible. Consciously direct your fury downward through your fists with your full force.

2. THE TENNIS RACKET RUMBLE

Take a tennis racket and beat the bed as powerfully as you can, again and again, making a loud noise (it should come from your gut) each time you deliver a blow. Use all your anger as energy and hit the bed as hard as you can.

3. VAH! SHAH! AGGRESSION RELEASE

Stand with knees slightly bent, feet apart, and shout or whisper, "VAH! SHAH! VAH! SHAH! VAH! SHAH! VAH! SHAH!" jabbing fiercely with your fists on each word, as short, sharp, and intense as you can make it. Do this twenty-six times.

4. BEAT 'EM UP BAT

If you don't have a tennis racket, roll up newspapers very tightly or use a cardboard mailing tube and GO!

5. TANTRUM

Lie on the bed or floor and pound your legs, fists, and feet continuously, yelling exactly like a small, angry child.

6. THE RUNNING-IN-PLACE PRESSURE RELEASE

Lean forward onto a desk, arms extended, and run in place five to ten minutes, making noises. Hold your breath ten to twenty counts (one per second), then release. (Don't do this if you have high blood pressure.)

7. THE HOSTILITY EXERCISE—"YOU BASTARD!"

If you hate to use the word *bastard*, you can substitute *rat*, which doesn't have quite the same lilt, but at least has the same open sound for the first syllable. Draw it out as long as possible with throat open

```
YOU   U    U    U    U    _____RRRA
A     A    A    TT!
```

Stand with feet firmly planted, about as wide as your shoulders, knees a trifle bent (to give you a good grip on the floor). Relax your hands at your sides, and begin to swing your arms up together in an arc, like a golf swing, from left to right. Practice a few times (bending your knees as you swing), swinging as high and free as you can. Breathe IN on the first swing to the left (mouth closed). Exhale on the second swing to the right, inhale (with mouth open) on the third swing to the left. THEN (after this three-swing preparation) on the fourth swing (right) shout as loud and as long as possible:

```
YOU   U    U    U   U B   AAA   A    A    A
S   -TARD!
```

(fourth swing	(fifth swing	(on a long exhale)
right)	left)	

Begin the whole sequence again with the three-swing preparation (inhale–exhale–inhale). Then

YOU U   U   U   U   B   AAA   A   A   A
S   -TARD!

(swing right) _ (swing left)

Repeat sequence at least ten times.
Important! Notice whether the sound of your voice is completely
coordinated with your body as you swing from one side to the
other. Stamp your foot for emphasis exactly at the top of the swing
when you say the word. Be sure to get everything working together. You may notice that you're holding back by tightening
your stomach or squeezing your throat. Or the words tumble out
before or after you stamp or have swung your arms. Make the
sound come from as deep as possible. Keep your throat totally
open and unconstricted and hurl it at the next block or at the
horizon. It's surprisingly tricky to coordinate. Any discoordina-
tion between the sound, the breath, the body, and the words will
weaken the anger release. To get the full benefit of this powerful
discharge it's all got to work together. Because so many mixed
messages about expressing anger were dinned into us as children,
we dilute the expression of our feelings by not letting everything
go at the same time (something we all knew how to do as
children). You may find you're stopping your breath between the
words *you* and *bastard*. It should run smoothly, one into the
other. Or you may stamp your foot before you say the word.
Once you get into the swing of it, you'll find it a lot of fun and
extremely satisfying. Make sure everything is happening *together*. (It can be startling for outsiders. Once at a large workshop, sixty people were all shouting "You bastard!" together
when the door opened. It was too late to stop a delegation of
Japanese teachers politely waiting to observe the class. They
looked a trifle stunned as they received the full brunt of sixty
enthusiastic people hurling "Youuuuu baaaaaastard!" in their
direction.)

Concentrating on the physical coordination focuses directly on
the release mechanism and bypasses the frustration of "stuckness"
that primal screaming or uncontrolled angry yelling produces.
Giving in to sheer fury can make us shake with bottomless, seem-
ingly endless spasms that often swell and intensify until we're
drained and *still not* satisfied. The advantage of the consciously

controlled release is that you feel the satisfaction of *directing* your most powerful negative feelings in a purposeful way toward maximum psychophysical release. Perhaps one reason why uncontrolled screaming anger is so upsetting is that it utilizes the same tight, only *partially* realized patterns of release that kept residual anger trapped in your body so long. In addition, focusing on the resentment content of rage feeds it further. The hostility exercises acknowledge the feelings and then concentrate your energy on achieving a complete body/voice/feeling release. The emphasis is not on outside factors (people or situations that "made you" angry) but on taking responsibility for discharging the anger and freeing the mind and body for other emotions. That's why the hostility exercises should be followed by the Anger Transformer (see p. 334) and the Great Wow!

THE GREAT WOW!

Crouch down near the floor. Begin very small and gradually increase the size and volume of your "wow." Think of it as excitement, anticipation, and pleasure. Take the adrenaline that you have released through the hostility exercises, and use it for joyous, uninhibited expression. (This completes the cycle of emotional transformation—from anger to celebration.) This transformation is crucial so you won't get trapped in an ascending spiral of escalating negative feelings.

The first "wow" is quiet, almost a whisper, with your hands opened out, palms away from you as you say the word. The second one is bigger, though still not voiced. The energy is increasing—all the "wows" are lyrically extended as though you were exclaiming at some great natural marvel: a mountaintop, a waterfall, a volcanic explosion. Do eight "wows," progressively louder and larger both with voice and body. The last shout is accompanied by a triumphant leap into the air, as high as you can. Shout as loud as you can make it, arms flung overhead, face upturned to the sky.

Some people frighten themselves the first time they hear their full voices and feel their bodies, breaths, and voices released all at once. Then an enormous exhilaration sets in; there's always a lot of laughter. People often feel silly at first. Invariably they find it's tremendously cathartic as well as a lot of fun. Lee said, "Oh, boy, for the first time all week I really feel I got my anger out. I feel tremendously energized. I was so tired when I came in!" Jason used a cardboard tube at the office after everybody had gone home the next time a problem came up with his associate. After he had whacked it so hard that it fell apart, he felt freed of his anger. Then he came up with a plan to give the other man more responsibility and at the same time remove him from a heavy traffic area where he grated on other people's nerves. Because Jason now felt "clear," he could present this arrangement neutrally, without anger, and the other man was satisfied, too.

May L. said she was able to assert herself quietly but firmly with her boss for the first time. "He listened to me," she said proudly. "I was neither overbearing nor tearful and apologetic; I got my points across."

Louis M., an advertising executive, did the hostility exercises in the men's room after running into a problem with the printer who hadn't completed a job the way he was supposed to. Having released his anger in the men's room,* Louis was able to communicate more information about the urgency of the job and the distress he felt that it wasn't up to standard. In an unprecedented move, the printer offered to do the whole thing over again for nothing. "That *never* would have happened before," Louis reported in amazement.

Callie O., who had a demanding, manipulative mother, was able, after doing the "You Bastard!" exercise, to smile and stand her ground when her mother began her usual entreaties and manipulations. She felt calm, amused, and in control instead of dissolving in tears or giving in as she usually did and getting a migraine headache.

At the end of the Charismedia course people often remark that this single exercise did more for them than any other. One man whom I had despaired of helping because he seemed very withdrawn and not particularly bright or articulate told us in his final group speech what the hostility exercises had done for him. "I can dance for the first time in my life! I was always too self-

---

* Since there were people around he used the Karate Chop, Vah Shah, and the Steam Engine to discharge anger, so no one heard him.

conscious before. Now I go disco dancing with my wife and she is delighted." This breakthrough had other effects. When we shared a group panel show, he turned out unexpectedly to be the wittiest member of the panel. I could hardly believe he was the same person.

To get the maximum mileage from the "You Bastard!" exercise, make sure your arms are very relaxed when they swing way up to the side. One woman objected that doing it in slow motion felt too "dancelike" to release her anger. I had suggested slow motion to help people release the tension in their arms. I added, "Then please intensify the momentum each time, so it *won't* feel lyrical. What would give you the right feeling?" I asked her. She thought a moment and said, "Getting ready for a pillow fight!" And she swung her arms in exactly the right free and easy full swing to the sides.

The power of an image is always the best way to get the information into your body. Then I realized that any completely expressed movement, if done very slowly but in continuous slow motion, will look dancelike and smooth! A discontinuous, jerky, or spastic motion won't. Take a great batter's swing or Kareem Abdul-Jabbar's leap for a basket or Jack Nicklaus's golf swing, show them in slow motion, and you'll see a dance, unmistakably liquid and molten.

When you've been able to use the hostility exercises to release your anger, recent and stored up, all the energy that was locked in your muscles and tense body will be available to you. If you want to use your anger productively when you're addressing a large or small group, your voice will be strong, vibrant, and sure. Your mind will be clear. The right words will be yours without effort. You will *choose* the way you express your anger (if you decide to) for maximum effect, instead of being shaken by it the way a bone is shaken by a dog. An interesting side effect is that your voice will become more varied, expressive, and energetic.

I've observed that people with monotonous voices have invariably been conditioned to repress anger. Not only is the negative side of their feelings unexpressed, but the positive feelings too. It's as though when some strong feeling is disapproved of, we unconsciously protect ourselves from criticism by hiding *all* strong feelings, including the positive ones. We lose the natural responsiveness of our voice to our feelings. To recover childhood's full spectrum of pleasurable expression, it's important to hear and experience yourself voicing those once-disapproved-of negative emotions. Given permission to express the least acceptable of feelings, the rest of the rich spectrum of tonally varied emotions is again available.

Then and only then is the sound of your feelings the sound of music, with all the richness, variety, and color of your full emotional range—your charisma.

10

The Feelings of Your Sounds

> For there is music wherever there
> is a harmony, order, or proportion:
> and thus far we may maintain the
> music of the spheres.
> — THOMAS BROWN

SOUND, which creates worlds, can draw people to you, enlarge your personal charisma. Its effect can be compelling, dramatic, as if when you vibrate to a certain wavelength, you irresistibly attract people.

"Yes, but aren't you born with whatever voice you have?" you ask. Yes and No! Most people do not really use the full power and range of their speaking voices. Strangely, this is even true for opera singers, whose singing voices are often so much richer and more interesting than their speaking voices that it's hard to guess it's the same person.

In my course for young singers and the Manhattan School of Music in New York (which I half whimsically entitled How to Act Although Singing), it amazed me that, more often than not, young singers would use a small, rather boring voice to speak, no matter how rich and splendid their singing voices were. This was more true of the women, possibly because their early conditioning as females was more powerful than their training as singers. It was almost as though they were in hiding from their full gifts.

Many people have told me that when they were children, they

were warned not to talk loudly, not to raise their voices, and, if they were girls, to be "ladylike". Just as a poet may be daring in print but terrified of expressing his/her feelings aloud, many women singers have an instinctive sense that it is socially acceptable to be powerful in singing but inappropriate or threatening to use their full voices in everyday life.

Not only women are programmed to be quiet and modest, most children also receive considerable social pressure not to "show off." Once you begin to guard the expression of your feelings, your voice too goes underground. The natural spontaneity of children is dampened, sometimes permanently. Their voices become careful, dull, with very little range or color.

What sounds "normal" to you is largely just what you're used to hearing. That's why so many people are shocked when they first hear themselves on a tape recorder. "But I *can't* have such a terrible accent as that!"

Unless you've had speech or voice training, the way you speak probably reflects pretty accurately the speech patterns of the place where you grew up and the people you grew up with, your family and peers. It's not just the way you pronounce words, but the much more subtle business of inflections, ranges, speed and emphasis. Most Americans have been exposed to standard "mid-Atlantic" speech on radio and TV. Yet their speech will still reflect their childhood homes, their educational backgrounds, and the speech of the people they spent the most time with.

Often people come to me and ask me to help them get rid of a regional or foreign accent. Most foreigners, acutely aware of their speech, don't realize that Americans in general are charmed by a foreign accent—as long as it's clear enough for them to understand.

For foreign accents there is a certain subliminal hierarchy of preference. British, French and Swedish accents are usually regarded as more glamorous than Spanish, Italian, or German. As George Orwell wrote in *Animal Farm*, everybody's equal—only some are more equal than others. Southerners have told me they felt northerners considered them not quite bright if they used their habitual speech rate. A person with a heavy Brooklyn or New Jersey accent may seem provincial, "dumb," or vulgar. A Mexican accent in California, a Puerto Rican one in New York, a black accent—alas, anywhere—may trigger prejudice. Sometimes fashions shift. Since Carter's presidency, a southern accent is more acceptable; you may even hear a commentator or newsperson with a slight southern lilt, which adds a nice variety to our increasingly homogenized society. Certainly it would be a shame if all regional differences were expunged.

Actors doing commercials are aware that sponsors love a midwestern accent. Their feeling is that most of the customers are out there in the heartland, and commercials should flatter them by sounding the way they do. Oh, there are a few characters in commercials from other parts of the country, but in general, the Midwest remains the most desired of accents in commercials, especially touting the virtues of soap and household cleaners.

When I went to Bennington College, I was exposed for the first time to the nasal semi-Britishism of the eastern seaboard upper-class accent. My classmates with that amazing (to me) nasal drawl had all gone to the small coterie of exclusive private schools, addressed each other as "Stokie" or "Smithie." Although everybody dressed in jeans, the subtle segregation by speech patterns was semiautomatic and inevitable.

In England, class distinctions based on speech are still quite rigid. Many working-class youngsters who attend public schools on scholarship are bitterly aware that speech is one of the dividers between the "ins" and the "outs." To some extent that has broken down since Twiggy and the Beatles. The rich infusion of talent from the non-U of British society has made Liverpool, Birmingham, and Manchester accents more familiar to everyone—and respectable. Even cockney speech is more accepted. Still, it's not likely Liverpool would be very welcome, even now, in the boardroom or a major corporation—unless they owned the corporation!

In this country some circles consider clear, mid-Atlantic speech "affected." Nevertheless a number of my students, determined to move up in the world by way of "improving their speech," successfully transformed their speaking style, and are very happy at the entree it has given them into circles which had been previously closed to them.

Changing your accent requires high motivation, lots of perseverance, and a good ear. It's hardest if you're surrounded by people who speak the way you want *not* to. They may think your desire to change is a criticism of them, and, subtly or not, discourage you, Still, some hardy souls succeed in pulling it off.

Diane L., a lovely young airline flight attendant, was in the habit of riding a motorcycle with her boyfriend on her days off. One day, dressed in her usual motorcycle gear of very brief shorts and a sweatshirt, she decided it would be fun to have dinner at a posh restaurant in the suburbs they had just passed.

"We walked in," she reported to me delightedly, "and I could see them getting ready to say, 'I'm sorry, we can't serve you.' But I just acted as if I belonged there. Using my new voice and speech, I told them we'd like to have dinner. They seated us and acted very respectful the rest of the evening. It was just great! I guess they figured if I wasn't somebody important I wouldn't have the nerve to come in dressed like that!"

Chalk up one more demonstration:

> **People do walk through the door of your expectations.**

According to the responses to the Charisma questionnaire, 90 percent felt that voice was an important element in charisma; 89 percent added that eloquence was probably a prime ingredient too. Most people in the United States, consciously or not, consider an English accent more elegant and eloquent. The famous drama teacher and actress Stella Adler was shopping in a fashionable Fifth Avenue store when someone asked her, "Pardon me, are you English?" To which the great lady replied disdainfully, "No, dahling, just affected!"

At the offices of the top executives in New York and California, it's a status symbol to have an English secretary. A British paper consultant tells me he's keenly aware what an advantage speech gives him in negotiations with his American colleagues.

Since the subtle messages of speech are such an integral part of your overall image, they contribute to your charisma or detract from it. Much depends on how people in your environment perceive your speech. That does *not* mean you should fake an English accent! It *does* mean that speaking clearly with an interesting, musical, and expressively varied voice is a tremendous asset. It also feels good!

My English consultant friend claims that, by and large, American businessmen tend to have extraordinary flat, uninteresting voices. Some people, even when they're talking about something they care about, sound as though they're issuing instructions ("Get me a dozen boxes of No. 10 A1").

In addition to obeying messages not to show off, many business people try too hard to seem "businesslike" or "professional." The professional societies—engineers, lawyers, urban planners, doctors, architects, all very left-brain-oriented professions—are full of people who speak with virtually no inflection. Their voices are so uninteresting they put an audience to sleep. Across the length and breadth of the land, charitable, fraternal, academic organizations are afflicted with speakers who are terrified of speaking and have never learned to do it well.

According to a study of over 3,000 people across the United States, 41 percent were more afraid of public speaking than any other single thing! In a British study by The London Sunday *Times* the women polled were far more fearful than the men. Fear of death rated only seventh on their list, just ahead of flying and loneliness, and after heights, insects and bugs, financial problems, deep water, and sickness.

Do you dread speaking in public? If the answer is yes, check your reasons:

1. I might make a fool of myself.
2. I'll forget what I wanted to say.
3. People won't listen to me.
4. My voice will crack.
5. People will find out I'm not as bright as they think.
6. I won't be able to express myself clearly. (Related to 1)
7. Other.

Instant Persuasion Power

All of us sound wonderful when we're enthusiastic. SO NOW LIST TEN THINGS YOU *LIKE* TO SAY. If you're not sure, close your eyes, breathe deeply, and let yourself remember the last time you enjoyed yourself. What did you say?

Statements such as:

1. I had a wonderful time.
2. I love you.
3. That's great.
4. You're wrong!
5. I've finished the job.
6. That's good.
7. I believe *I'm* next.
8. Will you go to hell!
9. Kiss me.

   10. You idiot!
   11. I can do it.
   12. I sold it!
   13. I love this restaurant.

Fill in your own list.

Say them aloud with enthusiasm. These examples, by the way, are all actual sentences various students gave during workshops.

Now list ten things you hate to say! Such as:
   1. I had a wonderful time.
   2. I love you.
   3. That's great.
   4. You're wrong.
   5. I'm wrong.
   6. I'm sorry.
   7. Kiss me.
   8. You idiot!
   9. Will you please help me?
   10. I don't want to see you anymore.
   11. I'm going to have to level with you.
   12. You don't understand what I'm trying to say.
   13. I don't get it.
   14. I can't do that.
   15. Other.

Write your own list. You'll have noticed that many sentences are on both lists! Some people love to say what others find difficult. This is a highly personal and profoundly important list for you. You may be surprised at some of the sentences you put on it!

The Pleasure Priority Sentence

Now pick the one in the first list that you can say with the most pleasure and enthusiasm. Say it over and over with mounting feeling. Notice the point where you begin to feel silly or the feeling is forced. Then go back to the point just before and recapture the full expressiveness of that one.

If you find you're losing the original feeling and sound of pleasure, stop. Close your eyes and revisualize yourself in the situation, time, and place when you first said it. Plunge on. Do you find it harder to say positive than negative things? Then practice the Great Wow! Do you find it hard to say negative things? You need courage from the Chutzpah exercises (in chapter 11). Of all the pleasurable sentences which do you like to say best?

Now that you've identified the Pleasure Priority Sentence, repeat it and notice how it sounds and feels as you say it. Escalate the pleasure; see how much you can increaes it without losing the genuine feeling. What's your face doing? Your eyes? Your voice? Hang on to the image of your happy experience when you first said the sentence. See yourself then. Be able to reproduce the tone of your voice, the twinkle in your eye, the enthusiasm you felt.

"But that would feel like acting," you say.

It's not acting. It's *reacting* or *reenaction.*

Practice several days. Also take time to spot new pleasure sentences in the course of your day. Write them down enjoy them, enlarge them. Your list:

1.

2.

3.

4. etc.

Whatever becomes *conscious* is then a *usable tool* for greater expressiveness.

You're increasing your charisma quotient when you increase the amount of pleasure you feel and express.

Experiment with different ways of expressing the pleasure. Vary the tone, the pitch, the inflection, and the speed. Try these on a tape recorder. Watch other people expressing pleasure: your child, your friends, strangers, people on TV. See if you can feel your way into their faces. How would it feel to use your face that way? You'll begin to explore new expressions that you haven't used before.

MIX and MATCH!

Now take one of your "disliked" sentences and say it in exactly the same tone and with the same expression you used for your Pleasure Priority Sentences.

Suppose you love to say "That's good!" Take one you hate to say, like "I'm sorry." Ordinarily, you probably mumble it while feeling apologetic or defensive and thoroughly uncomfortable. Now say, "That's good!" noticing how your voice and inflection sound. Immediately follow that with "I'm sorry!"—this time *using the same pleasantness and energy you used when you said "That's good!"*

It's much easier for someone to hear "I'm sorry" when it sounds pleasant and looks friendly, not sullen and grudging. This technique will detoxify a lot of your "hate to say" sentences and take them off other people's "hate to hear" list! Not every PP sentence will work, but you'll be able to find at least one that will. You can then choose the right sound you want, from a range of positive inflections. This suddenly opens up a number of brand-new possibilities and effective options.

For instance, if "I love this restaurant" was one of your PPs and "I don't get it" was one of your "hates," you'll sound very open and able to smile at yourself if you apply the inflection of No. 1 to No. 2. If "I've finished the job" was one of your PPs, it might go very well with "I don't want to see you anymore" or "I'm wrong" and beautifully with "I can't do that!"

Instead of sounding defeated, apologetic, or resentful, you will come across as unthreatened and able to admit a mistake cheerfully. If it's regret you're expressing, you'll sound—instead of indignant, reproachful, or defensive—adult and thoughtful. These are much better for your own self-esteem and face-saving for your listener.

On the other hand, if "You idiot" was a PP it might not sound good on "Kiss me!" (unless you want to be lightly exasperated or gaily commanding). If you had a little wine and the lights were low and you met the person of your dreams and then you said, "I had a wonderful time!" rather dreamily, THAT would apply marvelously to "Kiss me!" or "I believe *I'm* next" as a PP would apply perfectly to "That's great!" (if that's a negative one for you) or "Will you please help me?" (pleasant but not abject) or "I'm sorry" or "I'm wrong." But it probably wouldn't work quite as well on "You don't understand what I'm trying to say!" Try it; it's possible you *will* like it.

Now that you have the principle, you can really begin to be very effective saying the things that are hardest for you. This causes a lot of misunderstanding and unnecessary suffering. One of my clients, a department manager in a large corporation, called a man he admired very much to tell him the unpleasant news that the corporation would not be buying from him in the following year. The department manager, Jeff, felt very bad about this, particularly because he had been trying to avert the negative decision. The men were close enough for Jim, the supplier, to say to him, "Say, are you personally disappointed in me? You sound so cold, as though you're angry about something." Jeff was shocked. "Oh, my gosh, no, Jim! I just hated to have to tell you this!" In the Charismedia workshop, Jeff role-played, telling Jim the bad news with warmth in his voice so that the disappointing news wouldn't be twice as bad because he sounded unfriendly.

Homemade Opera

Sing Jeff's sentence in ten different ways. "Oh, but I can't sing!" you protest. Never mind. That doesn't matter in the slightest. Besides, I don't believe it! *Everybody* is capable of singing. Never mind that countless teachers and relatives may have told you you're a "listener" or "just stand there and move your mouth, but don't sing!" or "You have no voice!" Coleridge, an early putter-downer of bad singing, wrote caustically:

> Swans sing before they die—
>   'twere no bad thing
> Did certain persons die
>   before they sing!
> —("EPIGRAM ON A VOLUNTEER SINGER")

Never mind! If you can sustain sounds, you can sing. The rest is training your ear.

We all have an innate need to sing. It's part of the human capacity to express feelings. When a child is told "You can't sing!" a real violation of the spirit takes place, a secret, burning wound. Everyone experiences a deep yearning to utter lyric cries of emotion, pain or joy, in musical form. There are psycho-physical reasons for this. Since sustained sound uses much more breath than everyday speech, it offers emotional release, dis-charge of the psychophysical buildup of stress, and aesthetic satisfaction. Manfred Clynes suggested in his remarkable book, *Sentic Cycles*, that there is a model in the brain for all musical-emotional expression. That's why, when we hear a great artist expressing an emotion with precision and fullness, we *recognize* and are moved and cleansed by it.

We also tend to feel love for the artist. When teenagers swarm all over Mick Jagger, or opera fans go wild over Joan Sutherland or Luciano Pavarotti, they express a deep inner yearning of human nature.

Expression seems to be just as much a deep human need as eating and sleeping—sometimes even more important. You don't have to be great to sing, or dance. Just expressing feelings—especially in some kind of shaped form—not only eases emotional pain, but enhances feelings of innate self-worth. There is a profound satisfaction in shaping something beautiful or expressive from raw emotion. We feel it was somehow of value to have suffered, and the joy of communicating and connecting with other people's deepest emotions is incalculably great. Emotion "remembered in tranquillity" through art becomes a way of managing the world, of connecting with the meaning of existence.

The first Western nation to apply the awareness of music's importance on a nationwide scale was post–World War II Hungary. The Communist government offered Zoltán Kodály, their greatest living composer, the opportunity to revolutionize Hungary's musical education any way he liked.

Kodály knew that singing is profoundly valuable for children's mental health, the development of their concentration, capacity for self-esteem, and ability to get along well with people. He started the children off as early as kindergarten. Children between three and six years old sang every day, learned to improvise in song, and sang together. The especially talented ones were sent to special schools, as they are everywhere else in the world, but the extraordinary achievement in Hungary was a level of musical skill, expressiveness, and involvement for all children that has literally transformed the musical consciousness of the country.

When I visited Hungary a few years ago, I asked if I could observe an "ordinary" class of fourteen-year olds. I was curious, having heard about this amazing training, to hear what these young people could do. When I entered the music room, I was a little surprised to notice there was no piano or other instrument. The teacher began by asking one student to sing four bars in "the style of Bach." Tall and gawky, the boy stood up and unhesitatingly improvised a very graceful and rather elaborate melody of four bars in the style of Bach. Not only was his intonation excellent, but he was evidently enjoying himself and had no trouble doing the assignment.

Then the teacher pointed to another child and said, "Mari, will you please sing a counterpoint to the subject." To my amazement, Mari, a tall buxom girl with pigtails, got up and sang an ingenious counterpoint, on the spot, just as the teacher had asked her to do. Next came improvisations in the style of Mozart, then Beethoven. I was struck by the delight with which the students sang, and how perfectly in tune they were regardless of how involved the melodies became. I doubt if graduates of Juilliard or any other American conservatory could have done better or even as well. It was an astonishing hour.

Starting everybody off so young, no child is unable to sing. Even assuming an exceptionally high proportion of musically talented children in Hungary, it can't be statistically possible there are no "listeners"—as the ironic euphemism goes—in the whole country! It's simply assumed that everybody can learn to sing—and so everybody does.

Theater training has always realized the vital connection between speech and music. The great Russian director Stanislavski said, "Speech *is* music," and trained his company to sing so they would speak with a musical line, color, and feeling. Rhythm, tone, and movement added incomparable richness and expressive subtlety. The values of silence suddenly become more meaningful. Ralph Richardson, the great English actor, went so far as to say that "pauses are the most important part of speech." They help "impregnate the words with fresh inner content." A contemporary Japanese composer, Takemitsu, wrote that he wanted to achieve with his music "the eloquence of silence."

Stanislavski understood that deep feelings are released through the qualities of sounds themselves. In *Building a Character*, he wrote: "Do you realize that an inner feeling is released through the clear sound of the A (ah)? That sound is bound up with certain deep inner experiences which seek release and easily float out from the recesses of one's bosom. But there is another A sound. It is dull, muffled, does not float out easily but remains inside to rumble ominously—as if in some cavern or vault. There is also the insidious AAA which whirls out to drill its way into the person who hears it. The joyous A sound rises from one like a rocket, in contrast to the ponderous A which, like an iron weight, sinks in to the bottom of one's wellsprings."

Try these for yourself:

For instance, the euphoric AHHH—when you meet a dear friend you haven't seen for years—

"Ahhhhhhh! I'm so happy to see you!"

or the dull depressed groan of

"Ahhh, don't bother me! Agh, what's the use?"

(More like an uhh, preceded by a heavy sigh.)

How perceptive Stanislavski was when he said, "Do you not sense that particles of you are carried out on these vocal waves? These are not empty vowels, they have a spiritual content."

As the Italians who gave the world the art of bel canto know, singing is largely the art of sustaining vowels. People who haven't been used to singing usually alter the pitch or shape of the sounds and close them off quickly. Floating on the sustained sound is itself a form of trust. Vocally, it's like being on a swing —it puts you in touch with a feeling of soaring mastery and power. If the sound is placed right, an interesting thing happens —the note begins to float itself. It seems to grow out of the top of one's head, and you are surrounded by a sea of sound. The singer has become the sound. This is an indescribably exhilarating sensation. But how do you "place it right"?

THE TONAL TRAPEZE

To get in touch with that arcing loop of which you're only a small part, open your mouth just wide enough to say a smiling, easy *ahh*. Allow your jaw to relax; your tongue lies quietly at the bottom of your mouth. The back hinge of the jaw is wide enough for one finger to support the top jaw. Breathe with your mouth open in this position a few times, as softly and gently as you can. Gradually increase the amount of breath, then say *hhhhhhhhh*, as though you're laughing gently. Then begin singing *haaahh*—with as imperceptible an attack as you can manage. Let the *h* begin the sound. This way you keep the throat open, instead of starting with a glottal catch.

When the sound begins, nothing in the mouth or throat or tongue changes. Feel the sound filling your mouth and then penetrating the upper hard and soft palate and shooting up through the top of the head into the surrounding atmosphere. See where else you feel the vibration; you may find your shoulders, legs, or chest buzzing.

Keep the sound going until you've run out of air. Then, leaving your mouth and jaw in the same position, let the sound end, just fading away, melting into silence. Still not moving anything, allow the back of the throat to be an open door for your breath rising from the stomach. Don't shut it off or start the sound with the twitchy little glottis.

There's nothing intrinsically wrong with the glottal catch. But to produce a free, open vowel sound and gain access to the currents of breath from your lower abdomen, it's valuable to know how to begin a sound without a glottal catch (which always starts the sound in the throat). Save that for tremulous emotional moments—when it's very effective. You may find it hard at first to make a vowel sound *without* a glottal catch, but it will pay off in vocal freedom if you can. Here are some sentences to practice on. Have fun with them!

Glottal Nonstop Sentences

1. Esther idled away hours at antiques auctions.
2. Aunt Alice always inquired after all our affairs.
3. Almost everyone enjoys an evening of elegance.
4. Oscar outshines all other outstanding oboists (athletes, engineers, egotists).
5. Edward evidences every attribute of evasiveness.
6. Asters are arranged all over in extravagant abundance.
7. Archaeologists anticipate an enormous array of eye-opening artifacts.
8. Isabella always assured employers of unfailing ingenuity.
9. Each and every assignment energized eager actors.
10. I'd appreciate an uncluttered, uncomplicated existence once in a while.

N.B. If you have difficulty doing any of these:

1. Put an *h* before every vowel.
2. Try saying them without any consonants at all. It helps to put the thumb on the hard palate to do this—just hang the head on the thumb. Link all the sounds together.
3. Sometimes it helps to use arm movements.
4. A nice breathless sound to begin each vowel will help you get the hang of this.
5. Be as extravagant as possible in your inflections!

How to Sing Even Though You Can't

Let the back of your tongue press down as you breathe again and start a new sound with the breath *haaaaaah* ———. Starting softly, gradually increase the sound, filling the cavities of the head and the spaces around your head with the sustained sound of your *hahhhhhhhh.*

Begin with a note that's comfortable for you in the middle of your range. Sing that note five times, holding it each time as long as you can. Then start a new note, this time going as low as you can. Feel the sound spreading as you hold it, to your neck, shoulders, and chest, and then upward around your head. Feel the back of your head buzzing.

After you've tried that four or five times, keep the image of the sound permeating your head and ears and the crown of your head, in addition to the neck, chest, and shoulders. Then, still holding that feeling of vibrations in the entire upper body, spread them gradually through your waist and stomach. Feel your ribs and the sides of your spine opening, buzzing, and vibrating with the note you're singing. Really take time to visualize these vibrations opening and spreading your sound energy. Feel the ribs opening as though the air were pushing them apart.

If you aren't sure whether or not you actually feel the vibrations, just *imagine* that you do. Pretty soon you will be able to make every cell tingle with the dense intensity of your sound. Your body will feel both more porous and more intensely awake; it will be tuning into its own sounds. You'll notice that the sound feels different in different sections—it may tickle in some places, buzz in others, warm you at other points. All this is floated on the breath.

Your main task is not to interfere with the flowing diffusion of sound through your whole system. Let it flow!

THE SONIC EMBRACE

After doing the low *haah* ten times, close your eyes and feel your whole body tingling with the sounds; you'll feel wrapped in a kind of sonic embrace, very warm and cozy. Be sure to make the beginning and end of sounds as gentle as possible. Now hear the sounds continuing after you have stopped. Feel the space around your head and body and under your feet as completely filled in with vibrations, so that you're swimming in a thick sea of pulsing sound. Sit for two to ten minutes with eyes closed and enjoy the sensations of tingling and warmth and being massaged. Pay particular attention to your back (as though you were being stroked, a soft fur laid around you, or thousands of light fingertips gently caressing you). When you've stopped, release your stomach and breathe in very slowly through your lower belly with your mouth closed.

SONIC ACUPRESSURE MASSAGE

Every day in the shower, where the sound is glamorously amplified and everybody is a star, start with a hum that's very easy and check out how your body feels from the inside. Is there a pain, an ache? A slightly sore place somewhere? Send the hum there, a sonic messenger to massage and warm you where you need it most. When you find the right pitch, it will connect with the spot that hurts, almost as though locking into it. Visualize the hum dissolving the edges of the pain and spreading warmth all through your body.

Next, try it with an open *ah* sound. Look for the pitch that connects most deeply with your own vibratory rate. When it "hooks in" you can listen to it as though someone were giving you a giant sonic massage and all you have to do is allow yourself to enjoy it.

Now experiment with different pitches. Make them sound a little higher, a little louder. Stay with that new *haah*. Lower the back of your tongue *without* tensing the sides or the front. A neat trick! (If you can't do it at first, *imagine* it—pretty soon the muscles will wake up and respond.) Now see your body extending to each side as far as the walls, made of pure sound. Then imagine that it's extending up through the upper palate, up, up, out the top of your head. Hang on to the initial image. When you can keep those three directions vibrantly moving outward, then extend downward through the earth. If you're on the fifth floor of the building, make the sound go down below the basement!

Deepen the sound by flaring your nostrils, lifting your rib cage, and opening the "back nostrils" (inside the mouth). Hold it as long as you can. Afterward, sit and feel the sensations in your body. You may find parts of it waking up that you haven't been aware of before. You may feel excited. You may notice your heart beating faster. You may have a rush of unexpected emotion. When you bathe the body in sound, it triggers reservoirs of feeling. Let whatever wants to happen happen. You will probably feel distinct pleasure and tingling. Each day you try this, notice how the sensations change. Keep checking that your jaw is relaxed, the tip of your tongue relaxed, your breath as steady and even as you can make it, with the edges fading away and beginning again as imperceptibly as the sea fades into the horizon.

TONE TWINS

If there's another person around, try matching sounds. First he/she sings, then you match the sound as closely as you can. With your eyes closed, start the *ahhh* very softly, get louder, and then fade away and let your partner begin the sound exactly where you leave off. Then you pick up where she/he stops. Keep this seamless ribbon of sound going until you feel you're a helix of melody twining in and out between you and you can't tell where one leaves off and the other begins.

THE ENDLESS SOUND

Now put your palms against your partner's palms and start *ahhh-m* and feel the vibrations transfer between you, three to five minutes.

Then, putting your foreheads together gently, choose another pitch both of you are comfortable with. You'll find this very relaxing. Again continue for three to five minutes.

Now turn around and stand with your backs leaning against each other, your heads touching. In this position you may have to work a little harder to feel the vibrations as one body. Let the resonance of your backs enlarge the sounds you're feeling and making.

Now you both close your eyes and hear the sounds as though they were coming from some other source; you're simply the receiver or container. Again, don't change anything in your mouth, jaw, and tongue once you've set the shape of the *ahhhhh*. Let go of all judgments about whether your voice sounds "pretty" or not. Just keep your concentration focused on making the sounds as even as possible. If you make them louder, make the crescendo as gradual as you can. Notice what it takes *not* to clutch at the end of a sound. (Try to imagine your throat just as open at the back arch as your mouth is at the front). Let it end without changing anything in the position of your throat, tongue, mouth, or lips. If you notice an involuntary twitch or clutch somewhere, observe exactly where and what is happening, and the next time focus on eliminating it entirely. Even small changes in the position of your mouth, lips, tongue, or back of the throat can alter the sound. The idea is to sustain the sound *without any change* as long as possible—until it "hooks" in and floats itself.

You may find your head buzzing or even that you get a little dizzy—don't worry if that happens briefly. It merely means you're getting more oxygen than you're used to. If you get dizzy, breathe deeply (with closed mouth), pinch the flesh between your eyebrows sharply, and the dizziness will disappear.

Begin to hum and spread the hum throughout your backs. Then alternate with the *ahhhhhh*, spreading the buzzy vibration through every surface that touches your partner's back, and let it continue into the arms and hands. Keep your eyes closed so you can experience the sounds without being distracted. Feel every millimeter of the skin surface intensely alive with vibration.

THE ENDLESS WAVE

In Charismedia workshops, groups of people experiment with a continuous sound; they stand in two rows, their hands clasped, foreheads touching, eyes closed. They begin to hum. An immense wave of sound begins to permeate everyone's body; after five or ten minutes you feel as though you have one huge body which is bigger than all the individuals there and you're vibrating with all that power and energy. It's very powerful and pleasant, and afterward everybody's voice is clearer, more resonant, and everyone senses the group energy has made you feel more alive, more comfortable in your own body, and more relaxed with other people, somehow part of them at the same time.

Keep the sound going, either alone or with a partner or group, sustaining sounds as long as possible, moving in and out of existence as imperceptibly as possible—in a very real sense you begin to experience the flow of your own existence as pleasurable beyond words.

The benefits? Your breath control will increase greatly, your energy level will rise, you will feel more focused and centered, and your concentration will improve dramatically if you practice this every day. These experiences will also help you to speak in public with greater ease and courage. The risk of making sounds in public will seem a lot less dangerous. You are laying the groundwork for actually enjoying yourself while speaking up!

Pain-to-Pleasure Transformation

It is helpful not to say "I have a pain" but "there is a pain." Focus on the neutral energy, knowing that by centering on the feeling without identifying it as pain you intensify the energy and free it to be spread and diffused through every cell, until it harmlessly drifts into the air surrounding your body. Visualize it becoming a warm, viscous liquid like warm Jell-O, lapping at and supporting your body. If you think of pain as a form of energy that can be transformed to positive strength, the power of the feeling will begin to change into heat, which then feels pleasurable.

Remember, the pleasure and pain centers in the brain are very close, so these three steps help:

1. Focusing on the sensations, intensifying them
2. Spreading them throughout the body as energy, starting exhalation, and then—

3. Exhaling fully, passing out the diluted, diffused intensity like heat through cheesecloth, visualizing every cell as a fine, transparent network.

This sequence can change the experience of pain into something quite different. You may be aware of warmth or excitement or pleasure, even triumph!

YOU ARE A RADIANT CENTER MAKING THE WORLD YOURS

The next step is to feel that your inside and your outside are one with only a thin membrane of skin between. The hum is the vehicle of your merging. Feel your hum dissolving your boundaries. Put the center in:

a. the soles of your feet
b. your calves
c. your thighs
d. your genitals and buttocks (as you move up, keep the vibration in the lower areas and simply add and spread the hum)
e. your belly

BE YOUR OWN SUN:

f. your navel point: think of the hum as extending in a sunburst from your navel—in front, to the sides, and out to the back, as far as the horizon. Gradually make the rays longer and larger, until your navel point is the hot center of the radiant sun and you can feel the embracing rays of your own heat extending out toward infinity in every direction. You may feel prickly and tingly. Expand the prickle and tingle out to infinity.

Alternate *mmmmmm* with *ahhhhhh*. See which sound makes the sun more vivid. (The *ahhhhhh* and the *mmmmmmm* are now continuous.)

g. your solar plexus—feel the power of the center there radiating like thunderbolts in every direction.
h. your heart center—feel your heart grow bigger as though it were now enclosing your entire body, and your body is like a tiny figure inside the enormous gold heart, glowing and translucent. Now add the sun-center radiance from within the "little castle of the heart" and expand it through every individual pore in millions of tiny rays, and beyond the "heart-body" enclosing your body. Fill up every space outside your own,

above, to the back, the front, the sides, and below. Do this two ways: standing against someone else's back and also standing up alone.

i. the throat or expressive center—open the pathway to the gut and to the head simultaneously. See the great caverns of the mouth and head and throat extending up into the head and down into the body. Scoop out the whole inside of the mouth and throat with a yawn that reaches in a great curving embrace backward to the horizon as though the back of your neck were totally open. Keep that openness when the yawn is finished. Press down lower jaw toward the back of your neck. Let the *ahhhh* trigger new yawns each time—make each one bigger (and ruder!)—than the last. Let your eyes water. Let the sounds fill the spaces outside the body, still alternating between *ahhhh* and *mmmmm*. (When you close your lips for the hum, make sure you leave them full and relaxed, the tongue low in the mouth, throat even more open if possible.)

Cover every tiny pore on the back of your neck with vibrations shooting out like fireworks. The yawn makes your neck a wider and wider hollow column where the air passes from the lower part to the throat and head.

Let your arms float upward if they want to so there's the most stretch possible while your body is lapped around with the soft embracing airwaves. What color are they? (Some people find they change.) See how you can make the sound without tensing any part of your head, throat, neck, or tongue. Keep your ribs lifted; that'll lengthen the amount of breath you have.

BE YOUR OWN CATHEDRAL

A wonderful way to experience your sound and body fully while you find your ideal spinal alignment is to press your back against the wall, lower your weight, knees bent, feet apart about the same width as your shoulders. The spine, from the stomach and vertebra to the coccyx, makes contact with the wall, every vertebra pressing against it, arms relaxed. The head is a little away from the flat surface, growing organically out of the spine, eyes directly ahead. The shoulders do not touch the wall. In that position, the trunk is relaxed though pressed against the wall.

Sing *ahhhhhhhhhhhh . . . hmmmmmmmmmm* with an open throat (no glottal attack!), holding each note as long as you can, observing the sound vibrate on the roof of the mouth, hook in, and rise straight through the top of the head. Do this twenty-six times and you'll find you are in an altered state of consciousness. Your sense of using your whole body to SOUND your vibrations becomes a totally different experience of your own voice. You're your own cathedral. The limitless, echoing expanses of the sounds of your own breath and voice within your head and body and floating out around you energizing your environment will give you an expanded sense of lightness and power. Notice the moment when the sound seems to be singing itself. Allow it to float out and mingle with the sound of the room you're in. Soon the room will seem to be singing, not you. If you're singing with someone else, let the sounds mingle and match until you can't tell who is singing; the sound will fill the space between and around you.

After you've completed the twenty-six *ahhhh-mmmmmms*, listen to the vibration-rich silence. Feel your ears and body tingle, and notice every sensation that you experience. You'll feel expanded and abuzz. The air almost roars with the accumulation of sound.

Silence can never feel empty again after you've experienced this. You'll begin to notice that every silence has its own sound spectrum: the floor or a bone aching or creaking, the dry staccato twitch of a leaf or curtain, the velvet hum of a distant motor or current, the mordant squeal of a faraway dog, the hiss and moan and thump of internal tides, the polyphonic phrases of constant change expressed in faint cues and motifs, as elusive and varied as an atonal kaleidoscope, heard through water.

Now place your elbows on the wall on either side of your body and very gently—not changing your head or torso position at all—push off from the wall. Press hard away from the wall with your elbows, so the body remains aligned exactly the way it was when it was against the wall. Your pelvis is cupped like a palm or an ear, the lower back spread and wide, the stomach pressed in against the spine, the head rising from the torso like a flower at the end of its stem. When you feel your balance is just as solid as it was when you were leaning against the wall, very, very slowly straighten your knees until they're almost—but not quite—straight. Slowly lower your arms to the sides and relax them. Now observe how your body feels, scanning it from the inside.

You'll get a new sense of your optimum body alignment. Close your eyes and feel how comfortable it is to stand, both legs and feet supported by the ground, the head so centered that if you were to drop it on a straight line down the center of the body it would fall neatly between your feet after passing straight through your solar plexus and navel point and pubic bone.

Breathe in the sound-filled silence and exhale it through every pore to join the widening concentric circles of sound, traveling outward further and further with each breath. Each time you exhale, allow the breath to travel further outward and begin the next inhalation by scooping in the energy from that expanded circle.

Each time you exhale, let go more and more of the tensions in your body. Not only today's but all of the past's. Release old angers, fears, all irritations and annoyances, dissolving into the widening circles. As you enlarge the circles, change into a helix or spiral in a dense complexity of movement that finally weaves in and out in all the directions. See it rimmed in fire, edged with light, dancing, changing, constantly carrying your breath further out to the edges of the universe. Always widen it in all directions at once. . . .

Next, exhale and widen the circle to include first
  the room you're in
    then the building
      the block or open space
        the city or town
          the state
            the country
              the continent
                the oceans around the continent
                  the other continents
                    the world
                      the galaxies.

Rest in the simultaneous "being" in all this effortless flow as though your "body boundaries" now include entire galaxies. It's the universe breathing in and out, and your margins blur into a much larger consciousness. Through breathing you make the universe aware of itself. Feel space pouring through your bodilessness. You are now part of the largest universe imaginable.

BE YOUR OWN LULLABY

Sit or lie down for this. As you rest in this expanded pulsing sea, you may pick up the sounds of this process or experience the sounds as colors. Observe closely but don't force or direct anything. You may become suddenly aware, after some moments of not noticing your body, of a prickling of the hairs on the back of your neck or your foot falling asleep or some other reminder that you're back in your small form. Just notice it and release that sensation, whatever it is, with the next exhalation. Freeing it from its form in your body, send the feeling out and you may see it in its shadow form dancing outside the body, and then dissolve it in the seething energy sea—extra added power, density, and richness in the surrounding texture.

SONIC TRANQUILIZER

Variation I: Surrounded by the energy sea, with no effort in the throat, make the smallest, most continuous humming sound you can—as though the sound were coming from outside you. Keep experiencing the sound as if it were being generated *outside,* as if you were listening to a strange but deeply comforting steady sound coming from very far away. Like a foghorn heard in childhood while half asleep, signaling that someone was keeping watch, all was well. (We can paraphrase Meister Eckhart's famous "The eye with which I look at God is the same eye with which God looks at me" as "The sound with which I sing to God (or Nature) is the same as that which God sings to me.")

The detachment from one's own sound has a wonderfully calming effect. To hear the sound of one's own voice as though it were coming from outside has the effect of equalizing the energy outside and in. To sustain the feeling of this sound, you have to make the beginning and end as imperceptible as possible. If the sound was always there and you didn't start or end it, you can merge with it. It was always there, waiting to be uttered. One can only invent ("sound") what already exists. Acknowledging, giving it voice, makes it sing.

Variation II: Imagine you're going to focus in on *the* sound of the universe. When you match the pitch it will sing itself; you'll know by the way the inside and outside become the same. Listen to the silence and let your throat open to prepare itself. (Your mouth is open just a little.) When the pitch rises irresistibly from the silence, allow it to sound without planning or controlling it. Important: let it happen as though it had always existed (which indeed it has) and you've just permitted your body to resonate with it. Complete relaxation of the throat, lips, tongue, and shoulders is essential. Sometimes the sound may surprise you by being very high or then very low. The less you do, the better. Just allow it to continue as long as possible. Feel how it originates outside you and comes *into* you from all sides. It's not issuing from you. The pitch will probably be different on different days. Wait patiently for it to happen.

After this, sit very quietly and close off one nostril with your thumb and listen to the pitch of your breath. At first you may find it hard to tell what it is. But your breath, softly coming in and out of your nostrils, actually does have a pitch. Try the other one. The pitch will be middle C. Your breath sings! You have to be *very* quiet to hear it. The subtler the sounds you're attuned to, the more relaxed you are, the more power and sense of ease you can generate in your electromagnetic field. The more subtle your breath, the greater your power.

Results: GREATLY MAGNIFIED CHARISMA.

Variation III: LOVE SOUNDS.

Think of someone you love. Avoid thinking in words. See that person with as much sensory detail as possible: light, color, smell, sound, kinesthetic movement. Allow yourself to focus on all these impressions for a few moments, knowing that at a certain point a song will rise out of those impressions and shape itself without your doing anything but allowing it to flow out of you. All you have to do is to keep your awareness focused on the soft, warm feelings in your chest and wherever else they appear and simultaneously concentrate on the thought forms of the person you love.

Important: as soon as you feel your concentration slipping, or you become mesmerized or distracted by the act of singing or by the song, STOP! Refocus on the love you feel and the person who draws that love. You'll find that you're able to sustain the concentration more and more so that the song of your love sings itself with less and less interference. Use *lalala*. Using this syllable strengthens your electromagnetic field and compensates for any negative experience or feelings by stimulating the thymus and restoring the equilibrium of the left and right hemispheres. If you can't sing aloud or you're with other people, all you have to do is *think* the *lalala* and lightly tap your tongue over and over against the ridge just behind your front teeth as you do when you sing *lalala*, and the same revitalizing effect is produced.

As you focus on the image of a person you love, let the sound emerge from that image so that the song is coming into you and you hear it as it strikes off the image, not as though you had produced it at all. Start it quite softly so you don't have to worry about *making* the sound and the "edges" are imperceptible. This helps sustain the illusion that you're receiving the song fully formed rather than doing it yourself. Your heart expands with warmth, light, color, and sound. Spread the sound through your body. The love sounds sustain and float around you.

Sound plus visual imagination equals the experience. Now you know what it means when they say, "When you're in love, your heart sings!"

You can in fact produce the same feelings of euphoria; it's almost like *being* in love!

11

How to Conquer Stage Fright

"IF I HAVE a presentation to give, for days ahead I'm tense and nervous. No matter how much I prepare, it doesn't help. Sometimes the nervousness doesn't go away during the whole time I'm on."

"I'm always terrified before I go onstage."

"I can't bring myself to ask a question in class—or make a comment."

"I have such a bad case of stage fright I turned down a job I wanted because I'd have to speak in public."

"I want people to know what pain it costs me to perform! I'm always frightened before I go on."

"When I get up to speak in court, I feel I'm going to black out."

"My little girl said she didn't want to be a concert artist if she had to throw up like me every night before a concert."

"Before a job interview my head throbs, my heart beats terribly fast, my mouth is dry, and my knees shake."

"All I had to do was introduce the speaker, and I was paralyzed with fright. My stomach hurts. I can't catch my breath. My voice gets tight and high, my palms are wet. . . ."

"I forget what I was going to say."

"I can't remember the notes."

"After years of starring roles, I suddenly felt like a novice and couldn't remember my lines."

*

These confessions come from famous people and unknowns, people who're used to performing all the time and others who only occasionally need to face a small group in business or social affairs. Age, experience, sex—none of this alters the essential fact that nearly all of us suffer from stage fright at some time in our lives. I can't think of anybody who claims NEVER to have gone through it. I know several famous musicians who have given up playing in live concerts altogether because of their terror. Careers have tottered and even failed because of it. On the other hand, many stars claim it's essential for a good performance.

What *is* stage fright? The dictionary says, "The nervousness felt by a performer or speaker before an audience." Yet people who have never stepped on stage have felt it too—perhaps before meeting an important client or before their first date or before their wedding or before a battle or an athletic contest—even before sex. The fight-or-flight syndrome steps up the adrenaline and the release of hormones; all of your body and mind are gripped by a stress reaction. How you deal with it, whether you master it or not, can affect your life, career, health, and well-being.

Nobody really understands the mechanics or causes of stage fright very well. Oddly enough, there's very little research on the subject, although interest is growing as more and more people find they have to communicate with different groups and be able to talk on TV or at a PTA meeting or a business setting. Cable TV is expanding opportunities for "just plain folks" and people who never thought of themselves as performers to appear in public; the communications explosion is just beginning. So stage fright is a real concern to growing numbers of people.

The main causes seem to be:

1. Fear of not doing as well as you want to.
2. Insufficient or inadequate preparation.
3. Fear of what people (the audience) will think.
4. Earlier negative experiences.
5. Inadequate enjoyment of what you're doing (probably due to 1, 2, 3, or 4).

Many people in Charismedia workshops stand up at the beginning of the course and admit: "I always have to take Valium before I can speak in public."

"You'll never have to take one again!" I tell them. And after they learn how to calm themselves with breathing exercises and the other de-stressing techniques with which stress can be made manageable, they don't. Taking tranquilizers dulls your perceptions. It is far better to transform the energy of your nervousness into available adrenaline to energize your performance. (There has been much talk lately of a drug called Inderal to reduce nervousness; some psychopharmacologists claim it's effective and without side effects. But since nobody knows exactly how a drug may affect different people, certainly it's much safer to use control techniques that are nonpharmacological.) Changing your conceptualization, meditating, de-stressing your body, and controlling your breathing are simple, safe, effective; they require no equipment and cost nothing but time.

People who have had good experiences speaking or performing sometimes find it hard to understand why their less fortunate friends or colleagues are so terrified of getting up in public. An editor of *Fortune* who interviewed me and some of my students hinted in his article that people who were afraid of public speaking really only needed to "get hold of themselves." Himself a good speaker, he was unable to understand the problem, or believe there really is one! This, despite the fact that 41 percent of the U.S. population in a nationwide poll said they are more frightened of public speaking than any other single thing!

There are two types of stage fright: the kind that's worst beforehand and the kind that's most acute during performance. Some people begin to suffer days or weeks before their ordeal, some only moments before going on. Others are calm until they start, then are suddenly gripped by panic. Some feel it until they step onstage, then everything is all right (this pattern is most common with experienced performers). Many professionals recognize that the stress buildup can be a valuable source of heightened energy and performance readiness. "I need my nervousness to sharpen my responses onstage and make me a fine-tuned instrument for the role I am playing," remarked brilliant English actress Helen Burns.

Reactions are highly individual and variable even for the same person. Some lucky people claim they can't wait to get out onstage and only feel insecure when they haven't rehearsed enough and "done my homework." One woman in my class said she enjoys public speaking of any kind and will gladly address any group of any size, but she suffers all the agonies of stage fright when she has to take exams. A certain conductor found he was yawning and getting sleepy before performances—a kind of withdrawal.

Then there is the curious phenomenon of situation-specific stage fright; it only attacks in a particular environment. This type, I have found, always stems from one special, unpleasant early experience.

James F., a distinguished patent lawyer who took up a successful acting career late in life, confessed that although he loved performing and had no trouble from the time he was in college productions singing, dancing, and acting for thousands of people, one specific kind of situation—addressing a small group of his peers—made him so nervous that he had turned down the presidency of a nationwide law association. He even felt uncomfortable at meetings of his own firm! When I asked him if he could remember some early negative experience speaking in public, he said, "Yes, I remember now—I was in high school and I did something I shouldn't have—can't remember what. The assistant principal called me into his office and sternly informed me I would have to get up in the assembly on Monday morning and, *as punishment,* deliver some sort of speech. I have no idea now what it was about. All I know is that I was terrified of that assembly; I slunk in, somehow got through it, and crept out, feeling horribly humiliated and whipped. I never realized the connection before, but I see now that must have been a real injury. Later in college, my fraternity used to have weekly meetings in the living room and everybody was expected to get up and talk about something. I always sat there feeling scared and miserable. Somehow I managed to sneak out of the room every time without getting up and talking. And at the same time I was appearing in shows up and down the vaudeville circuit and loving it! I realize now all my life I've ducked that kind of situation if I could. It's a wonder people didn't realize! But it actually hampered my career." Here was a very cause-specific stage fright, which only affected him in situations vaguely similar to the one that had given him a bad experience.

Then there's reentry stage fright. No matter how experienced you are, if you've been away for a while, you may experience some of the nervousness and stage fright you felt when you first began. Performing isn't exactly like riding a bicycle! But the heebie-jeebies won't take as long to disappear as the first time. The experience and maturity you acquired in other areas of your life help to ease the transition.

Performers, if they talk about stage fright at all, tend to divide into two camps. Each side feels (somewhat snobbishly) superior to the other. The stage fright sufferers generally regard their agonies as somehow necessary and valuable and tend to disdain anybody who *doesn't* get nervous as insensitive, lacking in fineness of perception. The fearless ones are apt (like the *Fortune* editor) to be unsympathetic and find it difficult to understand why the others make such a fuss.

On evidence, whether or not you have stage fright does not seem to correlate with your artistic sensitivity, although it may reflect the state of your nervous system. Opera singer Richard Tucker was reputed to be "iron-nerved." He never lost his cool before or during a performance. Vladimir Horowitz suffered so badly from stage fright that for years he didn't play at all. (He returned to the concert stage when he suddenly began to enjoy sharing his music with a new generation of appreciative music lovers—his pleasure overrode his old fears.) Academy Award–winning actress Estelle Parsons told me matter-of-factly, "Stage fright is just part of your inner preparation and creativity." Pianist Abba Bogin said, "When I began my career, my left leg used to quiver badly during a concert, but, luckily, the audience couldn't see it because it was on the upstage side. I simply told myself to stop being such an idiot, and it stopped."

Usually (though not always) nervousness diminishes with increased experience. Sometimes a performer will be totally at home in one medium and suffer stage fright in another. Actors who have to appear on talk shows have come to me for help because they feel so uncomfortable and uncertain without a script. Peter Falk remarked on a talk show, "It's very difficult! I don't even know which camera to look at or if I should look at the camera at all!" An instrumentalist who turns to conducting may feel completely at ease on the podium, although subject to stage fright in solo recitals. I used to get nervous before singing, but not before acting (which seemed easy by comparison!). Whenever you don't feel your self-esteem is on the line you tend to be much less vulnerable to stage fright.

People who suffer from chronic stage fright usually have a scarcely heard tape going round in their heads. "They won't like me." "I'll make a fool of myself." "They'll think I'm boring." "I'm not good enough." Sometimes such a message is so ancient that you're not even aware of it, just of the physiological reactions it causes. If you're to give a talk you can install positive tapes instead. Say very consciously, loudly, and clearly, "I have something interesting and valuable to say, and people really want to hear it!" Then internalize it: put it on a cassette and play it to yourself over and over until you believe it! Repeat it silently, but with lots of conviction, just before you get up to speak.

Richard M., an amateur ornithologist, said, "I was afraid my bird slides were not good enough and that my group would think they were not up to their standards. Then I remembered to tell myself, 'I have something really interesting to show them, and they're very interested.' It was true! I can't tell you how that helped me! After that, everything was fine. It turned out they really did enjoy them."

Unfortunately, not all stage fright is that easily dispelled. Being thoroughly prepared is crucially important. For many people, preparation means overpreparation: learning their speech (or part) by rote and doggedly repeating it over and over until all the pleasure is gone out of it. Instead, if you can thoroughly *immerse* yourself in what you're doing, your pleasure in the talk (or music, play, or whatever) will protect you from many of the discomforts of nervousness. It's important to want to share your talk or your performance with others. "Love the art in yourself, rather than yourself in the art."

Composer-pianist-conductor Lukas Foss says, "Stage fright is very narcissistic. The more committed and dedicated, the more *serious* you are about music, the less you feel it. Of course, nothing is as awful as worrying whether or not you're going to be humiliated in front of an audience. One is much more likely to worry playing solo than when conducting. If I worry whether my fingers are going to hit all the notes, I become unserious. When I conduct, I'm worrying about other people—whether the horn will manage to hit the high note, whether the timpani will come in on the right beat, and so on. That's much more real because I'm thinking about the *music*. You have to be completely serious—the more dedicated you are, the less you think about yourself. No, I don't get stage fright onstage now. And I love a captive audience in the concert hall or in the classroom. I get nervous at home where I have to introduce people to each other at a party. I can never remember people's names!"

"Did you ever have stage fright when you were starting?" I asked him.

"When I was a little boy, my father told me, 'Look at the audience and imagine they're all naked!'" He laughed. "Somehow that made them much less frightening!"

The critical competitiveness that is the normal working atmosphere of many businesses, schools, and conservatories makes it hard to retain your joy in what you're doing. Luckily, the physiological changes that accompany stress can be eased or reversed through slow, deep breathing and preperformance exercises. When you discharge built-up tension through the Depressurizer, Karate Chop, the Steam Engine, the Elbow Propeller and the I Don't Care Swing, the Horse Laugh and the Wibble Wabble, you make the energy of your nervousness available to you again. You send oxygen to your brain, discharge lactic acid from your muscles, and stimulate your own energy level and desire to perform.

All creativity is born of excitement. Everybody who ever lived was conceived because some man got excited! The dopamine system of the brain is aroused by aggressive exercise. It's like a built-in "speed" drug. Serotonin released by "moving meditation" or even tennis, if you play with a certain detachment, behaves like mind-changing mescaline. Dr. Arnold J. Mandell of the University of California at San Diego School of Medicine says, "You can really manipulate these brain systems with exercise—and without drugs." Very competitive exercise has an "angry-upper" effect, which is then followed by depression, a "downer." But with a calm attitude, "you get high and you stay high. The elevated mood can last for days, even weeks."

Utilizing our new knowledge of how the brain functions, we can discharge the fright in stage fright through these powerful preperformance exercises. The next step is to calm your entire organism and normalize it, even bring it to a heightened state of optimum functioning through deep, even breathing. Add to this a meditation period and then a chant that reestablishes equilibrium of both hemispheres of the brain, and you're then able to enjoy the fruits of all your preparation. You'll be at your best—even though you don't feel like it!

I'll show you two kinds of anti–stage fright exercises—those you practice right before going on and those you settle into by practicing when you're not under stress so you can form new habits to call on when you need them.

Since most people don't breathe properly and are unaware of the profound connections between their state of mind and ability to function well, good breathing habits have to be learned when you have nothing else to think about, so you can concentrate on that process alone. The act of shifting concentration from your fears to the business of breathing is very comforting and supportive.

Knowing you can control at least *that* element gives you back your much-needed confidence. There is a third factor. It's impossible to be relaxed and anxious at the same time. If you can relax your muscles at will, then you can mentally rehearse the feared situation and see yourself going through it with complete success, visualizing every detail with pleasure and confidence. The moment you're aware of a problem in "seeing" or feel some nervous symptom overtake you (the familiar clutching at your throat or a sinking feeling in the stomach), you abandon the visualization and return to coaxing your body back to physical relaxation. Sure enough, you'll notice a slight clenching somewhere, a tiny grabbing at one set of muscles or another. By slowing your breathing and deliberately letting go of that tension spot or spots, you can again prepare yourself to "rehearse" when you are deeply relaxed.

The more you do it, the easier it'll get. When you're able to go through a whole performance mentally and with pleasure, just as though you were really experiencing it, you will have taken a tremendous step toward beating the problem. The body/mind doesn't know the difference—at that level—between real and imagined. It's just as though you had already *had* a good performance and experienced your own success. In a deep sense you have. When it comes time for the actual performance, it seems like *the second time*.

The more positive experiences you have, the less frightening your momentary inner leap of excitement will feel. Your stage fright will be transformed to stage readiness, that deliciously exhilarating feeling of being challenged and ready to do your best. Some people, like gamblers or racing car drivers, are "hooked" on this excitement.

A few summers ago, I found myself on a ski lift in Aspen, feeling very frightened in the open car and wondering how I'd gotten into that situation. There was no way I could get off. Close to panic, I forced myself to breathe very slowly and deeply. Suddenly an inspiration hit me. I'd pretend, like any nine-year-old, that I was a queen surveying her subjects ranged on the mountainside to greet me. It worked! As soon as I "saw" the massed throngs of my adoring people and felt their love and admiration supporting me, I straightened up and enjoyed the ride, though I was still aware of an undercurrent of acute danger. Dimly I recognized as distinctly familiar the transformation from paralyzing fear to a sense of being alive in a larger way than before, of being poised midway between peril and flying mastery. It was very much like stage fright and the transition to a good performance—on opening night!

Arrange Your Own Success—It's a Gift!

If numbers 1 and 3 are your main stage fright problems, the chances are they stem from number 4. You need long-range confidence building. This may mean that, in addition to meditation, chanting, breathing, and the stress-relief exercises, you have to program successes in a miniature version of your test situation. For instance, if you have a talk coming up in your work, offer to teach the children at a neighboring school something you know well, just to have the experience of presenting information publicly. Or start practicing telling stories to your friends and relatives when you're sure of getting appreciative responses.

You may need to use your imagination to find opportunities to volunteer your knowledge or skills in a less demanding situation than the one you face at work or socially. This practicing can help boost your confidence, especially when you give people something they need and would not have if you hadn't volunteered. You can always offer to read to patients in hospitals or spend a few hours a week telling stories to children at the library or nearest neighborhood center. Somebody somewhere needs and will appreciate a gift of your time, concern, and skills.

"When I finish my hour helping underprivileged school kids with their math problems," remarked Stuart S., a market analyst who regularly helped out at an inner-city school, "*I* feel good! It does as much for me as for them!"

Ruby R., a retired widow who had owned a cosmetics company, offered to teach teenage orphans in her community all about makeup. They were so happy to have her come and share her beauty secrets that her social confidence (which had plummeted after the death of her husband) rose sharply. Feeling useful and seeing how much her experience was appreciated, she no longer felt the stage fright and shyness she had been suffering on meeting new people in social situations since her husband's death. Connecting with others in a generous, giving way that uses some of your personal skills helps overcome the "narcissistic" fears of stage fright by increasing your own sense of real self-worth.

Every performance is a form of sharing with others. When you feel you're truly giving service and are a channel to transmit something of value, you're part of your own audience. That biorapport that's such an essential element of charisma rests on being able to overcome the "small self" stage fright because you're focused on something larger that you want to communicate to people. Getting your "small self" out of the way is the problem.

That old automatic fright response is left over from a time when your self-esteem was injured by a negative experience. "Every time I step on a platform, my heart jumps into my throat exactly as if my life were being threatened; it reminds me of the first public speaking experience I had when I was about nine—I stuttered and couldn't get the words out and everybody laughed at me," said Roland M., a management executive. By gritting his teeth and forcing himself, he managed to get through speaking engagements in his work without collapsing. But the internal cost was heavy: "I feel I'm going to die—it's ridiculous! Everybody thinks I'm calm, but I go through agonies. I've got to get over that! It really poisons my life every time I've got to get up and talk before a group." His Success Factor Workshop (see below) changed all that.

We all need a safe place to fail, where we won't be laughed at, fired, humiliated, or thrown out or killed if we make mistakes. NASA, the space agency, worked out some of the most complex and difficult explorations ever attempted. Mistakes are inevitable with so many unknown factors. Interestingly, they never use the word *failure* or even *mistake*. Their term is "negative successes." Can you see how this would alter attitudes toward a plan that hadn't succeeded? One can learn from it and go on without wasting energy on breast-beating, guilt, or shame. This creates a highly productive atmosphere in which risk taking is valued, not punished.

YOUR SUCCESS FACTOR WORKSHOP

If you have an early negative memory still triggering unwanted automatic responses like paralyzing stage fright, you can reprogram yourself through a Success Factor Analysis. Like all deconditioning processes, you start by relaxing totally.

1. Sit in a comfortable position, feet on the floor, hands relaxed on your lap. Starting with your feet and working your way up your body, deliberately release every muscle group in turn. (If you can't feel it, tense it first, then let go.)
2. Breathe very slowly and deeply, and mentally begin to count. On one inhalation: 1,000, 2,000, 3,000, 4,000, 5,000, 6,000. Hold for one beat, then exhale slowly, counting down: 6,000, 5,000, 4,000, 3,000, 2,000, 1,000. Repeat both sequences seven or eight times or until you are thoroughly relaxed. (Once you're used to doing it, you can put yourself into a relaxed state within two or three minutes.) At first it helps to hear another voice giving you gentle, complete directions on a relaxation tape. After a while, your body will get the idea and be able to do it by itself, having learned the specific steps from the tape. When you begin, it'll probably take about twenty-five minutes; later, you'll achieve total relaxation in about three minutes.
3. Now decide your objective. For instance: "I'd like to perform or speak in public without being paralyzed by stage fright." Raise your little finger when you've decided on your objective.

4. The part of you that always gets frightened was acting *to protect* you—a valid instinct of survival engendered by your first negative experience. What was she/he trying to protect you from? Call that part of you "Little ——— (your own first name)," and answer the question. The answer might be: "Little Tom wanted to save me from being criticized and mocked. I understand now that the fear was a protective measure so I wouldn't undergo such pain again." Raise your finger when you see this.

5. Ask Little ——— if she/he would be willing to *give up* this old way of "saving" you from destruction if Big ——— (you) could come up with a new form of protection that would be more appropriate and effective in your life now. Raise your finger when you have an agreement from Little ———

   IMPORTANT: If the part of you that is "Little ———" WON'T agree, ask her/him this question: "Would you be willing to TRY a new way and decide later if you think it's all right to give up the stage fright?" Usually, Little ——— will give this conditional agreement. Raise your little finger if it's all right to proceed.

6. Now, think back to the last time you felt completely comfortable and happy performing or talking to people. Raise your little finger when you've done this.

7. See yourself going through that experience in great detail. Hear it, see all the people who were there, see the appreciative expressions on their faces, remember how everything tasted, smelled, felt, where you were, what time of day or night it was—the entire scene. Take a few minutes to experience it as completely as you can. Enjoy it fully. Raise your little finger when you've done this.

8. Now, ask yourself: What were three qualities or personal resources that helped you in that situation and made it so successful and rewarding for you?"

   For instance, Neil S., a textile designer who wanted to be more spontaneous and comfortable talking to people, picked a time when he was made captain of his class at the age of fifteen. He decided that the three qualities he possessed then were resourcefulness, intelligence, and a genuine interest in people. He realized that he was using his intelligence and resourcefulness but, somehow, had lost contact with his interest in people.

   Having grown up on a Caribbean island, the son of a distinguished Anglo-Indian family, he was very conscious of social hierarchies, and when he came to this country, he was afraid to reveal himself to anyone lest people find him either superior or inferior! He was afraid that he might, in a new and unfamiliar society, make himself too vulnerable if he was spontaneous and open with people. "I thought people wouldn't be interested in my experience—I see now that that was when I began to lose interest in *them*. I became cold, shy, and mistrustful."

9. Now, ask yourself: How can I use these three qualities I've named as my best resources to learn a new way of handling the old challenge . . . for example, feel confidence instead of stage fright? How will these resources protect me against the "danger" of humiliation and satisfy the "Little" me?

> Neil's answer was: "I can prepare intelligently, use my resourcefulness to notice new points of interest I have in common with people, and trust my interest in people to arouse their interest in me."
>
> A singer's answer to this question was: "I have a beautiful tone, a great love of music, good judgment. The first and second are what I can count on to offer people in performance; the third will protect me from going out unprepared or from giving a bad concert. I got in touch with other resources I have, too. I'm creative and a damned good musician and I've worked hard so I deserve to succeed. I have an excellent stage presence, and I am grateful for the privilege of performing—after all, I waited on tables, did accounting, and other things that aren't any fun for me so that I could do this, which is what I love. I really want to do this! It helps a lot to realize that I'm *choosing* to sing because singing gives me more pleasure than anything else."
>
> A construction company executive said, "I have a keen knowledge of people, a thorough background in my business, and a likable personality. I realize I have a lot to contribute. I used to worry that my formal education wasn't good enough, and I was afraid to get up and speak. Now I see that I actually have experience of a wide range of people, and have been very successful in my business, and people really want to hear what I can tell them. And I do love to play the expert! So, I'm going to enjoy the opportunity next time."

If you find you perceive more than three resources, that's fine. Acknowledge them all and absorb them. If you have trouble finding three, use the one or two you are able to come up with. More will emerge later.

10. Now, keeping these three resources very much in mind, visual-

250

ize a situation coming up where you respond *in a new way,* using all your resources and enjoying it very much. See the situation in great detail: taste, smell, touch, colors, people, sounds, faces. Go through it just as you want it to happen, feeling just as comfortable and good about it as you did in the happy experience you remembered. Take a few minutes to do that. Enjoy it thoroughly; elaborate on it. Notice how much in command, how at ease, you are. Relive it. Raise your little finger when you've done this. (If it's a performance or a talk or a presentation or a meeting, SEE it happening with this new feeling of success that is you at your best—remembered from your success memory.)

11. Visualize another situation and go through it in the same way, utilizing your internal awareness of your success resources. Again, SEE, SMELL, TOUCH, TASTE, HEAR—*BE THERE.* Take five minutes to enjoy this.

12. Repeat the process, this time making your fantasy as satisfying as the best experience you ever had.

13. Now, notice how you are sitting. Don't move. Observe closely. This position is your Body Trigger, with which you'll always be able to activate your "Success Factors." Your head may be to one side, your fist on your chin. You may notice your arms are folded across your chest and your legs crossed. Just take careful note and, whenever you want to get back into that state of feeling unscared and in touch with your own charisma and personal power, assume this position and visualize your upcoming challenging situation. *The physiological reinforcement of your happy memories serves to lock in the new positive responses.*

14. Close your eyes and take a moment to get in touch with Little (you). Thank her/him for trying so hard in the past to protect you against humiliation and failure, and ask if she/he recognizes it's safe now to let go of the old Little (you) because you've found a better way. Assure Little (you) that you will always be there for protection and support, and that she/he has nothing to worry about anymore. This internal conversation can take place just with feelings—a wordless exchange which is nevertheless very real. Some people even feel their "Little Self" placing a small hand in theirs and expressing trust. It's amazing that one can feel very comforted and confident, having nurtured the small frightened person that, for most of us, still exists inside in some situations. Having taken care of your "child," the "child" will stop getting in the way of your grown-up self, knowing it's safe.

   If you had a skeptical, resistant inner Little Self, ask now, "Do you feel okay about changing the way you're going to protect me now?" If the "child" is still not sure, ask him/her to help you try out the new way anyway. Get a positive response. Thank your "child."

15. Periodically, when you have a performance or situation coming up that evokes some of the old stage fright, run through this process again to reinforce your success resources and rout the old shadow responses.

All successful performers eventually find ways to master their stage fright, though some never lose it completely. Everyone evolves his or her own "system." Know your own tension spots, use the exercises in this section, and experiment to see how they affect you. Then you can select and use those that work best and fastest for you.

Meditation is another important tool that demonstrably has reduced stress for thousands of people. It can give you just enough detachment to make all your preparation pay off. Meditation lowers blood pressure, slows the heartbeat, and gives you a deeper rest than normal sleep. Because there is usually a great deal of spontaneous, borderline imagery during meditation, the period of REM (rapid eye movement) imagery in sleep is unnecessary. You may well find, therefore, that you need far less sleep. I used to need eight hours' sleep. After a number of years of practicing meditation, I am perfectly happy with five. For a quick rest, I find that a ten-minute shoulder stand is as good as two hours' sleep.

The Alternate Breathing, the Right Nostril Breath, and the Breath of Fire are all fast energizers (See chapter 14).

When you prepare for a performance or an especially important presentation, interview, or meeting with people who make you nervous, don't forget the importance of eating and drinking wisely.

The most common cause of high stress in the United States is malnutrition, according to Dr. Warren M. Levin, an orthomolecular physician. Poor eating habits aggravate the effects of all other stressors on the system. Nutritionists emphasize the importance of avoiding "empty" calories (sodas and snack foods) as well as bleached flour, sugar, and refined foods. It's even more critical to eat wisely when you're under stress. Rushing and gulping food guarantees inadequate food absorption. Thorough chewing is necessary for good digestion. An enzyme called ptyalin in our saliva stimulates the production of hydrochloric acid in the stomach. It's only released by adequate chewing. (Try twenty times for each bite—it's a wonderful way to keep your weight down, too. It's difficult to overeat when you chew long and well.) We can't be well nourished without good digestion.

It's important to have fresh foods without additives and chemicals as the mainstay of your diet. Many stars drink fresh-squeezed vegetable juices, high in minerals and vitamins. Tennis pros claim that a carrot-celery cocktail gives them a great "lift" between matches. Many people are turning to vegetarianism. Meat, which takes days to digest, is frequently contaminated with hormones and chemicals, which then pass into our systems. The United States Senate Committee on Nutrition and Human Needs, headed by Senator George McGovern, strongly recommended less red meat and sugar and greater emphasis on whole grains and vegetables as a national health measure.

While we're constantly reminded that smoking is a deadly hazard to our health, many people don't know that it destroys the vitamin C in our bodies. Even nonsmokers lose vitamin C when exposed to other people's smoking.

NEVER EAT WHEN YOU'RE NERVOUS! If you're scheduled to speak after dinner, beware of overloading yourself with food. Eat very little and chew very thoroughly what you do eat. ("Chew your drink and drink your food!" Grandma used to caution.) Avoid iced drinks; ice chills your stomach and increases your discomfort. Skip liquor altogether. Heavy coffee drinking increases stress and nervousness and robs your system of B vitamins. Coffee is a drug that can make you a lot more jittery than you would otherwise be. If you're aware of being nervous, keep up the slow, even breathing; it'll do wonders. Peppermint tea, too, is soothing to the stomach, and stimulating. I always carry little bags of peppermint and chamomile tea with me when I travel; it's easy to get hot water and make tea yourself in hotels and coffee shops. Chamomile tea is soothing, too, but may make you sleepy. Try it at night for insomnia.

It's better to have small, light meals frequently than one heavy one. A few nuts and raisins, carrot sticks, alfalfa sprouts, an apple —these will give you quick energy when you're under stress without making you logy. When your stomach is busy digesting food, your mind can't be as alert as you'd like because blood is rushing to your stomach.

Somebody once estimated that the effect of a performance on an actor's nervous system is roughly equal to the shock of a minor car accident. This is true, to some degree, of all performances. You must treat your system with attention and intelligent care. A regular exercise routine (yoga, jogging, dance, or outdoor walking) is helpful for cutting down preperformance nervousness too because it improves the state of your entire nervous system. Above all, do the deep, slow breathing; that's the MASTER CONTROL.

Experiment with the stage fright exercises and suggestions given here to find the best combination and timing for you. Your stage fright preparation is absolutely essential for your best performance. Every artist develops certain preferred rituals and is meticulous about observing them.

Luciano Pavarotti loves to kid around in rehearsals, but prepares entirely alone and with great seriousness for an hour before every performance. Ballet star Alicia Markova always spent several hours immersing herself gradually in the role of Giselle. After a meal at two in the afternoon, singer Joan Sutherland takes a nap and doesn't eat again until after the evening's performance.

Plan intelligently to give yourself all possible support in terms of adequate rehearsal, de-stressing exercises, nutritional backup, chanting, meditation, or prayer.

When you want something more than you fear it, you can act freely.

Peter Serkin, the concert pianist son of distinguished pianist Rudolph Serkin and grandson of another great musician, Adolf Busch, rebelled against following the family tradition and dropped out of music for a year. He went to live in a little Mexican village where there was only the native music. One day, on a classical radio station, he heard a Bach *Brandenburg* Concerto and thought to himself, "How wonderful that I can make music like that!" He returned to his career, feeling now that he was choosing it himself. Music became his joy and stage fright took a back seat.

If you get nervous even practicing your presentation or performance, do your stage fright warm-ups before rehearsal. As a matter of fact, it's a good idea to do the warm-ups even if you're not nervous. You'll find you're able to work more efficiently and with a lot more pleasure. It seems so simple and natural when everything is going well that it's hard to realize what an extraordinary boost the de-stressing exercises will give you. We *are* under a lot of stress most of the time, and to recover the childlike spontaneity and pleasure in what we're doing and join that to the knowledge and skills of our adult achievement is a tremendous challenge.

Every moment is an experience in itself as well as preparation for the future. When you see the connections between your past successes and what you want to do, you can trust yourself more to bring the preparation you've already had to your new tasks.

Linda L., vice-president of a paper manufacturer, moaned, "When I have a presentation to prepare, I write everything out and memorize it, but it sounds dead and I feel miserable about it."

In Linda's Success Factor Workup, she remembered (as her three greatest resources) her sense of humor, her enjoyment of new experiences, and her pleasure in communicating with people. Then I asked her to talk on something she was passionate about. To her own surprise, she talked fluently with no notes whatever and very expressive body language on mountain climbing, her hobby.

"You see," I pointed out, "you just learned what your real style is—from your own spontaneous moments. That's the style you want to catch in your business talks. It's a lot easier and more natural than what you were trying to do. Don't write out the whole speech. Outline the points you want to make, know your first sentence and last, have notes only for statistics you want to refer to, rehearse six to eight times, and you're ready—not to lecture, but to talk to people! Every talk is a dialogue between you and the audience. Only you have to use your imagination to fill in what they would like to know and ask you."

Linda became an accomplished speaker for her company and, with her new ease and enjoyment of speaking in public, accepted the presidency of a major professional association.

Make Stage Fright a Tingle Instead of a Torture

1. Grab opportunities to talk to people on other subjects than the one you're required to do. Experience makes everything easier if it's good experience. The ease of speaking *when it doesn't matter* takes the pressure off. Having spoken comfortably where it wasn't required, having given a lot of pleasure to people who responded with appreciation, your confidence level will rise. Any success, even minor and unrelated, is wonderful preparation for more difficult challenges.

2. Do three nice things for someone else every day, for no reason, expecting nothing in return. (Try for a face-to-face exchange so you can enjoy the pleasure and warmth this will generate, first in yourself and then in others.) This too is confidence-building. You will have *acted,* instead of passively suffering fear and apprehension; this makes you feel more yourself, more powerful, generous, and charismatic. You will have done something because you chose to, regardless of what other people expected.

3. Sharing a laugh with people is profoundly helpful in reducing anxiety. Seize every opportunity to enjoy a light moment, even with people you only see briefly: taxi driver, postman, doorman, fellow passenger waiting at a bus stop. Establishing connections makes you feel you're supported, not alone. Brief, friendly encounters with strangers make audiences seem less strange and alien. Your private self has expanded a little in a warm outreach. The world itself seems suddenly more friendly. Then it's easier to share what you're doing with others and concentrate on shaping your "gift" to them, whatever the performance happens to be.

All this will help you get your small, frightened self out of the way and move out of the stage fright into the stage light, enjoying the warmth, connecting with your larger self, the one that makes you feel confident, at your best, and in touch with your audience, basking in the shared warmth of your moments together.

That's where your charisma can really shine, shedding light as well as warmth all around you!

Stage Fright Exercises

THE INFALLIBLE BUTTERFLIES CHASER

Great for last-minute (or earlier) preperformance nerves.

1. Stand with your feet apart, knees a little bent, back straight, arms relaxed and hanging loosely at your sides.
2. Without taking any additional breath, do ten short bounces, saying "Vuh!" on each. Do this as energetically as possible, making the *vuh* a short, sharp, forceful sound (coming from the gut).° Punch downward on each "Vuh" with both fists.
3. Relax and, with mouth closed, inhale slowly and very deeply.
4. Exhale in a steady stream (*sh-h-h-h*) with mouth slightly open, letting the body sink into the knees.
   Repeat three times; follow with long, slow breathing.

Follow immediately with the

SA-TA-NA-MA CHANT

This chant balances the two sides of your brain and provides a cooling, reassuring sense of smoothness and flow. It's particularly good when you're waiting to go onstage. It can be kept up under your breath and will keep you calm and steady in performance.

Ra means Sun; Ma means moon; SA TA NA MA is SAT NAM (truth essence) broken into component parts for the cycle of Birth, Life, Death, Rebirth. Hear the steady hum underneath the words, and keep that going. The sounds should be continuous, and each double syllable should take only the same time as each single, i.e., "Rama" and "Mama" are said twice as quickly as "Ra" and "Ma" so that all syllables take only about one half second.

Ra	Ra	Ra	Ra
Ma	Ma	Ma	Ma
Rama	Rama	Rama	Rama
Mama	Mama	Mama	Mama
SA	TA	NA	MA

Repeat for at least five minutes.

° If you're unable to manage ten bounces at first, do as many as you can and gradually work up to the full ten.

ENERGY EXPANDER

When you're weary, sleepy, or need energy,

1. Contract your middle as though it had been kicked by a horse, and at the same time, let out a short, sharp *huh* sound. Do as many as you can without breathing, gradually working up to at least ten.
2. Relax and inhale, expanding your abdomen and diaphragm.

Repeat ten times.

DEPRESSURIZER

1. Stand in a doorway and press your palms against the door-frame on both sides. Hold your breath and keep increasing the pressure—you'll feel warmth rushing to your face, head, and neck. Hold as long as you can.
2. Release totally, with a rush. Drop your hands as you exhale.
3. Inhale deeply.

Repeat three times.

KARATE CHOP

1. Stand with legs eighteen inches apart, bend your knees, clench fists at your sides next to your knees.
2. Pretend you're lifting a heavy bucket filled with sand in three short, sharp bursts of inhalation (mouth closed) so that by the third you're stretched upward, arms overhead as high as they will go, fists still clenched.
3. CRASH! Bring both fists down together in a tremendous karate chop, at the same time yelling, *"HEHHHHHHHH!"* or *"HÄHHHHHHHH!"*

Repeat five times.

STEAM ENGINE

1. Stand with legs eighteen inches apart, head erect, mouth closed. Make fists with both hands.
2. Pull right arm straight back and, at the same time, punch left arm forward (without leaning into it) as powerfully as possible, exhaling forcefully.

3. Draw left arm back, inhale as fists pass each other, and, as right arm punches forward, exhale forcefully. Maintain a steady, even rhythm, and keep the mouth closed.

Repeat as powerfully and steadily as you can for three to five minutes.

This produces tremendous energy discharge through chest, shoulders, arms, hands, and neck. Instantly enhances your courage and releases tension.

THE I DON'T CARE SWING

The ability to let go and release our effortfulness is essential to maintaining productivity. Any tension that is sustained without release will lead to reduced efficiency in functioning, and eventually stress the body/mind enough to produce an illness or breakdown. At the very least, we do not absorb information as well, listen as productively, think as creatively, or interact as effectively with others, unless we can achieve a childlike release of tension as often as necessary during our activities. Becoming aware of and sensitive to what your own biofeedback instrument—your body/mind—is registering is the first step to discharging the stress and renewing your energy. As children, we have natural anti-stressing techniques which we forget as we grow up. Getting in touch with the playful spirit and rebelliousness of a child is enormously rewarding and is an effective device for quick, efficient tension release.

1. Stand feet apart, approximately as wide as your shoulders. Slowly swivel whole torso/neck/head as one piece to one side, then the other, to feel what it is like to move the whole upper portion of your body as a unit. Do this a few times, slowly.
2. Now, let your arms swing from side to side, freely, at shoulder level, until they loosely wrap around your body, as you swing from side to side, torso/neck/head swiveling.
3. As your torso swings first to the left, then all the way to the right, "*I DON'T CARE!*" or "*NO, I WON'T!*" or "*YOU CAN'T MAKE ME!*" is shouted freely. Enjoy yourself! Do this at least twenty times. (Make sure that your head goes all the way around with the torso.)

Allow your eyes to unfocus as you swing and this becomes an effective eye-relaxing exercise as well.

THE CHUTZPAH (COURAGE) EXERCISE—THE ELBOW
PROPELLER

For stimulation of the chest and heart, relaxation of shoulder,
neck tension, and increasing ability to *take risks* and feel
energized:

1. Stand feet apart, knees slightly bent, elbows at sides, hands
   hanging limp from wrists.
2. Begin to rotate arms, leading with elbows in largest vertical
   circle possible, close to the body, ten times forward, then ten
   times backward—as rapidly and energetically as possible,
   mouth closed.
3. Finish with three long complete breaths (in and out) and
   relax.

This will give you instant alertness when you're tired, logy,
sleepy, or diffident, and step up your vitality.

More Stage Fright Exercises

I. Pointillist Necklace (Drunken Head Roll; see p. 322.) Three
   times in each direction.
II. Helium Ball Yawn (See p. 344.)
III. Head Alignment
   a. Drop head on chest.
   b. Slowly, slowly unroll neck from the back, keeping chin
      in, one vertebra at a time (eyes open), with the
      slowest possible continuous movement. When head
      is exactly at the end of the spine, like a flower at
      the end of its stem,
   c. Stop. Note position. Is it higher or lower than usual?
   d. Feel that you are looking straight ahead with your
      entire body—your head is very much part of the
      whole trunk.
   e. Maintain your open throat, straight back, proud head,
      and direct gaze. Notice the feeling of power and
      integration this gives you.
IV. PREPERFORMANCE LOOK
   a. Smile broadly.
   b. Drop smile from your mouth, but leave it in eyes and
      on cheekbones. Eyes sparkle; cheekbones are lifted
      and round.

    c. Inhale and feel the resultant look: "Something good is about to happen!" "I have a wonderful secret!" Great when you're being introduced on a dais, on TV, or at a party.

12

Breathing—The Bridge to Bio-Rapport

PNEUMA:
1. A breath, breathing.
2. Soul, spirit, according to some ancient philosophers, the universal spirit or primordial substance.
3. The life-giving principle, and the Spirit superior to both soul and body.

. . . An intermediate nature which, though distinct from the mortal Soul or Pneuma, is the source of vital activity.

—HIPPOCRATES

. . . A dream, a breath, a froth of fleeting joy.

—SHAKESPEARE,
The Rape of Lucrece, 212

BREATH is the link between body and mind. In the sea of emotion in which we live, breath is the intermediary that changes the chemistry of our consciousness.

For centuries yogis have known very detailed ways of controlling the body and the mind, and used elaborate breathing practices to produce whatever states of consciousness they wished. With our Western taste for mechanized technology, the simplicity of *breathing* still seems more primitive than using drugs, medicines, jogging, weights to harmonize, heal, and whole ourselves. It almost seems indecent to take breathing out of the quasi-military context which was, at least for most male Americans, their only introduction to this subject (except for a few crackpots and weirdos). "Suck in your gut!" "Shoulders back, stomach flat, and BREATHE!" barked the Marine sergeant. The harsh strain of effortful breathing, divorced from the tender belly and gut feelings, is an integral part of our jock sports, media blitz, driven business life, and stressed existence. In some way it's probably a legacy from our Puritan heritage. The delicate filaments of breath that have been known for centuries to mystical traditions as the doorway to expanded consciousness, long life, health, altered states, and remarkable feats were, in our macho society, invisible, even unthinkable.

For women, too, instruction would come as a tag-end reminder: "Mary, stand up straight and *breathe!*" or "Don't get angry—just take a deep breath and count to ten!" At the same time, everybody was told, "Hold in your tummy." So now we have a society of uptight people, cut off from their gut feelings. "Uptight" is a beautifully expressive description of what happens physically when people are tense. The entire center of gravity in the body (which ought to be two inches below the navel—what the Japanese call Hara and the Chinese the T'an Tsien) shifts upward because the stomach is held taut. Deprived of support and oxygen, the upper body is tight and strained.

The effects on personality are profound. Inside you're likely to feel nervous, anxious, worried, or irritable (if you're aware of your feelings). It's difficult to act spontaneously. When the pressure gets too intense you may blow up or withdraw from the situation. You look for distraction so you won't notice that you're pretty uncomfortable a lot of the time.

If you live in a city, the air isn't great to breathe anyway, so you avoid more than the absolute minimum. Who needs to inhale smog, gasoline, exhaust, and industrial fumes? Better to breathe as little as possible, except on vacations! (I once did a Broadway musical with Wally Cox, the comedian, who played his own sketch, which pretended to be a documentary about a young slum inhabitant. He came out on the stoop, looked around

—it was early morning—and took three slow, very guarded sniffs. Clearly that was his welcome to the day and all the breath it was safe to take. The audience howled with laughter—the recognition factor was high.)

We all know that you can live without food and drink for some time, but not without breathing. Just because we do take it so much for granted, it's hard for most people to realize how the very quality of their lives can change radically merely because they can control the quality of their breathing.

Most people breathe between twelve and eighteen breaths a minute. Take a moment to see how many breaths you take in one minute without making any special effort to slow down or otherwise alter your normal breathing pattern. You may notice, if you're paying attention, that your breath is uneven, choppy, or shallow; there may be a pause between the intake and the exhalation; you may find it's noisy or your nose is stuffed a good deal of the time. But that's nothing, just a minor inconvenience, not even worth bothering about—right? Wrong! We now know (and scientists are paying increasing attention to the little-noticed subtle interconnections between brain function and breath) that not only are all emotional states connected to particular breathing patterns, but that just by slowing and deepening your breathing you can:

overcome anger and fear
put yourself to sleep
expand your electromagnetic field
cure insomnia
lower high blood pressure
give yourself courage
alleviate pain
calm the nervousness of people around you
increase your personal charisma
stop smoking
strengthen your will
clear your mind
improve your digestion
regulate your heartbeat
calm your nervousness
increase your vitality and pleasure
improve mental functioning and concentration

Since we are creatures of rhythmicity, ebb and flow, systole and diastole, we need an alternation between effortless, relaxed deep breathing and at least ten minutes a day of continuous activity (if we're physically able, preferably around some greenery).

The vital quality of your personality, the alertness of your brain, the steadiness of your nerves all depend to a large extent on your breathing. With so many different interwoven systems contributing to the complicated interactions between our minds, bodies, spirits, and the society and time we live in, it's about the only one we can totally control and the only one that can change all the others.

Since all life follows rhythmic patterns, we "tune" to the patterns of the natural world and feel more connected with the vitality and rhythms of the universe when we increase the depth and vitality of our breathing. The passion for jogging that gripped the country is evidence of the need to reassert our natural sense of psychophysical aliveness in the face of increasingly denatured living conditions. Deadened commercial foods, stripped of nutrients and loaded with chemicals to guarantee a long shelf life; the increasing incidence of stress-related diseases (which account for 80 percent of our national mortality rate); the staggering costs of hospital care, drugs, and iatrogenic (doctor-induced) illness—all have at last alerted growing numbers of people to the need for taking responsibility for the quality of our own lives and health.

The simplest, most accessible tool for change is breathing. The simple, astonishing fact is that when you breathe seven breaths a minute or less, your entire metabolism changes, your personality is perceived differently, you'll be regarded as more composed, more authoritative and, oddly enough, more vivid; *and you are!* The breath is an incredibly subtle register of all the shifts in your thoughts and feelings. It's the single most potent tool for releasing your charisma.

Nervous or angry people breathe shallowly, mostly from the upper chest only. Depressed people have heavy, labored breathing. Recent studies confirm what everybody has always known: when you're happy you breathe deeply and fully. Chest breathing can, all by itself, produce unsteadiness of mind.

The average adult inhales about half a quart of air on each breath. This is shallow, chest breathing. With abdominal (deep chest) breathing, this can be doubled. With the Whole Body Breath (see pp. 326-7) you can take in three or four quarts of air. This is probably six to eight times what you're getting now. More air means better heart and lung condition, better skin, more complete digestion, improved morale. When the lungs are filled with air from the very bottom upward, they compress, giving a gentle massage to your heart. The diaphragm, too, by contracting and relaxing, massages the heart, liver, pancreas, and improves the functioning of the spleen, small intestine, stomach, and abdomen.

When I ask people in my Charismedia groups how they visualize breathing, most people smile and wave airily up and down the length of their bodies. A few suggest hesitantly that the movement of air is spherical, but they usually know this intellectually and can't put it into practice. When you ask a group to take a deep breath, the shoulders go up, they pull their stomachs in and stick their chests out with convulsive gasps. Then they look apologetic because, clearly, they can't go on doing that. It's too exhausting.

The Breath Balloon

The best way to discover how you're really meant to breathe is to lie down on the floor with your hands at your sides. If there is a hollow between the middle of your back and the floor, raise your knees until your back touches the floor along its whole length. Now, put one hand on your abdomen so you can feel and see the abdomen expand as you inhale.

Imagine that your entire lower abdomen and back is a beautiful balloon in your favorite color. It's going to fill up from the bottom (between your legs). Naturally, a balloon swells when it fills with air. Be prepared to feel your abdomen and sides swell evenly all around, exactly like a balloon. The mind can process millions of images in a microsecond, so this single image of your favorite-colored balloon will be the perfect wordless teacher for your new breathing process.

It's interesting that even old patterns are backed by a subconscious picture. Although they hadn't realized it before I asked, when people gestured in front of their bodies to show the vertical direction, they suddenly became aware that the picture represented the way they functioned. When you change your image, your body/mind instantly internalizes all the information necessary and is able to integrate it into a new process. If you described it in words it would take pages and pages and still would be very hard to follow. That's the great advantage of learning from a right-hemisphere image instead of a linear left-hemisphere model. Like a hologram, the information is compressed into a single image, which then breaks up into components to be reassembled where and when they're needed.

Think how difficult it would be to give a linear description of even such a simple process as walking or lifting a finger! I once spent two hours watching a swan on Central Park lake to see if I could predict the exact curve of its neck as it slowly lifted it, again and again, out of the water. Not being linear, that movement was astonishingly varied and subtle. Slow-motion photography would probably show that it was never exactly the same twice.

So it is with your breath balloon. If you visualize it as exactly and vividly as you can, you'll be able to get a uniform swelling of the whole area from the groin to the lower ribs, front, sides, and back in the most unforced and organic way. Then allow the top part of the balloon to expand your ribs and upper back as well. But it's important NOT to start the breath up there. If you do, you'll bypass the abdominal breathing and wind up with the old, hasty, shallow breath that only uses one-third of your lung capacity. That one's over before it's done you any good.

Before You Start Your New Breathing, Empty the Balloon. Most people never fully exhale. So many toxins are left stored in the body that there isn't enough room for new breath energy to come in, not to mention the residual tension that stays in the muscles if they're not "vacuumed" by breath. Exhale—and see and feel the balloon deflating until it's quite limp and flat. When you think you can't let any more air out, empty still more. *Then—*

Begin Filling the Balloon from the Bottom. The first part of the inhale should be almost imperceptible. The most common mistake people make is rushing convulsively as though there wouldn't be room or time to get enough air. Make the beginning of the breath the smallest, quietest you can. KEEP YOUR

MOUTH CLOSED. It's important to breathe through your nose. Put a small cushion under your head if you're more comfortable that way.

The Nose Knows

Your nose, you may be surprised to learn, performs close to thirty functions. It's the narrowest place in the respiratory tract and takes 150 percent of the effort that breathing through the mouth does (even if your nose doesn't feel stuffed up). Then why do it? There are profound reasons why it's important. We breathe 18–20,000 times a day, so mouth breathing requires a lot more energy. Your nose filters, moisturizes, directs air flow, conveys smells, warms the air, brings in oxygen, creates mucus, acts as a drainage passageway for the sinuses, and—most important—affects the nervous system.

We have an internal and an external nose. There we're unique. The ape, for instance, has no external nose. But the shape of our noses has a good deal to do with the climate our forebears came from. People from cold climates or very dry ones like the Middle East are apt to have long noses. In the tropics, the inhabitants have wide-open nostrils, since the air needs less processing. (For some inexplicable reason, however, a lot of Scandinavians have short noses.) The outside nose gathers the air and accelerates its flow into the cavity of the internal nose. The way that stream of air is aimed inside the head is extremely important.

The inside of the nose is a very complex, interesting place. The "floor" is also the roof of the mouth, the palate. If you move your tongue backward you find a place where suddenly the roof becomes softer. At the back of that is a little teardrop-shaped fleshy organ—the uvula. The roof of the nose is also the floor of the brain and the eyeball cavities, just the way the floor of the nose is the roof of the mouth. It's a kind of three-story house with the brain, eyes, and optic nerves on the top floor, the mouth on the bottom, and the nasal cavity in between.

Few people realize how closely related the internal nose is to the brain, the nervous system, and the pituitary gland (on the floor of the brain); the cranial olfactory nerve has nerve endings in the upper part of the compartment. The inside of the nose is bumpy, lumpy, and cleverly designed to move the air in certain directions. The turbinates, three shell-like bulges you can see if you tilt your head and look in the mirror, stir and circulate the air and protect the sensitive tissues of the lungs, adding moisture and humidity. The turbinates baffle the air, stir it up, and indirectly cause our winter-drippy noses (as you exhale, the moisture in the warm air condenses on the outside). The mucous membrane also helps the inside of the nose cleanse itself—because it picks up dust and microbes and, since it's always moving, carries the undesirable debris out. The "mucous blanket," as it is called, with its millions of cilia, minute hairlike structures, is a clever device for keeping all the microbes moving so they don't settle down and cause infection.

It's a brilliant system but it doesn't always work. If the mucus is too thick, it dries out and forms a crust; if it's too runny, you get a watery nasal drip.

What you eat has a great deal to do with the texture and amount of mucus. Milk products and citrus fruits like oranges, as well as sugary, starchy foods, produce a thicker mucus. The mucus is not only a secretion to protect our lungs, but excretion, when the other excretory organs (lungs, skin, bowels, kidneys, and uterus) can't rid the body of accumulated waste. Everything is connected. Processed foods clog the digestive system, antiperspirants prevent the skin from taking its share of excretory functions, lack of fiber causes constipation. The systems back up. The body responds by discharging quantities of mucus. That's how overeating, a poor diet, or constipation can produce a cold. Eating only greens for a day or two, cutting out meat and milk products, taking a laxative, drinking one teaspoon apple cider vinegar in water several times a day—these are quick ways to restore the body's alkaline balance and avoid the decline into colds and respiratory infections.

Most organs are echoes of others in body. The curve of the pelvis is repeated in the palm and the ear. The upper half of the body is a mirror image of the lower. The hands and feet are related—through both, pressure on sensitive points can relieve organs all over the body. The nose, interestingly, is related to the sex organs. Underneath the mucous membrane is a spongy layer of erectile tissue, which is also found in the genitals and breasts. Freud wrote about the interaction between the sex organs and the nose. Originally he developed his basic theory through correspondence with an ear, nose, and throat specialist, Wilhelm Fliess. They were both interested in the reflexes that link the nasal lining and reproductive organs. They found that they could "cure" menstrual cramps by anesthetizing certain parts of the lining of the nose. There is an interesting phenomenon called "honeymoon nose," familiar to ear, nose, and throat specialists. The continual sexual stimulation of the honeymoon period causes the erectile tissue of the nose to become chronically engorged, like aroused genitals.

The links with the brain are also profound. Usually the air flows through first the right, then the left nostril, alternating every ninety minutes to two hours. This is a natural biological rhythm, named "infradian rhythm" by Western scientists who "discovered" what the ancient yogis knew thousands of years ago. Certain activities are more appropriate for right-nostril flow, others for left. Research has shown that nostril dominance correlates with whichever brain hemisphere is more active.* Physiological and psychological states are reflected in nostril dominance. By controlling which nostril is functioning, it's possible to "tune" with the activity you're involved in. For instance, before eating the right nostril should be open; before drinking water, the left. Breathing through the left nostril generally connects with the right side of the brain and produces a quieter, more inner-directed state.

The cycle of breath alternation follows the cycle of the moon. At dawn there is a natural polarity of breath, depending on whether solar or lunar energy is dominant. The new moon initiates a left-nostril cycle; the full moon a right-nostril one. Solar energy is more constant; it's never altogether absent during the day, and its cycle lasts a year. The moon, of course, waxes and wanes regularly, and its 29½-day cycle governs the ocean's tides.

Since 70 percent of human body weight is water, the moon also affects us profoundly. The night of the full moon traditionally causes a kind of madness: dogs bay; people go haywire; these are times of high tides. In the darkest night, when the tides are at their lowest ebb, human emotional power is also at

* In other words, if you're breathing predominantly through the left nostril, the right hemisphere is more active and vice versa.

its weakest. More people die in the early hours before dawn than at any other time.

Swar (breath) Yoga details the best activities for whichever nostril is dominant. No need to worry if the wrong nostril is clear. (You can tell by closing off one side with one finger, and seeing if the air flow is cooler there than the other, or if the other side is more open. After some practice, you can check this out without closing off one nostril as you become more aware of the subtleties of breath flow.) There are several ways to change the flow of air from one side to the other. If you lie on your left side, the right side will open. The pressure on the arm and side of your chest sets up a reflex which automatically dilates the nostril that is up and closes off the lower one. This takes between three and ten minutes. Putting your knee or fist in your armpit will give you the same result.

After meals, lie on the left to stimulate the digestive process with the open right nostril. When you go to bed, if you lie on the left side for five or ten minutes, the opened right nostril will create increased body heat. When you're warm and comfortable, turn to the right; that lets the left nostril open. Then you're relaxed, calmed, and ready for sleep.

Sometimes the air will flow through both nostrils, but if one side is closed for as much as six to eight hours, some illness is on the way. The breath is related to the flow of energy (*prana*); imbalance always precedes the appearance of disease symptoms.

Right Breath	Left Breath
Left hemisphere dominant	Right hemisphere dominant
Sun	Moon
Electrical	Magnetic
Acidic	Alkaline
Hot	Cold
Operates after sunset	Operates after sunrise
Operates for one hour after sunrise following full moons	Operates for one hour after sunrise following the darkest night or new moon
Descending moon cycle	Ascending moon cycle
Fire	Water
Air	Earth
Sunday—east	Wednesday—west

Saturday—north	Thursday—south
Tuesday	Friday, Monday
Unstable short-term jobs for immediate profit	Peaceful long-term activities not for immediate gain
Eating, sleeping, defecating	Drinking, urinating
Bathing, studying	Playing music
Hatha Yoga	Getting married
Mantra chanting	Healing pain or depression

Both Operating at Once

Hemispheres in equilibrium
Operates exactly at sunrise and sunset
Operates briefly during the hourly transition from one nostril to the other
Ether
Concentration
Meditation
Worship

This calendar from Swar (breath) Yoga gives you an idea of the elaborate and precise correlations of nostril dominance with many activities and aspects of human existence. Great importance is given to living in harmony with natural cycles. That means getting up at least twenty minutes before sunrise every morning to prepare for the day, cleansed and sitting quietly. (At yoga ashrams, or spiritual communities, everybody gets up at 3:30 A.M. for a two-hour stint of chanting, exercise, and meditation. Many people in the West practice these disciplines, then go off to their work as lawyers, teachers, etc., like the rest of the world.)

If, when you wake up, the wrong nostril is dominant, change it right away; otherwise the day may be negative and present obstacles. When you get out of bed, first notice which nostril is more open and step out of bed on the corresponding foot. (Presumably "night people" are somewhat out of sync with natural cycles.) All this develops a much greater sensitivity to subtle cues of body, mind, and feeling, plus a host of strategies to cope with imbalances that arise.

One of the pleasantest pieces of advice out of this ancient tradition is this: on awaking, observe which nostril is open, then kiss the corresponding palm and stretch; you then give thanks for the day and step out of bed on, of course, the corresponding foot. A gentle salt-water nostril wash clears any mucus from the nose and leaves you feeling clearheaded and awake.

The constantly changing phenomenon of air flow is both cause and result of emotional, mental, and physiological states and functions. Rudolph Ballentine, M.D., and Swami Rama, in their book *Science of Breath*, write that "the pattern of engorgement in the turbinates and the resulting shape of air flow is apparently like a central clearinghouse, or switchboard, where all the body's functions are having an effect, and in turn being affected. Research has shown that the flow of air touching the surface of various areas of the turbinates triggers neuronal responses that set up reflexes throughout the body. In other words, a specific current of air sends out ripples into both the lungs and the nervous system that affect the whole person."

It's fascinating and awesome to realize how the smallest details are intimately connected with the most profound forces in the universe. Who could guess the critical role our noses play?

There is something faintly comic about the nose. It doesn't enjoy the dignity or respect of the eyes or mouth. It can be a source of embarrassment because it's so subject to dripping, running, and reddening. People are often dissatisfied with the shape of their noses (a fact which continues to enrich plastic surgeons). An exposed and dimly shamed air hovers about the nose, implying it is grateful to be admitted to polite company but may at any moment compromise its owner in some unexpected, indelicate, and socially or sexually unsuitable way. Moderate sneezing is acceptable, but blowing, picking, scratching, and fingering are distinctly out, and a possible source of sudden disgrace. And then there are the indignities of smells. Altogether an unreliable organ.

What has this slightly ridiculous, ingeniously designed body part to do with your charisma?

The nose is a humble but powerful asset in your arsenal of resources at your disposal for putting you at ease and making the most of your powers and ability to achieve bio-rapport with others. You just must understand how to control its whims.

That probably makes you laugh, or at least smile.

Whenever I first give the following exercises in my workshop, people snicker, look incredulous, amused, or otherwise indicate they feel foolish. But everybody quickly becomes an enthusiastic apostle once they've tried them. They're astoundingly simple and effective.

The Emotion Cooler

If you're feeling angry, upset, tearful, anxious, irritable, or nervous:

1. Put your right thumb on your right nostril, lightly closing it off.
2. Exhale. Inhale slowly through your left nostril only for twenty-six complete breaths.
   * Keep your mouth closed throughout.
   * Keep the breaths as long and even as you can.
   * Visualize the breath stream going up your nasal passages and across the corpus callosum to the right hemisphere of your brain, scooping it out as though there were nothing in it but limitless distances and pure, radiant energy.
   * If there is any obstruction in your nasal passage, *imagine* a tiny stream of air bypassing the blockage and making its way smoothly up into the right hemisphere.
   * With each exhalation, release all the tension, anger, annoyance, hurt, or other negative emotions you are feeling, and visualize it all draining out of your whole body, emptying from every pore. Each time you exhale, let go of more —not just what happened today, but last week, last year, and all of your life, until you are completely released and clear.
   * Stay empty for a second or two before you begin the next inhalation. Enjoy the increasing relaxation of your whole body and mind.

Allan S., a sales supervisor, said, "I often have difficult phone calls to make. One client particularly has a tendency to get abusive. He screams and yells over the phone. I tried the Emotion Cooler and found he didn't 'get to me.' I just let him rave on without saying a word, concentrating on exhaling what I was hearing so it wouldn't affect me. After a few minutes, he must have sensed something because he stopped, suddenly calmed down, and began to talk normally and reasonably."

Edith H., a junior high school teacher, told us, "One day I had an unpleasant argument with one of the students who was very rude and insolent. To my horror, I realized I was on the verge of tears. To cry at that moment would have been disastrous. I excused myself and went to the ladies' room to do the Emotion Cooler. In a very few minutes, when I had finished, I was calm and able to go back and discipline the student. If I had not done this, I'd have lost my authority entirely. I couldn't have pulled myself together if I hadn't done the exercise."

Another student did not get along well with her father. Now, when she spoke to him on the phone, she kept her thumb on her right nostril the whole time and breathed only through the left. "The first time I tried it, I had the first conversation with Dad since I moved away from home when I didn't either fight with him or cry. I realized suddenly that he was unhappy, too, and I could just listen without getting defensive."

For quick energy: Reverse the nostrils, i.e., close off the left one with your left thumb. This brings energy through the right-side nostril to the left hemisphere of the brain. Repeat twenty-six times.

The Magic Breath Exercise

Let's go back to the position you were in for the Breath Balloon. Lie on the floor, your back flat, hands relaxed at your sides or one hand on your abdomen to feel the breathing. I have a little jade statue of Buddha with a very fat belly; he's laughing. I ask my students to run their hands over it because it helps them get the feeling of the swelling breath and makes it easier for them to "internalize" it in their own bodies. (It's an excellent idea to record the counting for this exercise on tape and play it back as you do it, until you're accustomed to the rhythm and the sequence.)

1. Exhale completely—all the way down to the groin.
2. With the mouth closed, begin a very slow, even, continuous inhalation, counting to eight in about eight seconds. Imagine the balloon (in your favorite color) inflating smoothly and evenly from the very base of your groin, the air coming in at the bottom between your legs. This will relax the genitals too, where a good deal of tension is often held. Visualize the whole

process as completely and vividly as you can, seeing the balloon gradually expand to its full, round form, and then, on the exhale, slowly growing smaller and smaller and smaller until it's flat and empty.

3. Hold the "inflated" position for a count of four. If your shoulders have risen during the inhalation, relax them.

4. Begin to exhale with a slight hiss through a partly open mouth, making the sound as steady as a whistling teakettle, to a slow, even count of sixteen (sixteen seconds). If you run out of breath before the count, you probably let out too much air at the very beginning.

5. Repeat once: Breathe in—eight counts   (Mouth closed)
   Hold breath—four counts
   Exhale—sixteen counts   —with a hiss

6. Repeat twice, increasing the count to: Breathe in—ten counts
   Hold—five counts
   Exhale—twenty counts

7. Continue in this pattern, increasing the count as shown in chart below, doing each increase twice only. (If you cannot get to the inhale—twenty counts—go as high as you can. You'll find that your capacity will increase dramatically.)

Breathe in	Hold	Exhale	Repeat
8	4	16	2 times
10	5	20	2 times
12	6	24	2 times
14	7	28	2 times
16	8	32	2 times
18	9	36	2 times
20	10	40	2 times

Done just before bedtime, this is wonderful to give you a good night's sleep. It's also a great energizer in the morning. Like honey, which can tranquilize or energize, depending upon which the body needs, this Magic Breath will supply whatever your body needs most—relaxation or quickened energy. In addition, it teaches your body, muscles, and respiratory system how to utilize the expanded lungs and deepened abdominal breathing so necessary for your charisma.

Once you have mastered this exercise lying on the floor (the great advantage of learning it that way is that you actually feel the breath expanding your body against the floor, and you learn more of a "total body" sense of breathing), try it standing up, and then sitting, straight-backed, in a chair. Then you can use it in any tense situation. You will find, too, that it will calm people around you, although they are not aware of your doing anything or why their nervousness or irritability is changing into a more even emotional state.

The Chinese have a saying: "He who masters breathing can walk on the sand without leaving footprints."

The Magic Breath teaches your body how to isolate the shoulders (which tend to rise and try to get into the act) from the lower abdomen and diaphragm. The beauty of the low abdominal breathing is that it's invisible! You can practice it in the middle of a crowded room or a business meeting or at a party and no one will know you're doing anything special. You can do it walking to work, doing your chores, even jogging.

As you inhale, imagine that vital energy is entering your body with each breath and being circulated through your entire body with each breath. This is what in Oriental systems is called *prana* or *ch'i* or *ki*. It isn't chemical but spiritual, the elemental life-force of the universe. You can store up this energy with each deep breath you take and it will give you increased vitality, radiance, and composure—all vital components of your charisma.

Most people inhale about five to six quarts of air a minute. During strenuous exercise, it's possible to take in over 100 quarts of air. When you practice this deep breathing you can increase the amount of vital energy you are taking in to thirty or forty quarts of air. That produces a tremendous change in the way you feel and project to others.

Just as we are very sensitive to people's voices, we're also unconsciously responsive to their breathing patterns. We use terms like "Oh, he's so tense" or "She's so easy to be with," and the emotional response to life that we sense is expressed through people's breathing patterns, although we seldom realize it.

You may discover that it is difficult for you to take a really full, complete breath. Others find it hard to let go totally.

When you start breathing in these rhythmic patterns, you'll find that it has a profound effect on your confidence and well-being. If you happen to be a smoker you may spontaneously give up smoking. (As a friend of mine says, "You can never get enough of what you don't really need. The desire to smoke is partly a desire to get more breath. Since you get smoke, not breath, each time you puff, you need to keep coming back for more. Addiction means a desire that can never be satisfied. When you begin to breathe in this total way, for the first time you may find that you've gotten what you really craved, and the craving for cigarettes fades.") If you lack confidence, you'll find yourself becoming more sure of yourself, more assertive. If you fly off the handle, you'll notice you're able to control your temper much more easily.

Agnes D. told us in a Charismedia workshop: "I really have to tell you what an amazing change the breathing has brought about for me. I've been married about two years, and I've always been terribly jealous. I kept imagining what would happen if I found my husband with somebody else. I thought I'd kill him and then I'd probably die too. Well, last week the worst happened. He didn't come home and I found out he'd been with another woman. Then a funny thing happened. I'd been practicing the breathing and I did the Emotion Cooler and the Magic Breath when I spoke to him on the phone.

"Ordinarily I'd have ranted and raved, but I found myself talking to him very calmly. I asked him when he was going to be home so we could talk. I think he was surprised that I was so collected. Well, he came home and I was still doing the breathing, so I stayed calm. I never screamed or even cried or yelled. I'd thought I couldn't survive his infidelity. Now I found myself thinking, 'Gee, I wonder what he's like with this other woman? He must be a different person with her.' I was surprised to find I was interested and curious.

"Suddenly he seemed like an interesting stranger whom I didn't know very well. At the same time, I knew deep inside that I wasn't going to die of this, no matter what happened. I would be all right even if he left me. Never, never could I have imagined thinking that before! Well, he was so surprised at the calm way I acted that he began to talk to me; we talked all night. I think it's the best talk we ever had. I don't know what's going to happen, but I do know that whatever it is it'll be all right.

"I feel something very important has happened to me—it's as

though I found myself as a person. I could even see things from his point of view and understand his feelings without feeling mixed up and hurt and furious and wildly jealous the way I usually do. I feel very good about myself. It's like some new strong person inside me I didn't know was there and I'm proud of the way I behaved. I see him looking at me differently too. That's nice, but strangely enough, that's not the most important thing to me anymore."

Controlling your breathing gives you access to expanded aspects of your own personality. Your "witness" consciousness begins to operate. You become more objective, and once that happens you never feel as helpless and out of control again, even though you experience negative emotions.

Just as some people find it harder to take attention than to give it, some express through their shallow breathing the difficulty they have in asserting themselves. They lack the confidence to take a deep breath and live fully. It doesn't seem to matter whether you start from the inside or out. In fact, it's easier for many people to start with the breathing, and the opening up that begins to happen is effortless and remarkable. The quality of life changes.

Suddenly, a woman decides to go into business for herself, something she's always wanted to do but didn't have the courage to attempt. A young man who worked in a bank and hated it left to become a journalist. A pianist who had always been shy dared to form his own orchestra and was asked to head the jazz department of the university where he had been teaching; he also began to give TV lectures. People change careers, directions, take off forty pounds, begin to find themselves new, expanded lives—basically because the breathing put them in touch with their own gifts, their own charisma. Then they were able to go out and express it in their own lives.

People who find it difficult to exhale completely may have a rigid self-image. They're afraid to let go and express their real feelings. All the shouting, Karate Chop, hostility exercises, the Ape, the Great Wow!, the Infallible Butterflies Chaser help release feelings—which juices up the whole organism. When you raise the energy level, the sheer momentum of release breaks through old barriers. Suddenly it's easier for people to speak up, show their feelings, take risks, and begin to enjoy their own lives fully. The mysterious depths and colors of one's own personality begin to shimmer with inexhaustible radiance. Friends stop my students on the street and inquire if they've fallen in love or gotten a new job or been on vacation. Something, they sense, is different.

Having deeply de-stressed the body and mind, it's a short step to meditation. People begin to fall into it naturally when they do the slow breathing.

"Say, this feels familiar," someone will say. "I used to be in this state pretty often when I was a kid."

It's a good feeling. Everybody has had moments of complete concentration on something beautiful—music, a landscape, lovemaking. The selfless involvement is almost dreamlike, and people soon recognize that their most creative impulses come from that odd place just behind waking consciousness.

Since we are so result-oriented, we all need one place where we can trust our subconscious to come up with magical solutions, new perceptions, and an unprogrammed processing of the problems of one's life. The remarkable thing about our nervous systems is their natural tendency to evolve. Given half a chance, the nervous system takes precisely what it most needs from meditation. People who need stimulation become more lively. Those who need calming become calmer. It all happens without your doing anything at all except allowing yourself to be "empty" (which I know is very difficult).

There are many different mantras; TM assigns them by age and sex, other masters like Yogananda usually prefer one or two. I will use R A M (pronounced with a rolled *r*, the *ah* as in "far." If you prefer use So-Ham or Sat-Nam (truth essence). But once you choose your mantra, stay with it. The Sanskrit letters contain special qualities that produce specific effects on the body. It's best not to talk about your mantra, to keep the experience totally private. Your mantra should be exclusively associated with your private meditation, nothing else. Then the deep rest you get can be transferred to the day. It's like a still pool of clear water that you dip into whenever you need to, that gives you calm and peace in the midst of turmoil. It's good to meditate before breakfast and around five in the afternoon. Or before you go to sleep. You may find it keeps you up; generally the meditation will give you energy.

Prepare yourself by breathing ten breaths as slowly as possible. Or do alternate breathing. If you feel particularly distracted, do the active stage fright exercises first; when your body is tired, your mind will relax and let go more easily. Make sure you won't be disturbed for the next twenty minutes. Turn off the phone. Close the door. Loosen any tight clothing.

1. Sit with straight back, feet on the floor or cross-legged. Keep a watch on your lap or wrist.
2. Place hands on your knees, palms upward, first and second fingers touching lightly. Don't worry if they fall open later.
3. Close your eyes and roll them upward to the center of your forehead. This is known as the "third eye."
4. Begin to say "RRR-AHHHH-MMMMM RRAAHMMMM RRAHHHHMM." Roll the r slowly and evenly like a continuous hum. After a while, whisper it. Then repeat it silently in your mind, over and over.
5. When a thought crosses your mind—and many will!—just notice it and "get off the track." Go back to saying the mantra (which means "mind control"). Each time you find your mind wandering, observe that you're thinking of something else and, without getting annoyed at yourself, gently return to RAM.
6. Sit for twenty minutes. Open your eyes to check the time, and if it isn't time yet, close them again and return to the mantra. If you feel impatient, that's when you need the meditation most.
7. You may feel lightness or as though your body had disappeared. You may be aware of a sudden pain here or there or an itch. Remain as still as you can. The meditation puts you in touch with what your body is really experiencing. Each time will be different. Don't look for any special results. The important thing is to do it faithfully every day. Better: twice a day, early in the morning and late afternoon (—always before eating); don't meditate on a full stomach. If you have a performance or some special crisis coming up or you have insomnia, do an extra meditation.
8. When time is up, sit for a moment and enjoy the peace you feel. Never rush right out of a meditation; that shocks the nervous system. You have been in a deep state of awareness, even

> though you may feel you were on the verge of sleep and some-
> times thought of nothing at all. If the phone had rung or there
> had been another loud noise, it would have shocked you. If at
> the end of the meditation you feel very tired, that shows you
> that your mind and body were really exhausted. Lie down for
> five or ten minutes and you'll be completely refreshed. Most
> of the time the meditation will give you fresh energy.
>
> 9. Rub your hands together gently and stroke your face upward.
> Then sit for a few moments to allow your system to get used
> to waking consciousness again. Observe how the room looks to
> you now.

There is no substitute for regularity of practice. Find a time
when you can do it every day and make it a part of your routine.

Playwright John M. was en route to Florida when he saw a bad
review of his play, which had just opened there. Immediately, he
said, laughing ruefully, "I began to meditate on the plane. By
the time I got there, I had distanced it enough so the terrible
notice didn't bother me. It was very different from trying to tell
myself that I didn't care. I really didn't care!" Studies have
shown that meditators are able to resist shocks better than non-
meditators. The impact is the same, but they recover much faster.

Louise L., a retired fashion executive, asked if she could tell
the class her experience with the breathing and meditation one
day. "I have to tell you," she began, "that I used to be married
to a very difficult man. The last time I went to see him in New
York, I was so nervous I fell out of the cab and broke my wrist.
This time I prepared for days by doing the breathing and meditation. Well, I can't believe how calm I was. He never got my
goat once. In fact, he didn't want me to leave. We had a pleasant
dinner. At one point I thought, 'Oh, my goodness, I have no lip-
stick left,' and then I thought, 'That's all right, you're fine just
as you are.' And I really felt that; normally that would have
bothered me a lot, not to look my best. But the whole quality
of the evening changed. In fact, even when we were married,
we never had such a pleasant time!"

The idea is to gradually become so calm and compassionate
that there is no difference between meditation and nonmedita-
tion. You will find your intuition and creativity greatly enhanced.

"I get some of my best ideas when I'm meditating," Jana, a TV executive, remarked. When the mind is unstressed, the larger possibilities that were always implicit in the situation but were hidden suddenly emerge. Without effort.

Sometimes other people will notice the effect on you before you do yourself. Generally, however, there are small but dramatic changes in perception, in the "quality of life." Sometimes they happen immediately; sometimes it takes a while. Try the meditation for forty days. There is no question that you will find relaxation and interesting experiences at the "still point of the turning world."

Think Pink

The Rosicrucians, whose metaphysical knowledge is one of the oldest traditions in the West, have given us their knowledge of using color breathing for healing purposes. The power of thought to change matter, to heal, and to rejuvenate is very real. If a person you know is having emotional problems which are causing illness, you can visualize a pink or rosy pink color surrounding him. It's good to do this when you think the person is asleep, although he or she does not have to be in the same place or even in the same country to feel your healing thoughts. You must first meditate to clear your own consciousness, then visualize the person you want to help, sending a feeling of love to surround him, using the color which is most appropriate.

If the illness is not emotional but caused by physical debilitation, visualize a bright orange color. In Linda Clark's *Color Therapy* she describes the experiences of many people who have successfully used color breathing. One young woman wraps herself mentally with a spiral rainbow from head to foot before she leaves the house in the morning. Everywhere she goes, people are extremely friendly. The rainbow, she says, attracts people. Others use it to protect themselves from the drainage of energy in city crowds. Another protective device is to see yourself surrounded by white light—I have done this walking down a dark street late at night. Even people who can't see auras somehow sense this field around those who use it and they respond to it.

The rule is: heal yourself before you can heal other people. Meditation and the Anger Transformer will help. If you have a problem with someone and it seems impossible to resolve, prepare yourself to think of that person with love. Visualize her or him happy, smiling, at their best. Surround your friend with warm golden light. You may find the next time you see that person that the rift will be healed.

Using color with the long deep breathing seems to have a profound effect. (We know that the Kirlians have photographed auras in color.) Some of the results with color breathing to restore youthfulness are astonishing. Foods grown aboveground carry imprisoned sunlight. Sunlight, of course, is a source of vitamin D, and inhabitants of countries that are deprived of the sun for too long suffer from melancholy.

Yvonne Gary of Indiana has developed a system of color breathing for youthfulness and has reported some success at apparently reversing the aging process. Try it and see how it works for you.

1. Start by breathing very deeply and clearing your mind.
2. Choose an area to work on, perhaps bags under the eyes. Spread them smooth so you can see how the eyes would look without them.
3. Breathe in pink air (or a color you really like).
4. Hold your breath and visualize the skin as smooth and unwrinkled.
5. Exhale slowly. Repeat the breath and visualization twice more.
6. Now, take another area, and do three breaths there.
7. Try it when you wake up in the morning and just before going to sleep at night.

(It took her eight months to accomplish her objective. But it was worth it—her wrinkles and bags disappeared; her vitality and general health improved steadily.)

The desire to heal, to send love, is very powerful. If your intention is powerful, it will transcend space and time. Expanding your charisma with breathing and loving emanations will draw a responsive resonance from the world around you. It cannot be faked. When it's there, people feel it and respond to it intuitively. You have the light within. See it pouring down on you, limitless and golden, and "become the light." Then:

> When the heart is light, the breathing is light, for every movement of the breath affects the heart. In order to steady the heart, one begins by cultivating the breathing power. The heart cannot be influenced directly. Therefore the breathing power is used as a handle and this is what is called protecting the collected breathing power.
>
> —LAO-TZU

> When you fix your heart on one point, then nothing is impossible for you.
>
> —BUDDHA

> . . . The land that is nowhere, that is the true home. . . .
>
> —LAO-TZU

13

Your Persona: How to Match Your Inner and Outer Images

OUR INNER SENSE of ourselves is crucially important. We all have a complex, subtle "feeling sense" of what we are like inside. This is hard to put into words, yet it dramatically affects how we project our "image" to other people.

A lot of factors are obviously involved: how and with whom we grew up; the communication styles of our families and associates; our basic sense of enjoying life; our most hidden assumptions affect that image—what we project to others.

Charisma is to image as electricity is to the wire that carries it. Recognize it or not, everyone has a self-image and projects a persona that may or may not match the internal one. Are you projecting your charisma or the static that interferes with it? A lot is at stake. "Nobody," remarked Henry Kissinger, "gives prizes for lack of confidence."

You've seen how judgmentalism and lack of self-confidence interfere with your creativity, your health, your confidence, *and* your charisma. Ninety-five percent of the Charisma questionnaires cited "confidence" as a key factor in charisma. The color, shape, size, and nature of your charisma are unique because you're unique. So blanket instructions on what to do won't touch the central issue: defining (and realizing in action) who you really are.

You can define yourself according to your roles: "I am a businessman" or "I am a professional" or "I am a student" or "I am a mother" or "I am an artist," etc. Or you can define yourself according to your qualities: "I am a loving person," "I am a responsible adult," "I am a hard worker," or "I am an intellectual." Or, less favorably: "I am oversensitive," ". . . unstable," ". . . stubborn," etc. Astrological charts—"Are you a Gemini? I usually get along well with Gemini people" or "He's a Leo, that's why he's so domineering" or "I'm a home-loving Cancer person"— set up constellations of expectations that may reflect or influence your inner sense of yourself.

We now know, according to the principle of the hologram, that each part suggests the whole. The DNA contains the instruction for the whole organism. That's why one can "read" a person by analyzing his astrological chart; by observing body language and voice; by (if you're trained to understand the information) checking the iris of a person's eye. *Everything* is potentially a source of information about the whole person. According to our left-brain habits of thinking, we name four or five qualities or talents or predilections and come to a conclusion of some sort about ourselves or other people. The reality is much more complex, and harder to pin down.

In some of the other chapters in this book I've given you a lot of specific techniques to accomplish objectives we'd all like to see happen. Now I'll offer you an inventory to give you a positive inner sense of what you are really like. When you have put yourself in touch with very specific qualities that please you and that you connect with (you recognize and "own" them), it's possible to reprogram your inner image, that subtle-beyond-words computer. Through visualizing yourself in a different (perhaps only slightly different) way, you'll begin to project a different image. An image is very powerful; it can encapsulate an incredible amount of information in a microsecond. So when you imagine something deeply enough, in a relaxed state, with no forcing, you really *see* it as though it were happening right now. The mind/body programs this as a reality. That's how people with powerful dreams realize their ambitions. They "see" everything not as wishes but as reality. The mind and body only carry out the detailed subconscious instructions of the mental imagery. This is how healing can be programmed through imagery and also why TV and films affect us so profoundly.

The beautiful part is that everybody has the capacity to imagine. We do it all the time, sometimes without realizing it.

"Is that why I sometimes get my best ideas just as I'm dropping off to sleep?" asked a young corporate executive at one seminar.

"Yes, exactly!"

If you try to stop thinking altogether for a moment, you'll notice it's no use; thoughts and images flash into your brain anyhow. "Oh, I must take my coat to the cleaner's" is overlapped by a picture of your neighbor's dog racing past you that morning, a fight you had with the kids, and a dim awareness of six or seven other half-formed thoughts and elusive pictures that slip out and past your consciousness, some of them bearing no relation at all to the others or to your daily life. Out of this welter of information overload we can begin to solicit a useful randomness. This is not exactly free association, but it's more right-brain than linear thinking and gives us access to intuitive knowledge we didn't know we had.

I have found that when people in my Charismedia workshops fill in the upcoming Vocal Self-Portrait there's always a subtle but very real and *immediate* change in their voices and speaking styles. The process consists of two parts: first you write down the answers to the questionnaire; the second part is answered aloud. *The act of describing aloud your minute reactions to your thoughts and sensations has been found to enhance learning ability.* Apparently it works like this: the feeling state is a right-hemisphere activity; *describing* these feelings aloud involves the left-hemisphere processes. Any activity that uses *both* hemispheres improves the coordination and working efficiency of both. That's why when children learn to sight-sing and play an instrument at the same time, their general intelligence improves. Remember: the left cerebral cortex does the work with words, analytical thinking, logic, and analysis; the right deals with perspective, music, intuition, pattern recognition, insight, and the aesthetic sense. Most of our culture is left-brain–oriented. The counterculture tried to shut down the left brain through drugs to reach a right-brain experience. But this is just as big a mistake. You need the two working together to produce a high level of creative ability and intelligence.

Homemade Opera (see p. 228) is another method of stimulating your dual brain. Dr. Denis Gorges in Cleveland developed a brain synchronizer that allows the brain to synchronize its electric rhythms for both sides, as well as front and back, through sight and sound and magnetic field induction all working together. This improves communications within the brain and probably affects emotional balance and physiological well-being. One of the most fascinating training experiences I've had has been with Dr. Jean Houston, president of the Foundation for Mind Research, who, with her husband, Dr. Robert Masters, has done comprehensive work integrating the whole person through the body/mind connection. Their invaluable book. *Listening to the Body, the Psychophysical Way to Health and Awareness* (Delacorte, 1978), based on the fundamental principles of Moshe Feldenkrais (author of *Awareness through Movement*), details dozens of exercises to increase the subtlety, complexity, and creativity of body/mind functioning. Dr. Win Wenger, in his book *Beyond OK*, writes that he was amazed at the dramatic and lasting heightening of a wide spectrum of abilities as a result of describing spontaneous visual images aloud as people experienced them.

He writes: "Spontaneous visual imagery is a right-brain function; verbal description of such imagery is a left-brain function. Working that as one activity integrates functions from both sides. This integrative activity builds connectedness between the two hemispheres, and this improved connectedness *permanently* heightens general ability regardless of the particular activities and problems to which describe-as-you-observe mental-imaging is directed."

In Western culture, only poets, writers, and artists are accustomed to describing internal impressions and our *feel* for experiences. Yet this intuitive cross-sensing and pattern recognition is the ground from which all creativity and problem solving and insights, as well as sense of right/wrong, true/false, arise. If you have always wanted to learn to play the cello like Casals, then go to the cello with all the memories alive in your consciousness that you've ever had of hearing, seeing, and reading descriptions of wonderful cello playing. All that information is stored somewhere deep inside, and if you go through it with all your senses and then apply that to actual playing, you will learn about 100 times faster than the conventional way. The idea is to go back and forth from your "inner virtuoso" experience to your attempts to learn.

This clarifies why hero worship (or having a role model or guru) helps immeasurably in learning to become what one wants to. Not just information (left-brain) is being transmitted, but the complex feeling state of what it means to be or do as that person is or does.

In Bali, where children are taught to dance between six and eight, the teacher simply molds their bodies instead of giving a verbal explanation. At that age, the flexibility and plasticity of the mind and body are so great that the learning capacity is almost unlimited. This is the country where everybody is an artist, and nobody stops to ask if you are "talented." (Because everybody is!)

A simple way to practice visualization is to observe your "image-flow." Just breathe slowly and deeply, relaxing more and more with each exhalation. When an image flashes by, describe it aloud, whatever it is: some colors, a landscape, part of a face, some geometric shapes, whatever. If you keep describing it aloud, you will begin to get some interesting insights and a deep respect for the awesome richness of your inner images.

This is a good experience to share with a friend. Ask her/him to relax, breathe slowly and deeply with closed eyes. When you see a slight shift under the eyelids, that eye movement is the signal that your friend is experiencing a visual image of some kind, although he/she may not be aware of it. Sometimes you'll see changes in body position, breathing, or facial expression.

After you see any of these signs, ask quietly, "What was in your awareness then? What was your impression just now?" Encourage your partner to describe the visual impressions she/he is receiving as soon as she/he becomes aware of them, even if you don't ask. At first, your friend may protest, "I don't see anything." Quite soon, though, the images will start to come. If you see only some color, breathe in that color slowly and deeply a few times until the picture clears.

After a dozen experiences or so, pick one interesting image and ask for a more and more sensory-detailed picture of it. Special insights will surface when enough details are filled in. Suddenly, "the meaning" becomes clear.

Now have your partner do the same for you.

It was after experimenting with "image-flow" that I hit on the notion of using our capacity for image sensing to reprogram our voice sense. *This is one of the fastest and most effective ways to enhance your own vocal charisma.* It invariably produces rapid and subtle changes that are exactly what people have wanted for themselves.

Your Vocal Self-Portrait

(Write in your answers.)

What would my voice be if it were:

1. A material (i.e., wood, leather, stone, silk, rubber, corduroy, etc.)
2. A texture
3. An animal
4. A color
5. A landscape
6. A shape
7. A flower
8. A tree
9. A vehicle
10. A dance
11. A fragrance or smell
12. A tempo
13. Is your voice a musical instrument?
14. Is it warm or cold? Thick or thin?
15. Does it match your body?
16. Does it match your face?
17. Does it match your feelings?
18. Is it an effort?
19. Does it fully represent you?
20. Where does it come from? (throat, chest, head, etc.)
21. Is it big or small?
22. Strong or weak?
23. Is breathing easy or difficult?

Accept whatever images come to you—don't reject any even you think they're uninteresting!

* * *

In a Charismedia workshop, I asked everybody to describe their answers. Janet, a quiet, neat administrator, was first: "I saw my voice as nubby wool. Then I had an image of a fox, but I also had a fleeting image of a horse or a wolf." She hesitated. "I guess I like the fox running over cultivated terrain, but the strength and solidity and rhythmic gait of a horse—and the wildness of a wolf. Is that OK?"

"That's fine. This is your fantasy, so you can make it anything you please," I told her.

"I saw the color as deep blue, and it was pancake shape, thick, and cold. The flower is an organ pipe cactus. The fragrance was rich earth."

"Did you pick it because of the stickers?" asked another student.

"Well, more because of its rich solid base. But I guess," she admitted with a smile, "also because of the stickers. I like sounding a little prickly!" She couldn't feel an instrument. Her vehicle was a compact sports car going merrily over a hill.

Ellie, an extremely inhibited, shy, tall young woman of twenty, said her voice was corduroy, and the animal was a tiger, the shape an octagon, that it was thin and cold and her throat was the center. Her dance was also freeform and her flower was a tulip. The fragrance she thought of was a men's cologne. Her instrument was the drums and guitar, and her vehicle a Volkswagen. The smell was burning leaves.

Mel, a sixty-year-old amateur ornithologist who had at first looked skeptical and baffled, said, "I got fog; the color—blue; the animal—a bear; and it was thick and warm." He grinned with enjoyment. "I feel it in my whole head and throat, and it does match my face and body. The dance it most resembles is the rumba, and the vehicle is a boat."

"What kind of boat?" I pressed.

"Oh," he said, considering, "not a little boat—a yacht!"

"The tree is an oak, the smell is leather, and the rhythm is slow and even."

Having protested at first that he "couldn't think that way!" Mel, a retired engineer, found he could visualize quite easily and thoroughly enjoyed coming up with all these unexpected associations.

Natalie, an affable and very large fourth-grade teacher who had a decided dramatic flair and a strangely monotonous voice ("I feel really sorry for my kids, who have to listen to me all day!" she remarked), had the following list: "Velvet, or cotton corduroy, the color is yellow, the shape is a rectangle, the animal is either an elephant or a cat, the sound is thin and warm, it does *not* fully represent my feelings, I feel it in my forehead most. It does match my appearance." (This surprised me—since her voice was much more babyish than her large solidity would suggest.) "The smell is soap, pure castile. The flower is pussy willow and the tree is weeping willow. The rhythm is a slow, maddening, oscillating ceiling fan, and the dance is a fox-trot."

Jenny was next—a young chemist, who was sensitive, brilliant, and dedicated. Her voice was so thin and small she could barely be heard more than a few feet away. "I got an image of glassy ice, with cracks in it. A bird—a sea gull. The color was pale yellow—with splashes of violet. The shape—a narrow cylinder (like an attenuated wire). It is thin, cool. It doesn't fully represent my feelings, or match my face or body. It's too monotone. Sometimes it matches," she corrected herself. "I feel it in my throat and upper chest. Sometimes it's pleasurable to me, but I often find breathing an effort. I think of the waltz, and a plane."

"What kind?" I interrupted. "It's important to be as detailed as possible. A 747?"

"Oh, no," she laughed, "a Piper Cub. The smell is of pine needles, the tree is a pine tree, the flower is a petunia, and the tempo is staccato."

The whole class looked amazed. The images "fit" Jenny more perfectly than any description we could have come up with.

When asked to chart her vocal self-portrait, soft-voiced Celeste J., who has a gentle, self-effacing manner, remarked, "I can see easily the image that I would like to have, but an image for my voice the way it is now seems more difficult."

"You know," I told her, "there are no wrong or right choices. They only represent things the way you see them now and how you would like them to be. If you tried making new choices six months from now, your images *might* be entirely different. That's fine too!"

With some encouragement and prodding, she was able to come up with the following list: for texture, balsa wood, and for shape she selected round. The flower she chose was a daisy and the color was yellow; the landscape, Central Park. Then she decided to make some changes. The flower she preferred for her vocal image was the pussy willow and she chose ice blue instead of yellow. These two alterations seemed to mean the most to her. "Oh, and I'd like Newport instead of Central Park—I like the sense of adventure and the beauty of the sailboats, the cleaner whiteness, open sky, and the beautiful music. Oh, and I'd rather be a cello than a piccolo."

Suddenly, Celeste realized to her surprise that it had been quite easy to form an image of her voice as she saw it, the image that she would prefer.

"You're speaking in your new voice," I pointed out.

She laughed and protested, "I feel self-conscious!" Still, she went on talking.

"Do you hear the difference in her voice?" I asked, turning to the group.

"Yes. Her voice is deeper, more definite somehow."

"So is her whole personality!"

"More clarity. Crisper!"

"She sounds and looks more assertive now."

Celeste looked pleased. "Thank you, everybody," she said with a delighted smile. "I'm going to try to keep this new voice going all the time. It's the *me* I want to be."

Someone commented: "These are all such extraordinary self-portraits; we really get a rich, complex impression from all these associations." It was true. Their accuracy and subtlety were generally astonishing.

Celeste had anticipated the second part of the process. After a number of people had completed their self-portraits and described them to the group, I asked everybody to consider the following questions. Do this now at home.

Look over your list of written images. Then, again close your eyes and breathe deeply. Get an overall feeling about all the associations you decided on before.

1. What would you like more of in your voice?
2. What—if anything—do you want to give up to get that?
3. Can you feel or sense any other changes you'd like to make to have your ideal, charismatic voice?

4. Say them aloud and write them down. Be as detailed as possible, including your reasons.
5. Now hear your NEW, improved sound, visualizing yourself using it, with all the qualities you want enhanced or transformed as you just formulated them. Spend a few minutes, hearing and seeing and sensing yourself—in your mind's ear—expressing yourself in this new, more fully *you* way.
6. Now open your eyes and begin to speak IN THIS NEW VOICE. Share with us what changes you made.
7. Which of these images will you use to produce this new sound—and how?

Janet said, "I stayed with the fox, adding the freedom of the wolf and solidity of the horse, but I changed the color from blue to a much richer brown. Instead of the pancake, I prefer to have streamers. I like the thickness, but I changed the cold to warm and from the center of the sound in my chest, I expanded it to include my whole body, particularly the hands and feet, which almost never seem to get any circulation. They're always cold, and I can hardly feel them!"

"Good! Now when you want to quickly put yourself into this newly enlarged charismatic state, what will you do?"

"I'll use the streamers to spread the energy all over my body. Especially to my hands and feet."

"Right!" I was delighted that she had instantly seen the creative process she herself could use to transform her own functioning with an image that had meaning for herself.

"Do you notice how different your voice sounds?" I asked her.

She smiled happily. "Yes, it feels richer and more expressive."

Ellie was next, and she surprised everybody: "First of all, I'd like to change the corduroy to velvet. I want to keep the tiger, but I want to make the octagon a circle. From thin I want to change it to thick, from cold to warm. I'll keep the freeform dance, but I decided I would rather have a daisy than a tulip."

"Do you get a sense of why?" I asked.

"Yes." She hesitated a little. "It feels to me like a tulip is too closed—I want to be open and friendly. I'll keep the drums and guitar, but I'm going to change the Volkswagen to a Rolls-Royce."

"Hooray," cheered the class, "atta girl!"

Ellie grinned shyly. "Yeah, I like the quiet purring of a Rolls-Royce. It's very steady and reliable and luxurious, not uneven like I tend to be."

Her voice had taken on more color and definition and variety than we had ever heard before. Even her face was more expressive. The whole group could see the flowering of her personality just through this exercise.

Mel said, "Boy, I'd like to see you in six months, Ellie, if this is what you could accomplish in ten minutes!"

She blushed and looked pleased. "Yes," she admitted, "it feels really good!"

Natalie, the massive but pretty-faced teacher, said, "I want to get more *cat* in my voice. I don't need more elephant and I'd like to change the thinness. I'd like it to represent my feelings more, and to move the sound of it from my forehead to my legs and feet. I'd like less pussy willow and more of the weeping willow, with its long slender swaying branches and graceful trunk. Most of all," she paused mischievously, "I'd like to change the fox-trot to a tango! I want a slow, even tempo with a lot of depth."

"How are you going to put that into practice?" I asked her.

"Oh, I'm going to talk a lot lower," she said, "and with a lot more rhythmic variation to match the ebb and flow of my thoughts. I forgot to tell you the smell—it was of rich wood and the instrument is a cello!"

As she spoke she had taken on much more authority than usual. She suddenly seemed not just large, but important, not childish at all, a person to reckon with.

The group spontaneously applauded, and Natalie bowed with her usual sense of theater, this time without self-irony. She was assured and graceful.

Jenny said then, "I'd like mine to be silk instead of ice, with a liquid shimmer (no cracks!). I'm going to give my sea gull more room. I love the feeling of freedom and flight and the endless open sky all around for me to play and swoop in. Instead of a narrow cylinder I transformed into a kaleidoscope with rapid changes of color and pattern, constantly transforming without ever losing character or definition. I felt more crackle and crunch and I wanted to give up the coolness and the thinness and get more depth, more richness. From a triangle it became a xylophone, the iris changed to a peony, very full, womanly, and generous."

"When you felt yourself using this voice, how did you use this new knowledge?" I asked her.

"I was able to open up and express my thoughts and feelings with power and spontaneity. It felt marvelous!" Jenny's eyes were shining and her voice was noticeably stronger, firmer, and deeper than we had ever heard it.

This questionnaire has an amazing power to trigger a complex, rich awareness of inner gifts, which itself produces heightened confidence. The more specific the image, the more pleasure it gives. For instance, if your first definition of the vehicle is a train, ask, "What kind? How big? What era?" Jim, a brilliant wit and a highly successful literary agent, said at first only, "A train—long-distance." When I asked him to be more specific, he added more details: "A long, highly sophisticated train with an air of mystery and glamour—in fact, the Orient Express would be perfect!" Interestingly, Jim didn't have a particularly sensuous voice quality, but he was very pleased with his own sound. As he had been highly persuasive all his adult life, his images were rich and powerful—"velvet, lion, red, the flower a rose, the tree an oak." His inner self-perception actually communicated itself to his hearers, exactly as if he really had a beautiful voice. When I asked him if there was anything he wanted to change, he said no. The only thing he wanted to alter was a tendency to tire if he did long, sustained speaking. But since he never had to do this kind of speaking, he didn't feel he had a problem.

If you want to improve your voice, this questionnaire can help by eliciting powerful, self-chosen images with which you can produce the results you want, beginning immediately. Even the people who were very satisfied with their voices began to speak with more depth and variety. Laura, a business writer and executive who was also an artist and photographer, giggled with embarrassment when she began. "This is so revealing!" she remarked. But she, too, grew fascinated by her own choices and her voice began to take on more color, life, and richness from the multi-layered images that flooded her consciousness.

Universally, it seems to be a pleasurable, life-affirming procedure. For people who want to contact their charisma, it is an astonishingly effective and powerful tool. For those who are already sure of theirs, it's a surprising and many-textured confirmation of their own sense of strength.

There is another proof of the homeostatic tendency of the human organism to reach its healthy level of functioning. Every body who does the Vocal Self-Portrait experiences an increase in tonal variety, subtlety, and color (even those with monotonous voices), as well as more expressive and appealing rhythms and intensity All this suggests that we're really meant to be expressive and interesting—and are, by nature!

During a newspaper interview a few years ago, I remarked. "Nobody is boring!" The interviewer was skeptical.

"How can you say that?" she protested. "I know so many boring people!"

"Well, of course, we've all met 'boring people'!" I agreed. "But, inside, nobody's boring! Everybody is a maze of such incalculable richness and complexity that it's positively awesome!"

The Vocal Self-Portrait confirms my early feelings. The voice, as the most faithful, subtle index of inner intuition, is only the outward evidence of the limitless treasures of each individual's charisma.

Maggie H., a dynamic feminist, perceived her voice as coming "from the outside—at fingertip, outstretched, arm's length—from the electromagnetic field around me."

No two portraits were alike, although certain images appeared frequently. Some people chose one color, some several. Maggie asked for rich purple, deep brown, and silver. Some people smelled deep earth, burning leaves, fresh-baked bread, or cologne. Vehicles ranged from transatlantic liners to Model T's and kayaks or sleighs. Sometimes people would cross-sense; when asked what shape his voice was, Martin S., a banker and specialist in Japanese culture, saw a gyotan, a Japanese fruit with a particular ovoid shape. The literary agent chose for his tempo a "moderate, steady one—Big Ben." Others ranged from "boring ceiling fan oscillation" to "machine gun fire." Like the Vocal Self-Portrait, this exercise uses your own synergistic imagery to reach a new state of heightened awareness. At that level, not only is nobody boring, but everybody is a poet!

How to Find Your True Voice

Most people only use a fraction of their real voices. Do you know how yours really sounds?

The key to projection is relaxation and release of vibration. With your new interior image in mind, you're now going to connect to your inner sounding board and experience how your body and head feel when they are really resonating fully.

Is your voice harsh? Nasal? Too high? Too monotone? Breathy? Too thin? Too throaty? Uninteresting? Uneven?

To start off, let's get in touch with the sound as if it came from your gut. This will immediately double your power!

THE APE

Bend over from the waist and let your arms dangle. Let them fall as loosely as possible. Let your head drop too. Now, with a deep sound that comes from the lowest part of your abdomen, say: "HUHH! HUHH!! HUHH!!" The only thing that moves is your stomach; it moves sharply IN as you release the sound. The jaw is totally limp. When you've got that, jump with both feet at the same time you say the *huhh!* Now jump around the room, slowly (on both feet simultaneously), heavily, like an ape. Always sound the *huhh*s exactly as you come down on both feet. Keep your head and arms totally relaxed and dangling the whole time. (If they get stiff when you jump with both feet, practice relaxing them while standing upright.) Repeat ten times. Feel the sound go right through the floor. Feel it in your back as well.

THE SANTA CLAUS LAUGH

Once the Ape is easy for you, do a big *ho ho ho*, still keeping your jaw very limp for the *ho*s, standing upright this time. With each *ho*, your stomach moves in sharply, as though somebody kicked you and it recoiled. Keep the sound VERY big and deep, next door to a yawn. If it isn't deep enough, YAWN. Your throat probably isn't really open *enough*.

Can you make yourself yawn yet? Remember, if you draw your lips up off your teeth and stretch real wide, you should be able to start an involuntary yawn. If you can't, keep opening wider, until it begins to happen. When you yawn, notice how open the back of your throat gets. Now see if you can yawn with your mouth closed, just as you've done lots of times in a boring meeting! Put your fingers on the cords at the back of your neck (sides). You should feel them being pushed outward if the yawn is really wide enough. If at first you can't feel this opening, keep directing your attention to it and ask it to open—it will start to wake up and respond. This is very important for throat relaxation.

Whenever you're going to make a talk or presentation, practice pressing down your tongue and opening the back of your throat. That way, you'll prevent yourself from getting "strangled" by nervousness. By doing that before you get up to speak, you'll prevent trouble.

"When I get up to introduce speakers at the PTA, I feel my throat closing up," moaned Sally S.

"The same thing happened to me," Don B., journalist, added. "I thought I would die on camera. Then I did the Closed-Mouth Yawn and it opened up again. Boy, that was scary until I got that under control!" He now has a regular TV spot as a talk show commentator. Sally, who at first couldn't feel the back of her neck expanding with the Closed-Mouth Yawn, gradually was able to locate those muscles; she never had that trouble again.

NOW THE HELMET OF HUM

First hum, loose-lipped, thinking of something that turns you on. Then press lightly with your fingertips at the sides of your face, feeling the vibrations there. Then touch another spot. Then another: forehead, chin, nose, temples, top of the head, sides of the head, back of the head, back of the neck. In each area, if you don't feel as much vibration as you did in the first one, consciously SEND more to your fingers through that spot. Imagine that every pore on your face and scalp and neck is exuding electric vibrations *equally*.

THE DEAF-MUTE JACK AND JILL

Put your thumbs in your ears while your pinky fingers close off your nostrils. Gently! Now, keeping your mouth *closed*, yes, closed, say:

JACK AND JILL WENT UP THE HILL
TO FETCH A PAIL OF WATER
JACK FELL DOWN AND BROKE HIS CROWN
AND JILL CAME TUMBLING AFTER!

Say it as loudly and with as much vocal variation as you can. Naturally, you'll have to push hard to get your sounds through since all the openings are closed off.

1. Now take away your left thumb, keep everything else closed, and repeat the whole rhyme.
2. Put back the left thumb and take away the right and repeat the nursery rhyme. Notice whether there is a difference between how you hear on one side and the other.
3. Put back both thumbs, and remove the left pinky from your left nostril; now only the right one is closed off. Repeat the verse.
4. With thumbs still closing off the ears, remove the right pinky from the right nostril and repeat the verse. Notice any difference.
5. Now repeat with pinkies closing off both nostrils, but both ears open.
6. The same, but with only left nostril blocked off.
7. The same, but with only the right nostril blocked off.
8. Now, still with the mouth closed, but with ears and nostrils open, repeat, making it as articulate as you can without opening your mouth.
9. Open mouth, but keep teeth clenched and repeat the verse.
10. Now, finally, say it normally.

You'll be astonished at how loud your sound is after going through this sequence. Having forced the vibrations through the inside of your skull, you've experienced the head as a resonating cage of bones. Now you'll be able to EXPERIENCE the full resonance of your voice as it should sound.

Practice this sequence every day for three weeks, and it'll have an astonishing effect. Your voice will be large and resonant without effort!

THE HELMET OF HUM (continued)

1. Start humming again, jaw very relaxed, tongue low in mouth. Feel the hum at the top of the inside of your skull, at the back of your head, and around the sides.
2. Now hold up your palms two inches in front of your face and keep humming. Feel the entire surface of your hands massaged by the hum.
3. Move your palms away from your face a little further—perhaps four inches. Keep humming. Keep sending the vibrations to bathe your hands. At any point, if you can't feel the buzzing in your hands, move them closer again until you can.

4. Move the hands a little further away, then further until they're at arm's length. Make sure you can really feel the vibrations bathing the entire surface of your palms.

5. Slowly move the arms apart a little. STOP so the left palm (still facing you) is out about twelve inches from the left side of your head and the right palm on the opposite side is the same distance from the right side.

6. If that's still buzzing nicely, move the palms out to the sides at ear level, still looking straight ahead, and make the palms buzz out there.

7. Move them sideways around to the back and intensify your humming.

8. Move them above your head, first close, then as high as you can reach. Extend arms upward. Intensify humming.

9. Close your eyes and visualize the entire field around your head as a dense helmet of buzzing hum, at arm's length, in every direction: sides, top, and back. MAKE SURE YOU CAN REALLY FEEL YOUR PALMS BUZZ BEFORE YOU MOVE THEM TO THE NEXT POSITION A LITTLE FURTHER AWAY. ANYTIME YOU'RE NOT SURE YOU CAN FEEL THEM BUZZING, MOVE THEM CLOSER UNTIL YOU CAN FEEL THE BUZZING VIBRATION EASILY. You will generate a lot of tingling energy in your hands as well as around your head.

10. Now speak, sending the sound out *from the back of your head*, visualizing the sound radiating out from the back.

Your voice will feel and sound at least twice as strong and vibrant as usual. Practice this every day for a month, and your normal way of speaking will be dramatically improved. After that, you can probably maintain it without difficulty by doing it only once in a while to remind yourself of the way your expanded voice feels.

Now that you've relaxed your body with the Ape, felt the sound coming from your lower stomach, and activated the Helmet of Hum around your head, you're ready to combine the two for your newly expanded voice.

THE WHOLE BODY SOUND (be your own cathedral)

Sit or stand straight.

1. Put your left hand flat on your upper back and your right hand on your diaphragm, fingers spread so they are splayed across your stomach.

2. Now, say, as slowly and as sustained as possible, without any interruption of sound and so you can feel both hands vibrating: "AAAHHHHHHHHHHH-EEE WANNNNNNHHHHH-HHHHHHHHHHHHHNT (breathe) Toooooo FEEEEEEEEE-EEEEEEEEEEEEEEL (breathe) thuhhhhh SAHHHHHHHHH-HHHHHHHHOOND (breathe) of mahhhhhhheee VAWWW-WWWWWWWWWWWWWWWWWEEECE (breathe) Lah-hhhhhhhh-eeeke A WIHHHHHHHHHHHHHHHHHHHHHND (breathe) aaaaaaaaaaaand uhhhhhhhhh WAAAAAAAAAAAA-AYYYYYYYYYYYVE (breathe) THROOOOOOOOOOOOOO-UGH MAHHHHHHHHHHH-EEE (breathe) WHOOOOOO-OOOOOOOOOOOOOLE BOHHHHHHHHHHHHH-DEEE!" You're saying, "I want to feel the sound of my voice like a wind and a wave through my whole body," and you should experience your whole body sounding as though you're your own cathedral. Feeling your hands vibrate with your own sound is a very pleasurable sensation and will make you aware of the *back* of your body as a sounding board too. (Most of us feel as though the voice comes out of a narrow hole in the face!)

THE ENCHANTED STREAM

In bel canto singing (literally, "beautiful song") the Italians, the masters of this sustained and pure tonal style, taught the world that long, pure vowels are the secret of a beautiful, continuous, melodious sound. Most people who have not had voice training never really sustain *any* sounds long enough. The result tends to be choppy, disconnected, and unmusical.

To feel and produce the sustained sounds of the vowels flowing smoothly one into the next, sing the same sentence you did for the Whole Body Sound: "I want to feel the sound of my voice like a wind and a wave through my whole body." Only this time leave out all consonants! Like this:

"AHHHHHHHHHHHHHHHHHHHHHHHHEEEEEEEE AHHHHH-HHHHHHHHH (breathe) OOOOOOOOOO eeeeeeeeeeeeeeeeeeeee (breathe) uhhhhhhhhhhh ahhhhhhhhhhh uhhh ahhhhhhhhhhhh awwwwwwwwwwwweeeeeeeeeee (breathe) AHHHHHHHHHHH-HHHHHEEEEEE UHHHHHHHHHHHHHH IHHHHHHHHHHHH*
(breathe) ahhhhhhhhhhhhhhhhh uhhhhhhhhhhhhhhhh ayyyyyyyyyy-yyyyyyyyyyyyyyeeeee (breathe) ooooooooooooooooo ahhhhhhhhh-hhhe (breathe) uhhhhhhhhhhhhhhhhhhooooooooo ahhhhhhhhhhh-hhhhhhhhhheeeeeeeee!"

* like "pig"

If you do this right, you'll be able to feel the sound shooting right up through the top of your skull and also emanating from the sides and back of your head. It's exciting to feel this suddenly "take over" and become larger than you are!

When I studied opera on a Fulbright grant in Italy, my teacher had me practice all the early Italian art songs this way, with no consonants! At first it drove me crazy, but it was a marvelous way to learn how to connect the vowels in a pearly, unbroken line. Try doing this with the Glottal Nonstop Sentences (p. 232). Try it with *any* sentence. It's not easy! It requires considerable mental alertness. For instance, the sentence "It drove me crazy!" would read: "Ihhhhhhhhhhhhhhhhhhh oooooooooooooooooooo [uhh- hhhhooooo] eeeeeeeeeeee ayyyyyyyyyyyyyyyeeeeeeeeee!" The idea is to connect all the vowels on one breath, without inter- ruption.

Once you've practiced this sustained sounding, you'll enjoy speaking a lot more because of the secret melody underneath. And other people will find you infinitely more interesting to lis- ten to—without realizing why.

Remember, it's the sound (much more than the words) that seduces!

When you talk without these "underground melody streams," your speech is not only less musical but less interesting and sometimes even hard to understand. You never give the sound a chance to hook into the vibratory stream which, being closer to singing, is more expressive and a pleasure to feel and hear.

Part of the difficulty arises from the desire to enunciate clearly. If your tongue is agile, you can make clear sounds and yet not lose this all-important connecting stream. These exercises will help you maintain the personality expansion you experienced when you drew your Vocal Self-Portrait. Practicing these will make your new way of speaking feel comfortable, natural, and eventually automatic. If you exercise these new muscles and sen- sations of coordinated sound and body relaxation, your whole level of functioning will become more and more like your ideal vocal image. Otherwise, old habits can creep back and take over. As you build your new technique, the exercises will give you practical, multisensory image reinforcement.

The Vocal Self-Portrait invariably enhances self-esteem by giv- ing you a richer sense of your own nature. People are often surprised by the beautiful, satisfying memories it evokes, which are a source of refreshment, renewal, and growth. These self-chosen images are a sort of conscious cellular coding—a set of built-in, attainable instructions, portable, powerful, and private, to achieve your true charisma.

14

Your Charisma-cises

What to Do For:

1. STRESS: BEFORE
   when you are feeling nervous or apprehensive
2. STRESS: DURING
   when you are feeling uptight
3. STRESS: AFTER
   when you are feeling immobilized or exhausted
4. ANGER
   when you are feeling rage, indignation, or humiliation
5. QUICK ENERGY
   when you are feeling listless, dispirited, or tired
6. RELAXATION
   when you are feeling tension or exhaustion
7. VOCAL EASE
   when you want to release and develop your true voice
8. COURAGE
   when you want to be assertive, hold your own, or take risks
9. STAGE FRIGHT
   when you are feeling panic, alarm, or anxiety
10. MORE CONTROL OF YOUR LIFE
    when you want to expand your powers
11. MOOD CHANGE
    when you are feeling negative, sad, or depressed

12. GOOD RELATIONS WITH OTHERS
    when you want to be tuned in to others
13. PAIN
    when you are feeling physical distress or discomfort
14. BODY ALIGNMENT
    when you want to center and balance yourself
15. WAKING UP
    when you are feeling sleepy, tired, or lethargic
16. INDUCING SLEEP
    when you are feeling restless, fretful, or worried
17. BETTER SEX LIFE
    when you are feeling inhibited, bored, or distracted

101-Exercise Finder

Exercise	Section

••••••••• D •••••••••

••••••••• E •••••••••

••••••••• F •••••••••

••••••••• G •••••••••

••••••••• H •••••••••

••••••••• I •••••••••

Exercise	Section

Section 1 / *Stress: Before*

When you are feeling nervous or apprehensive

What Exercises to Do:

Basic Buddha Belly
Basic Breath Tranquilizer (Magic Breath)
Chutzpah Elbow Propeller
Golden Cocoon
Pointillist Necklace
Caveman Whump
I Don't Care Swing
Meditation on R-AAH-MM
Meditation on SO HAM
Meditation on SAT NAM

THE BASIC BUDDHA BELLY

How to Do It

Preparation: Sit on the edge of a chair, with your back straight and your feet on the floor. Clasp your hands around your lower abdomen, one on each side of your stomach (back of hands rest on legs).

1. Exhale fully with a big, audible sigh; deflate stomach all the way down to your groin, and stay empty a few seconds. Release any tightness you feel in your face, neck, jaw, shoulders, head, back, and chest.
2. Begin to inhale very slowly, with your mouth closed, feeling your lower abdomen swelling in your hands. Visualize the entire area from your groin to the rib cage as a balloon. Make the balloon a very beautiful, favorite color, and watch it inflate slowly and evenly all around, filling up from the bottom. (The air enters as though from between your legs.) Expand it totally.
   • Keep your shoulders relaxed. Don't let them hike up!
   • As you inhale, consciously draw in pure, fresh energy; feel it massage every cell, filling your body with vital force.
3. Hold for one slow count.

4. Exhale slowly, watching the balloon deflate, until your abdomen is completely flat.
5. Continue indefinitely. (Start with ten slow breaths.)

(If you experience a little light-headedness or dizziness when you first begin to breathe deeply in the Basic Buddha Belly, don't worry. You are simply taking in more oxygen than you are used to; with a little practice the sensation will disappear. Meanwhile, if you do feel dizzy, simply pinch the bridge of your nose between thumb and forefinger, breathe slowly, and the dizziness will subside.)

How It Helps

If it's done right, the Basic Buddha Belly will rid you of stress and recharge your entire system with energy. When you're sitting at a desk, it should be invisible. Breathing changes the chemistry of your consciousness. Most people breathe between twelve and eighteen times per minute. If you reduce your breaths to seven or less, you greatly increase your composure, stamina, intuition, and personal authority.

- You will feel less worn down by daily wear and tear.
- You will be a better listener, take in more information, and others will feel you are really understanding and responding to them.
- You prevent the escalation of stress.
- You'll be able to act on your intuition.
- You can keep up the breathing throughout conversations except when actually speaking.

BASIC BREATH TRANQUILIZER (magic breath)

How to Do It

Preparation: Lie on floor. Put a little cushion under your head or comfort. The important thing is to have your back flat. Raise our knees if you need to so you'll feel your whole spine touch-ng the floor.

1. Inhale, slowly and continuously, for eight counts. Visualize a rubber barrel filling with air all around or a balloon. Pick a lovely color! Feel your breath start sharply and evenly from the lowest point of the belly, just above the groin. (If you can't expand as long as eight counts, you just need to start

smaller. Make the beginning as subtle and imperceptible as you can. You're probably inhaling too fast!)
2. Hold breath for count of four.
  • Check to see if your shoulders are relaxed. (Drop them if they're tense.)
3. Exhale, with steady hiss, for sixteen. Make the breath as steady as a laser beam. Empty totally. (If you find you haven't enough breath left, you need to start more slowly. You're probably exhaling too fast. Husband your breath so it's very even.)
  • At the end of the count, your middle back or ribs will expand or lift, your chest and shoulders should remain quiet. If you find you're starting the breath in your chest or solar plexus, STOP. Start again.

NOTE: When you've experienced the breath pressing against the floor in back and learned how to isolate your lower belly so your shoulders don't get into the act and you can really feel the breath expanding through your whole body, then you can do this exercise sitting in a chair, standing, or walking.

HOW THESE EXERCISES HELP

Changing your breathing pattern combined with visualization gives you access to instantaneous de-stressing. It removes the buildup of lactic acid from your taut muscles, calms and oxygenates your whole system within seconds, lowers heart and pulse rate and cholesterol.

The entire system benefits from increased circulation of oxygen in the body. Learning to breathe and exhale fully will improve your health, stamina, creativity, and capacity to handle stress efficiently.

NOTE ON BREATHING EXERCISES

These must be practiced BEFORE you need them and frequently enough so they become automatic. Since the patterns are the reverse of the kind of breathing most people have been accustomed to all their lives, it takes a lot of practice to make thi much more organic and vital breathing perfectly automatic. It's worth the effort!

THE CHUTZPAH ELBOW PROPELLER

- Stimulates circulation in chest and heart
- Increases air intake, which releases tension and raises energy level
- Relaxes shoulder and head tension

How to Do It

1. Stand with your feet apart, knees slightly bent, elbows bent, and forearms raised, hands hanging limp from wrists (like a dog).
2. Begin to make vertical circles with your elbows, making the biggest circles possible, keeping elbows close to the body. Do backward ten times, then forward ten, as rapidly and energetically as possible.
   - Mouth is closed.
   - Bend your knees a little.
3. Stand still and take three long, slow, complete breaths (in and out) and slow your heartbeat—and relax.

How You Benefit

You'll feel energized immediately and will act freely—without being afraid! Great for your chutzpah (courage) level!

THE GOLDEN COCOON

How to Do It

1. Take a deep breath, exhale, and relax.
2. Visualize yourself surrounded by a radiant cocoon of deep golden relaxation. Feel it all around yourself; feel it particularly thick and golden wherever there is tension in your body. You're completely surrounded by this cocoon. It relaxes you completely. This is particularly good for dealing with irritable people; your cocoon protects and insulates you from them.
3. Now exhale and visualize all poisons, toxins, aggravation, anxiety, and tensions draining out of your body. After each exhalation, stay relaxed and empty for several seconds.
   - Relax shoulders, feet, hands, and back.
4. This breath needs to be practiced and mastered, for then you can truly breathe slowly and fully during all tense situations, which will keep you calm, authoritative, and in control.

- Your mouth should be closed when inhaling, but may be slightly open for exhaling.

5. Do ten to twenty-six complete breaths anytime during the day for a quick de-stressing and recharging your entire system with energy. (While sitting at a desk, if you do it right, this breathing is entirely invisible.)

6. After you've mastered this breath, you can add a heartbeat or pulse count to it.
   - On the inhale, count very slowly 1-2-3-4-5-6-7 pulse beats, hold 1.
   - Exhale very slowly in the same rhythm, 1-2-3-4-5-6-7 (make sure you are empty), hold 1.
   - Use this whenever you're not speaking and you need composure and alertness.

POINTILLIST NECKLACE

- Irons out all neck tension
- Relaxes shoulders
- Normalizes thyroid
- Calms and balances mind
- Helps you sleep
- Opens throat

How to Do It

1. Drop your head from the first vertebra until your chin practically rests on your chest. Imagine that there is a necklace around your clavicle and at each point on it someone will press gently and *that* will move your head. It'll start moving of its own weight without your help.

   Keep asking: Is my head as heavy as a cannonball? Is my neck as long as a giraffe's?

2. Now let it start moving around in the circle. Feel each point. Your head should move as slowly as possible without stopping. Don't turn it; let it *be* moved!

3. Circle three times clockwise, three times counterclockwise.
   - Breathe deeply, especially if your neck hurts. Open mouth slightly.
   - If it cracks, go back and "iron out" cracks.

CAVEMAN WHUMP

For anxiety in chest, beat your chest, shoulders, and back with your fists. This breaks up tight feelings, stimulates circulation, and opens your heart center.

I DON'T CARE SWING

How to Do It

1. Stand with feet apart (approximately the width of your shoulders). Swing your torso, neck, and head as one unit first to the left, then to the right.
2. Let your arms begin to swing freely, as your body turns from side to side, until they wrap loosely around you at shoulder level.
3. As your body swings from left to right and back, shout freely, "I don't care!" as loud as possible.
4. Enjoy yourself. Keep repeating. Switch to "No, I won't!" or "You can't make me!" if the impulse seizes you. Repeat twenty times or more.
   - Make sure your head follows your torso all the way around when you swing to each side.
   - Keep it as loose and free as you can.

How It Helps

Children have natural de-stressing techniques which we forget as we grow up. Getting in touch with the playful spirit and rebelliousness of a child is enormously rewarding, as well as an effective device for quick, efficient tension release.

MEDITATION I

How to Do It

1. Breathe slowly and deeply ten times, eyes closed.
2. Sitting with straight back, eyes closed, begin to repeat mentally, "Rr-ah-M," "R-ah-M," "Rrahm" (which is called a mantra).
3. When thoughts come into your mind, just notice, "Oh, that's a thought," and return to the mantra.
4. At the end of twenty minutes (keep a watch on your lap, close the door, and turn off telephones) rub your hands together, stroke your face gently upward, and, when ready, open your eyes. Don't rush.
5. Set aside regular time, before eating, morning, and early evening (or before bedtime) to meditate.
6. Let go of expectations. Your nervous system will take exactly what it needs from each meditation.
   - Allow yourself to stay as still as possible.
   - Boredom is a form of restlessness and indicates you need the meditation when you have the least patience for it. If you're very restless, jump rope, jog, or do strenuous exercise for ten or fifteen minutes before meditation.

How It Helps

By lowering your respiratory rate, blood pressure, heartbeat rate, meditation provides a deep rest for your mind/body. You then have more emotional margin and are less affected by stress. It's easier to take ups and downs calmly. In an emergency, meditate just before the important situation; in the long run, daily meditations will bring peace of mind and greater mental clarity.

MEDITATION II

How to Do It

1. When you choose a mantra, stick with it, and don't discuss it. It should be part of a completely private experience.
2. As you inhale, think SO; as you exhale, think HAM (pronounced *hum*). (So = that; Ham = I am.)
3. Repeat with the rising and falling of your breath over and over for ten, fifteen, or twenty minutes.

(The other directions are identical to Meditation I.)

MEDITATION III

1. Use the mantra SAT NAM
   (Sat = truth; NAM = essence).
2. The rest of the procedure is the same as I and II.

Stay with your mantra at least forty days to see results.

Section 2 / *Stress: During*

When you are feeling uptight

What Exercises to Do:

Basic Buddha Belly
Basic Breath Tranquilizer (Magic Breath)
Rushing Relaxation
Emotion Cooler
Heart Relaxer
Whole Body Breath

BASIC BUDDHA BELLY

See Section 1, STRESS: BEFORE, page 318, for this exercise.

BASIC BREATH TRANQUILIZER (magic breath)

See Section 1, STRESS: BEFORE, page 314, for this exercise.

RUSHING RELAXATION

When you are in a rush, have to get a thousand things done by yesterday, are late for an appointment, try this.

- You will be able to listen accurately, take in more information, respond with intuitive rightness.
- You will give the impression of being composed, calm, and authoritative, even in difficult situations.
- You will actually feel that way.

How to Do It

1. Walk quickly but breathe as SLOWLY AS POSSIBLE, expanding the abdomen as in the Basic Buddha Belly, imagining a colored balloon inflating and deflating. (Shoulders shouldn't ride up!) Start by counting four steps as you inhale. Then exhale evenly on eight steps. Work up to ten—inhale, twenty—exhale.
2. The faster you go, the slower you breathe. Continue indefinitely.
3. YOU MUST PRACTICE BEFORE YOU NEED IT, so you will be able to use it with ease and without thinking about it.

How It Helps

The brain uses three-quarters of your oxygen supply, so when you breathe shallowly under stress, the brain doesn't function well and memory and concentration suffer. The Rushing Relaxation assures you of an astonishing expansion of time, smooth functioning, steadiness, and calm. The increased oxygen intake steps up your mental efficiency.

EMOTION COOLER (or left-nostril breathing)

How to Do It

1. To calm your nerves or get over an emotional moment or give you strength for a difficult confrontation, place thumb on right nostril lightly blocking it off.

318

2. Exhale slowly, soundlessly, and completely through left nostril. "See" all toxins, poisons, stress, and negatives draining out of your body.
3. Inhale slowly and fully. "See" pure radiant energy filling your body.
4. Do 2–6 times.

How It Helps

By sending oxygen rapidly to the right hemisphere of the brain, this exercise acts quickly to stabilize your nervous system and even out emotional instability.

HEART RELAXER

How to Do It

1. Every half hour or so during your hectic day, suddenly drop your jaw.
2. At the same time, rotate your shoulders slowly in full, smooth, luxurious circles. Keep breathing smoothly!
   • Keep your jaw dropped.
3. Do six backward and six forward circles. Do this exercise every half hour, during a stressful day.

How It Helps

When your mind works intently, your jaw and shoulder muscles tense. You may also notice you're clenching your teeth and the backs of your shoulders feel tight and tense. The heart is ready to speed up and rush more blood to the fighting muscles. This "crouched for action" tension whips the heart into a spasm-ready state. The Heart Relaxer will relax the muscles in the backs of your shoulders (trapezius muscles), will alter the brain wave into a normally functioning pattern, and will relax your heart.

How You Benefit

You protect your heart, de-escalate your tension buildup, and at the same time increase efficiency and energy. Everything looks light and brighter. You can enjoy life again!

THE WHOLE BODY BREATH

Note to purists: this exercise tells you what happens in your body when you breathe fully and completely.

How to Do It

1. Sit or stand erect with spine straight, keeping your shoulders and arms relaxed.
2. Inhale steadily through the nostrils, expanding the lower belly. This fills the lower part of the lungs. The diaphragm drops and presses on the abdominal organs, pushing the stomach outward. Don't let your shoulders rise!
3. Continue to inhale slowly, filling the middle part of the lungs, pushing out the lower ribs, breastbone, and chest. Imagine that you're blowing up a balloon from the bottom.
4. Continue to inhale slowly, now filling the upper portion of the lungs, lifting the chest, including the upper six or eight pairs of ribs, which will move outward. In this final movement, the lower part of the abdomen will be slightly drawn in, which gives the lungs support and also helps to fill the highest part of the lungs.

    IMPORTANT: This is a continuous inhalation. Keep it very steady, smooth, flowing, and even—no jerks! Feel that you are drawing air in from the whole universe, up through the feet and legs, through your body and around your head—more and more energy is at your disposal each time you inhale this way.
5. Exhale slowly and evenly, without collapsing your chest. Draw in the abdomen slowly as the air leaves your lungs (imagine a balloon deflating). When air is completely exhaled, relax chest and abdomen, but don't collapse!
6. Stay empty briefly, then begin again.

How It Helps

This breath greatly increases lung capacity, exercises every rt of the lungs, including the most remote air cells. Your lung acity is greatly increased, your energy level vastly enhanced. s like an air laxative, cleaning and purifying the system! Holdg the breath a few seconds purifies the air still in the lungs from mer inhalations, discharges more accumulated stress and toxins an possible, fully oxygenates the blood, and leaves you more om to take in energy and strength on the next breath.

320

Section 3 / *Stress: After*

When you are feeling immobilized or exhausted

What Exercises to Do:

Chutzpah Elbow Propeller
Heart Relaxer
I Don't Care Swing
Neck and Shoulder Relaxer
Rag Doll Shakeout
Shoulder and Midback De-Tenser
Swinger
Whole Body Breath
Beat-Out Anger Release
Pressure Breaker
Cannonball Headroll
Instant Vacation

CHUTZPAH ELBOW PROPELLER

See Section 1, STRESS: BEFORE, page 321, for this exercise

HEART RELAXER

See Section 2, STRESS: DURING, page 326, for this exercise

I DON'T CARE SWING

See Section 1, STRESS: BEFORE, page 323, for this exercise
To give you instant alertness when you're tired or tense and
step up your vitality.

Effective eye-relaxing exercise, too. Do it before going to bed
(For best results, do 100 times.)

NECK AND SHOULDER RELAXER

How to Do It

1. Place head on right shoulder (keep shoulders relaxed, neck
   long). Swing in forward half circle to left shoulder. Do

THE I DON'T CARE SWING
Relieves stress and stage fright

How to do it

1. Stand with feet apart (approximately the width of your shoulders). Swing your torso, neck, and head as one unit first to the left, then to the right.

2. Let your arms swing freely, as your body turns from side to side, until they wrap loosely around you at shoulder level.

3. As your body swings easily from left to right and back, shout freely, "I don't care!" as loud as you can on each swing.

4. Enjoy yourself! Keep repeating. Switch to "No, I won't!" or "You can't make me!" or whatever rebellious phrase occurs to you. Repeat twenty times or more.

• Make sure your head follows your torso all the way round when you swing to each side.

• Keep it as loose and free as you can.

What it does

Children have natural de-stressing techniques which we forget as we grow up. Getting in touch with the playful spirit and rebelliousness of a child is enormously rewarding, as well as an effective device for quick, efficient tension release. You will feel relaxed and playful after it. Completely released of performance or perfectionist anxiety.

THE SUPER RAG-DOLL SHAKEOUT
Relieves stress, anger and stage fright

How to do it
First shake out one hand, then the other, then shake your head

like a rag doll (let your whole face — mouth, jaw and cheeks hang loose). Then shake out each leg (as you add each limb, keep up the one you began with!). Then hop, shaking the other foot. Then jump and wiggle your pelvis and throw your arms and elbows and hands all around every which way and make some noises while you're at it! Keep this up for 3 to 5 minutes.

What it does
• Changes your physical sense so that you can quickly relax your entire   body and face.

• Gives you sensations of freedom and ease you might have experienced as a child.

• Increases energy flow to every part of your body.

• Makes your body feel comfortable and uninhibited.

Doe Lang's, daughter, Andrea demonstrates this charisma-cise.

eight counts, and on eighth make complete circle with head. Reverse, starting on left shoulder. Swing to right eight counts, make complete circle on eighth.

2. Roll shoulders forward, shrug up, then roll back in one continuous movement.
    Inhale forward, exhale back.
    Reverse; start with shoulders back, shrug up, then roll shoulders forward.
    • Keep hands relaxed.

3. With feet apart, clasp your hands and extend arms straight back. Inhale and swing left.
    Exhale, and swing right as far as possible eight times.

4. Same position, arms out front, clasp hands and swing left (inhaling) and right (exhaling) eight times.

5. Same position. Clasp hands and stretch arms in back. Lean forward until nose almost touches the ground, stretching upward with arms. Inhale going down; exhale coming up. Repeat four times.

6. Same position; raise right hand over your head as high as you can, and, inhaling, swing it down to outside of left foot (knees straight!). Look back at raised arm. Exhale.
    Inhale and reverse, bringing left hand up over head to right foot. Try to touch ground outside each foot. Repeat sixteen times.

How These Help

They unkink tensions through shoulders, neck, and back, release energy flow, and relieve accumulated strain. Good for office break or anytime you need flexing and stretching.

RAG DOLL SHAKEOUT

How to Do It

1. First shake out one hand, then the other. Then shake your head like a rag doll (let your mouth hang loose). Then shake out each leg (just add each limb, keep shaking out the rest).

2. Then hop, shaking the feet. Then jump and wiggle your pelvis and throw your arms and elbows and hands all around every which way and make noises! Three to five minutes.

How It Helps

Every muscle and nerve in your body gets a workout. Your circulation increases. You breathe deeper, sending oxygen to every part of your body. You discharge all tensions completely.

How You Benefit

Your body no longer feels frozen, tight, tense, or tired. Your body and brain hum and buzz from the stimulating activity and you "loosen up." You're less withdrawn, you're not afraid, it's easier to "speak up," be spontaneous. You get instant energy.

SHOULDER AND MIDBACK DE-TENSER

1. Lean back on a desk or table, fingers facing forward, head down, knees slightly bent, body slumped (as though you were ashamed).
2. Inhale. Arch your body back, like a bow; drop your head back. Stretch. Straighten legs. Press toes against the floor.
3. Hold for a count of four and feel the stretch in your back muscles. To get the stretch higher or lower in your back, simply move your hands further apart or closer together. S-T-R-E-T-C-H!
4. Now, exhale, bend knees, come back to starting position.
5. Repeat sequence six to eight times.

SWINGER

1. Clasp your hands behind your back, and swing your whole torso and head to the left, breathing in. Then swing to the right as you exhale.
2. Do this twenty times. Imagine there's a point in the middle of your chest and you are suspended from the ceiling by a string that is attached there. Imagine the "wings" of your back touching as you swing.

WHOLE BODY BREATH

See Section 2, Stress: During, page 326, for this exercise.

THE BEAT-OUT ANGER RELEASE

Hit your bed or sofa with a tennis racket or rolled-up newspaper, mailing tube, or towel, while shouting, "NO!" or "I won't" or "Damn it" or "Bastard!"

You might also use the Karate Chop and the Steam Engine (see Section 4, Anger, pp. 333, 334).

Do this at least ten times.

Follow with slow, deep, even breathing.

THE PRESSURE BREAKER

- Increases tension of anger, then releases it
- Provides satisfying physical outlet for angry feelings
- (*Great* for complexion too!)

How to Do It

Put your hands on the floor, table, or arms of a chair (keep arms straight). Head is down. Clench fists if on table or chair. Press down. Inhale; hold breath. Jog in place twenty times as hard as possible, as though racing. Exhale all the way with a sigh. Then inhale, hold—jog thirty times, exhale; inhale and jog three to five times, exhale.

The harder you run, the harder you hold, the more release from tension you will get when you do exhale. Tighten everything—face, hands, and body—when you're running in place.

DON'T DO THIS IF YOU HAVE HIGH BLOOD PRESSURE!

Follow with slow, deep, even breathing.

CANNONBALL HEADROLL

How to Do It

1. Stand or sit straight. Drop your head on your chest. Feel the neck muscles stretch out. Keep breathing!
2. Roll head very, very slowly around, feeling base of motion as clavicle. Imagine a ball bearing inside your head. As the weight shifts, your head rolls. At each point on circle ask:
   - Is my head as heavy as a cannonball?
   - Is my neck as long as possible?

INSTANT VACATION

1. Close your eyes, breathe deeply, uncross your legs, relax every part of your body.
2. Go to your favorite natural place:
   - a beautiful garden
   - seashore
   - mountaintop

Be there completely. Feel the sun on your face or body, the breeze, the smell of flowers or pine. Hear the rustling of leaves or water or tide, whatever natural sounds belong in your vacation.

Section 4 / *Anger*

When you are feeling furious, indignant, or humiliated

What Exercises to Do:

"You Bastard!"
Karate Chop
Woodchopper
Steam Engine
Anger Transformer
World Heart Embrace
The Ape
Tranquilizing Triangle

"YOU BASTARD!"

- Powerfully releases tension buildup
- Satisfies need for strong, safe *discharge* of psychophysical tension buildup
- Teaches body/mind/voice/breath to act together—to expel anger

How to Do It

1. Swing arms freely from side to side a few times, loosely swiveling your head and torso. Breathe deeply and rhythmically as you do this. Bend knees as you swing, and breathe in as you swing left, out as you swing right.
2. Now swing more strongly, three more times. On the next swing (open mouth, getting ready to shout), in rhythm with your swing, shout "You . . ." and, as you swing the other way, shout "Bastard!" and stamp your feet. Let it come from your *gut!*
   - It's important to shout exactly with the rhythm of the swing.
3. Repeat until you've unloosed your anger and can shout it strongly. Keep your throat open: "You . . . bastard!"

How You Benefit

It's not easy to let go and not hold back if you're not used to expressing your anger openly—an invaluable exercise to help you

YOU DASTARD!
(or BASTARD, whichever you prefer)

How to do it   **Transforms anger**

Stand with feet firmly planted, about shoulder-width, knees a trifle bent (to give you a good grip on the floor). Relax your hands at
your sides, and begin to swing your arms up to the left like a golf
swing), as high and free as you can. Breathe IN on the first swing

to the left (mouth closed).
Exhale on the second swing
to the right, inhale (with
mouth open) on the third
swing to the left. THEN
(after the three-swing preparation) on the fourth swing
(to the right) shout as loud
and as long as possible:
YOU U U U U U
D AAA A A A A S -TARD!
(fourth swing—right)
(fifth swing—left)
(both on one long exhale)
Begin the whole sequence
again with the three-swing
preparation(inhale-exhale-
inhale). Then:
YOU U U U U U
D AAA A A A A S -TARD!

IMPORTANT! make sure
your breath, movement
(swings) and voice are
perfectly coordinated. If you find that the words are not in synch
with the motions, if they are coming before of after the gesture,
you've probably been programmed not to release anger as easily and
freely as a child. You may find that your throat tightens. It's important to open your throat and release the sound freely at exactly
the same time as the breath and the swing.

Benefits

A tremendous increase in spontenaity and freedom. (One man said
that after doing this exercise he was able to dance in public for the
first time in his life!)
NOTE: May be followed by an anger transformation exercise such
as The Great Wow! or the World Heart Embrace.

THE GROAN
Improves vocal ease, gives relaxation, channels anger

How to do it
Sit down comfortably in a chair or stand with your feet
slightly apart (knees bent). Place one hand on your stomach.

One hand on your
forehead. Close your eyes
and start to GROAN.
Groan softly.
(ENJOY IT.)

What it does
When you groan with
maximum vigor, your
voice gets connected to
your entire body, not just
your head, and you feel
the sound coming from
your entire body, not just
your head, and you feel
the sound coming from
your stomach and legs.
These vibrations add the
rich, deep, quality to
your voice that is so
exciting. Once you
become experienced, you will also feel when it's missing.

Benefits
You can eventually learn to control these vibrations and let
them "color" your speaking. When you have learned to
maximize the innate qualities of your voice, you'll be able
to communicate more effectively through the varieties you'll
find in your vocal intonations.

Doe Lang's, daughter, Andrea demonstrates this charisma-cise.

express your feelings and experience release of all that pent-up tension. When you're back in "neutral" you can deal with the situation more effectively.

THE KARATE CHOP

- Beats stage fright
- Discharges anger, hostility, or fear instantly
- Gives you immediate energy
- Gives you immediate courage

How to Do It

1. Stand with legs sixteen inches apart, knees bent. Hands are at sides—clench fists. With mouth closed, draw arms up in three short, powerful inhalations (as though pulling up heavy weight in a bucket) until you are stretched upward with fists overhead as high as they will go. Then:
2. CRASH! Bring both arms (fists powerful) down together in a tremendous karate chop, and say as loudly as possible, throat relaxed, "HAHHHHHHHHHHH!" (Bend your knees.)
3. Repeat five times as powerfully as you can.

THE WOODCHOPPER

- Regulates your biorhythms
- Stimulates adrenal glands in lower back, which control hormonal secretion rhythms
- Safely releases lactic acid from muscles
- Lets off steam, dissolves anger buildup, keeps you from being prey to your emotions, fills brain with fresh new blood

How to Do It

1. Stand with your feet fifteen to eighteen inches apart, toes pointing a little outward, knees almost straight but relaxed, and clasp your hands.
2. Inhale and swing your clasped hands as high over your head as they will go.
3. Immediately swing your clasped hands down between your legs as far as they will go, bending forward and exhaling. At the bottom of the swing, shout "HAH!" as loud as you can. (Your knees are bent.)
4. Inhale and swing hands up again overhead.
5. Repeat sequence without stopping, ten or twenty times.

Important! Keep mouth closed as you inhale, until you bring arms down for the "Hah!" More oxygen reaches the brain with the mouth closed, and the exercise is much more powerful.

THE STEAM ENGINE

- Releases blocked energy in chest, shoulders, neck, and arms
- Steps up oxygen intake
- Increases ability to take risks

How to Do It

1. Stand with legs approximately shoulder width, knees bent, head erect, mouth closed. Pull right arm straight back, and, at the same time, punch the left arm forward (without leaning into it) as powerfully as possible. Exhale powerfully.
2. Reverse: draw back left arm, inhale as fists pass each other, and exhale again as right arm punches forward. You will be exhaling with each punch. Rhythm is steady and even.
3. Start slowly. Continue as rapidly, powerfully, and steadily as you can for three to five minutes, MOUTH CLOSED!

How It Helps

This produces a tremendous charge of energy through the chest, shoulders, arms, hands, and neck.

ANGER TRANSFORMER

- Gets you back in "normal" fast and safely
- Discharges hormonal stress
- Lowers your blood pressure
- Satisfies need to "explode" with anger—safely

If you are feeling anger or there is somebody in your life who is the focus of negative feelings for you, before the World Heart Embrace, do this exercise:

1. Stand or sit. Bend arms at elbows and put your hands up about a foot in front of your face, palms facing away from you (as if somebody had said "stick 'em up").
2. Make little clockwise circles in the air with your hands (like polishing a window), gradually (with bent elbows) moving

your hands all the way toward the right. Your head follows,
eyes soft-focus.

3. When you get all the way to the right, make a sudden very violent pushing movement with both hands, straightening both
arms and pushing hard as though throwing away something you
want to get rid of. Push away your anger or negativity or the
person you're mad at. Throw it as far as possible, and make a
sound like *ugh* or *uhh*.

4. Immediately afterward, put your hands to the center again and
then, making counterclockwise circles, "polish" to the far left.
Then shove as hard and as suddenly as you can to the left,
pushing away your "enemy."

5. Repeat five times both ways.

6. Immediately after this, do World Heart Embrace.

WORLD HEART EMBRACE

* Converts energy of anger to positive love power
* Increases self-esteem
* Expands electromagnetic field

1. Inhale, feel yourself expanding, open your arms, embrace the
whole world, stretching out and up as though your heart center
is the world being stretched and opened. You become larger
than life.

2. Hold at least sixty seconds. Bring the world into your embrace,
gather that love, and lay it on your breast, your hands on your
chest, pressed gently one over the other.

3. Do this whole cycle four times, transforming the negative image
you have pushed away. Love it, bring it in, lay it on your heart,
transformed from hate to love.

NOTE: If you can't "let go" of the anger yet, repeat first exercise—jog, yell, hit bed with tightly rolled-up newspaper
(see Beat-Out Anger Release, page 330), and shout out.

Keep testing to see if you're ready to transform anger into love.

THE APE

* Releases deep body sound
* Loosens upper body rigidities
* Grounds and centers your energies
* Provides rapid deep release for muscular tension
* Reestablishes hormonal balance

- Gives body feeling of power and ease
- Disinhibits old constraints
- Releases anger through the feet°
- Stomping on floor—satisfying expression of strong emotion
- Balances overintellectualizing, counteracts worry

How to Do It

1. Bend over from waist, arms and head dangling loosely like an ape, knees slightly bent.
2. Now slowly jump heavily, landing on both feet at once, around the room, arms and head still dangling loosely. Stay relaxed, almost limp from the waist up.
3. With each jump, make a deep, open-throated grunt that you can feel way down in your stomach, your legs, your feet: "Ugh, ugh, ugh."°°
   - Make sure the grunt coincides exactly with your landing each time you jump.

TRANQUILIZING TRIANGLE

- Restores calm
- Sends blood to brain
- Increases mental alertness and memory

How to Do It

Stand with legs apart and put hands on floor. Keep legs straight (so you feel stretch in back of thighs). Let head dangle. Breathe slowly and deeply two to six breaths.

° Stamping on the floor provides a safe and satisfying "grounding" of anger, hostility, and frustration. This seems to be a universal expression, ranging all the way from a child's tantrums to jogging to the elaborate and precise rhythms drumming and rhythmic dancing use to express emotions and influence events, whether it's a war dance, a rain dance, or a fertility rite to insure a good crop.

°° Pope John Paul II, in his visit to the United States, surprised observers by uttering deep rhythmic grunts in response to audience adulation. This centered and protected him from the engulfing waves of sound bombarding him.

Section 5 / *Quick Energy*

When you are feeling low, depressed, or tired

What Exercises to Do:

> Emergency Energy Lift
> Fast Energizer
> Great Wow!
> I Don't Care Swing
> Karate Chop
> Tongue Tapping
> Zaps
> Zicker

EMERGENCY ENERGY LIFT (or right-nostril breathing)

How to Do It

1. Place left thumb on left nostril, lightly blocking it off. Exhale slowly through right nostril, imagining tiredness and strain leaving.
2. Inhale slowly through same nostril. Imagine new strength and energy coming into your body.
3. Repeat two to six times. YOU'LL FEEL NEW ENERGY!

FAST ENERGIZER

1. Inhale and tighten all the muscles in your face, neck, shoulders, hands, abdomen, buttocks, genitals, arms, legs, feet—all the muscles you can.
2. Hold as tight as you can and hold your breath for as long as you can.
3. Then—whoosh!—exhale with a big sigh and let go of all tensions.

THE GREAT WOW!

Take a deep breath. Now start softly, saying "Wow!" Repeat en times, getting louder and louder, more and more animated ach time, until you're leaping, jumping, and flinging your arms oward the ceiling each time you shout "WOW!"

I DON'T CARE SWING

See section 1, STRESS: BEFORE, page 323, for this exercise.

KARATE CHOP

See Section 4, ANGER, page 333, for this exercise.

TONGUE TAPPING

For quick energy, tap the tip of your tongue against the ridge behind your top front teeth, as though you were silently saying "La La La La La La La La" very rapidly.

How It Helps

The tapping stimulates the thymus gland and restores the balance between the two hemispheres of the brain. This produces a feeling of well-being.

ZAPS

Repeat over and over "ZAP! ZAP! ZAP!" getting louder with each one. As you say each "ZAP!" fling your arms in front of you, above, to the sides, everywhere—consciously "zapping" all obstacles with as much power and force as you can.

ZICKER (BUMBLEBEE)

Seated with a straight back on the edge of a chair, open your mouth and, with teeth closed, say "zzzzzzzzzzzzzzzzzzzzzzz," vibrating with the buzz as you get louder and louder. Feel the vibrations all through your head.

Now walk around the room buzzing.

Continue for three minutes.

How It Helps

It stimulates and wakes up energy all over your body, increases circulation, and unblocks energy channels.

THE WORLD HEART EMBRACE
Transforms anger and creates courage and confidence

The life-affirming gesture, the primal loving welcome of the eternal mother

How to do it

1. Relax yourself: see Ch. 4 & 5.
2. Stand up and stretch.
3. Inhale and hold out your arms as though you are embracing the universe. Really feel you're stretching to embrace the whole world. Hold your breath.
4. When you've held your breath as long as you can, slowly, lovingly, bring your arms down and fold your hands over each other and rest on your breast. Feel that you have brought the love of the whole world to your heart; feel the warmth of that love flowing into your whole body through your fingers.

5. Now stretch again and embrace the universe—allow all this concentrated love to sink in and nourish every cell of your body; spread it to your fingertips and your toes, to the top-most cell of your brain, and every single muscle, ligament, and neuron; feel it penetrate deep into the core of your being; feel all of you warmed and bathed in the comfort and radiance of that love...spread it with your soft full breath through your body and beyond all boundaries until the world and you are one—there is no distinction; all warmth and energy is flowing to you, through you, and you feel with every cell love pervading everything. . . .Do this 3 to 9 times.

On the 5th time, transform the negative image of person or thing you dislike (see pg. 146): zap it with the love you're radiating until it's atomized completely—dissolved in love—and lay it on your heart.

What it does

Muscle testing shows that merely seeing this gesture strengthens your life force. Making the movement opens your heart center and expands your electromagnetic field; your charisma is moving out to strengthen others. You enfold the world in your loving embrace. This has a wonderful healing effect for all kinds of situations.

NOTE: great after one of the anger dissipation exercises.

THE SECRET SMILE
To get in touch with your own pleasure

How to do it

Close your eyes, slowly, sensuously. Imagine a huge ball of helium in your open throat. With your lips loosely closed,

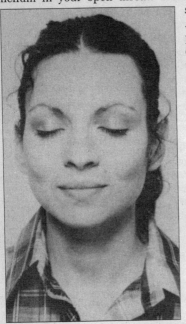

start HUMMING gently. As you begin to feel pleasurable vibrations all over your face and head, touch your face to intensify the sensation. Think of something you really enjoy. Maybe it's lying on the beach in the sun or eating your favorite dessert or being with someone you enjoy. It can be very private or personal. The important thing is to recall that particular pleasure and feel it. Spread it with the hum all through your face and head. Tingle all over with pleasure!

What it does

Be deliberately recalling some pleasurable experience in your mind, while humming, you can recreate all the relaxed body sensations that went with it the first time. IMPORTANT: When something pleasant happens to you, you automatically breathe deeply. When you are tense or afraid, your breath shortens.

Benefits:

Your pleasure trip only takes a minute. As you relax, you start to blossom. You know what to say. You are easier with people, more responsive, friendlier, more comfortable, and confident.

Doe Lang's, daughter, Andrea demonstrates this charisma-cise.

Section 6 / *Relaxation*

When you are feeling nervous tension or exhaustion

What Exercises to Do:

> Back Rock
> Basic Buddha Belly
> I Am at the Beach
> Infinite Shrug
> Laughing
> Piecemeal Poop-Out
> Prayer Pose
> Shoulder Rolls, Shrugs
> Portable Pleasure Producer
> Specific Tension Points

BACK ROCK

You massage all the sore points, stimulate the nerve endings all along the spine, and erase tension from your back and shoulders.

How to Do It

1. Lie on back, bend knees, bring them up to your chest, and clasp your hands around your knees.
2. Rock back and forth along the length of your spine. Feel each vertebra being massaged as you rock.
   - Don't forget to breathe deeply.

BASIC BUDDHA BELLY

See Section 1, STRESS: BEFORE, page 318, for this exercise.

I AM AT THE BEACH

Imagine you are at a beautiful sandy beach all by yourself. It's completely private, yours alone. Imagine trees around, decide what kind, and visualize them. See the flowers and the fish in the water. It's your favorite time of day. Imagine as clearly as possible everything you want to make this your perfect beach.

To get to your beach, you have only to close your eyes, breathe deeply, and say, "I am at the beach," and there you are.

Now, with your eyes closed, imagine yourself lying on the sand at your beach. Feel the warmth of the sun, hear the waves in the ocean, smell the salt water, feel the slight breeze on your body. Feel yourself relax totally in the sun.

Stay at the beach as long as you like. When you feel refreshed, open your eyes. You'll feel as if you had had a short, wonderful vacation.

THE INFINITE SHRUG

1. Sit with a straight back, eyes closed.
2. Breathing very slowly and deeply, begin to raise your shoulders as slowly as possible. It should take anywhere from five to fifteen minutes. Keep your arms, hands, and the rest of your body relaxed (especially the stomach!).
3. When they are touching your ears, hold your shoulders in this position for one minute.
4. Begin to lower your shoulders as slowly and continuously as you raised them, breathing deeply and evenly. (This should take as much time as raising them did—from five to fifteen minutes.)

How It Helps

This expands your sense of time, stimulates circulation, and releases deeply held tensions. Also sharpens concentration. Each person has a different—and fascinating—experience.

LAUGHING

- (A "soul bath")
- Relieves tension
- Steps up energy
- Dissolves anger

Laugh for three minutes. Start by just saying "ha, ha, ha," until you're genuinely laughing. Laughing continuously takes a lot of energy; it also produces a lot of energy by relaxing many involuntary muscles and stepping up oxygen consumption and circulation.

PIECEMEAL POOP-OUT

- Better than a nap—relaxes you totally
- Frees you from tension and worry

How to Do It

1. Lie on your back, arms at your sides, palms facing up. You might like to have some quiet, soothing music playing.
2. Take a few deep breaths from as low down in your body as you can.
3. Now say to yourself, "My feet are relaxed, they're feeling very heavy," and feel that happen. Breathe very slowly and deeply.
4. Now say to yourself, "Now my ankles are very relaxed. They feel very heavy." Feel your ankles relax and all tensions leave them. Continue through the whole exercise to breathe very slowly and deeply.
5. Continue in this way, saying "My ———— are relaxed," and then relaxing that part, in this order: lower legs, knees, upper legs, buttocks, genitals, lower back, upper back, belly, chest, hands, forearms, elbows, upper arms, shoulders, front of neck, scalp, forehead, eyes, cheeks, lips, chin, jaw.
6. Now put your concentration in your lower belly and feel it move out with the inhale and in with the exhale. Imagine that you are lying on an ocean and that the waves are moving your belly up and down, up and down. You are a small, light wave, bubbling buoyantly in the ocean—which supports you.
7. Take ten to fifteen minutes to do this deep relaxation. Then, open your eyes and sit up slowly.

How It Helps

As you slow down your breathing and put your attention in various parts of your body, you relax all tension.

How You Benefit

Better than a nap, you feel totally refreshed and relaxed, clear of the worries of the day.

PRAYER POSE

Sit on your knees, bend over, put your forehead on the ground, extend your arms and hands past head, palms together. Relax your stomach. Breathe slowly and deeply, until you feel relaxed, and then a little longer.

SHOULDER ROLLS, SHRUGS

1. Make six big backward circles with your shoulders, arms hanging loose, inhaling with mouth closed with each circle. Now make six circles forward, exhaling through your mouth with each circle.
2. Now shrug one shoulder up as you inhale strongly (mouth closed), then let it drop as you exhale sharply through your mouth.
3. Reverse.
4. Ten times for each shoulder.
5. Now shrug both shoulders as high as you can as you inhale strongly, and let them drop as you exhale sharply through your mouth. Three times.

PORTABLE PLEASURE PRODUCER

How to Do It

1. Close your eyes. Now imagine a huge ball of helium in your open throat.
2. With your lips loosely closed, start humming, increasing intensity as you begin to feel the vibrations all over your face and head. Touch your face, your cheeks, your forehead, your chin, your head, to intensify the vibration. Continue as you hum to imagine the helium ball in your throat.
3. Think of something you really enjoy. Maybe it's lying in a meadow or being with someone you enjoy or making love or eating your favorite dish. Whatever it is, recall that particular pleasure and feel it. Spread it with the hum all through your face and head. Tingle with pleasure.

How It Helps

When you're tense or afraid, your breath shortens. When something pleasant happens to you, you automatically breathe deeply. By deliberately recalling some pleasurable experience in your mind, while humming, you can recreate all the relaxed body sensations that went with it the first time.

Wherever You Feel Tension, Massage It!

Your own hands are your magic healing and tension-relieving tool. Breathe slowly and deeply as you massage yourself. Imagine, as you inhale, that the breath is flowing directly to and relax-

THE GREAT WOW!
For creating joy!

How to do it

1. Start by crouching and in a tone of wonder whisper "Wow, Wow," as you stand up.

2. Repeat ten times.

3. Each time the WOW should get louder until you leap in the air.

4. Take a deep breath, stretch, and jump into the air and shout
   "Wow! Wow! Wow!
      W-O-W W-O-W!
         W-AH-AH-OO!"

What it does
Your oxygen supply is stepped up, you are the crest of an energy high.

Benefits:
You have acccessed joy!—the most charismatic emotion. You've discharged any hidden tension you might have had in your body with a gradually escalating explosion of joy. This recharges your energy and gives you new sparkle and charisma. Now the world is yours.

Doe Lang's, daughter, Andrea demonstrates this charisma-cise.

INSTANT OPERA
Boosts courage

How to do it
When practicing a speech,
presentation, or dif-
ficult confrontation
or in the middle of
an angry argument,
sing your lines as
loud and extrava-
gantly as possible.
Use large arm
movements such as
swinging your arms.

What it does
You will find that
your rhythmic, tonal
and emotional
variety will greatly
expand without any
effort. Once you are
wildly extravagant
vocally, what is
"normal" for you will
will be more
interesting and varied than it was before "the opera." Your tonal
range will increase and your inflections will be more varied and
expressive. If you are angry, your anger will dissolve and you
will start to laugh. (One couple claimed it saved their marriage!)

Benefits
- Releases stress
- Makes you laugh
- Stimulates your confidence

The author, Doe Lang, demonstrates this charisma-cise.

ing the tense places, and that you diffuse and exhale through the entire body all fatigue, soreness, discomfort, and tension.

JAW RELEASER and YAWNS
See Section 7, VOCAL EASE, pages 343–44.

Section 7 / *Vocal Ease*

When you want to release and experience your true voice

What Exercises to Do:

This is a good sequence for throat, face, and jaw relaxation:

> Jaw Releaser
> Yawning:
>> Basic Yawn
>> Helium Ball Yawn
> Horse Laugh
> Idiot Fingers
> Wibble Wabble

Here's an excellent sequence for tonal color and variety:

> Portable Pleasure Producer
> "You Bastard!"
> Helmet of Hum
> Deaf-Mute Jack and Jill
> Glottal Nonstop Sentences

And miscellaneous others:

> Jogging before Speaking
> Crazy Scale
> Instant Opera
> Pointillist Necklace

JAW RELEASER

- Frees the tongue and jaw
- Relaxes tension of jaw and throat
- Increases blood circulation in throat (good for sore throat too!)

How to Do It

1. Open mouth wide; stick tongue out and downward.
2. At the same time, open your eyes wide. Hold tongue out for three breaths.
3. Now hold jaw still with finger, wag tongue from side to side and then up and down—without moving your jaw.
4. Now circle your tongue slowly and smoothly all around mouth, imagining tongue touching nose, cheeks, chin. Now circle the other way. Keep jaw still!

How You Benefit

Relieves throat tension, enabling you to speak more clearly and loudly.

YAWNING—INSTEAD OF CLEARING YOUR THROAT, YAWN!

If you have trouble starting the yawn, lift lips away from your teeth as though you were snarling, inhale deeply and open your throat wide, crinkle your nose and eyes, and then open your mouth as wide as you can so that the muscles in your neck stand out and you hear a roaring in your ears. Only by exaggerating the yawn can you really get into the feeling that will take over and thoroughly relax your whole face, neck, and throat.

Now do it with your mouth closed. Feel the muscular reactions. Your tongue is as low as possible at the back of the throat, lying on the bottom of the mouth; the tip is flat and the sides are in contact with all the gums. Press the middle of the tongue down hard.

HELIUM BALL YAWN

Now imagine there's a huge ball of helium in your mouth pressing the roof up, the back out against the back of the neck, and the sides and bottom down.

- These three release facial tension, prevent a "freeze"
- Relax face, tongue and lips, and throat
- Increase spontaneity

HORSE LAUGH

Start with your lips lightly together as though you were going to say p. Blow outward so your lips ripple continuously like a little motor.

IDIOT FINGERS

Move your index finger up and down rapidly across your absolutely lax lips, saying "BRRRRRRRRRRRRR."

WIBBLE WABBLE

Keeping your lips absolutely limp, shake your head. The lower part of your face will shake from side to side. If you're really relaxed you may even drool!

PORTABLE PLEASURE PRODUCER

See Section 6, RELAXATION, page 342, for this exercise.

"YOU BASTARD!"

See Section 4, ANGER, page 332, for this exercise.

HELMET OF HUM

- Relaxes throat, face, and head
- Provides feelings of pleasure, power, and confidence
- Stimulates
- Releases tension
- Generates energy and warmth

How to Do It

1. With lips loose, start humming loudly.
2. Put your hands on your cheekbones; feel the hum vibrating there. Now move your hands up and feel the vibrations of your forehead, on the top of your head, on the sides and back of your head.
3. Continue humming and now put your hands in front of your face, cupped, and feel the humming vibration fill them. Now move them further and further away in front of your face, still feeling the vibration filling them. If you lose the vibration, bring your hands closer to your face until you feel them again.
4. Send the vibration to your hands at arm's length. Then move your hands apart and to the sides, then move your hands above your head, then move your hands behind your head, making a huge helmet of hum all around your head. Feel that your head becomes a resonating cage of bones.

338

How This Helps

When you fill your head with humming vibrations, you can hear these vibes bounce off the different parts of your face and head.

DEAF-MUTE JACK AND JILL

See chapter 13, page 293, Your Persona—How to Match Your Inner and Outer Images, for this exercise.

GLOTTAL NONSTOP SENTENCES

See chapter 10, page 219, The Feelings of Your Sounds, for this exercise.

The voice is the first thing to shrink when you feel diffident or shy. These sentences help give your voice underlying melody and color.

JOGGING BEFORE SPEAKING

Jogging shakes up the accumulated rigidities and tensions, and lightens your approach to speaking. If you run in place before rehearsing, as part of your warm-up, you will find you are more in touch with your whole body, your voice will be louder and freer, and your gestures become larger and more relaxed and spontaneous. Practice singing and speaking while jogging in place. Follow with long, slow breathing.

CRAZY SCALE

Practice talking with the wildest extremes of pitch, going "crazily" up and down the scale. This gives you access to unsuspected tonal ranges of your own voice, and will add some new colors to the sound.

INSTANT OPERA

When practicing your speech, sing your lines as if they belonged to an opera. Use large arm movements. Having done that, you will find that your rhythmic variety and tonal possibili-

THE HELMET OF HUM
Improves vocal ease

- Relaxes throat, face and head
- Gives sensations of pleasure, juiciness and joy
- Raises energy level
- Releases power and confidence
- Raises energy level
- Dissolves body tension

How to do it

1. With lips loose, start humming loudly.

2. Put your hands on your cheekbones; feel the hum vibrating there. Now move your hands up and feel the vibrations on your forehead, on top of your head, on the sides and back of your head.

3. Continue humming powerfully and now cup your hands in front of your face and feel the humming vibrations fill them. Now move the hands further and further away from your face, expanding the vibrations to fill the space. If you lose the vibrating sensation, bring your hands closer to your face until you feel them again.

4. Keep stretching your arms until your hands are completely extended from your body. Send the vibration to your hands at extended arms' length.

5. While continuing to hum, slowly move your hands apart and to the sides, then above your head, then behind your head, making a huge helmet of hum all around your head. Feel your head become a resonating cage of bones.

How you benefit

When you fill your head with humming vibrations, you can hear these vibes bounce off the different parts of your face and head. You will feel expanded and secretly powerful. When you begin to speak your voice will have enlarged effortlessly about three times!

MARY HAD A LITTLE LAMB
Relieves stress, improves vocal ease

How to do it   1. Sit in a chair and close your eyes. Now think of things you enjoy. Close your mouth, put your thumbs in your ears and index finger lightly compressing each nostril. Start to HUMMMM so that you feel the soft buzzing sound inside your face and head.

Now with your mouth, nose and ears closed, recite your favorite

nursery rhyme as expressively as possible like "Mary had a little lamb, its fleece was white as snow...."

HINT: a lot of "Hummph"-ing helps here. Try it ten different ways. Fast, slow, excited, sad, angry, high and low, etc. The crazier the better.

2. Repeat it but take your thumb out of one ear. Notice the difference in the sound inside your head.

3. Release the other ear and repeat the rhyme. (Mouth and nostrils still closed)

4. Repeat: one nostril open. (Mouth still closed)

5. Repeat: the other nostril open.

6. Repeat: both nostrils open.

NOTE: each time make it as loud as you can.

7. Repeat: everything open your jaws and mouth closed.

8. Finally, open your mouth and say it aloud. It will probably come as a shock to you how loud and free it sounds.

What it does It's like discovering hi-fi amplifiers opening in your head. (Mary had a little lamb and a BIGGG voice). By expressing the widest range of your own vocal inflections through a familiar nursery rhyme, you will experience the amazing acoustic variations of your own head cavities. You will discover your true voice. Remember, use lots of energy and air even with the closed mouth.

Benefits • Your tonal range and variety will increase.

• Your inflections will be more interesting and expressive.

• A bigger, fuller, richer, more dynamic voice is yours. Are you prepared to be so fascinating? Don't be surprised if it doesnt scare you a little.

ties will expand without further effort. Once having been wildly extravagant vocally, what is "normal" will be more interesting and varied than it was before the exercise.

POINTILLIST NECKLACE

See Section 1, Stress: Before, page 322, for this exercise.

Since vocal freedom is impossible without relaxation in the throat, jaw, and neck, the Pointillist Necklace is very valuable here.

Section 8 / *Courage*

When you want to be assertive, hold your own, or take risks

What Exercises to Do:

There are two types of exercises for courage: those to be done just before a difficult encounter or a situation where you need courage, and those to be practiced daily to build up your general courage level.

For Emergency Courage

Chutzpah Elbow Propeller
Steam Engine
"You Bastard!"
I Don't Care Swing
Karate Chop

For Courage Buildup

Basic Buddha Belly
Meditation
Prespeech Visualization
Memorize Rhythmic Poetry—speak aloud every day
Hand Heartener
Sing

340

CHUTZPAH ELBOW PROPELLER
See Section 1, STRESS: BEFORE, page 321, for this exercise.

STEAM ENGINE
See Section 4, ANGER, page 334, for this exercise.

"YOU BASTARD!"
See Section 4, ANGER, page 332, for this exercise.

I DON'T CARE SWING
See Section 1, STRESS: BEFORE, page 323, for this exercise.

KARATE CHOP
See Section 4, ANGER, page 333, for this exercise.

BASIC BUDDHA BELLY
See Section 1, STRESS: BEFORE, page 318, for this exercise.

MEDITATION
See Section 1, STRESS: BEFORE, page 323, for this exercise.

PRESPEECH VISUALIZATION

Visualize the place where you'll be giving a speech. See it as a warm, cozy place. Imagine that the people who are there are all interested in hearing what you have to say, have only good wishes for your success and love in their hearts for you. This will enable you to let go of your fears and negative thoughts.

If you're confident and think other people think well of you, they'll step through the doors of *your* expectations.

MEMORIZE RHYTHMIC POETRY—SPEAK ALOUD EVERY DAY

Speaking poetry has a calming effect. It produces equilibrium in both sides of the brain. Therefore you feel less anxiety and tension.

HAND HEARTENER

Rub your hands together—harder. When they're quite warm, keep rubbing and imagine the warmth spreading all over your body.

Now reach up your hands as high as you can: imagine you are embracing the sun. Draw down that energy and place it on your heart and chest. Feel it warm you and glow, penetrating your back, spreading throughout your body.

This is also a good thing to do before speaking if you don't know what to do with your hands. They'll have so much warmth in them that they'll feel relaxed and natural!

SING

Singing is also excellent for calming the mind and establishing equilibrium in both sides of the brain. Also opens up the throat, improves breath control, and gives more color to your speaking voice.

Section 9 / *Stage Fright*

When you are feeling panic, alarm, or anxiety

What Exercises to Do:

There are exercises you can do right before you perform and exercises to do every day to make you feel more confident in general.

For preperformance

This is an excellent sequence:

    I Don't Care Swing   (see section 1)
    Woodchopper (4)
    Karate Chop (4)
    Steam Engine (4)

World Heart Embrace   (4)
Depressurizer   (9)

Here is another good sequence:

Horse Laugh   (7)
Idiot Fingers   (7)
Wibble Wabble   (7)
Chutzpah Elbow Propeller   (1)
Yawns   (7)
Butterflies Chaser   (9)
Preperformance Look   (9)
Chant "SA-TA-NA-MA," p. 264

For General Confidence

Speak Rhythmic Poetry   (8)
Sing   (8)
Meditate   (1)
Relaxation Rehearsal   (10)
Energy Expander, p. 265

THE INFALLIBLE BUTTERFLIES CHASER

Great for last-minute (or earlier) preperformance nerves.

1. Stand with your feet apart, knees a little bent, back straight, arms relaxed and hanging loosely at your sides.
2. Without taking any additional breath, do ten short bounces, saying "Vuh" on each. Do this as energetically as possible, making the *vuh* a short, sharp, forceful sound (coming from the gut).*
3. Relax and, with mouth closed, inhale slowly and very deeply.
4. Exhale in a steady stream ("sh-h-h-h-h") with mouth slightly open, letting the body sink into the knees.

Repeat three times; follow with long, slow breathing.

DEPRESSURIZER

1. Stand in a doorway and press your palms against the doorfram on both sides. Hold your breath and keep increasing the pressure—you will feel warmth rushing to your face, head, and neck Hold as long as you can.

* If you are unable to manage ten bounces at first, do as many as yo can and gradually work up to the full ten.

2. Release totally, with a rush.
3. Inhale deeply.

Repeat three times.

I DON'T CARE SWING
See Section 1, STRESS: BEFORE, page 323, for this exercise.

WOODCHOPPER
See Section 4, ANGER, page 333, for this exercise.

KARATE CHOP
See Section 4, ANGER, page 333, for this exercise.

STEAM ENGINE
See Section 4, ANGER, page 334, for this exercise.

HORSE LAUGH
See Section 7, VOCAL EASE, page 344, for this exercise.

IDIOT FINGERS
See Section 7, VOCAL EASE, page 345, for this exercise.

WIBBLE WABBLE
See Section 7, VOCAL EASE, page 345, for this exercise.

CHUTZPAH ELBOW PROPELLER
See Section 1, STRESS: BEFORE, page 321, for this exercise.

YAWNS
See Section 7, VOCAL EASE, page 344, for this exercise.

ENERGY EXPANDER
See chapter 11, page 265.

PREPERFORMANCE LOOK

1. Imagine something pleasant and smile.
2. Now drop the smile from your mouth, leaving it on the eyes and cheekbones. Gives you a dynamic, charismatic look. Everyone is drawn to an expression that says, "Something good is about to happen."

CHANT SA-TA-NA-MA

See chapter 7, page 264, for this exercise.

Section 10 / *More Control of Your Life*

When you want to expand your powers

What Exercises to Do:

Brain Cleaner
Creative Visualizations
Dream Machine
Electric Eye
Kinesthetic Body
Environmental Control
Golden Sunflower
Party Promoter
Relaxation Rehearsal
Onion Flower
Golden Cocoon
Infinite Shrug
Be Your Own Sun
Be Your Own Cathedral

BRAIN CLEANER

Close your eyes. Imagine a broom sweeping out sense after sense, sweeping out all the doors of your perceptions, your sight, your hearing, your smell, your taste, your kinesthetic feelings. This cleans out your senses, makes them fresh. Take three to five minutes for each sense. Breathe deeply. Open your eyes.

CREATIVE VISUALIZATIONS

1. Relax deeply.
2. Imagine a situation that is in the future, perhaps giving a presentation at work or meeting someone. Now imagine yourself giving this presentation (or whatever) with perfect calm and authority, and imagine the other people hearing it with interest. Put into your scenario whatever elements you want, and imagine yourself in the best possible light, doing the best job you can possibly do. The trick is to imagine specifically, to visualize clearly that you are as you would like to be.
3. Or remember a situation that has already happened that you were dissatisfied with. Go back over this situation in your mind, imagine it as you wish it had happened, imagining what you wish you had done or said, what you wish others had done or said. In this new scenario, be as you wish you could have been.
4. Both of these steps are rehearsals for the way you would like to be and can really be. They will help you to program yourself for success instead of failure by having success in your mind instead of the fear and subsequent image of failure. They help you to act differently than you would have otherwise.

DREAM MACHINE

At night before you go to sleep, say, "I'm going to remember my dream." Put paper and pen by your bed, or a tape recorder, and when you wake, immediately write down or tape what you remember of your dream. Then think of what this dream reminds you of and what associations you make. The dream doesn't have to be logical; it belongs to dream time, to the dream world.

Remembering your dreams puts you in touch with often hidden parts of your life, enriches your fantasy life, and gives you cues to intuition.

ELECTRIC EYE

Imagine that your eyes expand to the sides of your head. Now inhale through these enlarged eyes, taking in everything. This makes your eye and face muscles relax. You feel more open and expanded.

Now imagine a central eye in the middle of your forehead, like a big blue pearl. Connect this with the expanded large eyes. Feel that the light that comes in is an extraordinary, radiant light.

Now imagine that you have eyes in the back of your head and

can see everything in back of you. Feel that this makes your head feel light and spacious.

KINESTHETIC BODY

1. When you have some physical task to do (for instance, skating, dancing, walking across a stage), breathe deeply, imagine in your mind how the movement goes, and visualize yourself doing this movement as it should be done.
2. Then actually do the movement, as you have imagined and "programmed" yourself to do it. (This will erase previous "tapes" or memories of being awkward, clumsy, not able to do it, etc.)
3. Repeat imagining—deepening your sense of how it "feels" to do it marvelously. Use a mental picture of an "expert" or virtuoso doing it. If it's skiing, for instance, see Jean-Claude Killy skiing. If tennis, pick your favorite tennis stars—Bjorn Borg, Ilie Nastase, or whoever. Imagine you're inside *their* bodies—moving with perfect flowing grace and effectiveness.
4. Then go back to physically *doing* it!
5. Keep alternating—kinesthetic rehearsal and real practice.

ENVIRONMENTAL CONTROL

Listen to sounds, take them in, breathe them out completely. Don't resist them. For instance, in the subway where it's very noisy, breathe in these noises and let them go out. Don't tense against them. Feel the noise as energy and transform it into power by filtering it outward and equalizing the sound.

GOLDEN SUNFLOWER

Imagine a huge, very golden sunflower shining in your chest. See all the petals in great detail. When you meet someone (particularly if you are having trouble dealing with him or her), "see" a big golden sunflower shining in his/her chest too. Ignore negative messages from the top level (their mouths). Respond to their sunflower, too. Others will respond with more warmth and friendliness because you are "connecting" from your heart center —a great way to prevent yourself from getting "sucked in" by other people's negativity.

PARTY PROMOTER

Before you go to a party, imagine that the whole event is a show put on FOR YOUR BENEFIT. Therefore, WHATEVER HAPPENS at this party is happening for YOU.

You will find that instead of being worried, shy, or afraid, you will be interested in everything going on and enjoy the whole spectacle.

You let go of all expectations (future) and fears.

RELAXATION REHEARSAL

Tense and relax entire body, starting with toes and working upward.°

When you are deeply relaxed, visualize scene or talk you want to rehearse. See yourself going through it exactly as you'd like it to go; visualize every detail as if you were there. If you feel any nervousness or can't visualize—relax further or begin again. When you can easily go through entire scene, you're ready. Actual event will be easy—like the second time!

ONION FLOWER

Deeply relax. Now imagine your favorite flower. (Maybe a smooth yellow tulip, a fluffy white chrysanthemum?) Now BE that flower, use this flower for your image of yourself, focus on it, meditate on it.

When you're under stress you will be able to remember the image of your favorite flower and how it feels to be this flower. This will have an instant de-stressing and calming effect on you.

GOLDEN COCOON

See Section 1, STRESS: BEFORE, page 321, for this exercise.

INFINITE SHRUG

See Section 6, RELAXATION, page 340, for this exercise.

° Use relaxation tapes—Cassette Communications, 175 Fifth Avenue, New York, N.Y. 10010.

BE YOUR OWN SUN

See chapter 10, page 238, for this exercise.

BE YOUR OWN CATHEDRAL

See chapter 10, page 239, for this exercise.

Section 11 / *Mood Change*

When you are feeling negative, sad, or depressed

What Exercises to Do:

Letter from Your Higher Self
Lazy Lemon
Anger Transformer
Chutzpah Elbow Propeller
Emotion Cooler
World Heart Embrace
Centering with Sound
Calming Energizer
The Golden Light

LETTER FROM YOUR HIGHER SELF

Write yourself a letter of encouragement, as though your most developed self is addressing you. Acknowledge your fears, your good qualities (all of them), and express faith in and confidence in your abilities, efforts, and accomplishments. Make it as genuine, compassionate, and specifically supportive as you can. Write yourself what you would like most to hear, what you feel you need from the most supportive person you would like to have in your life. Keep this letter where you can reread it when you need to hear encouraging words.

Variation: tape the letter on a cassette and play it whenever needed.

LAZY LEMON

When you experience complete enjoyment through any of your senses, your breathing becomes deeper, your oxygen supply increases, tensions drain away.

- Helps you build up a satisfying field of pleasure, to be drawn on at will. An instant vacation—which breaks up and prevents stress buildup.
- Restores perspective and capacity to enjoy life.

How to Do It

1. Cut a fresh lemon or orange in half, or open a bottle of your favorite perfume.
2. Sit down in a comfortable position, close your eyes, relax your body, take deep breaths, enjoy fragrance.

ANGER TRANSFORMER

See Section 4, ANGER, page 334, for this exercise.

CHUTZPAH ELBOW PROPELLER

See Section 1, STRESS: BEFORE, page 321, for this exercise.

EMOTION COOLER

See Section 2, STRESS: DURING, page 325, for this exercise.

WORLD HEART EMBRACE

See Section 4, ANGER, page 335, for this exercise.

CENTERING WITH SOUND

Very effective when you're feeling scattered and want to center yourself.

1. Close your eyes, and sit with back and neck straight.
2. Inhale and exhale slowly and deeply three times.
3. Inhale and make a very low, deep *OM* sound. Feel the vibration cover the whole area from the base of your spine to your solar plexus (including the abdomen).
   Repeat twice more. Notice your feelings.

4. Inhale again and make a midrange *OM* sound. Let it vibrate through the heart center and chest.
Repeat twice more. Feel the effects.

5. Inhale and make a very high, loud *OM* sound. Make it vibrate through your whole head.
Repeat twice more. Observe your sensations. Open your eyes. You will feel strong, grounded, and confident.

CALMING ENERGIZER

This can be done anywhere you can close your eyes for fifteen minutes. Guaranteed to calm and refresh you.

1. Visualize a warm, glowing pink light around your heart center. Hold it there for a slow mental count of nine.

2. Move the glowing pink light to just over the top of your head, and hold it for a slow mental count of fifteen.

3. Surround your entire body with a field of glowing pink light; sit in the middle for a slow count of twelve.

4. Visualize a radiant blue light at your throat level, and hold it there for a slow count of nine.

5. Move the radiant blue light to just over your head and hold it there for a slow count of fifteen.

6. Surround your body with a field of radiant blue light; sit in the middle of it for a slow count of twelve.

7. Visualize a glowing white light at your forehead level; hold it there for a slow mental count of nine.

8. Hold the glowing white light just above your head for a slow count of fifteen.

9. Surround your body with a field of white light; sit in the middle of it for a slow count of twelve.

10. Observe how you feel and enjoy it, before opening your eyes.

THE GOLDEN LIGHT

1. Close your eyes. Sit with straight back.

2. Imagine that you are sitting on a soft white cloud, and gradually it lifts off the ground and soars up, up into the sky.

3. A great golden waterfall of warm light is high above you, cascading down. Your cloud approaches the base of the waterfall and the warm golden light pours down over your head.

4. You feel your skull, face, neck, shoulders, chest being bathed by the warm golden light. It pours down until it reaches the center (Tan T'ien) two inches below your navel. It rests there a moment.

5. Now the light rises to your waist, and divides in two—one part starts down your left side, the other down your right, down

     past the hips, thighs, knees, calves, ankles until the soles are bathed in the warm golden light. Pause.

6.   Now the light rises up the inside of each leg, until it reaches the crotch and meets again in the Tan T'ien.

7.   Then the light goes to the base of the spine and slowly moves up the spine, toward the middle of the back, the shoulders, and the base of the skull, rising, rising until it reaches the crown of your head. There it rests, bathing the entire head with its golden shower of warmth and light.

8.   Do this journey three times. You will feel peaceful and energized. If done nine times, you will move easily into deep meditation, and you will find your creativity and intuition are greatly enhanced.

THIS IS A WONDERFUL PREPARATION FOR MEDITATION OR A MEDITATION IN ITSELF.

Section 12 / *Good Relations with Others*

When you want to be tuned in to others

What Exercises to Do:

Fireworks Fling
Creative Visualizations
Golden Sunflower
Party Promoter
Anger Transformer
"You Bastard!"
Preperformance Look
Mirror Matching

FIREWORKS FLING

1.   Lightly curl your fists and fling your arms up into the air as you say "Ah!" Imagine a shower of fireworks issuing from your outspread fingertips as you fling them up in the air (at ninety degrees on either side of your head). Hold. Visualize the sparks cascading down all around you.

2.   Inhale (mouth closed) and bend your elbows, drawing in your arms close to the body again.

3. Repeat the "fling" on an "Ah!"
4. Do ten of these. Make each one bigger and more spectacular than the last.

CREATIVE VISUALIZATIONS

See Section 10, MORE CONTROL OF YOUR LIFE, page 353, for this exercise.

GOLDEN SUNFLOWER

See Section 10, MORE CONTROL OF YOUR LIFE, page 354, for this exercise.

PARTY PROMOTER

See Section 10, MORE CONTROL OF YOUR LIFE, page 355, for this exercise.

ANGER TRANSFORMER

See Section 4, ANGER, page 334, for this exercise.

"YOU BASTARD!"

See Section 4, ANGER, page 332, for this exercise.

PREPERFORMANCE LOOK

See Section 9, STAGE FRIGHT, page 352, for this exercise.

MIRROR MATCHING

See chapter 5, page 122, for this exercise.

Section 13 / *Pain*

When you are feeling physical distress

What Exercises to Do:

Drugless Painkiller
Pain-to-Pleasure Transformer
Piecemeal Poop-Out
Sonic Acupressure
Sore Throat Soother
Headache Remedy
For Toothache—EEEEEEEE
People Purr

DRUGLESS PAINKILLER

Sit or lie down, breathe deeply and slowly, relax. Now direct your brain to send endorphins, the body's own painkillers, to the spot that hurts. Visualize these endorphins as sparkling white lights going directly to the pain, absorbing the pain, dissolving the pain, and leaving sparkling white light in its place. Exhale the atomized pain.

PAIN-TO-PLEASURE TRANSFORMER

Ask: What message is this pain or illness trying to give me? What can I learn from it?

Focus on the energy of the feeling, without identifying with it as "your" pain. Intensify the energy and visualize it becoming a warm, viscous liquid (like Jell-O), lapping and supporting your body.

The pleasure and pain centers in the brain are very close. Concentrate on:

1. focusing on the sensations, intensifying them
2. spreading them throughout the body as neutral energy,

3. exhaling completely and passing the diluted, diffused intensity of that energy like heat through cheesecloth, visualizing every cell as a fine, transparent network
4. transforming the energy into white light and bathing the whole body in healing light

You may change the experience of pain into warmth, excitement—something actually akin to pleasure.

PIECEMEAL POOP-OUT

See Section 6, RELAXATION, page 341, for this exercise.

SONIC ACUPRESSURE

- Let the healing streams of water intensify the warm vibrations.
- Will relieve pain; make you feel pleasantly light, clear, and alert.
- Stimulates energy and well-being.

How to Do It

Get in a nice warm shower. Begin to hum (with relaxed, slightly parted jaws and loose lips). Feel the hum massaging the sides, back, and top of your head with soft, stimulating sonic "fingers" from the inside.

SORE THROAT SOOTHER

Put rubber band around second knuckle of thumb—nine minutes. Gargle with 1 tablespoon apple cider vinegar in glass of water—swallow (every hour).

Avoid meat, starches, sugar, citrus fruit, dairy products. Eat steamed greens (so body will become alkaline, not acid).

HEADACHE REMEDY

Visualize your pain, its exact dimensions, how big it is, where it's placed, what shape it is, what color it is. (Is it round, square, rectangular? Is it two inches or six inches? Is it yellow, green?) Now breathe slowly and deeply into the pain; imagine it getting smaller and smaller. Watch it disappear.

EEEEEEEEEE

For tooth pain, say "EEEEEEEEEE" in a high tone. Direct vibrations to painful area and visualize sound breaking up and dissolving pain. Match intensity of sound to pain—neutralizing it.

MISCELLANEOUS

If you're having trouble breathing, lie on your stomach with your head in your arms. Relax. Breathe deeply. Notice your belly expanding against the floor.

Try the PEOPLE PURR as a walking meditation. You purr as you walk along, very, very lightly. This keeps the expenditure of air very, very economical and even.

Section 14 / *Body Alignment*

When you want to center and balance yourself

What Exercises to Do:

> Pelvic Clock Rock
> Massage
> Belly Dancer's Bump
> Plumb Line
> Straight Standoff

PELVIC CLOCK ROCK

- Promotes sexual responsiveness
- Increases range of feeling and enjoyment
- Releases abdominal tension
- Promotes good digestion
- Improves coordination
- Helps you to enjoy dancing without self-consciousness

How to Do It

Feet slightly apart, imagine you are the center of a clock: 12:00 is in front of you, 3:00 at your side, 6:00 at back, 9:00 at the other side. Now move your pelvis around the clock, back the other way, very, very smoothly. Now try moving it from 12:00 to 3:00, from 9:00 to 12:00, from 9:00 to 6:00, etc., as though it were an oiled ball bearing. Try going from all hours to all others—smoothly and evenly.

MASSAGE

And don't forget massage for your body! You can massage yourself; your magic hands do know what to do. Even better, massage a friend and exchange massages. (Use only oils you could eat on your skin—almond, coconut, avocado, peanut—*not* mineral oil!)

BELLY DANCER'S BUMP

Stick your fanny out like a duck. (Don't tip forward with your torso!) Bring your pelvis sharply forward with a "bump." Don't move the top half of your body. This tucks your pelvis under and aligns your body, knees slightly bent, thighs under your shoulders.

PLUMB LINE

See chapter 5, page 119, for this exercise.

STRAIGHT STANDOFF—The Spine Lineup

1. Stand against a wall. Bend your knees. Press spine and small of your back against the wall. Breathe for a minute; pay attention to how this straight back feels.
2. In this position, sing "AHHHHHHH" as deeply and evenly as possible; then "MMMMMMMMMM"—two to six times.
3. Then push off with your elbows away from the wall, keeping the same alignment. Your pelvis is cupped like a palm, the lower back spread and wide, the stomach pressed in against the spine, the head rising from the torso like a flower at the end of its stem.
4. When you feel your balance is just as solid as when you were

pressed against the wall, slowly straighten knees until *almost* straight. Lower your arms slowly and relax them. Scan your body from the inside. See how it feels.

Section 15 / *Waking Up*

When you are feeling sleepy, tired, or lethargic

What Exercises to Do:

Alternate Breathing
Breath of Fire
Cat Crawl
Sunrise

ALTERNATE BREATHING

- Clears your head and nasal passages
- Balances your energies
- Oxygenates your brain
- Makes you feel alert and optimistic, calmer
- Makes you happy to start a new day

1. Close off right nostril lightly with right thumb. Exhale slowly and evenly through left nostril. Inhale slowly through same nostril.
2. With little finger of right hand (same hand), close off left nostril and exhale through right nostril. Inhale.
3. Again, thumb on right nostril, close it, exhale through left nostril, then inhale through same nostril. Then close left nostril as before and continue—five minutes (or until nose is clear).

- As you exhale, visualize poisons, phlegm, negativity leaving entire body.
  On inhale, visualize air being drawn into nasal passage, then up into head, clearing it and bringing oxygen and energy (prana) to brain. Then spread it through entire body.
- Move smoothly from thumb to pinky, only letting go of one nostril when you close off the other.

BREATH OF FIRE—FAST ENERGIZER, INSTANT WAKER-UPPER

- Cleanses entire bloodstream in three minutes
- Raises voltage of nervous system
- Increases circulation
- Releases old toxins from the lungs, blood vessels, mucous lining, and cells°

Important: Mouth is kept closed.

1. Exhale powerfully (with a short, sharp, unvoiced "HMH!") by pulling in the navel point and abdomen toward the spine (as though someone had kicked you in the solar plexus); immediately relax the abdomen and allow the breath to come in naturally and easily by itself (as part of the relaxation).
2. Then exhale again powerfully, and relax to inhale—this should be a continuous rhythm, fairly rapid (two to three breaths per second), with no pause between inhale and exhale.
   - Focus energy at the navel point—you should feel the pull of the muscles in that area. A steady, even rhythm is more important than speed.
3. Do this for one to three minutes.

Long-Range

Helps build endurance, stabilizes shaky nerves, generates mental and physical constancy. It can help you if you cannot keep a promise, intention, or train of thought without constant distraction. Great anytime you're tired, bored, or sleepy.

CAT CRAWL

- Gently stretches spine and body
- Eases transition from sleep to full alertness
- Gets the kinks out without strain

On your hands and knees begin to crawl very slowly around the room, so that your left knee is under chest and right leg is fully extended in back. Look over first one shoulder, then the other,

---

° If you are very toxic due to drugs, smoking, or poor nutrition, this exercise may stimulate a temporary self-toxification. To aid in cleansing increase the amount of exercise you normally do daily, and lighten your diet with vegetables, fruits, and nuts for a week or two. This helps your body drop the heavy load of toxins it has carried, without activating some illness to do the cleansing you ignored.

slowly twisting as far as you can. *Streeetch*. Change legs very slowly, being sure straight leg is totally extended.

Do ten times (each leg) as slowly and luxuriously as possible.

Variation

You can combine this with counting to your pulse or heartbeat. Exhale six beats, hold three; inhale six beats, hold three.

SUNRISE—SUPERENERGIZER

- Wakes you up
- Stimulates
- Centers your magnetic field
- Balances energies—anticipation for the day
- Gives you an optimistic energy to your day

Sit with a straight spine cross-legged or kneeling, eyes closed (fanny on heels).°

1. Extend arms out to sides at a forty-five-degree angle—thumbs pointing up, fists closed.
2. Do Breath of Fire for one minute (80–120 breaths). You will feel face and neck get warm.
3. Inhale deeply, while you bring straight arms up slowly over your head until thumbs meet. Hold six counts.
4. Exhale slowly while lowering arms straight out to sides—and then all the way down.

Section 16 / *Inducing Sleep*

When you are feeling restless, fretful, or worried

What Exercises to Do:

> To Sleep
> Presleep Rerun
> Sonic Tranquilizer

° You will feel like the sun yourself, surrounded by your own circle of warmth, energy, and radiance.

TO SLEEP

1. Don't eat for two hours before bedtime.
2. Drink chamomile, valerian, or passionflower tea.
3. Drink hot milk, with or without honey.
4. Do the Piecemeal Poop-Out (p. 341) to relax you.
5. Try tryptophane (in tablet form or in milk). It's a natural sleep inducer.
6. Lie on your left side and softly purr, feeling the vibration driving out all thoughts.
7. BE YOUR OWN LULLABY (see p. 242). Lie down, feel the sea of energy all around you, observe sounds, prickling of your hairs, small sensations . . . dissolve all thoughts with your purr.
8. Avoid stimulation or anxiety—provoking work, reading, or talking just before bedtime. Wind down. Put on soft soothing music or relaxation cassette. Let go of all worries—see them tied up in a huge garbage bag and floating up and away out of sight.

PRESLEEP RERUN

1. About an hour before you go to sleep, rerun the film of your day.
2. Sit or lie down; take a few deep, relaxing breaths. Begin in the morning, remember everything that happened that day.
3. Take note of the things that pleased you, that you liked. Acknowledge how great they were.
4. Look at the things that you were dissatisfied with, gently and without blame or guilt. Visualize how you would have liked them to be; make the scenario better than it was, making yourself and everyone else act the way you would have preferred.
5. Finish off the rerun with a thought of gratitude for the good things you experienced, for the lessons you received, for the problems you got to work on and began to solve.
6. This wipes clean your day, finishing up all the loose ends and worries, and allows you to sleep with a clear, relaxed mind. You wake up fresh in the morning, ready for the next day's movie!

SONIC TRANQUILIZER

See chapter 10, page 242, for this exercise.

Section 17 / *Better Sex Life*

When you are feeling inhibited, bored, or distracted

What Exercises to Do:

Pelvic Flow
Sensualizer
Pleasure Checklist
Belly Dancer's Bump
Pelvic Clock Rock

PELVIC FLOW

Undulate and weave around the room for ten minutes. Lie on the floor, lift pelvis, release spine. Let pelvis initiate the action. Move arms and legs smoothly and sinuously. Improvise without stopping. Move in ways you haven't done before and don't worry about how it looks. Feel good! Keep the movements very lazy, legato, and sinuous.

THE SENSUALIZER

Run your finger as lightly as you can down your own or a friend's arm and hand. Barely touch the skin. Do it very, very slowly; see if you can touch just the hairs. Let your friend do it to you.

PLEASURE CHECKLIST

Each day, at the end of the day, check whether you have had at least one pleasant experience of each of your senses:

Did I see something beautiful and feel pleasure today?
Did I taste something good and savor it today?
Did I smell something fragrant and enjoy it today?
Did I hear something beautiful and enjoy it today?
Did I touch something pleasurable and enjoy it today?

Did I feel any warm, loving thoughts and spread them through my body?

Keep a record for a week. If you notice that some of your senses get less pleasure than others, consciously make an effort to use those senses more and enjoy more with them.

BELLY DANCER'S BUMP

See Section 14, BODY ALIGNMENT, page 364, for this exercise.

PELVIC CLOCK ROCK

See Section 14, BODY ALIGNMENT, page 363, for this exercise.

- Increases your flexibility
- Increases your subtlety of movement
- Increases your ability to respond and feel pleasure

For a catalog of Charisma skills training tapes write to Charismedia, 610 West End Avenue, New York, NY 10024. (Please enclose a self-addressed, stamped envelope with your inquiry).

I will be delighted to receive your comments on your experiences and reactions to *The Secrets of Charisma*.

Doe Lang

The author, Doe Lang, Ph.D., and her daughter,
Andrea, have demonstrated the selected Charisma-cies
shown in this chapter. Her New York-based training
center, Charismedia, continues to help people explore
the enlightening processes in this book—opening new
doors of self-awareness, discovering and projecting
each person's true voice, enhancing confidence and
powers of communication, and accessing all the
elements of personal charisma needed to change our
lives and our world.

The author, Doe Lang, Ph.D., has taught charisma skills and leadership training for such clients as Honeywell, Xerox, government agencies and stars of entertainment and international politics. She has taught at Columbia University, Temple University and The New School. Dr. Lang has helped more than 100,000 people in all walks of life to be more comfortable, effective communicators —in business, in personal life and on TV! Her books are popular in 25 countries and 8 languages.